THE VAN DE WALLE PROFESSIONAL MATHEMATICS SERIES

VOLUME THREE

Teaching
Student-Centered
MATHEMATICS
Grades 5–8

JOHN A. VAN DE WALLE

Virginia Commonwealth University

LOUANN H. LOVIN

James Madison University

PEARSON

Boston | New York | San Francisco
Mexico City | Montreal | Toronto | London | Madrid | Munich | Paris
Hong Kong | Singapore | Tokyo | Cape Town | Sydney

Series Editor: Traci Mueller
Development Editor: Sonny Regelman
Editorial Assistant: James P. Neal, III
Marketing Manager: Jen Armstrong
Senior Editorial-Production Administrator: Donna Simons
Composition and Prepress Buyer: Linda Cox
Manufacturing Buyer: Andrew Turso

Cover Designer: Kristina Mose-Libon
Permissions Coordinator: William Walsh
Permissions Researcher: Renee Nicholls
Editorial-Production Service: Omegatype Typography, Inc.
Interior Designer: The Davis Group, Inc.
Illustrations: Omegatype Typography, Inc.
Electronic Composition: Omegatype Typography, Inc.

For related titles and support materials, visit our online catalog at www.abprofessionaled.com.

Library of Congress Cataloging-in-Publication Data

Van de Walle, John A.
    Teaching student-centered mathematics. Grades 5–8 / John A. Van de Walle and LouAnn H. Lovin.
        p. cm. — (Volume 3 of The Van de Walle professional mathematics series)
    Includes bibliographical references and index.
    ISBN 0-205-41797-3
    1. Mathematics—Study and teaching (Elementary)—United States.   I. Lovin, LouAnn H.   II. Title.

QA13.V35 2006
372.7—dc22

2005042917

Printed in the United States of America

20 21 22   EBM   14 13 12

BRIEF CONTENTS

CONTENTS

PREFACE

*A*nd once I had a teacher who understood. He brought with him the beauty
    of mathematics. He made me create it for myself. He gave me nothing,
    and it was more than any other teacher has ever dared to give me.

—Cochran (1991, pp. 213–214)

Math makes sense! This is the most fundamental idea that any teacher of mathematics
needs to believe and act on. It is through the teacher's actions that every student in his
or her own way can come to believe this simple truth and, more important, believe
that he or she is capable of making sense of mathematics. Helping students come to
this belief should be a goal of every teacher.

The title of this book, *Teaching Student-Centered Mathematics,* reflects our belief in
the best way for students to develop this confidence and understanding of mathematics. We believe that teachers must create an environment in which students are trusted
to solve problems and work together using their ideas to do so. Instruction involves
posing tasks that will engage students in the mathematics they are expected to learn.
Then, by allowing students to interact with and struggle with the mathematics using
their ideas and *their* strategies—a student-centered approach—the mathematics they
learn will be integrated with their ideas; it will make sense to them, be understood,
and be enjoyed.

Our Goals for the Book

For many teachers, the idea of allowing students to struggle with mathematics is
sometimes difficult to accept. "*How and why should I allow students to wrestle with problems and not show them the solutions? Where can the right kinds of tasks be found? Where*

can I learn the mathematics content information I really need in order to be able to teach in this way?" With these and other questions firmly in mind, we have three main objectives for this book:

1. To help teachers understand what it means to teach in a student-centered, problem-based manner. This is a theme that runs throughout the book. We have also tried to help you understand why this is the best method available for helping students understand mathematics.
2. To provide a reference book for all of the mathematics content found in fifth to eighth grades and the best information available concerning how children learn this content. We have tried to provide this information in a readable, useful manner, completely integrated with instructional strategies.
3. To provide a resource of simple, problem-based activities and tasks that can engage students in the mathematics that is important for them to learn.

These are also goals of my larger book, *Elementary and Middle School Mathematics: Teaching Developmentally (EMSM)*. Written primarily as a textbook for college courses about teaching mathematics, *EMSM* has also become popular as a resource book for classroom teachers. Therefore, it made sense to use that larger text as the basis for this series of books.

My first decision was to ask Dr. LouAnn Lovin to assist me in adapting *EMSM*. Together, we decided to use it as the foundation for each of the books in this series of three grade-banded books. In many instances we have used both text and activities exactly as they appear in the college text. Those of you familiar with that book will undoubtedly see overlap, as we included much of the material, both text and activities, from *EMSM*. However, we also quickly found that in order for the books to be more useful for the classroom teacher at the prescribed grade level, there were gaps to be filled, material to be rearranged, and language to be focused. As a result, we wrote new activities, expanded the mathematics, and in a few cases wrote almost completely new chapters. Unlike *EMSM,* this book is designed expressly for the classroom teacher at the fifth- to eighth-grade level. We hope you will find that this is a better resource for your purposes.

What You Will Find in This Book

We view this book as a primary resource for teachers. It is not simply a book of activities, although it has nearly 150 good and practical activities. It is not a book about content, although it addresses a deep understanding of mathematics and how children learn it. Nor is it a book about constructivist views of teaching, although it is firmly based on a constructivist view of how children learn. Rather, we have attempted to bring together all of these aspects of teaching student-centered, problem-based mathematics and integrate them in a manner that we hope is most helpful to you, the classroom teacher.

Foundations of Student-Centered Instruction

Chapter 1 is the only "general" chapter in the book. It describes four core ideas for effective mathematics teaching: knowledge of how children learn, an explanation of teaching mathematics through problem solving, suggestions for planning student-centered lessons, and strategies for assessment in a student-centered environment. We strongly believe that this is the most important chapter of the book. The remaining 11 chapters are based on these core ideas. We encourage you to read this chapter thoughtfully.

Big Ideas in Mathematics

Much of the literature espousing a student-centered approach suggests that teachers plan their instruction around "big ideas" rather than individual skills or concepts. At the start of every chapter after the first one, is a list of the key mathematical ideas associated with the chapter. Teachers find these lists beneficial because they focus thinking on the broader goals of a mathematics unit and, thus, keep both instruction and assessment on target.

Activities

Throughout Chapters 2 to 12 are numerous activities that can be directly adapted to lessons in your classroom. Most of the time you will find these set off from the text with a number and a title. Many additional ideas are described directly in the text or in the illustrations. Each of these is a problem-based task as described in Chapter 1.

It is important that you see these activities as an integral part of the text that surrounds them. The activities are inserted as examples to support the development of the mathematics being discussed and to show how children can be helped to learn that content. Therefore, we hope that you will not take any activity as a suggestion for instruction without reading carefully the full text in which it is embedded.

Following this Preface, you will find the Activities at a Glance chart, a list of all the named and numbered activities with a short statement of the mathematical goal for each. You may occasionally find that a topic you are teaching is not included in the list. For example, Chapter 2 contains only four activities. However, this chapter addresses fully the topic of whole-number computation and mental mathematics and provides clear guidance for instruction. The format of a boxed activity did not lend itself to the topic. Keep in mind that although this book addresses all of the big mathematical ideas in grades 5–8, it is not an activity book in the traditional sense.

Assessment Notes

We believe that in a student-centered environment assessment should be integral to instruction rather than an interruption or a test at the end of a unit. To teach in a student-centered manner demands listening carefully to the thinking of students (including paying attention to what they do and write) so that you can plan tomorrow's lesson, assist students, and communicate with parents. To aid in your listening, you will find assessment ideas located throughout Chapters 2 to 12.

Stop and Reflect

Reflective thinking is the key to effective learning. This is true not only for students but also for all learners. Throughout the book you will run across stop signs with questions that ask you to pause in your reading and reflect on some aspect of what you have read. These "stop-and-reflect" sections do not signal every important idea, but we have tried to place them where it seemed natural and helpful for you to slow down a bit and think.

Expanded Lessons

The activities in the book are written in a brief format so as not to detract from the flow of ideas. Details of how an activity should be implemented in the classroom are generally left to you with the assumption that your class is unique. The process of designing a good student-centered, problem-based lesson requires careful thought regardless of where the idea for the lesson comes from. By way of example, we selected one activity in each chapter and expanded it into a complete lesson plan, following the structure described in Chapter 1. We included lesson elements such as mathematical goals, notes on preparation, specific expectations for the students, and notes on assessment. Clearly, any lesson should be modified to suit the special needs of your class. We offer these examples as suggestions for making the many decisions involved in lesson planning. These Expanded Lessons are located at the ends of Chapters 2 to 12.

NCTM Standards Appendix

NCTM's *Principles and Standards for School Mathematics* (2000) has been a guiding force for reform in school mathematics and we feel that this book reflects that document. In Appendix A, you will find a copy of the appendix to the *Standards,* listing all of the content standards and goals for each of the four grade bands: pre-K–2, 3–5, 6–8, and 9–12.

Blackline Masters

Throughout the book are references to Blackline Masters that are useful for conducting the activities being discussed. In Appendix B, you will find thumbnails of all Blackline Masters assembled for your use. Go to the Companion Website at www.ablongman.com/vandewalleseries to download the full-sized versions. You may copy them freely for use in the classroom.

Acknowledgments

This series of books began as a straightforward and seemingly simple project: adapt *Elementary and Middle School Mathematics* to suit the needs of classroom teachers in three grade bands, K–3, 3–5, and 5–8. It was not nearly as simple as it initially seemed. I am indebted to a number of people who have helped to make the books a reality.

Two people at Allyn & Bacon have been truly indispensable. Our editor, Traci Mueller, has offered encouragement from start to finish. She has answered questions and helped with many big decisions. Our development editor, Sonny Regelman, is a master of detail and a font of good judgment. Her constant prodding and careful editing have become my safety net. Throughout the development of these books, and also

EMSM, we have become close professional friends. It has been a pleasure to continue my association with these and all of the people at Allyn and Bacon.

I would especially like to take this opportunity to offer a huge thank-you to my coauthor, Dr. LouAnn Lovin. In addition to contributing manuscript, LouAnn brought to this project a valuable second viewpoint on issues of mathematics and how best to help students learn. Without LouAnn's able collaboration, this series would probably not exist. More important, the books are significantly better for her efforts. Thanks, LouAnn!

To all of the teachers throughout the United States and Canada who have encouraged me and expressed their appreciation of the *EMSM* book, a special thanks. We hope that this book will be of even more help to you as you work with your students. Remember always to believe in kids. Allow them to think and to make sense of mathematics daily.

—John Van de Walle

ACTIVITIES AT A GLANCE

The table that follows lists all of the named and numbered activities in the book. In addition to providing an easy way to find an activity, the table provides the main mathematical goal or objective for each activity, stated as succinctly as possible. We hope this will be useful.

Rather than a book of activities, this is a book about teaching mathematics. Many practical and effective activities are used as examples. Every activity should be seen as an integral part of the text that surrounds it. Therefore, it is extremely important not to take any activity as a suggestion for instruction without reading carefully the full text in which it is embedded.

In addition to the named and numbered activities, the book is full of many more ideas for problem-based instruction that are found within the text and in the illustrations but without an activity name and number. Although we know you will find the activities in this table useful, you should see the table only as a listing of the named activities and not as an index to instructional ideas.

Chapter 4   Decimal and Percent Concepts and Decimal Computation

Chapter 8 Developing Measurement Concepts and Formulas

Chapter 10 Exploring Functions

Chapter 11 Exploring Data Analysis

Chapter 12 Exploring Concepts of Probability

ABOUT THE AUTHORS

John A. Van de Walle is Professor Emeritus at Virginia Commonwealth University. After 30 years with his university, Dr. Van de Walle continues to work with teachers at the K–8 level as a mathematics education consultant. He has taught mathematics to children at all levels, K–8. He is a coauthor of a mathematics series for K–6 (Scott Foresman) and the author of *Elementary and Middle School Mathematics: Teaching Developmentally*, the market-leading text and resource book on which this series is based.

LouAnn Lovin is a former classroom teacher and is currently an assistant professor in mathematics education at James Madison University, where she teaches mathematics methods and mathematics content courses for Pre-K–8 prospective teachers and has been involved in the mathematical professional development of teachers in grades 4–8. She is actively involved with NCTM and is also President of the Valley of Virginia Council of Teachers of Mathematics (V^2CTM). Her research interests are in the area of teacher knowledge, in particular, exploring the nature of the mathematical knowledge needed for effective teaching.

FOUNDATIONS OF STUDENT-CENTERED INSTRUCTION

What is basic in mathematics is as simple as this: *Math makes sense!* Every child in his or her own way can come to believe this. More important, every child can come to believe that he or she is capable of making sense of mathematics.

Students have to develop this understanding themselves. Their understanding and, thus, their confidence grow as a result of being engaged in doing mathematics. To teach effectively means to engage students at their level so they can create or develop new ideas to use and understand so they can make sense of mathematics.

The fundamental core of effective teaching of mathematics combines an understanding of how children learn, how to promote that learning through problem solving, and how to plan for and assess that learning on a daily basis. Information to help you with these four foundational components—children learning constructively, teaching with problems, planning lessons, and assessing where students are—are discussed in the next four sections of this chapter.

The remaining chapters of the book are designed to help you apply these core ideas to the content that you teach.

HOW CHILDREN LEARN AND UNDERSTAND MATHEMATICS

To put it simply, *children construct their own knowledge.* This is the basic tenet of the theory of learning called *constructivism.* In fact, not just children, but all people, all of the time construct or give meaning to things they perceive or think about. As you read these words, you are giving meaning to them. You are constructing ideas.

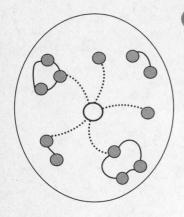

FIGURE 1.1 • • • • • • • • • •

We use the ideas we already have (gray dots) to construct a new idea (white dot), developing in the process a network of connections between ideas. The more ideas used and the more connections made, the better we understand.

Constructing Ideas

To construct or build something in the physical world requires tools, materials, and effort. Constructing ideas can be viewed similarly. The tools we use to build understanding are our existing ideas, the knowledge that we already possess. The materials may be things we see, hear, or touch—elements of our physical surroundings. Sometimes the materials are our own thoughts and ideas—existing ideas and thoughts used to modify other ideas. The effort that must be supplied is active and reflective thought. If minds are not actively engaged in thought, no effective learning occurs.

To get a notion of what it means to construct an idea, consider the diagram in Figure 1.1. Imagine that it represents a small portion of a student's knowledge concerning a collection of related ideas. The gray dots represent ideas that the student already has developed. The lines joining these dots represent connections between and among the ideas. Every idea or bit of knowledge that a person has is connected in at least some way to some other idea. No idea exists in complete isolation.

Now suppose that this person is trying to understand or learn or give meaning to a new idea, the one represented by the white dot in the diagram. The tools that are available to construct this idea are precisely the related ideas that the person already owns. As the existing ideas give meaning to the new idea, new connections are formed—the dotted lines in the diagram—between the new idea and the existing ones. The more existing ideas that are used to give meaning to the new one, the more connections will be made. The more connections made, the better the new idea is understood.

Understanding

It is possible to say that we know something or we do not. That is, knowledge is something that we either have or don't have. In contrast, *understanding* can be defined as a measure of the quality and quantity of connections that an idea has with existing ideas. Understanding is never an all-or-nothing proposition. It depends on the existence of appropriate ideas and on the creation of new connections (Backhouse, Haggarty, Pirie, & Stratton, 1992; Davis, 1986; Hiebert & Carpenter, 1992; Janvier, 1987; Schroeder & Lester, 1989). For example, consider the possibilities of seventh- or eighth-grade students computing the decimal product 37.6 × 1.4 as part of solving a story problem. Many will utilize the traditional algorithm. After multiplying and getting the digits 5264, some of these students may incorrectly recall a different decimal rule (i.e., align the decimal points), and as a result place the decimal point between the 6 and 4—526.4. Those using the algorithm correctly will count the two decimal places in the two factors and correctly determine the answer to be 52.64. Among these, a few may be able to connect the place counting with multiplying tenths by tenths to get hundredths. Still other students will rely on their number sense with decimals. These students know that 37.6 × 1.4 will have the same digits in the answer as the whole-number product, 376 × 14. After computing that product, 5264, they place the decimal by estimation—the answer has to be between 1 × 37 and 2 × 37 or between 37 and 74. Therefore, the answer must be 52.64. Due to the nature of the problem being solved, some students may have seen that an estimated answer is all that is necessary and not bothered to compute with pencil and paper. One of several possible estimates is based on the easier product, 40 × 1.4.

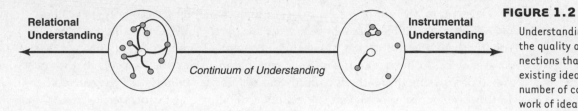

Relational Understanding

Instrumental Understanding

Continuum of Understanding

FIGURE 1.2 • • • • • • • • • • • •

Understanding is a measure of the quality and quantity of connections that a new idea has with existing ideas. The greater the number of connections to a network of ideas, the better the understanding.

Since 4 × 14 is 56, an estimate of 55 or 56 is used. Each of these students brings a different set of dots to this task. Each "understands" decimal computation in a different way.

Another way to think about an individual's understanding is that it exists along a continuum (see Figure 1.2). At one extreme is a very rich set of connections. The understood idea is associated with many other existing ideas in a meaningful network of concepts and procedures. Hiebert and Carpenter (1992) refer to "webs" of interrelated ideas. Clearly, our goal for children is that each new mathematical idea be well understood—that it be embedded in as rich a web of related mathematical ideas as possible.

At the other end of the continuum, ideas are completely isolated or nearly so. Here we find ideas that have been rotely learned. Due to their isolation, poorly understood ideas are easily forgotten and are unlikely to be useful for constructing new ideas.

For instance, consider the concept of "ratio" as constructed by a student in the sixth grade. Often initial ideas about ratio are connected directly to fractions. With only this connection, comparing ratios is not any different than comparing fractions. But there are many ideas to connect to ratio. For example, ratios can be

- comparisons of the part-to-whole variety, as in number of girls to the size of the class
- comparisons of different types, such as girls to boys, or peanuts to cashews
- percents
- rates, such as miles per gallon or dollars per pound
- scale drawings, connecting ratio to the geometric concept of similarity

Ratios can be compared in a wide variety of ways, each of which is connected to one or more different ideas about what a ratio is. The web of potential ideas connected to a ratio can grow large and involved. Students who possess only a few of these ideas understand ratio less well than those who possess a lot of these ideas. And understanding is not only a matter of quantity but also of quality. We want the things that students relate to an idea to be those that are most helpful and useful. Research suggests that students who come to think of a ratio as a singular entity rather than as two distinct numbers or quantities are much more likely to be capable of proportional reasoning, a hallmark achievement of the middle grades.

Computational procedures also provide a good place to see how understanding can differ from one student to another. In the previous example of decimal products, it is clear that the more connections with the meanings of decimals and the meaning of multiplication, the more efficient and less error-prone students are likely to be. The same is true of ratio. Those with minimal understanding are more likely to use a cross-product approach to make comparisons while others may use estimation, percent equivalents, common numerators, unit rates, and even other methods depending on the numbers and the circumstances.

Of course, we cannot "see" a student's understanding. We can only make inferences about what it may be. When students are given problems without directions for solving them, the assumption is that students use the ideas they have, whatever those ideas may be. In the case of traditional computational rules, the danger is that we may see students using the methods correctly but not understanding what they are doing. In this case, our inference about student understanding may be incorrect.

Classroom Influences on Learning

The theory of constructivism suggests that we cannot teach students by telling. Rather, we must help them construct their own ideas using the ideas that they already own. This does not mean that we simply let students play around and hope that they will magically discover new mathematical ideas. On the contrary the manner in which you conduct your class plays an enormous role in what is learned and how well it is understood. Let's examine three factors that influence learning:

- student reflective thinking
- social interaction with other students in the classroom
- the use of models or tools for learning (manipulatives, symbolism, computer tools, drawings, and even oral language)

Each factor impacts what and how well students learn. Each one is significantly influenced by you, the classroom teacher.

Reflective Thought

 Stop for a moment and see if you can come up with a good definition of reflective thinking. What does that phrase mean to you?

Whatever your description of reflective thinking, it almost certainly involves some form of mental activity. It is an active, not a passive, endeavor. You may have said that it involves figuring something out or trying to connect ideas in your head. You may have used the words "ponder" or "consider." What you just did to try to come up with a definition of reflective thinking almost certainly involved reflective thinking.

If we assume that constructivist theory is correct, then we want students to be reflective about the ideas they need to learn. For a new idea you are teaching to be interconnected in a rich web of interrelated ideas, children must be mentally engaged. They must find the relevant ideas they possess and bring them to bear on the development of the new idea. In terms of the dots in Figure 1.1, we want to activate every gray dot a student has that is related to the new white dot we want them to learn. The more relevant gray dots used—the more reflective thinking—the better the new ideas will be constructed.

But we can't just hold up a big THINK sign and expect students to ponder the new thought. The challenge is to get them mentally engaged. As you will see later in this chapter and throughout this book, the key to getting students to be reflective is to engage them in problems that force them to use their ideas as they search for solutions and create new ideas in the process. Two other related activities are also encouraged: writing about solutions to problems and having discussions with the rest of the class. Each is a method of promoting reflective thinking. Each should be built into most of your lessons.

Students Learning from Others

Reflective thought and, hence, learning are enhanced when the learner is engaged with others working on the same ideas. Students reside in classrooms. An interactive, thoughtful atmosphere in a classroom can provide some of the best opportunities for learning.

A worthwhile goal is to transform your classroom into what might be termed a "mathematical community of learners," or an environment in which students interact with each other and with the teacher. In such an environment students share ideas and results, compare and evaluate strategies, challenge results, determine the validity of answers, and negotiate ideas on which all can agree. The rich interaction in such a classroom significantly raises the chances that productive reflective thinking about relevant mathematical ideas will happen.

The Interaction of Students' Ideas with the Ideas of Others

Piaget helped us to focus on the cognitive activity of the child and to begin to understand how an individual uses ideas in a reflective manner to construct new knowledge and understanding. Vygotsky focused on social interaction as a key component in the development of knowledge. Vygotsky viewed the ideas that exist in the classroom, in books, and those shared by teachers and other authorities as distinct from the ideas constructed by the child. The well-formulated ideas that are external to the child he called *scientific concepts,* whereas those developed by the child (in the manner described by Piaget) he called *spontaneous concepts.*

Vygotsky talked about these two types of concepts as working in opposite directions, as shown in Figure 1.3. The scientific concepts work downward from external authority. As such, they impose their logic on the child. The spontaneous concepts bubble upward as a result of reflective activity. In Vygotsky's *zone of proximal development,* the child is able to meaningfully work with the scientific concepts from outside. Here the child's own conceptual understanding is sufficiently advanced to begin to take in the ideas from "above."

It is not necessary to choose between a social constructivist theory that favors the views of Vygotsky and a cognitive constructivism that is built on the theories of Piaget (Cobb, 1996). In a classroom mathematical community of learners, students' learning is enhanced by the reflective thought that social interaction promotes. At the same time, the value of the interaction for individual students is determined to a large extent by the ideas that each individual brings to the discussions. When, for any given child, the conversation of the classroom is within his or her zone of proximal development, the best social learning will occur.

Classroom discussion based on students' own ideas and solutions to problems is absolutely "foundational to children's learning" (Wood & Turner-Vorbeck, 2001, p. 186).

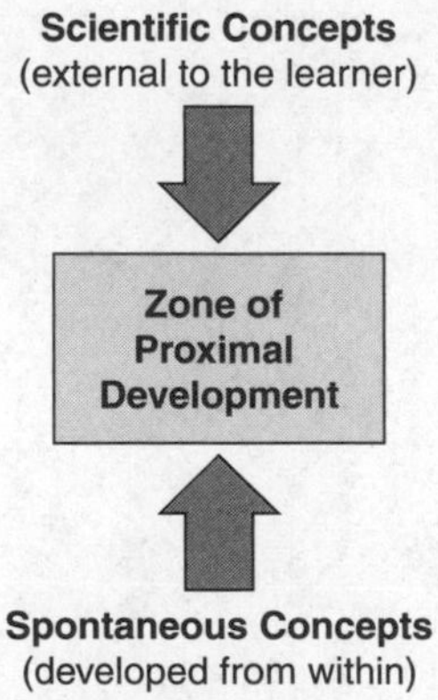

Scientific Concepts
(external to the learner)

Zone of Proximal Development

Spontaneous Concepts
(developed from within)

FIGURE 1.3 • • • • • • • • •

Vygotsky's zone of proximal development is the place where new external ideas are accessible to the learner with those ideas already developed.

Mathematical Communities of Learners

In the wonderful book *Making Sense* (Hiebert et al., 1997), the authors describe four features of a productive classroom culture for mathematics in which students can learn from each other as well as from their own reflective activity.

1. Ideas are important, no matter whose ideas they are. Students can have their own ideas and share them with others. Similarly, they need to understand that they can also learn from the ideas that others have formulated. Learning mathematics is about coming to understand the ideas of the mathematical community.
2. Ideas must be shared with others in the class. Correspondingly, each student must respect the ideas of others and try to evaluate and make sense of them. Respect for the ideas shared by others is critical if real discussion is to take place.
3. Trust must be established with an understanding that it is okay to make mistakes. Students must come to realize that errors are an opportunity for growth as they are uncovered and explained. All students must trust that their ideas will be met with the same level of respect whether they are right or wrong. Without this trust, many ideas will never be shared.
4. Students must come to understand that mathematics makes sense. As a result of this simple truth, the correctness or validity of results resides in the mathematics itself. There is no need for the teacher or other authority to provide judgment of student answers. In fact, when teachers routinely respond with "Yes, that's correct," or "No, that's wrong," students will stop trying to make sense of ideas in the classroom and discussion and learning will be curtailed.

Classrooms with these characteristics do not just happen. The teacher is responsible for creating this climate. It happens over time in two ways. First, there must be some direct discussion of the ground rules for classroom discussions. Second, teachers can model the type of questioning and interaction that they would like to see from their students.

Tools for Learning

It would be difficult for you to have become a teacher and not at least heard that the use of manipulatives, or a "hands-on-approach," is the recommended way to teach mathematics. There is no doubt that these materials can and should play a significant role in your classroom. Used correctly, they can be a positive factor in children's learning. But they are not the cure-all that some educators seem to believe them to be. It is important that you have a good perspective on how manipulatives can help or fail to help children construct ideas.

Models Are Not the Same as Concepts

Conceptual knowledge of mathematics consists of logical relationships constructed internally and existing in the mind as a part of a network of ideas. It is the type of knowledge Piaget referred to as *logico-mathematical knowledge* (Kamii, 1985, 1989; Labinowicz, 1985). By its very nature, conceptual knowledge is knowledge that is understood (Hiebert & Carpenter, 1992). Ideas such as three-fourths, trapezoid, tenths, hundredths, thousandths, product, and ratio are all examples of mathematical relationships or concepts.

Figure 1.4 shows the three blocks commonly used to represent ones, tens, and hundreds in the elementary grades. By middle school, virtually all students have seen pictures of these or have used the actual blocks. For many, the names of these blocks (ones, tens, and hundreds) may be more significant to them than the relationships. The blocks are not the same things as ones, tens, and hundreds. In fact, in the later grades, the same blocks are often used with the flat or a large cube representing one and the others correspondingly representing decimal values. The mathematical concept of a tenth is that *ten tenths are the same as one*. Tenth is not a rod. The concept of tenth is found in the relationship between the rod and the flat. This relationship called "tenth" must be created by students in their own minds. The blocks may help students "see" and talk about the relationships, but what they see are blocks, not concepts.

As another example, consider the rectangles in Figure 1.5. If we call rectangle B "one" or a "whole," then we might refer to rectangle A as "one-half." The idea of "half" is the *relationship* between rectangles A and B, a relationship that must be constructed in our mind. It is not in either rectangle. In fact, if we decide to call rectangle C the whole, A becomes "one-fourth." The rectangles did not change in any way. The concepts of "half" and "fourth" are not in the rectangles; we construct them in our mind. The rectangles may help us "see" the relationships, but what we see are rectangles, not concepts.

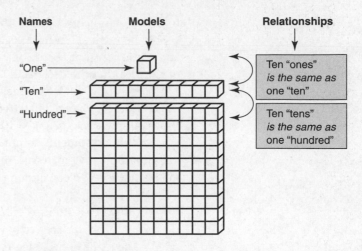

FIGURE 1.4 •

Objects and names of objects are not the same as relationships between objects.

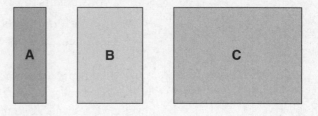

FIGURE 1.5 •

Three shapes, different relationships.

With this understanding we can define a model as follows: A *model* for a mathematical concept refers to any object, picture, or drawing that represents the concept or onto which the relationship for that concept can be imposed. In this sense, any two objects can be a model for the fraction one-fourth as long as a 4-to-1 relationship can be imposed on them.

It is incorrect to say that a model "illustrates" a concept. To illustrate implies showing. That would mean that when you looked at the model, you would see an example of the concept. Technically, all that you actually see with your eyes is the physical object; only your mind can impose the mathematical relationship on the object (Thompson, 1994). For a person who does not yet have the relationship, the model does not illustrate the concept *for that person*. In contrast, when you see a bicycle, what you see is in fact an example of the physical concept of *bicycle*. But unlike physical concepts, there are no physical examples of mathematical concepts. Mathematical concepts are relationships constructed in a person's mind.

Models and Other Tools for Learning

Hiebert and his colleagues (1997) argue that the concept of model should be expanded to include oral language, written symbols for mathematics, and any other tools that can help students think about mathematics. Certainly, calculators can and should be included in this broad definition of mathematical tools. For example, the automatic constant feature of a calculator can assist students in the development of the idea that the decimal 0.01 is a relatively small quantity. If students press 1 ⊞ 1 ⊟ ⊟ . . . , they can quickly make the calculator count to 100. However, if the constant is changed to 0.01—that is, press .01 ⊞ .01 ⊟ ⊟ . . . —then it requires ten thousand presses to count to 100.

Although students do not see concepts by seeing mathematical models or by handling manipulative materials, these various tools can help them learn important mathematical ideas in several important ways:

- Ideas that students are in the process of developing can be tested to see if they "fit" or work correctly when applied to a model that the teacher or other students have suggested represents that idea.

- It is often easier for students to think through a problem or task by use of an appropriate model or tool.

- Tools are especially helpful in communicating ideas that are otherwise difficult for students to talk about or write about.

- Simple drawings of counters, base-ten blocks, number lines, or fraction pieces can help students who are trying to record their ideas.

As students use a tool to represent an idea, their work or reflective activity can help develop meaning for the tool in their own minds. As these meanings for tools are developed, they also become more useful as a tool for further learning. That is, students must both develop meanings *for* tools and meaning can be developed *with* tools.

Procedural Knowledge as a Tool

Procedural knowledge of mathematics is knowledge of the rules and the procedures that one uses in carrying out routine mathematical tasks and also of the symbolism that is used to represent mathematics. Procedural knowledge of mathematics plays a very important role both in learning and in doing mathematics. For example, algorithmic procedures help do routine tasks easily and, thus, free students' minds to concentrate on more important tasks. Symbolism is a powerful mechanism for conveying mathematical ideas to others and for "doodling around" with an idea as students do mathematics. But even the most skillful use of a procedure will not help develop conceptual knowledge that is related to that procedure (Hiebert, 1990). Doing repeated division of fraction exercises will not help students understand why they are inverting the divisor. In fact, students who are skillful with a particular procedure are very reluctant to attach meanings to it after the fact. It is generally accepted that procedural rules should never be learned in the absence of a concept, although, unfortunately, that happens far too often.

Using Models in the Classroom

Mathematical concepts that students are in the process of constructing are formulated little by little over time. As students actively reflect on their new ideas, they test them out through as many different avenues as we might provide. This is where the value of student discussions and a mathematical environment comes in. Talking through an idea, arguing for a viewpoint, listening to others, and describing and explaining are all mentally active ways of testing an emerging idea against external reality. As this testing process goes on, the developing idea gets modified, elaborated, and further integrated with existing ideas. When there is a good fit with external reality, the likelihood of a correct concept being formed is good.

Models and mathematical tools in the more general sense can play this same role as a testing ground for emerging ideas. Tools can be thought of as "thinker toys," "tester toys," and "talker toys." It is difficult for students (of all ages) to talk about and test out abstract relationships using words alone. Models give learners something to think about, explore with, talk about, and reason with.

Introducing Models and Making Them Available

We can't just give students a set of fraction bars or two-color counters and expect them to develop the mathematical ideas that these materials can potentially represent. When a new model or new use of a familiar model is introduced into the classroom, it is generally a good idea to explain how the model is used and perhaps conduct a simple activity that illustrates this use.

For example, suppose that you have begun to discuss negative quantities or integers in your sixth-grade class. You have talked about real-world examples such as floors below ground level or the idea of debits and credits in a balance sheet. Now you want students to see how integers work in arithmetic the same as whole numbers do. You introduce the idea that two-color counters (yellow on one side, red on the other) can be used to represent positive and negative quantities respectively. With the class you discuss how 7 red and 5 yellow illustrate negative two (–2) just as does a set of only 2 red chips or even a set of 52 red and 50 yellow. With this understanding of the model, you give students the task of finding sums and differences involving integers. Students may choose to use the chips, they may choose to use a number line (another model for integers you may have discussed), or they may select to use no model. Once you are comfortable that the models have been explained, you should not force their use on students. Rather, students should feel free to select and use models that make sense to them. In most instances, not using a model at all should also be an option. The choice a student makes can provide you with valuable information about the level of sophistication of his or her reasoning.

Although the free choice of models should generally be the norm in your classroom, you can often ask students to use a model to show their thinking. This will help you find out about a child's understanding of the idea and also his or her understanding of the models that have been used in the classroom.

The following are simple rules of thumb for using models:

- Introduce new models by showing how they can represent the ideas for which they are intended.

- Allow students (in most instances) to select freely from available models to use in solving problems.

- Encourage the use of a model when you believe it would be helpful to a student having difficulty.

Assessment Note

Lesh, Post, and Behr (1987) talk about five representations for concepts, two of which are manipulative models and pictures. (See Figure 1.6.) Their research has found that students who have difficulty translating a concept from one representation to another are the same students who have difficulty solving problems and understanding computations. As students move between and among these representations of concepts, there is a better chance of a concept being formed correctly and integrated into a rich web of ideas.

Translation activities can be used for lessons or for diagnosis. For example, students may be given 3 flats, 6 longs, and 4 tinies (base-ten blocks). Their task may be to write the number that tells how many longs in all (symbols), show the same number on a number line (a different manipulative), and write a sentence in which that number is used and makes sense (real-world situation).

Think about the translation tasks when you want to do a short interview with a student to find out more about his or her thinking. How a student represents ideas in various forms and explains why these representations are similar or different can often provide you with valuable information about what misconceptions he or she may have and what type of activity to use to help.

Incorrect Use of Models

The most widespread error that teachers make with manipulative materials is to structure lessons in such a manner that students are being directed in exactly how to use a model, usually as a means of getting answers. There is a natural temptation to get out the materials and show children exactly how to use them. Students will blindly follow the teacher's directions, and it may even look as if they understand. A rote procedure with a model is still just that, a rote procedure (Ball, 1992; Clements & Battista, 1990).

A natural result of overly directing the use of models is that students begin to use them as answer-getting devices rather than as thinker toys. When getting answers rather than solving problems becomes the focus of a lesson, students will gravitate to the easiest method available to get the answers. For example, if you have carefully shown and explained how to compute integer sums and differences with a number line, then that method is the procedure they will most likely select. (Integers are discussed in Chapter 12.) Little or no reflective thought will go into exploring the concepts involved, with the result that little understanding will be constructed.

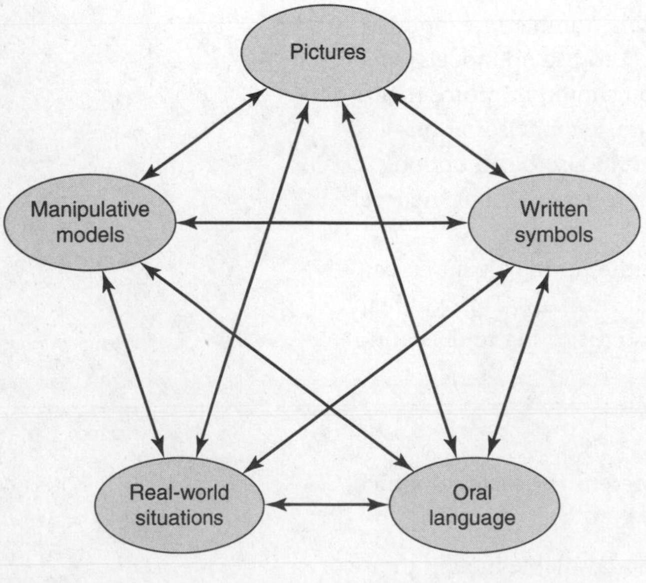

FIGURE 1.6 ●

Five different representations of mathematical ideas. Translations between and within each can help develop new concepts.

TEACHING WITH PROBLEMS

Understanding should be a goal for all of the mathematics we teach. This message of NCTM's *Principles and Standards for School Mathematics* (2000) is a goal with which it is difficult to argue. For many years and continuing today, didactic, top-down, do-as-I-show-you instruction has been the norm in the United States. The results have not been positive except for our brightest students and those who memorize rules well. There must be a better method of teaching.

The single most important principle for improving the teaching of mathematics is to *allow the subject of mathematics to be problematic for students* (Hiebert et al., 1996). That is, students solve problems not to apply mathematics but to learn new mathematics. When students engage in well-chosen problem-based tasks and focus on the solution methods, what results is new understanding of the mathematics embedded in the task. When students are actively looking for relationships, analyzing patterns, finding out which methods work and which don't, justifying results, or evaluating and challenging the thoughts of others, they are necessarily and optimally engaging in reflective thought about the ideas involved. The appropriate dots in their cognitive structure are acting to give meaning to new ideas. *Most, if not all, important mathematics concepts and procedures can best be taught through problem solving.*

Problem-Based Tasks

A *problem* is defined here as any task or activity for which the students have no prescribed or memorized rules or methods, nor is there a perception by students that there is a specific correct solution method (Hiebert et al., 1997).

A problem for learning mathematics also has these features:

- *The problem must begin where the students are.* The design or selection of the task should take into consideration the current understanding of the students. They should have the appropriate ideas to engage and solve the problem and yet still find it challenging and interesting. In other words, it should be within their zone of proximal development.

- *The problematic or engaging aspect of the problem must be due to the mathematics that the students are to learn.* In solving the problem or doing the activity, students should be concerned primarily with making sense of the mathematics involved and thereby developing their understanding of those ideas. Although it is acceptable and even desirable to have contexts or external conditions for problems that make them interesting, these aspects should not overshadow the mathematics to be learned.

- *The problem must require justifications and explanations for answers and methods.* Students should understand that the responsibility for determining if answers are correct and why rests with them. Students should also expect to explain their solution methods as a natural part of solving problems.

It is important to understand that mathematics is to be taught *through* problem solving. That is, problem-based tasks or activities are the vehicle through which your curriculum can be developed. Student learning is an outcome of the problem-solving process.

Teaching with problem-based tasks is student centered rather than teacher centered. It begins with and builds on the ideas that children have available—their dots, their understandings. It is a process that requires faith in children, a belief that all children can create meaningful ideas about mathematics.

Learning Through Problem Solving: A Student-Centered Approach

Let's look into a hypothetical sixth-grade classroom near the middle of the year. The students have been working on fractions, especially equivalent fraction concepts. Prior to that, students had engaged in many number sense challenges with fractions. For example, students each drew a line segment on their paper. Assuming that the segment was $1\frac{2}{3}$ units long, they were to draw a line segment that was just 1 unit long and explain their reasoning. They had also spent considerable time comparing fractions and in so doing had used a variety of strategies.

These experiences have helped students develop ideas about fractions, including the meanings of the numerator and denominator. They have been taking fractions apart in various ways as they sorted fractions as those close to 0, $\frac{1}{2}$, and 1. Their work with equivalent fractions was focused on the idea that there can be two or more fractions that stand for the same quantity. These are their gray dots—their ideas about fractions. Each child's unique collection of ideas is connected in different ways. Some ideas are well understood, others less so; some are well formed, others still emerging. Some students are more reliant on the use of models, others less so.

The students in the class have not been taught the typical algorithms for addition or subtraction of fractions. In the previous lesson the students had been given this problem.

> Carla and her brother ordered two small pizzas, one pepperoni and the other cheese. The pizzas were the same size. They each had some of both pizzas. Carla only ate $\frac{1}{2}$ of a pizza while her brother ate $\frac{5}{6}$ of a pizza. How much pizza did they eat together?

Almost all pairs of students had solved the problem, but no group had gotten a common denominator. For instance, some split $\frac{5}{6}$ into $\frac{1}{2}$ and $\frac{2}{6}$, and then added $\frac{1}{2}$ and $\frac{1}{2}$ and $\frac{2}{6}$. Others used pie pieces and saw the same thing—that there was an easy $\frac{1}{2}$ in $\frac{5}{6}$. Still others took $\frac{1}{6}$ from the $\frac{1}{2}$ to make a whole. This was more difficult because they had to figure out what was left from the $\frac{1}{2}$.

Since the teacher wanted to develop the usual common denominator approach, on this day she revisited the pizza problem but changed the numbers to $\frac{1}{4}$ and $\frac{2}{3}$. She decided that if the students could solve it, this problem would likely force the concept of common denominators. Some students relied on models and a few groups asked for hints. As the teacher observed the work, she gave some groups a transparency on which to record their work for sharing. These are the groups that are the first to share their ideas with the class. Although this is a hypothetical class, the following solutions are not unusual.

STOP Before reading further, see how many different ways you can think of to solve this problem $(\frac{1}{4} + \frac{2}{3})$.

Group 1: The answer is a little less than one whole pizza. We knew that $\frac{2}{3}$ was $\frac{1}{3}$ away from a whole. But $\frac{1}{3}$ is more than $\frac{1}{4}$. So if you stick $\frac{1}{4}$ onto the $\frac{2}{3}$, you will have a little space left. We didn't have time to figure an exact answer. Another group adds that the missing piece is $\frac{1}{12}$ so the answer is $\frac{11}{12}$.

Group 2: We tried to use our pie pieces and make both fractions the same color (type of fraction). We started with the fourths but they don't work on the $\frac{2}{3}$. Then we just kept trying smaller and smaller pieces until we came to the twelfths. We could fit 3 on the $\frac{1}{4}$ and 8 on the $\frac{2}{3}$ so we had 11 in all—$\frac{11}{12}$.

Group 3: We tried to find names for the fractions that were the same. We changed $\frac{1}{4}$ to $\frac{2}{8}$ but could not change $\frac{2}{3}$ to eighths. Then we tried sixths but that doesn't work for fourths. Finally we got to twelfths. You can change $\frac{1}{4}$ to $\frac{3}{12}$ and $\frac{2}{3}$ to $\frac{8}{12}$. That makes $\frac{11}{12}$ in all.

The teacher's objective is for students to see the value of a common denominator for adding and subtracting fractions. This is the white dot that the class has been constructing with each student developing his or her own ideas. By allowing children to solve the problem in their own way, each student is essentially required to use his or her own particular set of gray dots to give meaning to the solution strategy.

During the discussion periods of classes such as this one, ideas continue to grow. Students may hear and understand a clever idea that they could have used but that did not occur to them. Other students actually begin to create new ideas to use as they hear (usually after numerous lessons) the strategies used by their classmates. Perhaps earlier they had simply not been able to use or understand these ideas. Some in the class may hear excellent ideas from their peers that do not make sense to them. These students are simply not ready or do not have the prerequisite concepts to construct these new ideas. On subsequent days there will be similar opportunities for all students to grow at their own pace based on their own understandings. It is important to listen each day to the methods students are using to see if your objectives are actually being developed. In this example, the earlier task of $\frac{1}{2} + \frac{5}{6}$ did not achieve the desired results.

In classrooms such as the one just described, teachers begin *where the students are*—with *their* ideas. They do this by allowing students to solve problems or approach tasks in ways that make sense to them. The students have no other place to turn except to their own ideas.

Show and Tell: A Teacher-Directed Approach

In contrast to the student-centered class just described, let's consider how a lesson with the same basic objective might look using a teacher-directed approach.

The teacher distributes fraction pie pieces to all students. She reads the Carla pizza problem using the numbers $\frac{1}{4}$ and $\frac{2}{3}$. In each pair of students, one is told to model the fraction $\frac{1}{4}$ and the other the fraction $\frac{2}{3}$. "In order to add the two fractions we have to have both fractions shown with the same types of pieces—we have to get common denominators." Beginning with thirds, then fourths, fifths, sixths, and so on, the students try successively smaller pieces from their kit. Eventually they arrive at twelfths to exactly cover both fractions.

Two students are asked to come to the board to write the equivalent fraction equations for each of the two fractions:

$$\frac{1 \times 3}{4 \times 3} = \frac{3}{12} \qquad\qquad \frac{2 \times 4}{3 \times 4} = \frac{8}{12}$$

The teacher explains how these two equations can be used to rewrite the original problem with common denominators. "Now that we have common denominators, we can add the numerators and get the answer to the problem." Students agree that 3 and 8 is 11 and that the answer is $\frac{11}{12}$.

Next, students are given five similar problems to do with the models. Students work in pairs and record answers on their papers. The teacher circulates and helps students having difficulty by guiding them through the same steps indicated by her earlier questions.

 Think about what you like and do not like about this lesson. How is it different from the earlier example? On what ideas will the students be focusing?

In this lesson the teacher and students are using manipulatives in a very conceptual manner. The process of equivalent fractions and common denominators is "seen" as students find like-color equivalents for the fractions using the pie pieces. After one or two lessons similar to this one, most of the class will learn how to add fractions with unlike denominators. This is a typical example of what often is viewed as an excellent lesson.

But let's examine this lesson more closely. The students were told that they had to get like denominators or same-sized pieces. There is little help beyond the models for how to go about finding these common denominators and no reasons for doing so are offered. The rule of adding the numerators is also given as obvious. The teacher receives no information about the ideas that individual students may have. The teacher can only find out who has and who has not been able to follow the directions. The assumption is that those students who solve the problems correctly also understand. However, many students (including some of those who do the problems correctly) will not understand and will be reinforced in their belief that mathematics is a collection of rules to be learned. Everyone in the class must do the problem the way that makes sense to the teacher rather than the way that makes sense to him or her. No student is given the opportunity to find out that his or her own personal ideas count or that there are sometimes other good ways to solve the problem. This disenfranchises the student who needs to continue working on the development of basic fraction ideas as well as the student who could easily find one or more ways to do the problem mentally if only asked to do so. Rather, students are likely to use the same tedious method to add $\frac{1}{2}$ and $\frac{3}{4}$ that should easily be done mentally.

The Value of Teaching with Problems

There is no doubt that teaching with problems is difficult. Tasks must be designed or selected each day, taking into consideration the current understanding of your students and the needs of your curriculum. It is hard to plan more than a few days in advance. If you are using a traditional textbook, modifications will need to be made. However, there are excellent reasons for making the effort.

- *Problem solving focuses students' attention on ideas and sense making.* When solving problems, students must necessarily reflect on the mathematics inherent in the problems. Emerging ideas are more likely to be integrated with existing ones, thereby improving understanding. In contrast, no matter how skillfully you explain ideas and offer directions, students will attend to the directions but rarely to the ideas.

- *Problem solving develops the belief in students that they are capable of doing mathematics and that mathematics makes sense.* Every time you pose a problem-based task and expect a solution, you say to students, "I believe you can do this." Every time the class solves a problem and students develop their understanding, confidence and self-esteem are enhanced.

- *Problem solving provides ongoing assessment data.* As students discuss ideas, draw pictures or use manipulatives, defend their solutions and evaluate those of others, and write reports or explanations, they provide a steady stream of valuable information. That information can be used for planning the next lesson, helping individual students, evaluating their progress, and communicating with parents.

- *Problem solving is an excellent method for attending to a breadth of abilities.* Good problem-based tasks have multiple paths to the solution, from simple or inefficient to clever or insightful. Each student gets to make sense of the task using his or her own ideas. Furthermore, students expand on these ideas and grow in their understanding as they hear and reflect on the solution strategies of others. A teacher-directed approach ignores diversity to the detriment of most students.

- *Problem solving engages students so that there are fewer discipline problems.* For most students, the process of solving problems in ways that make sense to them is intrinsically rewarding. There is less reason to act out or to cause trouble. Real learning is engaging whereas following directions is often boring.

- *Problem solving develops "mathematical power."* Students solving problems will be engaged in all five of the process standards described in the NCTM *Principles and Standards* document: problem solving, reasoning, communication, connections, and representation. These are the processes of doing mathematics.

- *It is a lot of fun!* After experiencing teaching in this manner, very few teachers return to a teach-by-telling mode. The excitement of students developing understanding through their own reasoning is worth all the effort. And, of course, it is fun for the students.

A Three-Part Format for Problem-Based Lessons

It is useful to think of problem-based lessons as consisting of three main parts: *before, during,* and *after.* (See Figure 1.7.)

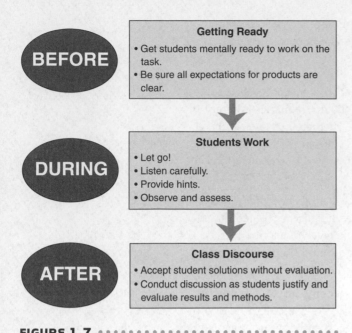

FIGURE 1.7 •

Teaching through problem solving suggests a simple three-part structure for lessons.

If you allot time for each before, during, and after segment, it is quite easy to devote a full period to one seemingly simple problem. The same three-part structure can be applied to small tasks, resulting in a 10- to 20-minute mini-lesson. A mental mathematics activity is a good example of such a mini-lesson.

The Before Phase

You have three tasks to accomplish here: get students mentally prepared for the task, be sure the task is understood, and be certain that you have clearly established your expectations beyond simply getting an answer.

Get Students Mentally Prepared

You want to be sure that whatever ideas students have about the mathematics in the task for the day are "up and running" in their heads. There are several possible strategies you might consider.

- Begin with a simple version of the task you intend to pose. For example, suppose your students are going to order a list of five fractions using only informal methods. You might begin with several pairs of fractions, each lending itself to a different strategy: $\frac{3}{4}$ or $\frac{3}{7}$, $\frac{2}{3}$ or $\frac{4}{9}$, $\frac{7}{8}$ or $\frac{5}{6}$. Alternatively, if you want students to explore area and perimeter relationships on dot grids, you might have them make a rectangle with a specific perimeter, such as 12. A quick discussion of results will help students realize that there can be more than one rectangle with a given perimeter, alerting them to the coming task.

- You might begin a lesson by posing the task right away and then brainstorming solution strategies. For example, if the task involves gathering data and selecting appropriate statistics to compute, you might ask students to think about the statistical techniques that they have learned recently and briefly discuss what each approach can tell them about the data. Brainstorming works best when the task has multiple solution paths that students may not necessarily think of without some prompting.

- For tasks involving a single computation such as $3\frac{1}{4} \times 1\frac{1}{2}$, you can have students think about the size of the answer—is it more or less than 3? More or less than 6? You may even have students tell what they think the answer is since many will be able to compute mentally. This does not spoil the task for others or "give away the answer." Remember, students must explain the reasoning they use to get the answer. It is helpful for students to hear ideas before they are left completely on their own.

Be Sure the Task Is Understood

You must always be sure that students understand the problem or task before setting them to work. Remember that their perspective is different from yours.

Discuss briefly what information is provided in the problem and help students clarify what the problem is asking. Go over vocabulary that may be troubling. Having students restate the problem in their own words forces them to think about the problem in a more complete manner.

Establish Expectations

Every task should require more of students than simply the answer. Minimally, students should be prepared to explain their thinking to the class. Whenever possible, some form of writing that shows how students have solved the problem should be included as part of the task. Whatever the expectations, written work, or preparation for discussion, they must be made clear at the outset.

There are important reasons for requiring more than just answers. Students preparing to explain and defend their answers will spend time reflecting on the validity of their results and will often make revisions even before sharing them. They will have a greater interest in the class discussion because they will want to compare their solution with others' solutions. When an explanation is included as part of what is required by the task, especially if it is in the form of writing and drawings, students will have "rehearsed" for the class discussion and be ready to participate. Students should be expected to show the ideas and the work that they have considered even when they are unable to fully solve a problem.

Requesting that students use words, pictures, and numbers to explain their thinking also has the effect of placing an emphasis on process. Students need to know that their thinking and that of their classmates is at least as important as answers.

As students become more accustomed to writing, consider replacing the instruction "Show how you got your answer" with "Explain why you think your answer is correct." With the former direction, students may simply record their steps ("First we did, and then we . . ."). The focus needs to shift to justification and reasoning rather than simply a record of what was done, especially if students are apt to use a traditional algorithm.

A fifth-grade class was asked to solve this problem in two ways: *Mark bought $1\frac{1}{4}$ pounds of candy for his mom. The candy looked so good that he ate $\frac{7}{8}$ of a pound of it. How much does he give to his mom?* Many students attempted or correctly used a standard subtraction algorithm for mixed numbers as one method. However, not a single drawing or other explanation could be found in the class for the algorithm. As shown in Figure 1.8, Christian makes an error with the algorithm but draws a correct picture showing $4\frac{1}{4} = \frac{34}{8}$, resulting in a correct answer of $\frac{27}{8}$. However, he is not confident in his drawing and crosses it out. A drawing method used by many in the class involved taking the

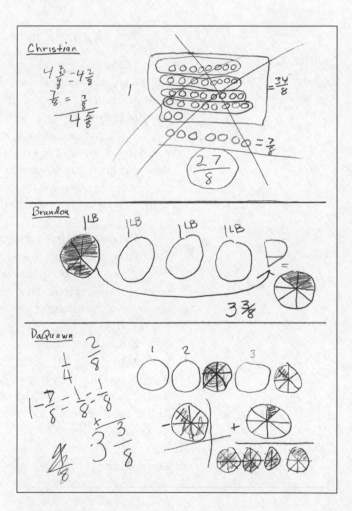

FIGURE 1.8 •

Fifth-grade students show how they solved the problem $4\frac{1}{4} - \frac{7}{8}$. For most students, their methods based on drawings have little to do with their symbolic algorithms. The work of DaQuawn, a student who struggles, is an exception.

A THREE-PART FORMAT FOR PROBLEM-BASED LESSONS

$\frac{1}{8}$ left from the $\frac{7}{8}$ and adding it onto the $\frac{1}{4}$ as shown in Brandon's drawing. Only DaQuawn does this first in a symbolic manner. His "second method" is a drawing supporting his work. When DaQuawn shares with the class he says, "I took this from eighths so I could minus it from $\frac{7}{8}$. That leaves $\frac{1}{8}$. Then change [points to quarter circle] to $\frac{1}{8}$. Minus $\frac{1}{8}$ from . . . No, add it to $\frac{1}{8}$ equals $\frac{2}{8}$ plus $\frac{1}{8}$ equals $\frac{3}{8}$." The teacher notes that DaQuawn "struggles with reading and writing although has good number sense." This teacher correctly values students' thinking and distinguishes it from their abilities to express ideas.

These examples not only illustrate how written work can force students to explain their thinking, but they also illustrate that students have great difficulty with any explanation for algorithms that they have not developed themselves.

For some tasks you may decide to forgo written work. If so, strongly consider using a "think-pair-share" approach, requiring students to reflect on results before sharing. This causes students to defend their ideas to a peer and prepares them to talk to the class.

The During Phase

The most important thing for you to do here is to *let go!* Give students a chance to work without your guidance. Give them the opportunity to use *their* ideas and not simply follow directions. Your second task is to *listen*. Find out how different children or groups are thinking, what ideas they are using, and how they are approaching the problem.

You must demonstrate confidence and respect for your students' abilities. Set them to work with the expectation that they will solve the problem. Students must deeply believe that the teacher does not have a predetermined or preferred method for solving the problem. If they suspect otherwise there is no reason for them to take risks with their own ideas and methods.

Provide Hints but Not Solutions

How much help to give students is always an issue. Should you let them stumble down the wrong path? Do you correct errors you see? Always keep in mind that as soon as students sense that you have a method of solving the problem, they will almost certainly stop searching for their own methods because they are convinced that your way must be best.

Before being tempted to help or provide a suggestion, first find out what ideas the student or group has. Try to construct any hints on ideas that you hear them considering. "If you think an equivalent fraction might help, then go ahead and try it and see how that turns out." Notice that a phrase like this does not suggest that the student's idea is right or wrong, only that he or she needs to continue with it rather than wait for sanction from you.

You might suggest that the students try using a particular manipulative or drawing a picture if that seems appropriate. For example, if students cannot decide how to work on a percent story problem, the suggestion of a simple drawing showing the parts and the whole can give them some confidence and ideas. (Refer to Chapter 6 for development of this approach.)

Encourage Testing of Ideas

Students will look to you for approval of their results or ideas. Consistently avoid being the source of "truth" or of right and wrong. When asked if a result or method is correct, ask, "How can you decide?" or "Why do you think that might be right?" or "I see what you have done. How can you check that somehow?" Even if not asked for an opinion, asking, "How can we tell if that makes sense?" reminds students that answers without reasons are not acceptable.

Listen Actively

This is one of two opportunities you will get in the lesson (the other is in the discussion period) to find out what your students know, how they think, and how they are approaching the task you have given them. You might sit down with a group and simply listen for a while, have the students explain what they are doing, or take notes. If you want further information, try saying, "Tell me what you are doing," or "I see you have drawn a number line. Can you show me how you are using it?" You want to convey a genuine interest in what students are doing and thinking. This is *not* the time to evaluate or to tell students how to solve the problem.

The After Phase

Plan ample time for this portion of the lesson and then be certain to *save* the time. It is not necessary to wait for every student to finish. Often this is when the best learning will take place. Twenty minutes or more is not at all unreasonable for a good class discussion and sharing of ideas. This is not a time to check answers but for the class to share ideas. Over time, you will develop your class into a community of learners who together are involved in making sense of mathematics. This atmosphere will not develop easily or quickly. You must teach your students about your expectations for this time and how to interact with their peers politely, attentively, and critically.

Engage the Full Class in Discussion

You may want simply to list answers from all of the groups and put them on the board without comment. Following that, you can return to one or more students to get explanations for their solutions or to explain their processes.

When there are different answers, the full class should be involved in the discourse concerning which answers are correct. Allow those responsible for the answers to defend them and then open the discussion to the class. "Who has an idea about this? George, I noticed that you got a different answer than Tomeka. What do you think of her explanation?"

One of your functions is to make sure that all students participate, that all listen, and that all understand what is being said. Encourage students to ask questions. "Pete, did you understand how they did that? Do you want to ask Mary a question?"

A second suggestion is to begin discussions by calling first on the students who tend to be shy or lack the ability to express themselves well. Rowan and Bourne (1994) note that the more obvious ideas are generally given at the outset of a discussion. When asked to participate early and given sufficient time to formulate their thoughts, these reticent students can more easily participate and, thus, be valued.

Make it a habit to ask for explanations to accompany *all* answers. Soon the request for an explanation will not signal an incorrect response, as students initially believe. Many incorrect answers are the result of small errors in otherwise excellent thinking. Likewise, many correct answers may not represent the insightful thinking you might have assumed. A child who has given an incorrect answer is very likely to see the error and correct it during the explanation. Try to support students' thinking without

A THREE-PART FORMAT FOR PROBLEM-BASED LESSONS

evaluating responses. "Does someone have a different idea or want to comment on what Daniel just said?" All children should hear the same teacher reactions that only the so-called "smart kids" used to hear.

Use Praise Cautiously

Be an attentive listener to all ideas, both good and not so good. Praise offered for a correct solution or excitement over an interesting idea suggests that the student did something unusual or unexpected. This can be negative feedback for those who do not get praise.

In place of praise that is judgmental, Schwartz (1996) suggests comments of interest and extension: "I wonder what would happen if you tried" or "Please tell me how you figured that out." Notice that these phrases express interest and value the student's thinking. They also can and should be used regardless of the validity of the responses.

Teachers' Questions About Problem-Based Teaching

A problem-based approach to teaching is a new idea to many teachers. Even for those who have been working at it for some time, there are stumbling blocks and doubts that arise. Here are a few questions that are often raised by teachers and our answers to them.

 After reading each of the following questions, pause first to consider your personal response. Then compare your thoughts with the ideas suggested.

What Can I Tell Them? Should I Tell Them Anything?

When teaching through problem solving, one of the most perplexing dilemmas is how much to tell or not to tell. To tell too little can sometimes leave students floundering and waste precious class time. A good rule of thumb is that you should feel free to share relevant information as long as the mathematics in the task remains problematic for the students (Hiebert et al., 1997). That is, "information can and should be shared as long as it does not solve the problem [and] does not take away the need for students to reflect on the situation and develop solution methods they understand" (p. 36).

According to Hiebert et al., three specific types of information can and should be shared:

1. *Mathematical conventions.* Students must be told about the social conventions of symbolism and terminology that are important in mathematics. For example, the order of operations is a convention. Definitions and labels are also conventions.

2. *Clarification of students' methods.* You should help students clarify or interpret their ideas and perhaps point out related ideas. Discussion or clarification of students' processes focuses attention on ideas you want the class to learn. Care must be taken that attention to one student's ideas does not diminish those of other students or suggest that one method is the preferred approach.

3. *Alternative methods.* You can, with considerable care, suggest to students an alternative method or approach for consideration. You must be very cautious in not conveying to students that their ideas are second best. Nor should students ever be forced to adopt your suggestion over their own approach. In contrast, try this: "The other day I saw some students in another class solve a problem this way. (Show the method.) What do you think of that idea?"

How Will I Be Able to Teach All of the Basic Skills?

There is a tendency to believe that mastery of the basics is incompatible with a problem-based approach or that drill is essential for basic skills. However, the evidence strongly suggests otherwise. First, drill-oriented approaches in U.S. classrooms have consistently produced poor results (Battista, 1999; Kamii & Dominick, 1998; O'Brien, 1999). Short-term gains on low-level skills may possibly result from drill, but even state testing programs require more.

Second, research data indicate that students in constructivist programs based on a problem-solving approach do as well or nearly as well as students in traditional programs on basic skills as measured by standardized tests (Campbell, 1995; Carpenter, Franke, Jacobs, Fennema, & Empson, 1998; Hiebert & Wearne, 1996; Silver & Stein, 1996). Any deficit in skill development is more than outweighed by strength in concepts and problem solving.

Finally, traditional skills such as basic fact mastery and computation can be effectively taught in a problem-solving approach (for example, see Campbell, Rowan, & Suarez, 1998; Huinker, 1998).

Why Is It Okay for a Student to "Tell" or "Explain" but Not for Me?

There are three answers to this question. First, students will question their peers when an explanation does not make sense to them, whereas explanations from the teacher are nearly always accepted without scrutiny—even when they are not understood. Second, when students are responsible for explaining, class members develop a sense of pride and confidence that *they* can figure things out and make sense of mathematics. Third, having to explain forces the student who is doing the explaining to clarify his or her thoughts.

This Approach Takes More Time. How Will I Have Time to Cover Everything?

The first suggestion is to teach with a goal of developing the "big ideas," the main concepts in a unit or chapter. Most of the skills and ideas on your list of objectives will be addressed as you progress. If you focus separately on each item on the list, big ideas and connections—the essence of understanding—are unlikely to develop. Second, with a traditional approach far too much time is spent reteaching because students don't retain ideas. Time spent up front to help students develop meaningful networks of ideas drastically reduces the need for reteaching, thus creating time in the long term. You must have faith that time invested in concept development will create time later.

Do I Need to Use a Problem-Based Approach Every Day?

Yes! Any attempt to mix problem-based methods with traditional teaching by telling will cause difficulties. Consider the response of Mokros, Russell, and Economopoulos (1995):

> In classrooms where both approaches are used to teach a skill, children become confused about when they are supposed to use their own strategies for figuring out a problem and when they are supposed to use the officially sanctioned approach. Children get the sense that:
>
> - Their own approach to problem-solving is merely "exploration," and they will later learn the "right way."
>
> - Their own approach isn't as good as the one the teacher shows.
>
> - The teacher didn't really mean it when he or she said there were lots of good strategies for solving problems like 34 × 68. (p. 79)

Is There Any Place for Drill and Practice?

Yes! However, the tragic error is to believe that drill is a method of developing ideas. Drill is only appropriate when (a) the desired concepts have been meaningfully developed, (b) students already have developed (not mastered) flexible and useful procedures, *and* (c) speed and accuracy are needed. Watch children drilling basic facts who are counting on their fingers or using some other inefficient method. What they may be improving is their ability to count quickly. They are not learning their facts.

If you consider carefully these three criteria for drill, you will likely do much less of it than in the past.

My Textbook Is a Traditional Basal. How Can I Use It?

Traditional textbooks are designed to be teacher directed, a contrast to the approach you have been reading about. But they should not be discarded. Much thought went into the content and the pedagogical ideas. Your book can still be used as a prime resource if you think about translating units and lessons to a problem-oriented approach.

Adopt a *unit perspective.* Avoid the idea that every lesson and idea in the unit requires attention. Examine a chapter or unit from beginning to end and identify the two or three *big ideas,* the essential mathematics in the chapter. (Big ideas are listed at the start of each of the remaining chapters in this book. These may be helpful as a reference.) Temporarily ignore the smaller subideas that often take up a full lesson.

With the big ideas of the unit in mind, you can now do two things: (1) adapt the best or most important lessons in the chapter to a problem-solving format and (2) create or find tasks in the text's teacher notes and other resources that address the big ideas. The combination will almost certainly provide you with an ample supply of tasks.

What Do I Do When a Task Bombs or Students Don't "Get It"?

There may be times when your class simply does not solve the problem during the class period, but not as often as you might suspect. When it does happen, do not give in to the temptation to "show 'em." Set the task aside for the moment. Ask yourself why it bombed. Did the students have the ideas they needed? How did students attempt the task? Occasionally we need to regroup and offer students a simpler related problem that gets them prepared for the one that proved difficult. When you sense that a task is not going anywhere, listen to your students and you will know where to go next. Don't spend days just hoping that something wonderful might happen.

PLANNING IN A PROBLEM-BASED CLASSROOM

Teaching with a problem-based approach requires more time for planning lessons than simply following the pages in a traditional text. Every group of students is different and each day is best built on the actual growth of the previous day. Choices of tasks must be made daily to best fit the needs of your students.

Planning Problem-Based Lessons

The outline in Figure 1.9 illustrates suggested steps for planning a lesson. The first four steps involve the most thought and are the most crucial. The next four steps follow from these initial decisions and will assure that your lesson runs smoothly. Finally, you can write a concise lesson plan that will be easy to follow.

Step 1: ***Begin with the Math!*** Articulate clearly the ideas you want students to learn as a result of the lesson. Think in terms of mathematical concepts, not skills. Describe the mathematics, not the student behavior.

But what if a skill is the intended outcome? Often state or local objectives are written in procedural terms (e.g., "The student will be able to . . ."). Perhaps you want students to be able to solve proportions. Rather than a page of proportions to solve according to your rules, consider tasks that require proportional reasoning. If your students need to compute areas of standard figures, have them develop formulas themselves. Providing formulas into which students "plug and chug" is counterproductive. For these and every other skill there are underlying concepts and relationships. Identify these concepts at this step of your planning.

Step 2: ***Think About Your Students.*** What do your students know or understand about this topic? Are they ready to tackle this bit of mathematics or are there some background ideas that they have not yet developed?

Be sure that the mathematics you identified in step 1 includes something new or at least slightly unfamiliar to your students. At the same time, be certain that your objectives are not out of reach. For real learning to take place, there must be some challenge, some new ideas—even if it is simply

FIGURE 1.9 • • • • • • • • • • • •

Planning steps for thinking
through a problem-based lesson.

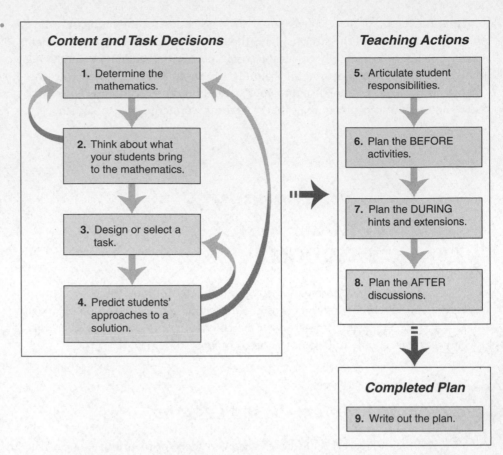

seeing an old idea in a new format or with a different model. If necessary,
now is the time to revisit step 1 and make adjustments in your goals.

Step 3: ***Decide on a Task.*** Keep it simple! Good tasks need not be elaborate.
Often, a simple story problem is all that is necessary as long as the solution involves children in the intended mathematics. Do not feel com-
pelled to search through books for clever or elaborate tasks.

Keep the content foremost in mind. Frantically searching through
books for a problem can be a waste of time due to the difficulty of finding a
task that meets your needs. Teachers frequently realize the task that looked so
good in the resource did not exactly get at the intended mathematics.

Good tasks can often come directly from your text. A direct-instruction
lesson can be modified to allow students to wrestle with the main idea. This
book is full of tasks and is intended as a resource for you. NCTM has numerous publications with excellent ideas. Children's literature can often inspire
great tasks. There are many excellent resource books but stick with those that
allow the mathematics to be problem based. The longer you have had to
build a repertoire of task ideas from journals, resource books, conferences,
and in-service, the easier this important step in planning will become.

Step 4: ***Predict What Will Happen.*** You have made hypotheses about what your
students know and have selected a task. Now use that information and
think about all of the things your students are likely to do with this task.
If you catch yourself saying, "Well, I hope that they will . . . ," then *stop*.
Predict! Don't hope!

Does every student in your class have a chance of engaging in this problem in some manner that is meaningful? Although students may each tackle the task differently, don't leave your struggling students to flounder. Perhaps you want to provide for modifications in the task for different students. (See the discussion of diversity later in this chapter.) This is also a good time to think about whether your students will work alone, in pairs, or in groups. Group work may assist students in need of some extra help.

If your predictions are beginning to make you uneasy about your task, this is the time to revisit the task. Maybe it needs to be modified, or perhaps it is simply too easy or too difficult.

These first four decisions define the heart of your lesson. The next four decisions define how you will carry out the plan in your classroom.

Step 5: ***Articulate Student Responsibilities.*** You always want more than answers. For nearly every task, you want students to be able to tell you

- What they did to get the answer
- Why they did it that way
- Why they think the solution is correct

Decide how you want students to supply this information. If responding in writing, will students write individually or prepare a group presentation? Will they write in their journals, on paper to be turned in, on a page you prepare that includes the problem, or perhaps on acetate that can be used for sharing with the class?

You may choose to have students simply report or discuss their ideas without writing. Although this option may occasionally be adequate, it should not be used often. The reflective value of written work is too great to ignore. Students are less likely to be prepared for discussion if they have not written out their ideas. Writing is a form of rehearsal for discussions.

Step 6: ***Plan the Before Portion of the Lesson.*** Sometimes you can simply begin a lesson with the task and articulation of students' responsibilities. But, in many instances, you will want to orient students' thinking with a related task or warm-up exercise. After presenting the task, will you "let go" or do you want students to brainstorm solutions or estimate answers? (See the earlier discussion of the "before phase" of a lesson on p. 16.)

Consider how you will present the task. Options include having it written on paper, taken from their texts, shown on the overhead, or written on the board or overhead projector.

Step 7: ***Think About the During Portion of the Lesson.*** Look back at your predictions. What hints or assists can you plan in advance for students who may be stuck? Are there particular groups or individual students you wish to specially observe or assess in this lesson? Make a note to do so. Think of extensions or challenges you can pose to students who finish quickly.

Estimate how much time you think students should be given for the task. It is useful to tell students in advance. Some teachers set a timer that all students can see. Plan to be flexible, but do not use up your discussion period.

Step 8: ***Think About the After Portion of the Lesson.*** How will you begin your discussion? One option is to simply list all of the different answers from groups or individuals, doing so without comment, and then returning to students or groups to explain their solutions and justify their answers.

You may also begin with full explanations from each group or student before you get all the answers. Will you record on the board what is being said or have students write on the board or show their work in other ways?

Plan an adequate amount of time for your discussion. A good average is about 15 to 20 minutes.

Step 9: *Write Your Lesson Plan.* If you have thought through these steps, a plan is simply a listing of the critical decisions you have already made. The outline shown here is a possible format:

- The mathematics or goals
- The task and expectations
- The *before* activities
- The *during* hints and extensions for early finishers
- The *after*-lesson discussion format
- Assessment notes (what to be looking for, students to watch)

Note that at the end of each of the remaining chapters of this book, we have selected an activity from the chapter and expanded it into a complete lesson plan utilizing this structure.

Variations of the Three-Part Lesson

Certainly, not every lesson is developed around a task given to a full class. This is especially true in the primary grades. However, the basic concept of tasks and discussions can be adapted to most any problem-based lesson.

Mini-Lessons

Many tasks do not require the full period. The three-part format can be compressed to as little as 10 minutes. You might plan two or three cycles in a single lesson. For example, consider these tasks:

- On your geoboard make two figures, one with rotational symmetry but not line symmetry and the other with line symmetry but not rotational symmetry.

- I want to reduce this drawing on the photocopier so that it will fit inside of a 6-inch square. (Pass out drawing.) By what percentage should I reduce it and keep the drawing as large as possible?

These are worthwhile tasks that do not require a full period to do and discuss. A think-pair-share strategy is useful for these shorter tasks.

Computer Activities and Games

There is no reason in a problem-based classroom to abandon the use of the many computer activities (applets) that focus on a small conceptual area of content. Nor are games necessarily inappropriate. The before portion of a lesson adapted for computer tasks or games generally happens with the whole class when you explain the activity or show briefly how the applet works.

A game or other repeatable activity may not look like a problem, but it can nonetheless be problem based. The determining factor is this: Does the activity cause students to be reflective about new or developing mathematical relationships? If the activity merely has students repeating a procedure without wrestling with an emerging idea, then it is not a problem-based experience. For example, the electronic activities ("e-examples") in the NCTM *e-Standards* or the Illuminations Web site can often be used more than once and still maintain a problem-based spirit for students who have not yet mastered the ideas. (See www.NCTM.org.) When selecting games, look for those that cause students to reflect on ideas rather than those that simply provide drill.

The time during which students are working on the computer or playing games is analogous to the during phase of a lesson. A discussion with students who have been working on a task, the after phase, is just as important for computer tasks and games. Generally, you can wait until all students in the class have worked at the same game or activity and have a full group discussion. Computer tasks should always involve a problem, and these can be discussed like any other problem. For games, ask about strategies that were helpful or ideas that were discovered.

Just as with any task, some form of recording or writing should be included with computer tasks. Students solving a problem on a computer can write up what they did and explain what they learned. Students playing a game can keep records and then tell about how they played the game—what thinking or strategies they used.

Diversity in the Classroom

Perhaps one of the most difficult challenges for teachers today is to reach all of the students in their increasingly diverse classrooms. Every teacher faces this dilemma because every classroom contains a range of student abilities and backgrounds.

Interestingly, a problem-based approach can be the best way to attend to the range of students. In the problem-based classroom, children make sense of the mathematics in their way, bringing to the problems only the skills and ideas that they own. The sophistication of the methods and approaches used will vary in accord with the range of ideas found within the class. In contrast, in a traditional, highly directed lesson, it is assumed that all students will understand and use the same approach and the same ideas. Students not ready to understand the ideas presented by the teacher must focus their attention on following the rules or directions in a mindless manner. This, of course, leads to endless difficulties and leaves many students behind or in need of serious remediation and reteaching.

In addition to using a problem-based approach, specific things you can do to help attend to the diversity of learners in your classroom include:

- Making sure that problems have multiple entry points.
- Plan differentiated tasks.
- Use heterogeneous groupings.

Plan for Multiple Entry Points

Step 4 in the planning guidelines suggests that you predict how all of the students in the class are likely to approach the task you've selected. Many tasks can be solved with a range of strategies. This is especially true of computational tasks in classes in which student-invented methods are encouraged and valued. For many tasks, the use or nonuse of manipulative models is all that is necessary to vary the entry point. Other students can be challenged to devise rules or to use methods that are less dependent on manipulatives or drawings. When considering a task, think of the least sophisticated method of solution you can imagine. Will this method provide an entry for your struggling students? Is there a clever method or extension you can imagine that will challenge your more able students?

Plan Differentiated Tasks

The idea here is to plan a task with multiple versions; some less difficult, others more so.

For many problems involving computations, you can insert multiple sets of numbers. In the following problem, students are told that the first pair of numbers ($4\frac{1}{2}$ and $\frac{3}{4}$) are the easiest problem and each pair gets successively more difficult. They are permitted to select the numbers they wish. If they finish, they can try a second problem.

· ·

The restaurant manager has $\{4\frac{1}{2}, 3\frac{2}{3}, 2\frac{1}{4}\}$ quarts of ice cream left in the freezer. If it takes $\{\frac{3}{4}, \frac{2}{3}, \frac{2}{3}\}$ of a quart to make an ice cream pie, how many pies can he make? Include fractional parts of a pie if there is any leftover ice cream.

· ·

In this example, it is not immediately clear why each problem is harder than the preceding one. However, if students are inventing division strategies or are using drawings or manipulatives, there is a definite progression of difficulty. Because all students are working on what is conceptually the same problem, all will be able to participate in the discussion. Even if the task is not embedded in a story problem, three or four similar computations can be presented in increasing order of difficulty.

As another example, consider the task of finding areas of irregular polygonal shapes. Figure 1.10 shows three shapes that could be offered. Students might all begin with Figure 1.10a and see how many they can solve.

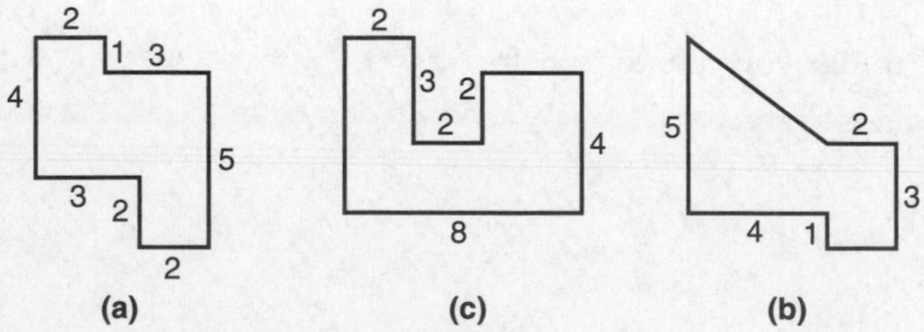

Use Heterogeneous Groupings

Avoid ability grouping! Trying to split a class into ability groups is futile; every group still has diversity. It is demeaning to those students not in the top group. Students in the lower group will not experience the thinking and language of the top group, and top students will not hear the often unconventional but interesting approaches to tasks in the lower group. Furthermore, having two or more groups means that you must diminish the time you can spend with each group.

It is much more profitable to capitalize on the diversity in your room by using pairs or cooperative

FIGURE 1.10 ·

Area tasks of increasing difficulty, left to right. Students solve as many as they can. Tasks of varying difficulty are one method of addressing diversity in the classroom while allowing all students to wrestle with the same basic concepts.

groups that are heterogeneous. Try to pair students in need of help with capable students but also students who will be compatible and willing to assist. Students will find that everyone has ideas to contribute. This does not mean that every cooperative group need be of mixed ability. Some teachers find it useful to vary this approach, sometimes grouping children more homogeneously and other times heterogeneously.

ASSESSMENT IN A PROBLEM-BASED CLASSROOM

In a problem-based approach, teachers often ask, "How do I assess?" The question stems from the realization and acceptance of the fact that the traditional skill-oriented testing fails to adequately tell what students know.

Both the *Assessment Standards for School Mathematics* (1995) and *Principles and Standards for School Mathematics* (2000) stress that the line between assessment and instruction should be blurred. Teaching with problems allows us to blur that line. Assessment need not look different from instruction. The typical approach of an end-of-chapter test of skills may have some value but it is not appropriate as the main method of assessment. Assessment can and should happen every day as an integral part of instruction. If you restrict your view of assessment to tests and quizzes, you will miss seeing how assessment can help students grow and inform instruction. "Assessment should focus on what students *do know* instead of what they *do not know*" (NCTM, 1989).

Appropriate Assessment

An *appropriate assessment task* refers to a task or problem that allows students to demonstrate what they know. Both you and your students must see it as an integral part of the learning process.

If you take a problem-based approach to instruction but most of your assessments focus on recall and closed-response items, you are sending mixed messages to your students. Recall and skill assessments tell students that what is valued is getting answers. Soon they will not be willing to solve problems or engage in class discussions but rather will insist that you simply "show them how to get the answers."

Assessment Tasks

Recall that a problem was any task or activity for which the students have no prescribed or memorized rules or specific correct solution method. The same definition should be used for assessment tasks. Perhaps you have heard about *performance assessment tasks* or *alternative assessments*. These terms seem to refer to tasks that are in some way different from those used in instruction. They should not be different! An assessment task should be a performance task as should problem-based tasks for learning.

Good tasks—for either instruction and/or assessment purposes—should permit every student in the class, regardless of mathematical prowess, to demonstrate his or her knowledge, skill, or understanding. Lower-ability students should be encouraged to use the best ideas they possess to work on a problem, even if these are not the same skills or strategies used by others in the room. When problem-based tasks are used for assessment and evaluation, then rather than find out what students *do not know* (e.g., he can't do percent problems), you will have a broad description of the ideas and skills each student possesses—what they *do know* (e.g., he understands fraction problems; does not see percents as fractions; some confusion with decimals).

Tasks used in this way focus attention on the thinking and processes that students use in solving tasks. The percentage of correct responses is a very incomplete picture of what a student knows. However, the potential data about your students can and should come daily as you "listen" in as many ways as possible to the methods that your students use to grapple with the tasks you give them.

Collecting Assessment Data

In some instances, the real value of a task or what can be learned about students will come primarily during the discussion in the after phase of your lesson. At other times the best assessment data will be in the written work that students do. To consistently receive valid data, it is important that you develop in your students the habit of adding justifications to their answers and listening to and evaluating the explanations of others.

The amount of information available from students, both from their written work and their discussions, is voluminous. However, you must find ways to record it so that you have the information when you need it. Your memory of what transpired today may be sufficient for planning tomorrow's lesson. However, to help with grades and parent conferences, you need records. Here are some ideas:

- Make a habit of recording quick observational data. There are lots of options. A full class checklist with space for comments is one method. Another is to write anecdotal notes on address labels and stick them into binders.

- Focus on big ideas rather than small skills. For example, "is working on estimation to place decimal point in computations" is more helpful than "performs decimal computation with 70% accuracy."

- You need not assess every child on every task. By focusing on big ideas, you will not feel required to check on every student on any given day. Make a habit of selecting a small number of students to focus on during a lesson. Gather data on a big idea over a week or so.

- Save or make copies of student work that indicates well the thinking of a child. There may be days when you announce to students that you are going to keep their written work in their folders. However, some students may produce better work the next day or will have done better thinking the day before. Use written work to show what students know.

- Use traditional tests for skills that you feel are essential. Use this technique sparingly.

Rubrics and Their Uses

Appropriate assessment tasks yield an enormous amount of information that cannot be evaluated by simply counting correct answers. We need to find ways to manage this information and make it useful. One important tool is a rubric.

A *rubric* consists of a scale of three to six points that is used as a rating of performance rather than a count of how many items are correct or incorrect. The rating is applied by examining total performance on a single task as opposed to counting the number of items correct.

Simple Rubrics

The following simple four-point rubric was developed by the New Standards Project and is used by many teachers and some school districts:

4   Excellent: Full Accomplishment

3   Proficient: Substantial Accomplishment

2   Marginal: Partial Accomplishment

1   Unsatisfactory: Little Accomplishment

This four-point rubric allows a teacher to rate performances using a double-sort technique as illustrated in Figure 1.11. The broad categories of the first sort (*Got It* or *Not Yet*) are relatively easy to discern. The scale then allows you to separate each category into two levels as shown. Some teachers use a 4+ rating to note truly exceptional performance. A rating of 0 can be given for no response or effort or for responses that are completely off task.

The advantage of the four-point scale is the relatively easy double sort that can be made. The first sort, between those who have basically developed the idea from those students who need further experiences or instruction, is most important for judging how to pace your lessons and identifying students in need of additional instruction.

3   Above and beyond—uses exemplary methods, shows creativity, goes beyond the requirements of the problem

2   On target—completes the task with no more than minor errors, uses expected approaches

1   Not there yet—makes significant errors or omissions, uses inappropriate approaches

The exact rubric you use is less important than having a well-understood method of communicating with your students and parents and making it easier for you to record assessment data.

FIGURE 1.11 • • • • • • •

With a four-point rubric, performances are first sorted into two categories. Each performance is then considered again and assigned to a point on the scale.

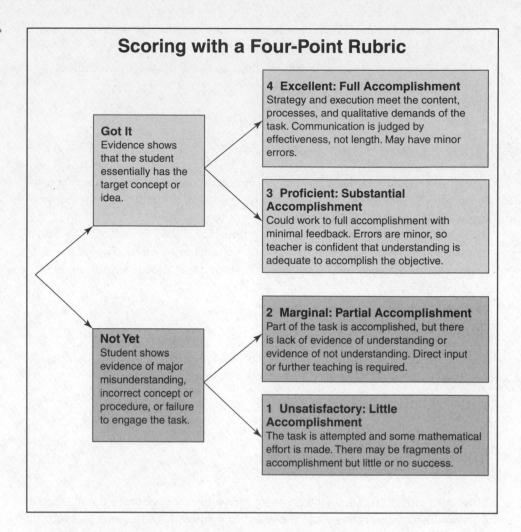

Scoring with a Four-Point Rubric

Got It
Evidence shows that the student essentially has the target concept or idea.

4 Excellent: Full Accomplishment
Strategy and execution meet the content, processes, and qualitative demands of the task. Communication is judged by effectiveness, not length. May have minor errors.

3 Proficient: Substantial Accomplishment
Could work to full accomplishment with minimal feedback. Errors are minor, so teacher is confident that understanding is adequate to accomplish the objective.

Not Yet
Student shows evidence of major misunderstanding, incorrect concept or procedure, or failure to engage the task.

2 Marginal: Partial Accomplishment
Part of the task is accomplished, but there is lack of evidence of understanding or evidence of not understanding. Direct input or further teaching is required.

1 Unsatisfactory: Little Accomplishment
The task is attempted and some mathematical effort is made. There may be fragments of accomplishment but little or no success.

Involve Students with Rubrics

In the beginning of the year, discuss your general rubric with the class. You may find that your students respond more to phrases like "Wow," "Got It," "Not Quite," and "Need Help." Post the rubric prominently. It is possible to use the same rubric for all subjects. If you do not teach your students all day, discuss this with the other teachers in your grade level. It can be helpful to students if the words for evaluation that students hear are the same throughout the day. In your discussion, let students know that as they do activities and solve problems in class, you will look at their work and listen to their explanations and occasionally provide them with feedback in terms of the rubric rather than as a letter grade or other evaluative mark.

Make it a habit to discuss performance on tasks in terms of the general rubric. You might have students rate their own work according to the rubric and explain their reasons for the rating. You can have class discussions about a task that has been done and what might constitute good and exceptional performance.

A rubric is much more than a grade. It is a meaningful and helpful form of communication with your students (and their parents). It should let students know how well they are doing and encourage them to work harder. When their performance is less than okay, students should understand not that they have failed but that there are ideas they need to work on. Your task is to see that they get that opportunity and your help.

You do not need to use rubrics with every task. Nor is it necessary to reserve rubrics for assessments that you want to grade. If you are using the four-point rubric just described, the language of the rubric can be used informally with your students. "Maggie, that paper is only a 2. I know you can do better."

The rubric scale can also be used in your observation recordings. If you describe the task at the top of a class roster, then it is easier and faster to record a 2, 3, or 4 next to a name than it is to write out a detailed comment.

Diagnostic Interviews

An interview is simply a one-on-one discussion with a student to help you see how she is thinking about a particular subject, what processes she uses in solving problems, or what attitudes and beliefs she may have. It may be as short as 5 to 10 minutes.

Many teachers avoid interviews because of time constraints. This is unfortunate because interviews have the potential to give you information that you simply cannot get in any other way. Think of interviews as a method to be used for only a few students at a time—not for every student in the class. You can interview a single student while the rest of the class is working on a task.

The most obvious reason to consider an interview is that you need more information concerning a particular student and how he or she is constructing concepts or using a procedure. Remediation will almost always be more successful if you can pinpoint *why* a student is having difficulty before you try to fix the problem.

A second reason is to get information either to plan your instruction or to assess the effectiveness of your instruction. For example, are you sure that your students have a good understanding of equations and variables, or are they just doing the exercises according to rote rules?

Planning an Interview

There is no magic right way to plan or structure an interview. In fact, flexibility is a key ingredient. You should, however, have some overall game plan before you begin and be prepared with key questions and materials. Begin an interview with questions that are easy or closest to what the student is likely to be able to do, usually some form of procedural exercise. For numeration or computation topics, for example, begin with a pencil-and-paper computation. When the opening task has been completed, ask the student to explain what was done. "How would you explain this to a fifth grader?" "What does this (point to something on the paper) stand for?" "Tell me about why you do it that way." At this point, you may try a similar task but with a different feature; for example, after doing $\frac{2}{3} \times \frac{1}{4}$, try a problem with mixed numbers. With mixed numbers, the algorithm cannot be immediately applied. Does the student change the problem to improper fractions or use the whole numbers and fractions separately?

The next phase of the interview might involve models or drawings that the student can use to demonstrate understanding of the earlier procedural task. Decimals and percents might be explored with base-ten materials or 10 × 10 grids. There are numerous models for fractions, and it may be useful to see if one model is more meaningful than another. Be careful not to interject or teach. The temptation to do so is sometimes overwhelming. Watch and listen. Next, explore connections between what was done with models and what was done with pencil and paper. Many students will do the very same task and get two different answers. Does it matter to the student? How is the discrepancy explained? Can the student connect actions using models to what he or she wrote or explained earlier?

Alternative beginnings to an interview include making an estimate of the answer to either a computation or a word problem, doing a computation mentally, or trying to predict the solution to a given task. Your goal is not to use the interview to teach but to find out where the student is in terms of concepts and procedures at this time.

Suggestions for Effective Interviews

The following suggestions have been adapted from excellent discussions of interviewing children by Labinowicz (1985, 1987), Liedtke (1988), and Scheer (1980).

- *Be accepting and neutral as you listen to the child.* Smiles, frowns, or other body language can make the child think that the answer he or she gave is right or wrong. Develop neutral responses such as "Uh-huh," "I see," or even a silent nod of the head.

- *Avoid cuing or leading the child.* "Are you sure about that?" "Now look again closely at what you just did." "Wait. Is that what you mean?" These responses will indicate to students that they have made some mistake and cause them to change their responses. This can mask what they really think and understand. A similar form of leading is a series of easily answered questions that direct the student to a correct response. That is teaching, not interviewing.

- *Wait silently.* Give the student plenty of time before you ask a different question or probe. After the student makes a response, wait again! This second wait time is even more important because it allows and encourages the student to elaborate on the initial thought and provide you with more information. Wait even when the response is correct. Waiting can also give you a bit more time to think about the direction you want the interview to take. Your wait time will almost never be as long as you imagine it is.

- *Do not interrupt.* Let children's thoughts flow freely. Encourage students to use their own words and ways of writing things down. Interjecting questions or correcting language can be distracting to students' thinking.

- *Use imperatives rather than questions.* Say, "show me," "tell me," "do," or "try," rather than "can you?" or "will you?" In response to a question, the child can simply say no, leaving you without information.

- *Avoid confirming a request for validation.* Students frequently follow answers or actions with, "Is that right?" This query can easily be answered with a neutral, "That's fine," or "You're doing okay," regardless of whether the answer is right or wrong.

Interviewing is not an easy thing to do well. Many teachers are timid about it and fail to take the time. But not much damage is possible, and the rewards of listening to children, both for you and your students, are so great that you really do not want to pass it up.

Grading

Myth: A grade is an average of a series of scores on tests and quizzes. The accuracy of the grade depends primarily on the accuracy of the computational technique used to calculate the final numeric grade.

Reality: A grade is a statistic that is used to communicate to others the achievement level that a student has attained in a particular area of study. The accuracy or validity of the grade depends on the information that is used in preparing the grade, the professional judgment of the teacher, and the alignment of the assessments with the true goals and objectives of the course.

Confronting the Myth

Most experienced teachers will say that they know a great deal about their students in terms of what the students know, how they perform in different situations, their attitudes and beliefs, and their various levels of skill attainment. Unfortunately, when it comes to grades, they often ignore this rich storehouse of information and rely on test scores and rigid averages that tell only a small fraction of the story.

The myth of grading by statistical number crunching is so firmly ingrained in schooling at all levels that you may find it hard to abandon. But it is unfair to students, to parents, and to you as the teacher to ignore all of the information you get almost daily from a problem-based approach in favor of a handful of numbers based on tests that usually focus on low-level skills.

Grading Issues

Some hard decisions are inevitable for effective use of the assessment information gathered from problems, tasks, and other appropriate methods to assign grades. Some decisions are philosophical, some require school or district agreements about grades, and all require us to examine what we value and the objectives we communicate to students and parents.

Using rubric scales to provide feedback and to encourage a pursuit of excellence must also relate to grades. However, "converting four out of five to 80 percent or three out of four to a grade of C can destroy the entire purpose of alternative assessment and the use of scoring rubrics" (Kulm, 1994, p. 99). Kulm explains that directly translating rubrics to grades focuses attention on grades and away from the purpose of every good problem-solving activity, which is to strive for an excellent performance. When papers are returned with less than top ratings, the purpose is to help students know what is necessary to achieve at a higher level. (This purpose must be explicitly communicated to students and parents.) Early on, there should be opportunities to improve based on feedback. When a grade of 75 percent or a C– is returned, all the student knows is that he or she did poorly. If, for example, a student's ability to justify his own answers and solutions has improved, should he be penalized in the averaging of numbers that includes a weaker performance early in the marking period?

What this means is that grading must be based on the performance tasks and other activities for which you assigned rubric ratings; otherwise, students will soon realize that these are not important scores. At the same time, they need not be added or averaged in any numeric manner. The grade at the end of a unit or chapter should reflect a holistic view of where the student is now relative to your goals for that unit.

The grades you assign should reflect all of your objectives. Procedural skills remain important but should be weighted in proportion to other goals in keeping with your value system. If you are restricted to assigning a single grade for mathematics, different factors probably have different weights or values in making up the grade. There are no simple answers to how you balance all of your objectives—concepts, skills, problem solving, communication, and so on. However, these questions should be addressed at the beginning of the grading period and not the night you set out to assign grades.

A multidimensional reporting system is a big help. If you can assign several grades for mathematics and not just one, your report to parents is more meaningful. Even if the school's report card does not permit multiple grades, you can devise a supplement indicating several ratings for different objectives. A place for comments is also helpful. This form can be shared with students periodically during a grading period and can easily accompany a report card.

GET STARTED

In this chapter we have briefly touched on the foundational ideas of how children learn, teaching through problem solving, planning problem-based lessons, and assessment. It may take some time for you to completely adopt these ideas and approaches. Some things may make more sense to you than others. It may be discomforting to give up methods with which you've become familiar. It is hard to think of allowing—even planning for—the students in your room to struggle. Most people get into teaching because they want to help students learn. To not show them a solution when they are experiencing difficulty seems almost counterintuitive.

It is unrealistic to think you could simply read this chapter and then turn around and become a problem-based teacher. However, if you give this approach a fair chance and try to apply your understanding of how children learn to your daily teaching, your students will reward you with their performance, enthusiasm, and understanding. No, it will not happen overnight. But now is the time to begin—so get started!

As reflective thinking is the key ingredient in student learning, so also is reflection necessary to improve as a teacher. Do not be discouraged by lessons that did not go as you planned. Rather, ask yourself what happened and why. How could you have changed the lesson to make it better? How will you apply what you learned to the next lesson?

Social learning is also an important tool for teachers. Get other teachers on your grade level or in your school to try new ideas together. Talk informally about what seems to make a good lesson and what gets in the way. Use the planning guide discussed in this chapter to create lessons together. Don't try to jointly plan every lesson—just one every two or three weeks. Then have everyone teach the same lesson and compare notes. Make revisions based on your experiences. File these "special" lessons away and use them next year.

In addition to simply getting started and trying these ideas, the most important ingredient is to *Believe in your kids!* Your students can think and can make sense of mathematics—*all of your students*. Some may learn more slowly or create different approaches that have never occurred to you, but they all can think and they all can learn. By allowing the mathematics to be problem based for students every day, we demonstrate our belief every day in their abilities to do and learn mathematics. Just give them the chance and let them amaze you.

FLEXIBLE STRATEGIES FOR WHOLE-NUMBER COMPUTATION

Much of the public sees computational skill as the hallmark of what it means to know mathematics at the elementary and middle school levels. Although this is far from the truth, the issue of computational skills with whole numbers is, in fact, a very important part of the curriculum.

Rather than a single method of multiplication (or any operation), the most appropriate method can and should change flexibly as the numbers and the context change. In the spirit of the *Standards,* the issue is no longer a matter of "knows how to multiply three-digit numbers"; rather it is the development over time of an assortment of flexible skills that will best serve students in the real world.

It is quite possible that you do not have these skills, but you can acquire them. Work at them as you learn about them. Equip yourself with a flexible array of computational strategies.

Toward Computational Fluency

With today's technology the need for doing tedious computations by hand has essentially disappeared. At the same time, we now know that there are numerous

big ideas

1 Flexible methods of computation involve taking apart and combining numbers in a wide variety of ways. Most of the partitions of numbers are based on place value or "compatible" numbers—number pairs that work easily together, such as 25 and 75.

2 Invented strategies are flexible methods of computing that vary with the numbers and the situation. Successful use of the strategies requires that they be understood by the one who is using them—hence, the term *invented.* Strategies may be invented by a peer or the class as a whole; they may even be suggested by the teacher. However, they must be constructed by the student.

3 Flexible methods for computation require a good understanding of the operations and properties of the operations, especially the commutative property and the distributive property for multiplication. How the operations are related—addition to subtraction, addition to multiplication, and multiplication to division—is also an important ingredient.

4 The traditional algorithms are clever strategies for computing that have been developed over time. Each is based on performing the operation on one place value at a time with transitions to an adjacent position (trades, regrouping, "borrows," or "carries"). Traditional algorithms tend to make us think in terms of digits rather than the composite number that the digits make up. These algorithms work for all numbers but are often far from the most efficient or useful methods of computing.

methods of computing that can be handled either mentally or with pencil-and-paper support. In most everyday instances, these alternative strategies for computing are easier and faster, can often be done mentally, and contribute to our overall number sense. The traditional algorithms (procedures for computing) do not have these benefits.

Consider the following problem.

Becky earns $28 each week babysitting. How much money will she earn in 7 weeks?

 Try solving the babysitting problem using some method other than the one you were taught in school. If you want to begin with the 8 and the 7, try a different approach. Can you do it mentally? Can you do it in more than one way? Work on this before reading further.

Here are just three of many methods to solve the computation in the babysitting problem:

7 × 20 is 140 and 7 × 8 is 56. 140 and 56 is 196.

7 × 30 is 210, subtract two 7s gives 196.

7 25's is 175, plus seven 3s gives 196.

Strategies such as these can be done mentally, are generally faster than the traditional algorithms, and make sense to the person using them. Every day, students and adults resort to error-prone, traditional strategies when other, more meaningful methods would be faster and less susceptible to error. Our goal is to help our students develop numerical power—the ability to work flexibly and easily with numbers, not the ability to repeatedly perform the same procedure. Flexibility with a variety of computational strategies is an important tool for successful daily living. It is time to broaden our perspective of what it means to compute.

Invented Strategies

Carpenter, Franke, Jacobs, Fennnema, and Empson (1998) refer to any strategy other than the traditional algorithm and that does not involve the use of physical materials or counting by ones an *invented strategy*. We will use this term also, although *personal and flexible strategies* might be equally appropriate. At times, invented strategies are done mentally. For example, 75 + 19 can be done mentally (75 + 20 is 95, less 1 is 94). For 847 + 256, some students may write down intermediate steps to aid in memory as they work through the problem. (Try that one yourself.) In the classroom, some written support is often encouraged as strategies develop. Written records of thinking are more easily shared and help students focus on the ideas. The distinction between written, partially written, and mental is not important, especially in the development period.

Not all students invent their own strategies. Strategies invented by class members are shared, explored, and tried out by others. However, no student should be permitted to use any strategy without understanding it.

Mental Computation

A mental computation strategy is simply any invented strategy that is done mentally. What may be a mental strategy for one student may require written support by another. Initially, students should not be asked to do computations mentally, as this may threaten students who have not yet developed a reasonable invented strategy. At the same time, you may be quite amazed at the ability of students (and at your own ability) to do computations mentally.

Try your own hand with this example:

$$73 + 98$$

 For the addition task just shown, avoid the temptation to do the standard procedure in your head. What number is 98 close to that would make this computation easier to do?

When the computations are a bit more complicated, the challenge is more interesting and generally there are more alternatives, as we saw in the babysitting problem.

As your students become more adept, they can and should be challenged from time to time to do appropriate computations mentally. However, do not expect the same skills of all students.

Contrasts with Traditional Algorithms

There are significant differences between invented strategies and the traditional algorithms.

1. *Invented strategies are number oriented rather than digit oriented.* For example, an invented strategy for 68 × 7 begins 7 × 60 is 420 and 56 more is 476. The first product is 7 times *sixty,* not the digit 6, as would be the case in the traditional algorithm. Using the traditional algorithm for 45 + 32, students never think of 40 and 30 but rather 4 + 3. Kamii, long a crusader against standard algorithms, claims that they "unteach" place value (Kamii & Dominick, 1998).
2. *Invented strategies are left-handed rather than right-handed.* Invented strategies begin with the largest parts of numbers, those represented by the leftmost digits. For 26 × 47, invented strategies might begin with 20 × 40 is 800, providing some sense of the size of the eventual answer in just one step. The traditional algorithm begins with 7 × 6 is 42. By beginning on the right with a digit orientation, traditional methods hide the result until the end. Long division is an exception.
3. *Invented strategies are flexible rather than rigid.* Invented strategies tend to change with the numbers involved in order to make the computation easier. Try each of these mentally: 465 + 230 and 526 + 98. Did you use the same method? The

traditional algorithm suggests using the same tool on all problems. The traditional algorithm for 7000 – 25 typically leads to student errors, yet a mental strategy is relatively simple (Carroll & Porter, 1997).

Benefits of Invented Strategies

The development of invented strategies delivers more than computational facility. Both the development of these strategies and their regular use have positive benefits that are difficult to ignore.

- *Base-ten concepts are enhanced.* There is a definite interaction between the development of base-ten concepts and the process of inventing computational strategies (Carpenter et al., 1998). "Invented strategies demonstrate a hallmark characteristic of understanding" (p. 16). The development of invented strategies should be integrated with the development of base-ten concepts.

- *Invented strategies are built on student understanding.* Students rarely use an invented strategy they do not understand. In contrast, students are frequently seen to use traditional algorithms without being able to explain why they work (Carroll & Porter, 1997).

- *Students make fewer errors with invented strategies.* Data collected by Kamii and Dominick (1997) provide some hard evidence for this claim. With traditional algorithms, students tend to develop systematic errors or "buggy algorithms" that they use again and again. Careless errors often result from confusion with carried digits or column alignment. Systematic errors are not typical of invented strategies.

- *Invented strategies serve students at least as well on standard tests.* Evidence from reform programs, in which students develop invented strategies, suggests that students not taught traditional algorithms fare about as well in computation on standardized tests as students in traditional programs (Campbell, 1996; Carroll, 1996, 1997; Chambers, 1996). As an added bonus, students tend to do quite well with word problems, since they are the principal vehicle for developing invented strategies. The pressures of external testing do not dictate a focus on the traditional algorithms.

When teachers first see alternative methods for computation, many think that the methods are too difficult and confusing for students. First of all, these invented strategies are built on students' ideas and understanding. Second, these alternative methods for computation tend to be more difficult and confusing for *us*, not the students, because we are more familiar and comfortable with the standard procedures. Before you reject the idea of helping your students develop invented strategies, walk through the standard procedure for multiplying, say, 23 by 57. Consider the procedure from a student's perspective. The standard procedures for computation are very efficient algorithms that have developed over the years. One of the benefits of the standard procedures is that they are efficient—they use the least number of pencil strokes to complete the computation. However, the biggest difficulty in learning the standard procedures is also connected to this efficiency: The efficiency masks the meaning, so learning how to do the procedures is often about memorizing the steps to complete the computation. Spending time developing invented strategies can lay the groundwork for teaching the standard procedures in a meaningful way.

Traditional Algorithms

In everyday life, the need for a traditional algorithm generally increases as the number of digits or complexity of a necessary computation increases. It is difficult to compute 486 × 372 without a digit-oriented algorithm. Similar statements are true of division. For addition and subtraction, one can easily argue that well-understood and practiced invented strategies are more than adequate. Since we have grown up with the traditional algorithms, abandoning them is difficult to imagine.

By fifth or sixth grade, it is almost certain that your students have been exposed to the traditional algorithms for whole numbers. More than likely, students have not only been taught these algorithms but also have come to believe that these are the "right" ways to compute. These are the methods that previous teachers have taught them. Once having begun with traditional methods, it is extremely difficult to suggest to students that they learn other methods. Notice how difficult it is for you to begin computations by working from the left rather than the right and to think in terms of whole numbers rather than digits. These habits, once established, are difficult to break.

Traditional algorithms are in no way evil, and so to forbid their use is somewhat arbitrary. However, students who have become familiar with a traditional method often resist the invention of more flexible strategies. What do you do then?

First and foremost, apply the same rule to traditional algorithms as to all strategies: *If you use it, you must understand why it works and be able to explain it.* In an atmosphere that says, "Let's figure out why this works," students can profit from making sense of these algorithms just like any other. But the responsibility should be theirs, not yours.

Accept a traditional algorithm (once it is understood) as one more strategy to put in the class "tool box" of methods. But reinforce the idea that like the other strategies, it may be more useful in some instances than in others. Pose problems where a mental strategy is much more useful, such as 504 – 498 or 75 × 4. Discuss which method seemed best. Point out that for a problem such as 4568 + 12,813, the traditional algorithm has some advantages. But in the real world, most people do those computations on a calculator.

As already noted, you should probably not make a big distinction between mental methods and invented strategies. However, by the middle grades, encouraging students to do computations mentally may be necessary in order to wean them from their reliance on traditional strategies. Even then, students' first attempts at mental strategies are often an attempt to "see" their familiar traditional algorithm in their heads. Explain that this is not what you mean by doing a computation mentally since what they are doing is using a mental blackboard. You may have to offer some examples.

Development of Invented Strategies: A General Approach

Students do not spontaneously invent wonderful computational methods while the teacher sits back and watches. Among different reform or progressive programs, students tended to develop or gravitate toward different strategies suggesting that teachers and the programs do have an effect on what methods students develop. This section discusses general pedagogical methods for helping students develop invented strategies.

Motivating Students to Use Invented Strategies

Because your students have likely adapted standard procedures for computation and may not have a well-developed sense of number, you should begin by asking your students to come up with alternative ways to add or subtract multidigit numbers. These experiences will help them begin to pull numbers apart in a less threatening context. Once they have become confident with alternative ways to add and subtract multidigit numbers, they will be more willing and able to find alternative approaches to multiply and divide multidigit numbers.

First of all, students need to be convinced that the standard algorithms for addition and subtraction are not always the best strategies to use. Although speed should not always dictate the method used—especially if it interferes with sense making—you can use it to convince students that alternative methods might be better to use in some situations. Form three "teams": one team that has to use the standard algorithms to do computations; one team that has to use calculators; and one team comprised of you, the teacher, who will use alternative ways to compute—so choose the numbers in the computation carefully! (Possible computations are 98 + 22; 45 + 75; 83 – 44.) If you would prefer to form the third team using students, form the team with students who already use alternative strategies. The "team" who correctly completes a computation first earns a point.

As the third team begins to earn more and more points, students in the other groups may begin to protest that the competition is not fair because they are using faster ways to do the computations. At some point, ask students to think (either in pairs or small groups) about alternative ways to do a particular computation. Have students share and discuss various approaches. You will find more details about invented strategies for adding and subtracting multidigit numbers later in the chapter.

This competition serves at least three purposes: (1) it allows for the introduction of alternative strategies; (2) it illustrates that alternative strategies can be faster and somewhat easier to perform; and (3) it also illustrates that the calculator is not always the fastest way to do a computation.

Use Story Problems Frequently

When computational tasks are embedded in simple contexts, students seem to be more engaged than they are with bare computations. Keep in mind that the numbers used in the story problems can influence the strategies used to do the computation. For example, consider 298 × 42. Since 298 is so close to 300, students can think 300 × 42 and then subtract 2 × 42. For 41 × 16, they can multiply 41 × 8 to get 328 and then double it to get 656. Students can choose an approach that best fits the numbers in the given problem. Use this to your advantage if you want a particular strategy to surface. Furthermore, the choice of story problems influences the strategies students use to solve them. Consider these problems:

Max had already saved 68 cents when Mom gave him some money for running an errand. Now Max has 93 cents. How much did Max earn for his errand?

> **George took 93 cents to the store. He spent 68 cents. How much does he have left?**

The computation 93 − 68 solves both problems, but the first is more likely than the second to be solved by an add-on method. In a similar manner, fair-share division problems are more likely to encourage a share strategy than a measurement or repeated subtraction problem.

Children's literature can play a very useful role in helping you develop problems for your invented strategies and mental computation lessons. Your simple story problems every day may be great, but students deserve a change. There are a great many fascinating books that involve large numbers and opportunities to compute. Some are about real data, and others are fictional. *Cookies* by Jaspersohn is one such example.

This is the true story of Wally Amos and his Famous Amos Chocolate Chip Cookies. (Are you interested already?) The text includes a large number of color and black-and-white photos that show the production and distribution of Famous Amos cookies. Because it is filled with facts about the cookies—numbers sold, number the average person eats in a year, and so on—you can easily pose questions that require computation and that students will find interesting. Although actual computations can be done on a calculator, this context clearly suggests that estimates and round numbers make more sense. As you discuss ideas generated by the book, some computations can be done mentally to determine exact answers. Other computations will be estimates. Students can extend the story to a project to research cookie consumption in their home, data from grocery stores about other cookies, or the number of trucks or miles required to get cookies to market. The possibilities are endless.

Not every task need be a story problem. Especially when students are engaged in figuring out a new strategy, bare arithmetic problems are quite adequate.

Use the Three-Part Lesson Format

The three-part lesson format described in Chapter 1 is a good structure for an invented-strategy lesson. The task can be one or two story problems or even a bare computation but always with the expectation that the method of solution will be discussed. Sometimes you can provide variations with different numbers to different groups to adjust for difficulty.

Allow plenty of time to solve a problem. Listen to the different strategies students are using, but do not interject your own. Challenge able students to find a second method or improve on a written explanation. Students who finish quickly may share their methods with others before sharing with the class.

The most important portion of the lesson comes when students explain their solution methods. Help students write their explanations on the board or overhead. Encourage students to ask questions of their classmates. Occasionally have the class try a particular method with different numbers to see how it works. When students find a particular idea worthwhile, record it on a "strategies chart." Remember, not every student will invent strategies. However, students can and will try strategies that they have seen and that make sense to them. Make a firm rule that *no one may use a strategy that he or she does not understand.*

DEVELOPMENT OF INVENTED STRATEGIES: A GENERAL APPROACH

Assessment Note

Parents are perhaps more interested in their children's computational skills than in any other area. It is quite easy to give a test of computation like those provided in traditional textbooks. When students do well on these tests, parents are pleased. But what do you know when students do not do well? At best you can make inferences based on the papers turned in. You can look for basic-fact errors and carelessness or perhaps find a systematic error in an algorithm. What you do not know is how children are solving these problems and what ideas and strategies they have developed that are useful or need further development.

Ongoing Assessment

When computational strategies and algorithms are developed in the manner suggested in this chapter, every day you are presented with a wealth of assessment data. The important thing is to gather, record, and use these data for individual students the same as you would for tests and quizzes.

As you walk around in the during portion of your lessons, and also in the after portion when children explain their computation strategies and reasoning, you can make notes on a chart similar to the one in Figure 2.1. Make a new chart each week but keep the old ones to provide evidence of growth over time. These charts can be useful for grading and for parent conferences. There is no harm in giving an occasional quiz or test of computational skills. But avoid giving more value to tests simply because they are objective. Compare the results with the information you have gathered through observation. Did you get any new information? Were the results consistent? If not, why not?

FIGURE 2.1 • • • • • • • •

A checklist with space for comments or notes lets you record daily observations of students' progress toward computational fluency.

Topic: Invented strategies for multiplication / Student	Multiplies two-digit by two-digit numbers	Methods used	Flexibility in choosing a method (circle one, 1 being highest)			Comments
Lalie			1	2	3	
Pete			1	2	3	
Sid			1	2	3	
Marissa			1	2	3	

Invented Strategies for Addition and Subtraction

Research has demonstrated that students will invent a lot of different strategies for addition and subtraction. Your goal might be that each of your students has at least one or two methods that are reasonably efficient, mathematically correct, and useful with lots of different numbers. Expect different students to settle on different strategies.

Mental computation should be encouraged. However, recording of strategies on the board not only helps communicate ideas but also helps students who need the short-term memory assistance of recording intermediate steps.

Adding Two-Digit Numbers

For the examples that follow, a possible recording method is offered. These are intended to be suggestions, not prescriptions. Students have difficulty inventing recording techniques. If you record their ideas on the board as they explain their ideas, you are helping them develop written techniques. You may even discuss recording methods with individuals or with the class to decide on a form that seems to work well. Horizontal formats encourage students to think in terms of numbers instead of digits. A horizontal format is also less likely to encourage use of the traditional algorithms.

Students will often use a counting-by-tens-and-ones technique for some of these methods. That is, instead of "46 + 30 is 76," they may count "46 ⟶ 56, 66, 76." These counts can be written down as they are said to help students keep track.

Figure 2.2 illustrates four different strategies for addition of two two-digit numbers. The following story problem is a suggestion.

....

The two Scout troops went on a field trip. There were 46 Girl Scouts and 38 Boy Scouts. How many Scouts went on the trip?

....

The *move to make ten* and *compensation* strategies are useful when one of the numbers ends in 8 or 9. To promote that strategy, present problems with addends like 39 or 58. Note that it is only necessary to adjust one of the two numbers.

 Try adding 367 + 155 in as many different ways as you can. How many of your ways are like those in Figure 2.2?

Invented Strategies for Addition with Two-Digit Numbers	

Add Tens, Add Ones, Then Combine
 	
  46 + 38
 	
40 and 30 is 70.
6 and 8 is 14.
70 and 14 is 84.
	Move Some to Make Tens
	
	  46 + 38
	
	Take 2 from the 46 and put it with the 38 to make 40. Now you have 44 and 40 more is 84.

Add On Tens, Then Add Ones
 	
  46 + 38
 	
46 and 30 more is 76.
Then I added on the other 8.
76 and 4 is 80 and 4 is 84.
	Use a Nice Number and Compensate
	
	  46 + 38
	
	46 and 40 is 86.
	That's 2 extra, so it's 84.

FIGURE 2.2 • • • • • • • •

Four different invented strategies for adding two two-digit numbers.

Subtracting by Counting Up

This is an amazingly powerful way to subtract. The concept is the same as the think-addition strategy students used for their basic facts. It is important to use *join with change unknown* problems or *missing-part* problems to encourage the counting-up strategy. Here is an example of each.

Sam had 46 baseball cards. He went to a card show and got some more cards for his collection. Now he has 73 cards. How many cards did Sam buy at the card show?

Juanita counted all of her crayons. Some were broken and some not. She had 73 crayons in all. 46 crayons were not broken. How many were broken?

The numbers in these problems are used in the strategies illustrated in Figure 2.3.

Take-Away Subtraction

Using take-away is considerably more difficult to do mentally. However, take-away strategies are common, probably because students have been taught that take-away is the meaning of subtraction. Four different strategies are shown in Figure 2.4.

There were 73 children on the playground. The 46 second-grade students came in first. How many children were still outside?

The two methods that begin by taking tens from tens are reflective of what most younger students do with base-ten pieces. The other two methods leave one of the numbers intact and subtract from it. Try 83 – 29 in your head by first taking away 30

FIGURE 2.3 ········

Subtraction by counting up is a powerful method.

Invented Strategies for Subtraction by Counting Up	
Add Tens to Get Close, Then Ones 73 – 46 46 and 20 is 66. (30 more is too much.) Then 4 more is 70 and 3 is 73. That's 20 and 7 or 27. $46 > 20$ $66 > 4$ $70 > 3$ $73 \underline{} 27$	**Add Ones to Make a Ten, Then Tens and Ones** 73 – 46 46 and 4 is 50. 50 and 20 is 70 and 3 more is 73. The 4 and 3 is 7 and 20 is 27. 73 – 46 $46 + 4 \rightarrow 50$ $+ 20 \rightarrow 70$ $\underline{+ 3 \rightarrow 73}$ 27
Add Tens to Overshoot, Then Come Back 73 – 46 46 and 30 is 76. That's 3 too much, so it's 27. 73 – 46 $46 + 30 \rightarrow 76 - 3 \rightarrow 73$ $30 - 3 = 27$	Similarly, 46 and 4 is 50. 50 and 23 is 73. 23 and 4 is 27. $46 + 4 \rightarrow 50$ $50 + 23 \rightarrow 73$ $23 + 4 = 27$

FIGURE 2.4 · · · · · · · · ·

Invented Strategies for Take-Away Subtraction	

Take Tens from the Tens, Then Subtract Ones
 	
    73 – 46
 	
70 minus 40 is 30.
Take away 6 more
is 24.
Now add in the
~~3~~ ones   27.
 	
$$73 - 46$$
$$70 - 40 \rightarrow 30 - 6 \rightarrow$$
$$24 + 3 \rightarrow 27$$
 	
Or
 	
70 minus 40 is 30.
I can take those 3 away,
but I need 3 more
from the 30 to make 27.
 	
$$\begin{array}{r} 7\cancel{3} \\ -46 \\ \hline 30 \\ -3 \\ \hline 27 \end{array}$$
	Take Away Tens, Then Ones
	
	    73 – 46
	
	73 minus 40 is 33. $73 - 40 \rightarrow 33 - 3$
	Then take away 6:
	3 makes 30 and $30 - 3 \rightarrow 27$
	3 more is 27.
	
	Take Extra Tens, Then Add Back
	
	    73 – 46
	
	73 take away 50 is 23. $73 - 50 \rightarrow 23 + 4$
	That's 4 too many.
	23 and 4 is 27. 27
	
	Add to the Whole If Necessary
	
	    73 – 46 +3
	
	Give 3 to 73 to make 76. $73 - 46$
	76 take away 46 is 30. $76 - 46 \rightarrow 30$
	Now give 3 back $\longrightarrow$ 27.
	              $-3 \rightarrow 27$

Take-away strategies work reasonably well for two-digit problems. They are a bit more difficult with three digits.

and adding 1 back. This is a good mental method when subtracting a number that is close to a multiple of ten.

 STOP Try computing 82 – 57. Use both take-away and counting-up methods. Can you use all of the strategies in Figures 2.3 and 2.4 without looking?

Extensions and Challenges

Each of the examples in the preceding sections involved sums less than 100 and all involved *bridging a ten;* that is, if done with a traditional algorithm, they require carrying or borrowing. Bridging, the size of the numbers, and the potential for doing problems mentally are all issues to consider.

Bridging

For most of the strategies, it is easier to add or subtract when bridging is not required. Try each strategy with 34 + 52 or 68 – 24 to see how it works. Easier problems instill confidence. They also permit you to challenge your students with a "harder one." There is also the issue of bridging 100 or 1000. Try 58 + 67 with different strategies. Bridging across 100 is also an issue for subtraction. Problems such as 128 – 50 or 128 – 45 are more difficult than ones that do not bridge 100.

Larger Numbers

Try seeing how *you* would add and subtract three-digit numbers without using the traditional algorithms: 487 + 235 and 623 – 247. For subtraction, a counting-up strategy is usually the easiest. Occasionally, other strategies appear with larger numbers. For example, "chunking off" multiples of 50 or 25 is often a useful method. For 462 + 257, pull out 450 and 250 to make 700. That leaves 12 and 7 more $\longrightarrow$ 719.

Activities for Flexible Thinking

In addition to the ideas from the preceding section, middle grades students may also need experiences to help them develop flexibility with numbers so that they can and will create those flexible approaches.

An important focus involves thinking about a number in terms of two parts, especially thinking about a missing part, which is the agenda of the next several activities.

Often in computations it is useful to recognize that a number can be made up of a "nice" number and some more. The nice part (maybe a multiple of 50 or 100) is dealt with first and then the smaller leftover piece can be considered.

ACTIVITY 2.1

50 and Some More

Say a number between 50 and 100. Students respond with "50 and _____." For 63, the response is "50 and 13." Use larger numbers and have students split the number at the highest increment of 50. For example, for 482, students respond "450 and _____." For 327, students respond "300 and _____."

Nice numbers also are often broken apart in computations. The next two activities are extremely useful for developing the thinking required for counting-up approaches to subtraction. Introduce these activities to the full class using the overhead projector. Have students share their thinking strategies.

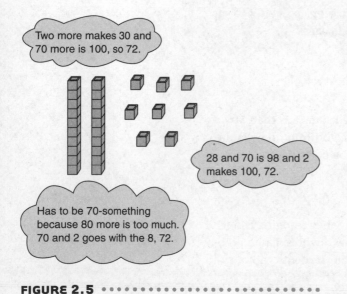

ACTIVITY 2.2

The Other Part of 100

One student makes a two-digit number. Then both students work mentally to determine what goes with the amount to make 100. They write their solutions on paper and then check to see if the total is 100. Students take turns making the original number. If needed, show the given part of 100 on the overhead using base-ten models. Figure 2.5 shows three different thought processes that students might use.

Being able to give the other part of 100 is so useful in invented strategies that students should get quite good at it.

If your students are adept at parts of 100, you can change the whole from 100 to another number. At first try other multiples of 10 such as 70 or 80. Then extend the whole to any number less than 100.

FIGURE 2.5 ••••••••••••••••••••••••••••

Using base-ten pieces to help think about the "other part of 100."

 Suppose that the whole is 83 and you start with 36. What goes with 36 to make 83? How did you think about it?

What you just did in finding the other part of 83 was subtract 36 from 83. You did not borrow or regroup. Most likely you did it in your head. With more practice you and students can do this very quickly and with ease.

Compatible numbers for addition and subtraction are numbers that go together easily to make nice numbers. Numbers that make tens or hundreds are the most common examples. Compatible sums also include numbers that end in 5, 25, 50, or 75, since these numbers are easy to work with as well. The teaching task is to get students accustomed to looking for combinations that work together and then looking for these combinations in computational situations.

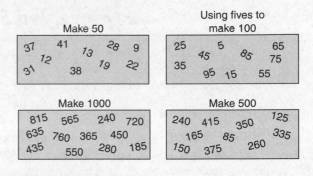

FIGURE 2.6 •

Compatible-pair searches.

ACTIVITY 2.3

Compatible Pairs

Searching for compatible pairs can be done as a worksheet activity or with the full class using the overhead projector. Prepare a transparency or duplicate a page with a search task. Five possibilities of different difficulty levels are shown in Figure 2.6. Students call out or connect the compatible pairs as they see them.

Here are two more activities that combine some of the ideas we have been exploring.

ACTIVITY 2.4

Calculator Challenge Counting

Students press any number on the calculator (e.g., 17), then + 8. They say the sum before they press =. Then they continue to add 8 mentally, challenging themselves to say the number before they press =. They should see how far they can go before making a mistake.

The constant addend in "Calculator Challenge Counting" can be any number, even a two- or three-digit number. Try 20 or 25. Try 40 and then 48. As an added challenge, after a student has progressed eight or ten counts, have the student reverse the process by pressing − followed by the same number and then =, =, ... Discuss patterns that appear.

Watch for students who are merely counting on. This strategy works but is not very efficient and will not help students improve their number sense. Encourage them to think about pulling one number apart to build the other number up to the next ten.

Although activities like those in this section can be done independently or in pairs, it is good to occasionally do them with the full class so that strategies can be discussed. The discussion provides students opportunities to consider new strategies and provides you opportunities to assess students' progress toward flexible thinking.

INVENTED STRATEGIES FOR ADDITION AND SUBTRACTION

Invented Strategies for Multiplication

Computation strategies for multiplication are considerably more complex than for addition and subtraction. Often, but by no means always, the strategies that students invent are very similar to the traditional algorithm. The big difference is that students think about numbers, not digits. They always begin with the large or left-hand numbers.

For multiplication, the ability to break numbers apart in flexible ways is even more important than in addition or subtraction. The distributive property is another concept that is important in multiplication computation. For example, to multiply 43 × 5, one might think about breaking 43 into 40 and 3, multiplying each by 5, and then adding the results. Students require ample opportunities to develop these concepts by making sense of their own ideas and those of their classmates.

EXPANDED LESSON

(pages 64–65)
The expanded lesson for this chapter uses story problems to help students explore strategies for multiplication of whole numbers.

Multiplication by a Single-Digit Multiplier

It is helpful to place multiplication tasks in contextual story problems. Let students solve the problems in ways that make sense to them. Do not be concerned about mixing of factors (6 sets of 34 or 34 sets of 6). The types of strategies that students use for multiplication are much more varied than for addition and subtraction. However, the following three categories can be identified from the research to date.

Complete-Number Strategies

Students who are not yet comfortable breaking numbers into parts using tens and ones will approach the numbers in the sets as single groups. For students who think this way, Figure 2.7 illustrates two methods they may use. These students will benefit from listening to students who use base-ten strategies.

Partitioning Strategies

Students break numbers up in a variety of ways that reflect an understanding of base-ten concepts, at least four of which are illustrated in Figure 2.8. The "By Decades" approach is the same as the standard algorithm except that students always begin with the large values. It extends easily to three digits and is very powerful as a mental math strategy. Another valuable strategy for mental methods is found in the "Other Partitions" example. It is easy to compute mentally with multiples of 25 and 50 and then add or subtract a small adjustment. All partition strategies rely on the distributive property.

Compensation Strategies

Students look for ways to manipulate numbers so that the calculations are easy. In Figure 2.9, the problem 27 × 4 is changed to an easier one, and then an

---

Complete-Number Strategies for Multiplication

$$63 \times 5$$

```
   63
 + 63
 ────
  126
 + 63
 ────
  189
 + 63
 ────
  252
 + 63
 ────
  315
```

```
63 ⟩ 126
63
         ⟩ 315
63 ⟩ 126
63
         ⟩ 189
63
```

FIGURE 2.7

Students who use a complete-number strategy do not break numbers apart into decades or tens and ones.

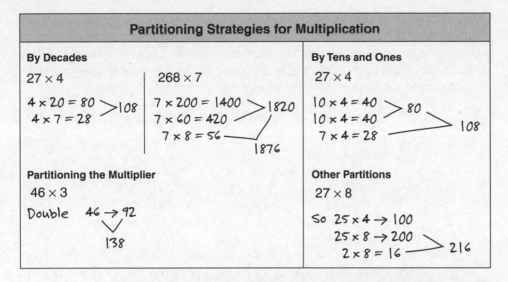

Partitioning Strategies for Multiplication

By Decades

27×4

$\begin{array}{l} 4 \times 20 = 80 \\ 4 \times 7 = 28 \end{array} \Big\rangle 108$

268×7

$\begin{array}{l} 7 \times 200 = 1400 \\ 7 \times 60 = 420 \\ 7 \times 8 = 56 \end{array} \Big\rangle \begin{array}{l} 1820 \\ 1876 \end{array}$

Partitioning the Multiplier

46×3

Double $\quad 46 \rightarrow 92$

138

By Tens and Ones

27×4

$\begin{array}{l} 10 \times 4 = 40 \\ 10 \times 4 = 40 \\ 7 \times 4 = 28 \end{array} \Big\rangle \begin{array}{l} 80 \\ \end{array} \Big\rangle 108$

Other Partitions

27×8

So $\begin{array}{l} 25 \times 4 \rightarrow 100 \\ 25 \times 8 \rightarrow 200 \\ 2 \times 8 = 16 \end{array} \Big\rangle 216$

Compensation Strategies for Multiplication

27×4

$\begin{array}{l} 27 + 3 \rightarrow 30 \times 4 \longrightarrow 120 \\ 3 \times 4 = 12 \longrightarrow -12 \\ \hline 108 \end{array}$

250×5

I can split 250 in half and multiply by 10.
$125 \times 10 = 1250$

17×70

$3 \times 70 \searrow$

$20 \times 70 \longrightarrow 1400 - 210 \longrightarrow 1190$

FIGURE 2.8 • • • • • • • •

Numbers can be broken apart in different ways to make easier partial products, which are then combined. Partitioning by decades is useful for mental computation and is very close to the standard algorithm.

FIGURE 2.9 • • • • • • • •

Compensation methods use a product related to the original. A compensation is made in the answer, or one factor is changed to compensate for a change in the other factor.

adjustment or compensation is made. In the second example, one factor is cut in half and the other doubled. This is often used when a 5 or a 50 is involved. Because these strategies are so dependent on the numbers involved, they can't be used for all computations. However, they are powerful strategies, especially for mental math and estimation.

Cluster Problems

In the fifth grade of *Investigations in Number, Data, and Space* (one of the NSF-supported, reform curricula), one approach to multidigit multiplication is called "cluster problems." This rather unique approach to the topic encourages students to use facts and combinations that they know or can easily figure out in order to find the answers to more complex computations. For example, consider the following cluster found in a fifth-grade lesson:

$$10 \times 32$$
$$5 \times 32$$
$$20 \times 32$$
$$30 \times 32$$
$$35 \times 32$$

INVENTED STRATEGIES FOR MULTIPLICATION

The goal is to figure out the last product. Students solve all of the problems and explain what problems were helpful in solving the last problem. Not every problem in the clusters needs to be used to solve the final problem. If students wish to add other problems to the cluster to aid in their solution to the final problem, they are encouraged to do so.

Here are three cluster problems taken from a fifth-grade worksheet.

10 × 18	400 × 9	2 × 72
5 × 18	500 × 9	10 × 72
50 × 18	90 × 9	5 × 72
2 × 18	8 × 9	20 × 72
20 × 18	2 × 9	200 × 72
40 × 18	**498 × 9**	210 × 72
45 × 18		**215 × 72**
47 × 18		

It is useful to have students make an estimate of the final product before doing any of the problems in the cluster. Students should be encouraged to add problems to the cluster if they need them and here is a good example. Think how you could use 10 × 34 (and some other related problems) to find 34 × 25.

The cluster-problem approach begins with students being provided with the cluster of problems. After they have become familiar with the approach, students should make up their own cluster of problems for a given product. At first, have students brainstorm clusters together as a class.

 First, solve the preceding clusters. Now, try your hand at making up a cluster of problems for 86 × 42. Include all problems that you think might possibly be helpful, even if they are not all related to one approach to finding the product. Then use your cluster to find the product. Is there more than one way?

Here are some problems that might be in your cluster.

2 × 80   4 × 80   2 × 86   40 × 80   6 × 40   10 × 86   40 × 86

Of course, your cluster may have included products not shown here. All that is required to begin the cluster-problem approach is that your cluster eventually leads to a solution. Besides your own cluster, see if you can use the problems in this cluster to find 86 × 42.

Cluster problems help students think about ways that they can break numbers apart into easier parts. The strategy of breaking the numbers apart and multiplying the parts—the distributive property—is an extremely valuable technique for flexible computation. It is also fun to find different clever paths to the solution. For many problems, finding a workable cluster is actually faster than using an algorithm.

Two-Digit Multipliers: The Area Model

A problem such as this one can be solved in many different ways:

The parade had 23 clowns. Each clown carried 18 balloons. How many balloons were there altogether?

Some students look for smaller products such as 6 × 23 and then add that result three times. Another method is to do 20 × 23 and then subtract 2 × 23. Others will calculate four separate partial products: 10 × 20 = 200, 8 × 20 = 160, 10 × 3 = 30, and 8 × 3 = 24. And still others may add up a string of 23s. Two-digit multiplication is both complex and challenging. But students can solve these problems in a variety of interesting ways, many of which will contribute to the development of the traditional algorithm or one that is just as efficient. Time devoted to working on these tasks is well spent because of the enhanced number sense that students develop.

A valuable exploration is to prepare large rectangles for each group of two or three students. The rectangles should be measured carefully, with dimensions between 25 cm and 60 cm, and drawn accurately with square corners. (Use the corner of a piece of poster board for a guide.) The students' task is to determine how many small ones pieces (base-ten materials) will fit inside. Wooden or plastic base-ten pieces are best, but cardboard strips and squares are adequate. Alternatively, rectangles can be drawn on base-ten grid paper (see Blackline Masters), or students can simply be given the task verbally: *What is the area of a rectangle that is 47 cm by 36 cm?*

Many students will fill the rectangle first with as many hundreds pieces as possible. One obvious approach is to put the 12 hundreds in one corner. This will leave narrow regions on two sides that can be filled with tens pieces and a final small rectangle that will hold ones. Especially if students have had earlier experiences with finding products in arrays, figuring out the size of each subrectangle is not terribly difficult. The sketch in Figure 2.10 shows the four regions.

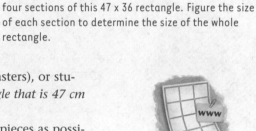

FIGURE 2.10 • • • • • • • • • • • • • • • • • • •

Ones, tens, and hundreds pieces fit exactly into the four sections of this 47 x 36 rectangle. Figure the size of each section to determine the size of the whole rectangle.

BLM 1

 STOP **If you did not already know the algorithm, how would you determine the size of the rectangle? Use your method (not the standard algorithm) on a rectangle that measures 68 cm × 24 cm. Make a sketch to show and explain your work.**

As you will see in the discussion of the traditional algorithm, the area model leads to a fairly reasonable approach to multiplying numbers, even if you never have students "carry," which is a source of many errors.

The Traditional Algorithm for Multiplication

The traditional multiplication algorithm is probably the most difficult of the four algorithms if students have not had plenty of opportunities to explore their own strategies. The multiplication algorithm can be meaningfully developed using either a repeated addition model or an area model. For single-digit multipliers, the difference is minimal. When you move to two-digit multipliers, the area model has some advantages. For that reason, the discussion here will use the area model.

One-Digit Multipliers

Although most students in fifth through eighth grades have been taught the steps to the standard procedure for multiplication, we suggest that you introduce the area model using one-digit multipliers. The smaller numbers make it easier for students to make a transition from thinking about digits to thinking about the value of the numbers. You will also find that for one-digit multipliers, students' invented strategies are very similar to those developed using the area model.

Begin with Models

Give students a drawing of a rectangle 47 cm by 6 cm. *How many small square centimeter pieces will fit in the rectangle?* (What is the area of the rectangle in square centimeters?) Let students solve the problem in groups before discussing it as a class.

As shown in Figure 2.11, the rectangle can be "sliced" or separated into two parts so that one part will be 6 ones by 7 ones, or 42 ones, and the other will be 6 ones by 4 tens, or 24 tens. Notice that the base-ten language "6 ones times 4 tens is 24 tens" tells how many *pieces* (sticks of ten) are in the big section. To say "6 times 40 is 240" is also correct and tells how many units or square centimeters are in the section. Each section is referred to as a *partial product.* By adding the two partial products, you get the total product or area of the rectangle.

BLM 1

To avoid the tedium of drawing large rectangles and arranging base-ten pieces, use the base-ten grid paper found in the Blackline Masters. On the grid paper, students can easily draw accurate rectangles showing all of the pieces. Check to be sure students understand that for a product such as 74 × 8, there are two partial products, 70 × 8 = 560 and 4 × 8 = 32, and the sum of these is the product. Do not force any recording technique on students until they understand how to use the two dimensions of a rectangle to get a product.

Develop the Written Record

When the two partial products are written separately as in Figure 2.12a, there is little new to learn. Students simply record the products and add them together. As illustrated, it is possible to teach students how to write the first product with a carried digit so that the combined product is written on one line. This traditional recording scheme is known to be problematic. The little carried digit is often the source of difficulty—it gets added in before the second multiplication or is forgotten.

There is absolutely no practical reason why students can't be allowed to record both partial products and avoid the errors related to the carried digit. When you accept that, it makes no difference in which order the products are written. Why not simply permit stu-

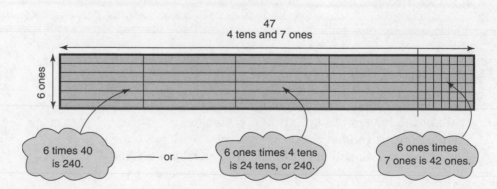

FIGURE 2.11

A rectangle filled with base-ten pieces is a useful model for two-digit-by-one-digit multiplication.

47
4 tens and 7 ones

6 ones

6 times 40 is 240.

— or —

6 ones times 4 tens is 24 tens, or 240.

6 ones times 7 ones is 42 ones.

dents to do written multiplication as shown in Figure 2.12 without carrying? When the factors are in a word problem, chart, or other format, all that is really necessary is to write down all the partial products and add. Furthermore, that is precisely how this is done mentally.

Most standard curricula progress from two digits to three digits with a single-digit multiplier. Students can make this progression easily. They still should be permitted to write all three partial products separately and not have to bother with carrying.

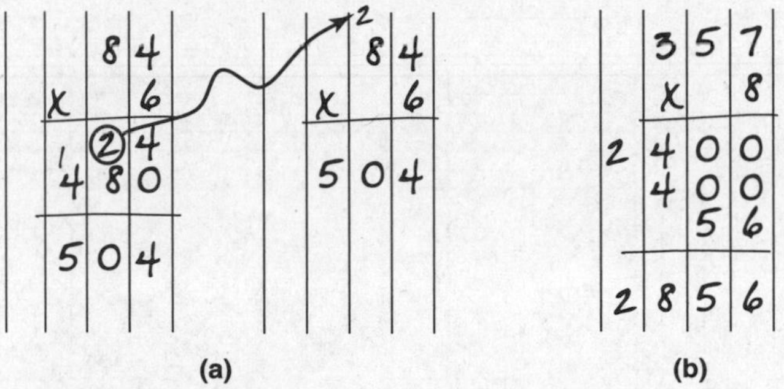

Two-Digit Multipliers

With the area model, the progression to a two-digit multiplier is relatively straightforward. Rectangles can be drawn on base-ten grid paper, or full-sized rectangles can be filled in with base-ten pieces. There will be four partial products, corresponding to four different sections of the rectangle.

Figure 2.13 also shows the recording of four partial products in the traditional order and how these can be collapsed to two lines if carried digits are used. Here the second "carry" technically belongs in the hundreds column but it rarely is written there. Often it gets confused with the first and is thus an additional source of errors. The lower left of the figure shows the same computation with all four products written in a different order. This is quite an acceptable algorithm. In the rare instance when someone multiplies numbers such as 538 × 29 with pencil and paper, there would be six partial products. But far fewer errors would occur, requiring less instructional time and much less remediation.

(a) **(b)**

FIGURE 2.12 •••••••••••••••••••••••••••••••

(a) In the standard form, the product of ones is recorded first. The tens digit of this first product can be written as a "carried" digit above the tens column. (b) It is quite reasonable to abandon the carried digit and permit the partial products to be recorded in any order.

Invented Strategies for Division

Even though many adults think division is the most onerous of the computational operations, it can be considerably easier than multiplication. Although most students are introduced to the long-division algorithm by fourth grade, it remains mysterious and a source of errors for many. Therefore, we suggest you take the time to revisit division using a more conceptual approach.

Sharing and Measurement Problems

There are two concepts of division. First there is the partition or fair-sharing idea, illustrated by this story problem:

••

The bag has 783 jelly beans, and Aidan and her four friends want to share them equally. How many jelly beans will Aidan and each of her friends get?

••

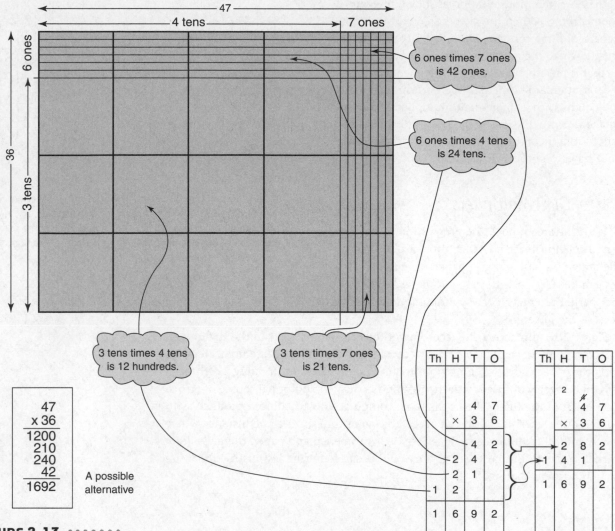

6 ones times 7 ones
is 42 ones.

6 ones times 4 tens
is 24 tens.

3 tens times 4 tens
is 12 hundreds.

3 tens times 7 ones
is 21 tens.

```
    47
  x 36
  1200
   210
   240
    42
  1692
```
A possible
alternative

Then there is the measurement or repeated subtraction concept:

Jumbo the elephant loves peanuts. His trainer has 625 peanuts. If he gives Jumbo 20 peanuts each day, how many days will the peanuts last?

Students should be challenged to solve both types of problems. However, the fair-share problems are often easier to solve with base-ten pieces. Furthermore, the traditional algorithm is built on this idea. Eventually, students will develop strategies that they will apply to both types of problem, even when the process does not match the action of the story.

Figure 2.14 shows some strategies that students have used to solve division problems. The first example illustrates 92 ÷ 4 using base-ten pieces and a sharing process. A ten is traded when no more tens can be passed out. Then the 12 ones are distributed, resulting in 23 in each set.

In the second example, the student sets out the base-ten pieces and draws a "bar graph" with six columns. After noting that there are not enough hundreds for each kid, he splits the 3 hundreds in half, putting 50 in each column. That leaves him with 1 hundred, 5 tens, and 3 ones. After trading the hundred for tens (now 15 tens), he gives 20 to each, recording 2 tens in each bar. Now he is left with 3 tens and 3 ones, or 33. He knows that 5×6 is 30, so he gives each kid 5, leaving him with 3. These he splits in half and writes $\frac{1}{2}$ in each column.

The student in the third example is solving a sharing problem but tries to do it as a measurement process. She wants to find out how many 8s are in 143. Initially she guesses. By multiplying 8 first by 10, then by 20, and then by 14, she knows the answer is more than 14 and less than 20. After some more work (not shown), she rethinks the problem as how many 8s in 100 and how many in 40.

Missing–Factor Strategies

You can see in Figure 2.14a how the use of base-ten pieces tends to lead to a digit-by-digit strategy—share the hundreds first, then the tens, then the ones. Although this is precisely the conceptual background behind the traditional algorithm, it is digit oriented as opposed to an approach that helps students think of the whole value of the dividend. In Figure 2.14c, the student is using a multiplicative approach. She is trying to find out "what number times 8 is close to 143 with less than 8 left over." This is a good method to suggest to students. It will build on their multiplication skills, it is a method that lends itself to mental estimation, and it can work quite well for most purposes.

 Before reading further, consider the task of determining the quotient of 318 ÷ 7 by trying to figure out *what number times 7 (or 7 times what number)* is close to 318 without going over. Do not use the standard algorithm.

There are several places to begin solving this problem. For instance, since 10×7 is 70 and 100×7 is 700, it has to be between 10 and 100, probably closer to 10. You might start adding up 70s:

$$
\begin{array}{l}
70 \\
+\ 70 \text{ is } 140 \\
+\ 70 \text{ is } 210 \\
+\ 70 \text{ is } 280 \\
+\ 70 \text{ is } 350
\end{array}
$$

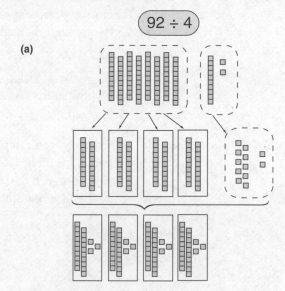

(a) 92 ÷ 4

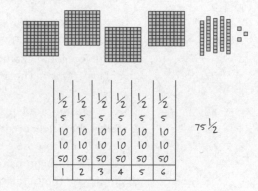

(b) 453 ÷ 6
(share with 6 kids)

$\frac{1}{2}$	$\frac{1}{2}$	$\frac{1}{2}$	$\frac{1}{2}$	$\frac{1}{2}$	$\frac{1}{2}$
5	5	5	5	5	5
10	10	10	10	10	10
10	10	10	10	10	10
50	50	50	50	50	50
1	2	3	4	5	6

$75\frac{1}{2}$

(c) 143 jelly beans shared with 8 kids

Try $14 \times 8 \rightarrow 112$
12 groups of 8 is 96.
12 groups in 100 leaves 4.
 5 groups of 8 is 40.
And 3 more left over.
12 + 5 is 17 with 7 left.

FIGURE 2.14 ·

Students use both models and symbols to solve division tasks.

Source: Adapted from *Developing Mathematical Ideas: Numbers and Operations, Part I: Building a System of Tens Casebook,* by D. Schifter, V. Bastable, & S. J. Russell. Copyright © 1999 by the Educational Development Center, Inc. Published by Dale Seymour Publications, an imprint of Pearson Learning. Used by permission.

INVENTED STRATEGIES FOR DIVISION

So four 70s is not enough and five is too much. It has to be forty-something. At this point you could guess at numbers between 40 and 50. Or you might add on 7s. Or you could notice that forty 7s (280) leaves you with 20 plus 18 or 38. Oh—five 7s will be 35 of the 38 with 3 left over. In all, that's 40 + 5 or 45 with a remainder of 3.

Another starting point might be 50 × 7. This beginning likely indicates that 40 × 7 will be the largest multiple of ten.

This missing-factor approach is likely to be invented by some students if they are solving measurement problems such as the following:

Grace can put 6 pictures on one page of her photo album. If she has 82 pictures, how many pages will she need?

Alternatively, you can simply pose a task such as 82 ÷ 6 and ask students, "What number times 6 would be close to 82?" Then continue from there.

Another approach to developing missing-factor strategies is to use cluster problems as discussed for multiplication. (See p. 51.) Here are two examples:

$$
\begin{array}{cc}
100 \times 4 & 10 \times 72 \\
500 \div 4 & 5 \times 70 \\
4 \times 25 & 2 \times 72 \\
6 \times 4 & 4 \times 72 \\
\mathbf{527 \div 4} & 5 \times 72 \\
& \mathbf{381 \div 72}
\end{array}
$$

Notice that the missing-factor strategy is equally good for one-digit divisors as two-digit divisors. Also notice that it is okay to include division problems in the cluster. In the foregoing example, 125 × 4 could easily have replaced 500 ÷ 4 and 400 ÷ 4 could replace 100 × 4. The idea is to keep multiplication and division as closely connected as possible.

Cluster problems accentuate a flexible approach to computation, helping students realize that there are many different good ways to compute. Another way to develop flexibility is to pose a division problem (or a multiplication problem) and have students solve the problem using two different approaches. Of course, neither of the methods should use the traditional algorithm or a calculator.

 Solve 514 ÷ 8 in two different nontraditional ways. Your ways may converge in similar places but begin with different first steps—or they may be completely different.

Here are four possibilities and there are certainly others:

$$
10 \times 8 \qquad 400 \div 8 \qquad 60 \times 8 \qquad 480 \div 8
$$

You should try to solve 514 ÷ 8 beginning with each of these starting points.

When students are first asked to solve problems using two methods, they often use a primitive or completely inefficient method for their second approach. For example, to solve 514 ÷ 8, a student might perform a very long string of subtractions (514 − 8 = 506, 506 − 8 = 498, 498 − 8 = 490, and so on) and count how many times he subtracted 8. Others will actually draw 514 tally marks and loop groups of 8. These students have not developed sufficient flexibility to think of other efficient methods. To help with this, pose problems along with two or three starting points and have students use each of the starting points to solve the problem. Your class discussions will help students begin to see more flexible approaches.

The Traditional Algorithm for Division

If you have been working along with the examples and approaches in this section, we hope you are convinced that students can use invented strategies for both one-digit divisors and two-digit divisors as long as the dividends are less than 1000 and a whole-number quotient with a remainder is all that is required. That is, it is not significantly faster to do 738 ÷ 43 by the traditional algorithm than to use a missing-factor approach. (Try it!) Notice that while doing the traditional algorithm you also have to do 308 ÷ 43, another problem as hard as the original. That is, the task often does not get easier as you go along. Compound this with the abundant difficulties of the traditional algorithm and the concomitant reteaching that inevitably takes place.

However, many will argue that students simply must have a more efficient method of dividing than those suggested here. Furthermore, if the curriculum requires division with decimal divisors or quotients are to be carried out to get decimal results (in contrast to whole-number remainders), an argument can possibly be made for teaching a traditional algorithm. Therefore, we share with you one approach to the traditional long-division algorithm. Since the algorithm most often taught in textbooks is based on the partition or fair-sharing concept of division, that is the method described here. (Some teachers may want to explore a repeated-subtraction algorithm that is very much like a missing-factor approach with partial products recorded in a column to the right of the division computation. See Figure 2.15 for an example.)

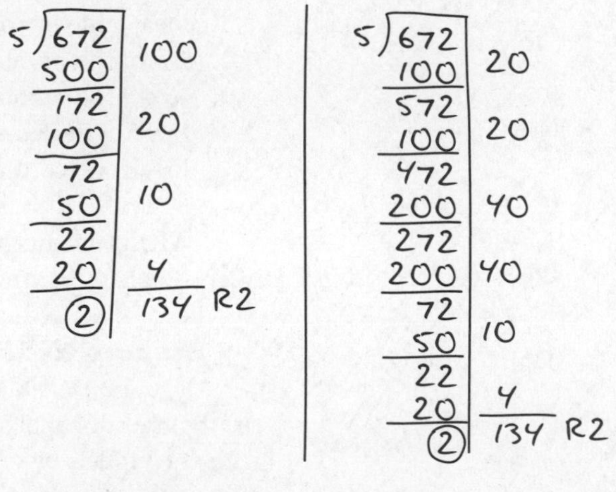

One-Digit Divisors

Typically, the division algorithm with one-digit divisors is introduced in the third grade. If done well, it should not have to be retaught, and it should provide the basis for two-digit divisors. Again, students in the upper grades who are having difficulty with the division algorithm can benefit from a conceptual development.

Begin with Models

Traditionally, for a problem such as 4)583, we might say "4 goes into 5 one time." This is quite mysterious to students. How can you just ignore the "83" and keep changing the problem? Preferably, you want students to think of the 583 as 5 hundreds, 8 tens, and 3 ones, not as the independent

FIGURE 2.15

In the division algorithm shown, the numbers on the side indicate the quantity of the divisor being subtracted from the dividend. As the two examples indicate, the divisor can be subtracted in any amounts desired.

THE TRADITIONAL ALGORITHM FOR DIVISION

digits 5, 8, and 3. One idea is to use a context such as candy bundled in boxes of ten with 10 boxes to a carton. Then the problem becomes *We have 5 boxes, 8 cartons, and 3 pieces of candy to share between 4 schools evenly.* In this context, it is reasonable to share the cartons first until no more can be shared. Those remaining are "unpacked," and the boxes shared, and so on. Money ($100, $10, and $1) can be used in a similar manner.

 Try the distributing or sharing process yourself using base-ten pieces (or draw squares, sticks, and dots). Use the problem 583 ÷ 4. Try to talk through the process without using "goes into." Think sharing.

Language plays an enormous role in thinking about the algorithm conceptually. Most adults are so accustomed to the "goes into" language that it is hard to let it go. For the problem 583 ÷ 4, here is some suggested language as you work through the task:

- *I want to share 5 hundreds, 8 tens, and 3 ones among these four sets. There are enough hundreds for each set to get 1 hundred. That leaves 1 hundred that I can't share.*
- *I'll trade the hundred for 10 tens. That gives me a total of 18 tens. I can give each set 4 tens and have 2 tens left over. Two tens is not enough to go around to the four sets.*
- *I can trade the 2 tens for 20 ones and put those with the 3 ones I already had. That makes a total of 23 ones. I can give 5 ones to each of the four sets. That leaves me with 3 ones as a remainder. In all I gave out 1 hundred, 4 tens, and 5 ones with 3 left over.*

Develop the Written Record

The recording scheme for the long-division algorithm is not completely intuitive. You will need to be quite directive in helping students learn to record the fair sharing with models. There are essentially four steps:

1. *Share* and record the number of pieces put in each group.
2. *Record* the number of pieces shared in all. Multiply to find this number.
3. *Record* the number of pieces remaining. Subtract to find this number.
4. *Trade* (if necessary) for smaller pieces and combine with any that are there already. Record the new total number in the next column.

When students model problems with a one-digit divisor, steps 2 and 3 seem unnecessary. Explain that these steps really help when you don't have the pieces there to count.

Record Explicit Trades

Figure 2.16 details each step of the recording process just described. On the left, you see the traditional algorithm. To the right is a suggestion that matches the actual action with the models by explicitly recording the trades. Instead of the somewhat mysterious "bring-down" procedure, the traded pieces are crossed out, as is the number of existing pieces in the next column. The combined number of pieces is written in this column using a two-digit number. In the example, 2 hundreds are traded for 20 tens, combined with the 6 that were there for a total of 26 tens. The 26 is, therefore, written in the tens column.

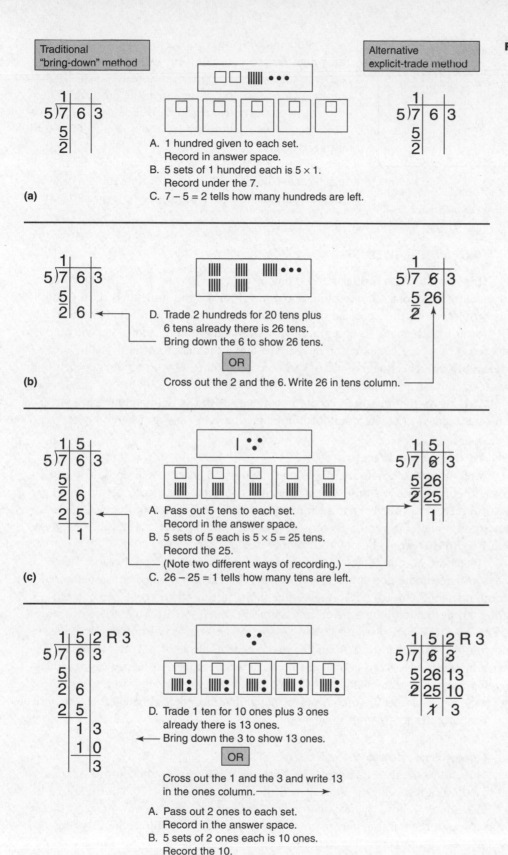

FIGURE 2.16 • • • • • • • • • • •

The traditional and explicit-trade methods are connected to each step of the division process. Every step can and should make sense.

Traditional "bring-down" method

Alternative explicit-trade method

(a)

A. 1 hundred given to each set. Record in answer space.
B. 5 sets of 1 hundred each is 5×1. Record under the 7.
C. $7 - 5 = 2$ tells how many hundreds are left.

(b)

D. Trade 2 hundreds for 20 tens plus 6 tens already there is 26 tens. Bring down the 6 to show 26 tens.

OR

Cross out the 2 and the 6. Write 26 in tens column.

(c)

A. Pass out 5 tens to each set. Record in the answer space.
B. 5 sets of 5 each is $5 \times 5 = 25$ tens. Record the 25. (Note two different ways of recording.)
C. $26 - 25 = 1$ tells how many tens are left.

(d)

D. Trade 1 ten for 10 ones plus 3 ones already there is 13 ones. Bring down the 3 to show 13 ones.

OR

Cross out the 1 and the 3 and write 13 in the ones column.

A. Pass out 2 ones to each set. Record in the answer space.
B. 5 sets of 2 ones each is 10 ones. Record the 10.
C. Subtract 10 from 13. There are 3 ones left.

THE TRADITIONAL ALGORITHM FOR DIVISION

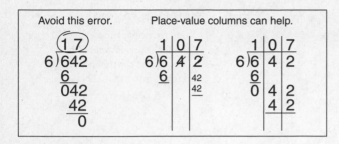

FIGURE 2.17 •

Using lines to mark place-value columns can help avoid for-getting to record zeros.

Students who are required to make sense of the long-division procedure find the explicit-trade method easier to follow. It is important to spread out the digits in the dividend when writing down the problem. (The explicit-trade method is a Van de Walle invention. It has been used successfully in grades 3 to 8. You will not find it in textbooks.)

Both the explicit-trade method and the use of place-value columns will help with the problem of leaving out a middle zero in a problem (see Figure 2.17).

Two-Digit Divisors

There is almost no justification for having students master the division algorithm with two-digit divisors. A large chunk of the fourth, fifth, and sometimes sixth grades is frequently spent on this outdated skill. The cost in terms of time and students' attitudes toward mathematics is enormous. Only a few times in any adult's life will an exact result to such a computation be required and a calculator not be available. If you can possibly influence the removal of this outdated skill from your school's curriculum, you are encouraged to speak up.

With a two-digit divisor, it is hard to come up with the right amount to share at each step. A guess too high or too low means you have to erase and start all over.

An Intuitive Idea

Suppose that you were sharing a large pile of candies with 36 friends. Instead of passing them out one at a time, you conservatively estimate that each person could get at least 6 pieces. So you give 6 to each of your friends. Now you find there are more than 36 pieces left. Do you have everyone give back the 6 pieces so you can then give them 7 or 8? That would be silly! You simply pass out more.

The candy example gives us two good ideas for sharing in long division. First, always underestimate how much can be shared. You can always pass out some more. Second, if there is enough left to share some more, just do it! To avoid ever overestimating, always pretend there are more sets among which to share than there really are. For example, if you are dividing 312 by 43 (sharing among 43 sets or "friends"), pretend you have 50 sets instead. Round *up* to the next multiple of 10. You can easily determine that 6 pieces can be shared among 50 sets because 6 × 50 is an easy product. Therefore, since there are really only 43 sets, clearly you can give *at least* 6 to each. Always consider a larger divisor; *always round up*. If your underestimate leaves you with more to share, simply pass out some more.

Using the Idea Symbolically

These ideas are used in Figure 2.18. Both the traditional method and the explicit-trade method of recording are illustrated. The rounded-up divisor, 70, is written in a little "think bubble" above the real divisor. Rounding up has another advantage: It is easy to run through the multiples of 70 and compare them to 374. Think about sharing base-ten pieces (thousands, hundreds, tens, and ones). Work through the problem one step at a time, saying exactly what each recorded step stands for.

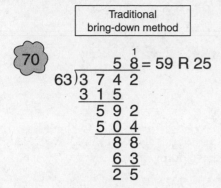

Traditional
bring-down method

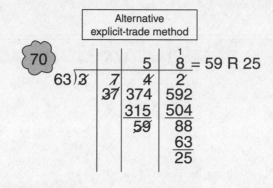

Alternative
explicit-trade method

FIGURE 2.18 • • • • • • •

Round the divisor up to 70 to think with, but multiply what you share by 63. In the ones column, share 8 with each set. Oops! 88 left over, just give 1 more to each set.

It reduces the mental strain of making choices and essentially eliminates the need to erase. If an estimate is too low, that's okay. And if you always round up, the estimate will never be too high. Nor is there any reason ever to change to the more familiar approach. It is just as good for adults as for children. The same is true of the explicit-trade notation. It is certainly an idea to consider.

EXPANDED LESSON

Multiplication Strategies

GRADE LEVEL: Fifth or sixth grade.

MATHEMATICS GOALS

- To develop strategies for two-digit multiplication of whole numbers in a conceptual manner.
- To develop the distributive property of multiplication.

THINKING ABOUT THE STUDENTS

Students have mastered most of their basic multiplication facts and understand that multiplication can be thought of as repeated addition. They understand that length times width gives the area of a rectangle. Most have been using the traditional algorithm but have little or no conceptual understanding of it.

MATERIALS AND PREPARATION

- Prepare a transparency with the problems in the lesson.
- Make the following materials available for student use: copies of base-ten grid paper (see Blackline Master 1) and base-ten models (ones, tens, and hundreds). Students will use these as options.

- -

lesson

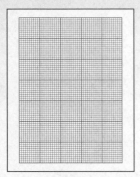

BLM 1

BEFORE

Begin with a simpler version of the task:

- Explain that for today, the usual method of multiplying numbers is "outlawed." (Indicate the traditional method of multiplication on the board.)
- Pose the following task to students and ask them to think of two different ways to solve the task other than the "old way":

    Raymond bought a sheet of stamps. There are 8 stamps to a row. His sheet has 14 rows of stamps. How many stamps did Raymond buy?

- After students have had time to work on the task, discuss the various ways they used to find the answer. List on the board the models and strategies students used. If no one uses an array with some attention to 8 times 10 and 8 times 4, draw a sketch like this and see if it might prompt a different approach.

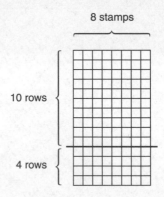

The Task

- Pose the following two problems to students. The problems may cause different strategies.

    During the school fund-raiser, 17 students in the school each sold 26 rolls of wrapping paper. How many rolls of wrapping paper were sold by this group of students?

    Nathan was helping his dad lay tile on the basement floor. They had figured out that they needed 15 rows of 37 tiles. How many tiles do they need?

Establish Expectations

- As before, students are not permitted to use the traditional algorithm for today. Students should solve the problems using any strategy that they can explain meaningfully. Explain that while they may not need to use models to determine the answer, sometimes models can be helpful to show others the reasoning involved. Today you want words, pictures or drawings, and numbers to explain their calculations.

DURING

- Students who have no strategy other than the traditional algorithm will be the biggest challenge. Ask them to use numbers and words to show you what the problem means rather than how to solve it. Return to these students and help them build a method on their ideas.
- Look for students who are using different strategies to solve the problem. Capitalize on the various strategies in the "after" portion of the lesson.

AFTER

- Ask various students to share their strategies for determining the answer to the tasks. Ask the class to comment or ask questions about each strategy.
- When discussing the strategies, encourage students to look for similarities and differences across the different methods.

ASSESSMENT NOTES

- Are students looking for ways to break numbers apart to make computations easier? Or are they using a digit-oriented approach? The use of tens or multiples of tens in most any way will usually lead to a good strategy.
- Although many students will likely know the standard algorithm for multiplication, activities like this can help them better understand the algorithm and the meaning of multiplication. Resistance to anything other than the standard algorithm may be a sign that their number sense is not very well developed.
- Look for students who reason through the task without the use of drawings. If their reasoning is valid, do not force them to use models to determine the answer. Eventually the goal is to have students mentally work through these kinds of tasks in a valid and efficient manner.

• •

next steps

- For students who are experiencing difficulty thinking of different ways to approach the task, work on developing their number sense with multidigit addition problems using mental methods or invented strategies other than the traditional algorithm. Students may be more willing to take risks with multidigit addition and can learn the value of breaking numbers into parts.
- Continue to pose different story problems to students, keeping in mind that the story problem often influences the choice of the model that students choose to use.
- The physical models that students use can build toward more efficient mental strategies. Eventually move students toward developing those mental strategies that do not require a physical model.

FRACTION CONCEPTS AND COMPUTATION

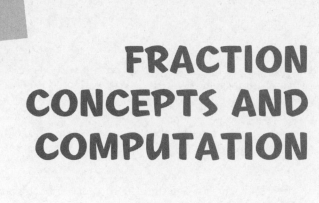

ractions have always represented a considerable challenge for students, even into the middle grades. This lack of understanding is then translated into untold difficulties with fraction computation, decimal and percent concepts, the use of fractions in measurement, and ratio and proportion concepts.

There is substantial evidence to suggest that the use of models in fraction tasks is important. Unfortunately, many teachers in the upper grades, where manipulative materials are not as common, fail to use models for fraction development. Models can help students clarify ideas that are often confused in a purely symbolic mode. Sometimes it is useful to do the same activity with two quite different models; from the viewpoint of the students, the activity is quite different. In this chapter we will distinguish among three types of models: area or region models, length models, and set models.

big ideas

1 The denominator of a fraction indicates by what number the whole has been divided in order to produce the type of part under consideration. Thus, the denominator is a divisor. In practical terms, the denominator names the kind of fractional part that is under consideration. The numerator of a fraction counts or tells how many of the fractional parts (of the type indicated by the denominator) are under consideration. Therefore, the numerator is a multiplier—it indicates a multiple of the given fractional part.

2 Two equivalent fractions are two ways of describing the same amount by using different-sized fractional parts. For example, in the fraction $\frac{6}{8}$, if the eighths are taken in twos, then each pair of eighths is a fourth. The six-eighths then can be seen to be three-fourths.

3 The meanings of each operation on fractions are the same as the meanings for the operations on whole numbers. Operations with fractions should begin by applying these same meanings to fractional parts.

- For addition and subtraction, it is critical to understand that the numerator tells the number of parts and the denominator the type of part.

- For multiplication by a fraction, it is useful to recall that the denominator is a divisor. This idea allows us to find parts of the other factor. (See p. 95.)

- For division by a fraction, the two ways of thinking about the operation—partition and measurement—are extremely important. The partition or fair-sharing concept of division will lead to a very different division procedure than will the measurement or repeated subtraction concept.

4 Estimation of fraction computations is tied almost entirely to concepts of the operations and of fractions. A computation algorithm is not required for making estimates. Estimation should be an integral part of computation development to keep students' attention on the meanings of the operations and the expected size of the results.

Understanding Fraction Symbols

Fraction symbolism represents a fairly complex convention that is often misleading to children. It is well worth your time to ensure students have developed a strong understanding of what the top and bottom numbers of a fraction tell us.

It is assumed that students in grades 5–8 have constructed the idea of *fractional parts of the whole*—the parts that result when the whole or unit had been partitioned into *equal-sized portions* or *fair shares*.

Fractional-Parts Counting

Counting fractional parts to see how multiple parts compare to the whole creates a foundation for the two parts of a fraction. Students should come to think of counting fractional parts in much the same way as they might count apples or any other objects. If you know the kind of part you are counting, you can tell when you get to one, when you get to two, and so on. Students who understand factional parts should not need to arrange pie pieces into a circle to know that four fourths make a whole.

Display some pie-piece fraction parts in groups as shown in Figure 3.1. For each collection, tell students what type of piece is being shown and simply count them together: "*one*-fourth, *two*-fourths, *three*-fourths, *four*-fourths, *five*-fourths." Ask, "If we have five-fourths, is that more than one whole, less than one whole, or the same as one whole?"

As students count each collection of parts, discuss the relationship to one whole. Make informal comparisons between different collections. "Why did we get almost two wholes with seven-fourths, and yet we don't even have one whole with ten-twelfths?"

Also take this opportunity to review the concept of mixed fractions. "What is another way that we could say seven-thirds?" (Two wholes and one more third or one whole and four-thirds.)

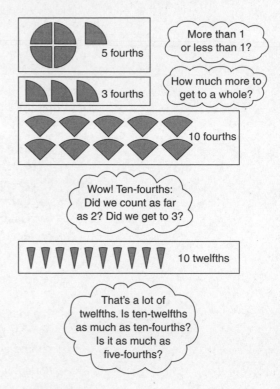

FIGURE 3.1

Counting fractional parts using an area model.

Top and Bottom Numbers

The way that we write fractions with a top and a bottom number and a bar between is a convention—an arbitrary agreement for how to represent fractions. (By the way, always write fractions with a horizontal bar, not a slanted one. Write $\frac{3}{4}$, not 3/4.) As a convention, it falls in the category of things that you simply tell students. However, a good idea is to make the convention so clear by way of demonstration that students will tell *you* what the top and bottom numbers stand for. The following procedure is recommended even if your students have been "using" symbolic fractions for several years.

Display several collections of fractional parts in a manner similar to those in Figure 3.1. Have students count the parts together. After each count, write the correct fraction, indicating that this is how it is written as a symbol. Include sets that are more than one, but write them as simple or "improper" fractions and not as mixed numbers.

Include at least two pairs of sets with the same top numbers such as $\frac{4}{8}$ and $\frac{4}{3}$. Likewise, include sets with the same bottom numbers. After the class has counted and you have written the fraction for at least six sets of fractional parts, pose the following questions:

What does the bottom number in a fraction tell us?

What does the top number in a fraction tell us?

Before reading further, answer these two questions in your own words. Don't rely on formulations you've heard before. Think in terms of what we have been talking about—namely, fractional parts and counting fractional parts. Imagine counting a set of 5 eighths and a set of 5 fourths and writing the fractions for these sets. Use children's language in your formulations and try to come up with a way to explain these meanings that has nothing to do with the type of model involved.

Here are some reasonable explanations for the top and bottom numbers.

- *Top number:* This is the counting number. It tells how many shares or parts we have. It tells how many have been counted. It tells how many parts we are talking about. It counts the parts or shares.

- *Bottom number:* This tells what is being counted. It tells what fractional part is being counted. If it is a 4, it means we are counting *fourths;* if it is a 6, we are counting *sixths;* and so on.

This formulation of the meanings of the top and bottom numbers may seem unusual to you. It is often said that the top number tells "how many" (this phrase seems unfinished) and the bottom tells "how many parts it takes to make a whole." This may be correct but can be misleading. For example, a $\frac{1}{6}$ piece is often cut from a cake without making any slices in the remaining $\frac{5}{6}$ of the cake. That the cake is only in two pieces does not change the fact that the piece taken is $\frac{1}{6}$. Or if a pizza is cut in 12 pieces, two pieces still make $\frac{1}{6}$ of the pizza. In neither of these instances does the bottom number tell how many pieces make a whole.

There is evidence that an iterative notion of fractions, one that views a fraction such as $\frac{3}{4}$ as a count of three things called *fourths,* is an important idea for children to develop (Post, Wachsmuth, Lesh, & Behr, 1985; Tzur, 1999). The iterative concept is most clear when focusing on these two ideas about fraction symbols:

- The top number *counts.*

- The bottom number tells *what is being counted.*

The *what* of fractions are the fractional parts. They can be counted. Fraction symbols are just a shorthand for saying *how many* and *what.*

Smith (2002) points out a slightly more "mathematical" definition of the top and bottom numbers that is completely in accord with the one we've just discussed. For Smith, it is important to see the bottom number as the divisor and the top as the multiplier. That is, $\frac{3}{4}$ is three *times* what you get when you *divide* a whole into four parts. This multiplier and divisor idea is especially useful when students are asked later to think of fractions as an indicated division; that is, $\frac{3}{4}$ also means 3 ÷ 4.

Numerator *and* Denominator

To count a set is to *enumerate* it. *Enumeration* is the process of counting. The common name for the top number in a fraction is the *numerator*.

A $1 bill, a $5 bill, and a $10 bill are said to be bills of different denominations. Similarly, the word *denomination* is used to differentiate among branches of religions (such as Baptists, Presbyterians, Episcopalians, and Catholics). A denomination is the name of a class or type of thing. The common name for the bottom number in a fraction is the *denominator*.

The words *numerator* and *denominator* have no common reference for children. Whether these words are used or not, the words themselves will not help young children understand the meanings.

Mixed Numbers and Improper Fractions

In the fourth National Assessment of Educational Progress, about 80 percent of seventh graders could change a mixed number to an improper fraction, but fewer than half knew that $5\frac{1}{4}$ was the same as $5 + \frac{1}{4}$ (Kouba et al., 1988a). The result indicates that many children are using a mindless rule that is in fact relatively easy to construct.

If you have counted fractional parts beyond a whole, your students already know how to write $\frac{13}{6}$ or $\frac{11}{3}$. Ask, "What is another way that you could say 13 *sixths?*" Students may suggest "two wholes and one-sixth more," or "two plus one-sixth." Explain that these are correct and that $2 + \frac{1}{6}$ is usually written as $2\frac{1}{6}$ and is called a *mixed number.* Note that this is a symbolism convention and must be explained to children. What is not at all necessary is to teach a rule for converting mixed numbers to common fractions and the reverse. Rather, consider the following task.

ACTIVITY 3.1

Mixed-Number Names

Give students a mixed number such as $3\frac{2}{5}$. Their task is to find a single fraction that names the same amount. They may use any familiar materials or make drawings, but they must be able to give an explanation for their result. Similarly, have students start with a fraction greater than 1, such as $\frac{17}{4}$, and have them determine the mixed number and provide a justification for their result.

Repeat the "Mixed-Number Names" task several times with different fractions. After a while, challenge students to figure out the new fraction name without the use of models. A good explanation for $3\frac{1}{4}$ might be that there are 4 fourths in one whole, so there are 8 fourths in two wholes and 12 fourths in three wholes. The extra fourth makes 13 fourths in all, or $\frac{13}{4}$. (Note the iteration concept playing a role.)

There is absolutely no reason ever to provide a rule about multiplying the whole number by the bottom number and adding the top number. Nor should students need a rule about dividing the bottom number into the top to convert fractions to mixed numbers. These rules will readily be developed by the students but in their own words and with complete understanding.

Calculator Fraction Counting

Calculators that permit fraction entries and displays are now quite common in schools. Many, like the TI-15, now display fractions in correct fraction format and offer a choice of showing results as mixed numbers or simple fractions. Counting by fourths with the TI-15 is done by first storing $\frac{1}{4}$ in one of the two operation keys: $\boxed{\text{Op1}}$ $\boxed{+}$ 1 $\boxed{\text{n}}$ 4 $\boxed{\text{d}}$ $\boxed{\text{Op1}}$. To count, press 0 $\boxed{\text{Op1}}$ $\boxed{\text{Op1}}$ $\boxed{\text{Op1}}$ . . . . The display will show the counts by fourths and also the number of times that the $\boxed{\text{Op1}}$ key has been pressed. Students should coordinate their counts with fraction models, adding a new fourths piece to the pile with each count. At any time the display can be shifted from mixed form to simple fractions with a press of a key. The TI-15 can be set so that it will not simplify fractions automatically, the appropriate setting prior to the introduction of equivalent fractions.

Fraction calculators provide a powerful way to help children develop fractional symbolism. A variation on Activity 3.2 is to show children a mixed number such as $3\frac{1}{8}$ and ask how many counts of $\frac{1}{8}$ on the calculator it will take to count that high. The students should try to stop at the correct number $\frac{25}{8}$ before pressing the mixed-number key.

Parts-and-Whole Tasks

The exercises presented here can help students develop their understanding of fractional parts as well as the meanings of the top and bottom numbers in a fraction. Models are used to represent wholes and parts of wholes. Written or oral fraction names represent the relationship between the parts and wholes. Given any two of these—whole, part, and fraction—the students can use their models to determine the third.

Any type of model can be used as long as different sizes can represent the whole. Traditional pie pieces do not work because the whole is always the circle, and all the pieces are *unit fractions*. (A *unit fraction* is a single fractional part. The fractions $\frac{1}{3}$ and $\frac{1}{8}$ are unit fractions.)

Examples of each type of exercise are provided in Figure 3.2, Figure 3.3, and Figure 3.4. Each figure includes examples with a region model (freely drawn rectangles), a length model (Cuisenaire rods or fraction strips), and set models. Use 11 colors of poster board to make fraction strips to use instead of Cuisenaire rods. Double the length of the rods. For example, the light green rod (1 cm by 3 cm) becomes a strip 2 cm by 6 cm. Make a pink strip 2 cm by 24 cm for a "12 rod."

It would be a good idea to work through these exercises before reading on. For the rectangle models, simply sketch a similar rectangle on paper. For the rod or strip models, use Cuisenaire rods or make fraction strips. The colors indicated correspond to the actual rod colors. Lengths are not given in the figures so that you will not be tempted to use an adult-type numeric approach. If you do not have access to rods or strips, just draw lines on paper. The process you use with lines will correspond to what is done with rods.

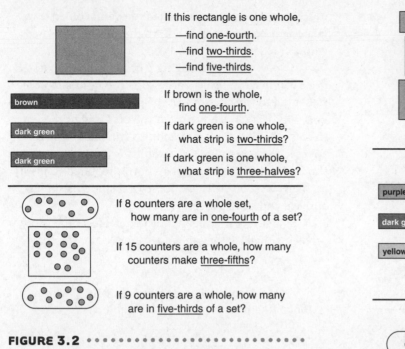

If this rectangle is one whole,
—find <u>one-fourth</u>.
—find <u>two-thirds</u>.
—find <u>five-thirds</u>.

If brown is the whole,
find <u>one-fourth</u>.

If dark green is one whole,
what strip is <u>two-thirds</u>?

If dark green is one whole,
what strip is <u>three-halves</u>?

If 8 counters are a whole set,
how many are in <u>one-fourth</u> of a set?

If 15 counters are a whole, how many
counters make <u>three-fifths</u>?

If 9 counters are a whole, how many
are in <u>five-thirds</u> of a set?

FIGURE 3.2 •

Given the whole and the fraction, find the part.

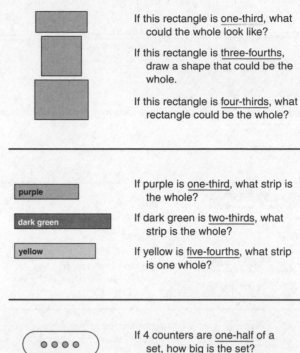

If this rectangle is <u>one-third</u>, what
could the whole look like?

If this rectangle is <u>three-fourths</u>,
draw a shape that could be the
whole.

If this rectangle is <u>four-thirds</u>, what
rectangle could be the whole?

If purple is <u>one-third</u>, what strip is
the whole?

If dark green is <u>two-thirds</u>, what
strip is the whole?

If yellow is <u>five-fourths</u>, what strip
is one whole?

If 4 counters are <u>one-half</u> of a
set, how big is the set?

If 12 counters are <u>three-fourths</u> of
a set, how many counters are in
the full set?

If 10 counters are <u>five-halves</u> of a
set, how many counters are in
one set?

FIGURE 3.3 •

Given the part and the fraction, find the whole.

The questions that ask for the fraction when given
the whole and part require a lot of trial and error. Be sure
that appropriate fractional parts are available for the region
and length versions of these questions.

By its very nature, a fraction is associated with a
whole, of which it is a part. Many times it is assumed that
what constitutes the whole is understood. Tasks that ask
for the whole when the part and the fraction are given (see Figure 3.3) make it apparent to students that fractions are defined in relation to a whole. Furthermore, many
students assume that given a particular manipulative, the whole must always be the
same. Although the whole cannot change within a given computation with fractions,
it certainly need not be fixed for a given model. In Figure 3.5, everyday items, such as
graham crackers and wrapped candy, are used to pose this same type of question that
asks students to determine the size of the whole.

**Before reading on, take a moment to work through these tasks. Using the same
items to identify a different whole requires flexible thinking that can be more
difficult than it appears. Figure 3.6 shows the associated whole for one of these
fractions in the given context.**

Sometimes the whole seems so obvious that it appears unnecessary to identify
it. For example, it is reasonable to assume that an entire graham cracker with four sections is the whole. However, when making s'mores, some people break the four sections
into two pieces and the half can now be thought of as the whole. Many mistakes and

UNDERSTANDING FRACTION SYMBOLS

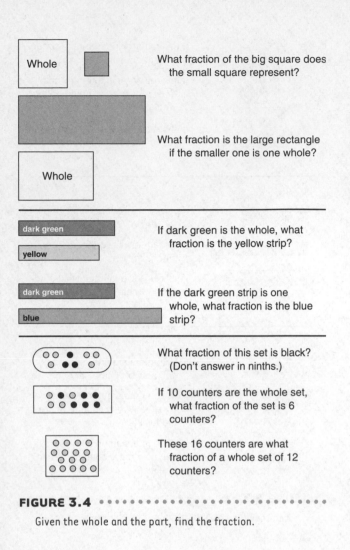

What fraction of the big square does the small square represent?

What fraction is the large rectangle if the smaller one is one whole?

If dark green is the whole, what fraction is the yellow strip?

If the dark green strip is one whole, what fraction is the blue strip?

What fraction of this set is black? (Don't answer in ninths.)

If 10 counters are the whole set, what fraction of the set is 6 counters?

These 16 counters are what fraction of a whole set of 12 counters?

FIGURE 3.4 •

Given the whole and the part, find the fraction.

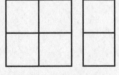

If this is *two-fifths* of the graham crackers, what would the whole look like?

If this amount of graham crackers is equal to *three*, what would the whole look like?

Graham Crackers

If this amount of candy is *one and one-eighth* of all the candy, how much candy was there?

If this amount of candy is *one-half* of what we had, how much did we have?

Packaged Candy

FIGURE 3.5 •

Possible everyday items to use in finding the whole when given the part and the fraction.

misconceptions can be corrected or even avoided if we take the time to pay attention to the whole associated with a fraction.

Two or three challenging parts-and-whole questions can make an excellent lesson. The tasks should be presented to the class in just the same form as in the figures. Physical models are often the best way to present the tasks so that students can use a trial-and-error approach to determine their results. As with all tasks, it should be clear that an explanation is required to justify each answer. For each task, let several students supply answers and explanations.

Sometimes it is a good idea to create simple story problems that ask the same questions.

• •

Mr. Samuels has finished $\frac{3}{4}$ of his patio. It looks like this:

Draw a picture that might be the shape of the finished patio.

• •

The problems can also involve numbers instead of models:

• •

If the swim team sold 400 raffle tickets, it would have enough money to pay for new team shirts. So far the swimmers have $\frac{5}{8}$ of the necessary raffle tickets sold. How many more tickets do they need to sell?

• •

With some models, it is necessary to be certain that the answer exists within the model. For example, if you were using fraction strips, you could ask, "If the blue strip (9) is the whole, what strip is two-thirds?" The answer is the 6 strip, or dark green. You could not ask students to find "three-fourths of the blue strip" because each fourth of 9 would be $2\frac{1}{4}$ units, and no strip has that length. Similar caution must be taken with rectangular pieces.

Questions involving unit fractions are generally the easiest. The hardest questions usually involve fractions greater than 1. For example, *If 15 chips are five-thirds of one whole set, how many chips are in a whole?*

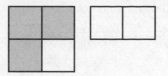

If the given amount equals $\frac{2}{5}$, then, since $\frac{2}{5}$ is *two* parts, the given amount is twice $\frac{1}{5}$. The shaded amount equals $\frac{1}{5}$.

FIGURE 3.6 • • • • • • • •

Finding the whole if the given amount of graham crackers is two-fifths. This same reasoning can be used for the tasks in Figure 3.3.

The whole is equal to five of these fifths.

However, in every question, the unit fraction plays a significant role. If you have $\frac{5}{3}$ and want the whole, you first need to find $\frac{1}{3}$.

Avoid being the answer book for your students. Make students responsible for determining the validity of their own answers. In these exercises, the results can always be confirmed in terms of what is given.

Fractions in textbooks and even some of the activities in this chapter lack context. Context takes children away from rules and encourages them to explore ideas in a more open and informal manner. The way that students approach fraction concepts in these contexts may surprise you. The following activity uses literature to provide an excellent context for discussing fractional parts of sets and how fractional parts change as the whole changes.

ACTIVITY 3.3

Sharing Camels

As a class, read the story "Beasts of Burden" in the book *The Man Who Counted: A Collection of Mathematical Adventures* (Tahan, 1993). This story is about a wise mathematician, Beremiz, and the narrator, who are traveling together on one camel. They are asked by three brothers to solve an argument. Their father has left them 35 camels to divide among them in this way: one-half to one brother, one-third to another, and one-ninth to the third. Have students grapple with this situation to try to come up with a solution. Make sure to discuss students' approaches and their conjectures before changing the number of camels. Try to choose the number of camels based on students' conjectures so they have an opportunity to test their hunches. For example, if students claim that they cannot divide an odd number of camels (e.g., 35) in half, they may state that the starting number has to be even. So start with an even number of camels, say 34 or 36. Or students may claim that the starting number must be divisible by three since there are three brothers. In this case, start with a number such as 33. Students should share what they think they have discovered as each number is tested. No matter how many camels are involved, the problem of the indicated shares cannot be resolved. (Why does this happen?)

 Before going further, try the preceding activity. What do you discover as you test various numbers? Why can you not find a number that will work?

The problem of the indicated shares cannot be resolved because the sum of $\frac{1}{2}$, $\frac{1}{3}$, and $\frac{1}{9}$ will never be one whole. No matter how many camels are involved, there will always be some "left over." Bresser (1995) describes three full days of wonderful discussions with his fifth graders, who proposed a wide range of solutions. Bresser's suggestions are worth considering.

Fraction Number Sense

The focus on fractional parts is an important beginning. But number sense with fractions demands more—it requires that students have some intuitive feel for fractions. They should know "about" how big a particular fraction is and be able to tell easily which of two fractions is larger.

Benchmarks of Zero, One-Half, and One

The most important reference points or benchmarks for fractions are 0, $\frac{1}{2}$, and 1. For fractions less than 1, simply comparing them to these three numbers gives quite a lot of information. For example, $\frac{3}{20}$ is small, close to 0, whereas $\frac{3}{4}$ is between $\frac{1}{2}$ and 1. The fraction $\frac{9}{10}$ is quite close to 1. Since any fraction greater than 1 is a whole number plus an amount less than 1, the same reference points are just as helpful: $3\frac{3}{7}$ is almost $3\frac{1}{2}$.

ACTIVITY 3.4

Zero, One-Half, or One

On the board or overhead, write a collection of 10 to 15 fractions. A few should be greater than 1 ($\frac{9}{8}$ or $\frac{11}{10}$), with the others ranging from 0 to 1. Let students sort the fractions into three groups: those close to 0, close to $\frac{1}{2}$, and close to 1. For those close to $\frac{1}{2}$, have them decide if the fraction is more or less than $\frac{1}{2}$. The difficulty of this task largely depends on the fractions. The first time you try this, use fractions such as $\frac{1}{20}$, $\frac{53}{100}$, or $\frac{9}{10}$ that are very close to the three benchmarks. On subsequent days, use fractions with most of the denominators less than 20. You might include one or two fractions such as $\frac{2}{8}$ or $\frac{3}{4}$ that are exactly in between the benchmarks. As usual, require explanations for each fraction.

The next activity is also aimed at developing the same three reference points for fractions. In "Close Fractions," however, the students must come up with the fractions rather than sort them.

ACTIVITY 3.5

Close Fractions

Have your students name a fraction that is close to 1 but not more than 1. Next have them name another fraction that is even closer to 1 than that. For the second response, they have to explain why they believe the fraction is closer to 1 than the previous fraction. Continue for several fractions in the same manner, each one being closer to 1 than the previous fraction. Similarly, try close to 0 or close to $\frac{1}{2}$ (either under or over). The first several times you try this activity, let the students use models to help with their thinking. Later, see how well their explanations work when they cannot use models or drawings. Focus discussions on the relative size of fractional parts.

Understanding why a fraction is close to 0, $\frac{1}{2}$, or 1 is a good beginning for fraction number sense. It begins to focus on the size of fractions in an important yet simple manner. The next activity also helps students reflect on fraction size.

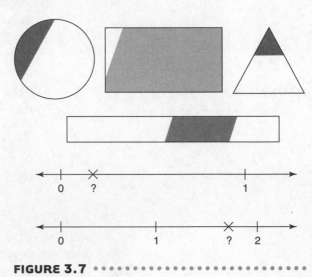

ACTIVITY 3.6

About How Much?

Draw a picture like one of those in Figure 3.7 (or prepare some ahead of time for the overhead). Have each student write down a fraction that he or she thinks is a good estimate of the amount shown (or the indicated mark on the number line). Listen without judgment to the ideas of several students, and discuss with them why any particular estimate might be a good one. There is no single correct answer, but estimates should be "in the ballpark." If children have difficulty coming up with an estimate, ask if they think the amount is closer to 0, $\frac{1}{2}$, or 1.

FIGURE 3.7 •

About how much? Name a fraction for each drawing and explain why you chose that fraction.

Thinking About Which Is More

The ability to tell which of two fractions is greater is another aspect of number sense with fractions. That ability is built around concepts of fractions, not on an algorithmic skill or symbolic tricks.

Concepts, Not Rules

Children have a tremendously strong mind-set about numbers that causes them difficulties with the relative size of fractions. In their experience, larger numbers mean "more." The tendency is to transfer this whole-number concept to fractions: Seven is more than four, so sevenths should be bigger than fourths (Mack, 1995). The inverse relationship between number of parts and size of parts cannot be told but must be a creation of each student's own thought process.

ACTIVITY 3.7

Ordering Unit Fractions

List a set of unit fractions such as $\frac{1}{3}$, $\frac{1}{8}$, $\frac{1}{5}$, and $\frac{1}{10}$. Ask children to put the fractions in order from least to most. Challenge children to defend the way they ordered the fractions. The first few times you do this activity, have them explain their ideas by using models.

Which fraction in each pair is greater? Give one or more reasons. Try not to use drawings or models. <u>Do</u> <u>not</u> <u>use</u> common denominators or cross-multiplication. Rely on concepts.

A. $\frac{4}{5}$ or $\frac{4}{9}$ G. $\frac{7}{12}$ or $\frac{5}{12}$

B. $\frac{4}{7}$ or $\frac{5}{7}$ H. $\frac{3}{5}$ or $\frac{3}{7}$

C. $\frac{3}{8}$ or $\frac{4}{10}$ I. $\frac{5}{8}$ or $\frac{6}{10}$

D. $\frac{5}{3}$ or $\frac{5}{8}$ J. $\frac{9}{8}$ or $\frac{4}{3}$

E. $\frac{3}{4}$ or $\frac{9}{10}$ K. $\frac{4}{6}$ or $\frac{7}{12}$

F. $\frac{3}{8}$ or $\frac{4}{7}$ L. $\frac{8}{9}$ or $\frac{7}{8}$

FIGURE 3.8 •

Comparing fractions using concepts.

This idea is so basic to the understanding of fractions that arbitrary rules ("Larger bottom numbers mean smaller fractions") are not only inappropriate but dangerous. Come back to this basic idea periodically. Children will seem to understand one day and revert to their more comfortable ideas about big numbers a day or two later.

You have probably learned rules or algorithms for comparing two fractions. The usual approaches are finding common denominators and using cross-multiplication. These rules can be effective in getting correct answers but require no thought about the size of the fractions. This is especially true of the cross-multiplication procedure. If children are taught these rules before they have had the opportunity to think about the relative size of various fractions, there is little chance that they will develop any familiarity with or number sense about fraction size. Comparison activities (which fraction is more?) can play a significant role in helping children develop concepts of relative fraction sizes. But keep in mind that reflective thought is the goal, not an algorithmic method of choosing the correct answer.

Before reading further, try the following exercise. Assume for a moment that you know nothing about equivalent fractions or common denominators or cross-multiplication. Assume that you are a fourth- or fifth-grade student who was never taught these procedures. Now examine the pairs of fractions in Figure 3.8 and select the larger of each pair. Write down or explain one or more reasons for your choice in each case.

Conceptual Thought Patterns for Comparison

The first two comparison schemes listed here rely on the meanings of the top and bottom numbers in fractions and on the relative sizes of unit fractional parts. The third and fourth ideas use the additional ideas of 0, $\frac{1}{2}$, and 1 as convenient anchors or benchmarks for thinking about the size of fractions. Comparing two fractions can strengthen and develop a general sense of fractions. Strict adherence to a common denominator rule sidesteps these benefits.

1. *More of the same-size parts.* To compare $\frac{3}{8}$ and $\frac{5}{8}$, it is easy to think about having 3 of something and also 5 of the same thing. It is common for children to choose $\frac{5}{8}$ as larger simply because 5 is more than 3 and the other numbers are the same. Right choice, wrong reason. Comparing $\frac{3}{8}$ and $\frac{5}{8}$ should be like comparing 3 apples and 5 apples.

2. *Same number of parts but parts of different sizes.* Consider the case of $\frac{3}{4}$ and $\frac{3}{7}$. If a whole is divided into 7 parts, the parts will certainly be smaller than if divided into only 4 parts. Many children will select $\frac{3}{7}$ as larger because 7 is more than 4 and the top numbers are the same. That approach yields correct choices when the parts are the same size, but it causes problems in this case. This is like comparing 3 apples with 3 melons. You have the same number of things, but melons are larger.

3. *More and less than one-half or one whole.* The fraction pairs $\frac{3}{7}$ versus $\frac{5}{8}$ and $\frac{5}{4}$ versus $\frac{7}{8}$ do not lend themselves to either of the previous thought processes. In the first pair, $\frac{3}{7}$ is less than half of the number of sevenths needed to make a whole, and so $\frac{3}{7}$ is less than a half. Similarly, $\frac{5}{8}$ is more than a half. Therefore, $\frac{5}{8}$ is the larger fraction. The second pair is determined by noting that one fraction is less than 1 and the other is greater than 1.

4. *Distance from one-half or one whole.* Why is $\frac{9}{10}$ greater than $\frac{3}{4}$? Not because the 9 and 10 are big numbers, although you will find that to be a common student response. Each is one fractional part away from one whole, and tenths are smaller than fourths. Similarly, notice that $\frac{5}{8}$ is smaller than $\frac{4}{6}$ because it is only one-eighth more than a half, while $\frac{4}{6}$ is a sixth more than a half. Can you use this basic idea to compare $\frac{3}{5}$ and $\frac{5}{9}$? (*Hint:* Each is half of a fractional part more than $\frac{1}{2}$.) Also try $\frac{5}{7}$ and $\frac{7}{9}$.

How did your reasons for choosing fractions in Figure 3.8 compare to these ideas? It is important that you are comfortable with these informal comparison strategies as a major component of your own number sense as well as for helping children develop theirs.

Tasks you design for your students should assist them in developing these and possibly other methods of comparing two fractions. It is important that the ideas come from your students and their discussions. To teach "the four ways to compare fractions" would be adding four more mysterious rules and would be defeating for many students.

ACTIVITY 3.8

Choose, Explain, Test

Present two or three pairs of fractions to students. The students' task is to decide which fraction is greater (choose), to explain why they think this is so (explain), and then to test their choice using any model that they wish to use. They should write a description of how they made their test and whether or not it agreed with their choice. If their choice was incorrect, they should try to say what they would change in their thinking. In the student explanations, rule out drawing as an option. Explain to students that drawings are sometimes inaccurate and can lead to faulty conclusions for these tasks.

Rather than directly teach the different possible methods for comparing fractions, select pairs that will likely elicit desired comparison strategies. On one day, for example, you might have two pairs with the same denominators and one with the same numerators. On another day, you might pick fraction pairs in which each fraction is exactly one part away from a whole. Try to build strategies over several days by the appropriate choice of fraction pairs.

The use of a model in Activity 3.8 is an important part of students' development of strategies as long as the model is helping students create the strategy. However, after several experiences, change the activity so that the testing portion with a model is omitted. Place greater emphasis on students' reasoning. If class discussions yield different choices, allow students to use their own arguments for their choices in order to make a decision about which fraction is greater.

The next activity extends the comparison task a bit more.

Line 'Em Up

Select four or five fractions for students to put in order from least to most. Have them indicate approximately where each fraction belongs on a number line labeled only with the points 0, $\frac{1}{2}$, and 1. Students should include a description of how they decided on the order for the fractions. To place the fractions on the number line, students must also make estimates of fraction size in addition to simply ordering the fractions.

Including Equivalent Fractions

The discussion to this point has somewhat artificially ignored the idea that students might use equivalent fraction concepts in making comparisons. Equivalent fraction concepts are such an important idea that a separate section is devoted to the development of that idea. However, equivalent fraction concepts need not be put off until last and certainly should be allowed in the discussions of which fraction is more.

Smith (2002) thinks that it is essential that the comparison question is asked as follows: "Which of the following two (or more) fractions is greater, *or are they equal?*" (p. 9, emphasis added). He points out that this question leaves open the possibility that two fractions that may look different can, in fact, be equal.

In addition to this point, with equivalent fraction concepts, students can adjust how a fraction looks so that they can use ideas that make sense to them. Burns (1999) told of fifth graders who were comparing $\frac{6}{8}$ to $\frac{4}{5}$. (You might want to stop for a moment and think how you would compare these two.) One child changed the $\frac{4}{5}$ to $\frac{8}{10}$ so that both fractions would be two parts away from the whole and he reasoned from there. Another changed both fractions to a common *numerator* of 12.

Be absolutely certain to revisit the comparison activities and include pairs such as $\frac{8}{12}$ and $\frac{2}{3}$ in which the fractions are equal but do not appear to be. Also include fractions that are not in lowest terms.

Only One Size for the Whole

A key idea about fractions that students must come to understand is that a fraction does not say anything about the size of the whole or the size of the parts. A fraction tells us only about the *relationship between* the part and the whole. Consider the following situation.

Mark is offered the choice of a third of a pizza or a half of a pizza. Since he is hungry and likes pizza, he chooses the half. His friend Jane gets a third of a pizza but ends up with more than Mark. How can that be? Figure 3.9 illustrates how Mark got misdirected in his choice. The point of the "pizza fallacy" is that whenever two or more fractions are discussed in the same context, the correct assumption (the one Mark made in choosing a half of the pizza) is that the fractions are all parts of the same size whole.

Comparisons with any model can be made only if both fractions are parts of the same whole. For example, $\frac{2}{3}$ of a light green strip cannot be compared to $\frac{2}{5}$ of an orange strip.

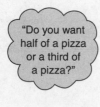

"Do you want half of a pizza or a third of a pizza?"

One-half of a pizza

One-third of a pizza

What assumption is made when answering this question?

FIGURE 3.9 •

The "pizza fallacy."

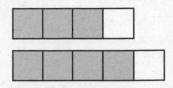

Since it has more, four-fifths is bigger than three-fourths.

FIGURE 3.10 • • • • • • •

A student compares $\frac{3}{4}$ and $\frac{4}{5}$.

Assessment Note

It is a good idea to periodically pose tasks in which students are required to draw representations of the fractions they are comparing. Consider the drawing in Figure 3.10, where a student has compared $\frac{4}{5}$ to $\frac{3}{4}$. What insights into his understanding does this student's work provide?

This student came to the correct conclusion but in an erroneous way. It appears that the student used "fractional pieces" of the same size to build his representations, resulting in two different wholes. His representations suggest that he may not realize that the wholes should be the same size within any given situation such as a comparison or computation.

Circular pie pieces and fraction bars can mask this misconception because the size of the whole circle or whole rectangle is fixed, eliminating the need for the student to think about the relative sizes of the associated wholes. Providing outlines of the wholes for students also diverts the focus from the size of the wholes.

Estimation

A frequently quoted result from the Second National Assessment (Post, 1981) concerns the following item:

Estimate the answer to $\frac{12}{13} + \frac{7}{8}$. You will not have time to solve the problem using paper and pencil.

Here is how 13-year-olds answered:

Response	Percent of 13-Year-Olds
1	7
2	24
19	28
21	27
Don't know	14

A later study of sixth- and eighth-grade Taiwanese students included this same item. The results were nearly identical to those in the NAEP study (Reys, 1998). In the Taiwanese study, a significantly higher percentage of students (61 percent and 63 percent) was able to correctly compute the sum, a process that requires finding the common denominator of thirteenths and eighths! Notice that to estimate this sum requires no skill whatsoever with computation—only a feeling for the size of the two fractions.

The development of fraction number sense should most certainly include estimation of fraction sums and differences—even before computational strategies are introduced. The following activity can be done regularly as a short full-class warm-up for any fraction lesson.

ACTIVITY 3.10

First Estimates

Tell students that they are going to estimate a sum or difference of two fractions. They are to decide only if the exact answer is more or less than one. On the overhead projector show, for no more than about 10 seconds, a fraction addition or subtraction problem involving two proper fractions. Students write down on paper their choice of more or less than one. Do several problems in a row. Then return to each problem and discuss how students decided on their estimate.

Restricting Activity 3.10 to proper fractions keeps the difficulty to a minimum. When students are ready for a tougher challenge, choose from the following variations:

- Use fractions that are less than one. Estimate to the nearest half $(0, \frac{1}{2}, 1, 1\frac{1}{2}, 2)$.
- Use both proper and mixed fractions. Estimate to the nearest half.
- Use proper and mixed fractions. Estimate the best answer you can.

In the discussions following these estimation exercises, ask students if they think that the exact answer is more or less than the estimate that they gave. What is their reasoning?

Figure 3.11 shows six sample sums and differences that might be used in a "First Estimates" activity.

 Test your own estimation skills with the sample problems in Figure 3.11. Look at each computation for only about 10 seconds and write down an estimate. After writing down all six of your estimates, look at the problems and decide if your estimate is higher or lower than the actual computation. Don't guess! Have a good reason.

In most cases students' estimates should not be much more than $\frac{1}{2}$ away from the exact sum or difference.

FIGURE 3.11 • • • • • • • • • • • • •

Fraction estimation drill.

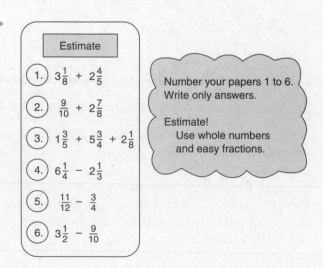

Estimate

1. $3\frac{1}{8} + 2\frac{4}{5}$
2. $\frac{9}{10} + 2\frac{7}{8}$
3. $1\frac{3}{5} + 5\frac{3}{4} + 2\frac{1}{8}$
4. $6\frac{1}{4} - 2\frac{1}{3}$
5. $\frac{11}{12} - \frac{3}{4}$
6. $3\frac{1}{2} - \frac{9}{10}$

Number your papers 1 to 6. Write only answers.

Estimate!
Use whole numbers and easy fractions.

Equivalent-Fraction Concepts

STOP How do you know that $\frac{4}{6} = \frac{2}{3}$? Before reading further, think of at least two different explanations.

Concepts Versus Rules

Here are some possible answers to the question just posed:

1. They are the same because you can reduce $\frac{4}{6}$ and get $\frac{2}{3}$.
2. If you have a set of 6 things and you take 4 of them, that would be $\frac{4}{6}$. But you can make the 6 into groups of 2. So then there would be 3 groups, and the 4 would be 2 groups out of the 3 groups. That means it's $\frac{2}{3}$.
3. If you start with $\frac{2}{3}$, you can multiply the top and the bottom numbers by 2, and that will give you $\frac{4}{6}$, so they are equal.
4. If you had a square cut into 3 parts and you shaded 2, that would be $\frac{2}{3}$ shaded. If you cut all 3 of these parts in half, that would be 4 parts shaded and 6 parts in all. That's $\frac{4}{6}$, and it would be the same amount.

All of these answers are correct. But let's think about what they tell us. Responses 2 and 4 are very conceptual, although not very efficient. The procedural responses, 1 and 3, are quite efficient but indicate no conceptual knowledge. All students should eventually be able to write an equivalent fraction for a given fraction. At the same time, the rules should never be taught or used until the students understand what the result means. Consider how different the algorithm and the concept appear to be.

Concept: Two fractions are equivalent if they are representations for the same amount or quantity—if they are the same number.

Algorithm: To get an equivalent fraction, multiply (or divide) the top and bottom numbers by the same nonzero number.

In a problem-based classroom, students can develop an understanding of equivalent fractions and also develop from that understanding a conceptually based algorithm. As with most algorithms, a serious instructional error is to rush too quickly to the rule. Be patient! Intuitive methods are always best at first.

Equivalent-Fraction Concepts

The general approach to helping students create an understanding of equivalent fractions is to have them use models to find different names for a fraction. The following activities are possible starting places.

ACTIVITY 3.11

Different Fillers

Using an area model for fractions that is familiar to your students, prepare a worksheet with two or at most three outlines of different fractions. Do not

(continued)

limit yourself to unit fractions. For example, if the model is circular pie pieces, you might draw an outline for $\frac{2}{3}$, $\frac{1}{2}$, and $\frac{3}{4}$. The students' task is to use their own fraction pieces to find as many single-fraction names for the region as possible. After completing the three examples, have students write about the ideas or patterns they may have noticed in finding the names. Follow the activity with a class discussion.

In the class discussion following the "Different Fillers" activity, a good question to ask involves what names could be found if students had any size pieces that they wanted. For example, ask students "What names could you find if we had sixteenths in our fraction kit? What names could you find if you could have any piece at all?" The idea is to push beyond filling in the region in a pure trial-and-error approach.

The following activity is just a variation of "Different Fillers." Instead of a manipulative model, the task is constructed on dot paper.

BLM 10

ACTIVITY 3.12

Dot Paper Equivalencies

Create a worksheet using a portion of either isometric or rectangular dot grid paper. (These can be found in the Blackline Masters.) On the grid, draw the outline of a region and designate it as one whole. Draw a part of the region within the whole. The task is to use different parts of the whole determined by the grid to find names for the part. Figure 3.12 includes an example drawn on an isometric grid. Students should draw a picture of the unit fractional part that they use for each fraction name. The larger the size of the whole, the more names the activity will generate.

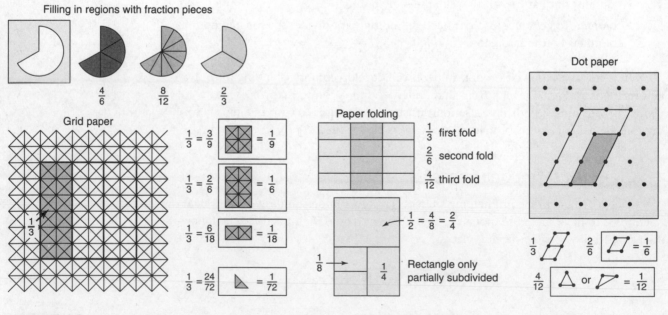

FIGURE 3.12

Area models for equivalent fractions.

The "Dot Paper Equivalencies" activity is a form of what Lamon (2002) calls "unitizing," that is, given a quantity, finding different ways to chunk the quantity into parts in order to name it. She points out that this is a key ability related not only to equivalent fractions but also to proportional reasoning, especially in the comparison of ratios. (See also Lamon, 1999 a, b.)

Length models can be used to create activities similar to the "Different Fillers" task. For example, as shown in Figure 3.13, rods or strips can be used to designate both a whole and a part. Students use smaller rods to find fraction names for the given part. To have larger wholes and, thus, more possible parts, use a train of two or three rods for the whole and the part. Folding paper strips is another method of creating fraction names. In the example shown in Figure 3.13, one-half is subdivided by successive folding in half. Other folds would produce other names and these possibilities should be discussed if no one tries to fold the strip in an odd number of parts.

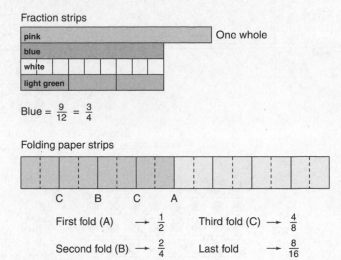

FIGURE 3.13 •••••••••••••••••••••••••••••••

Length models for equivalent fractions.

The following activity is also a unitizing activity in which students look for different units or chunks of the whole in order to name a part of the whole in different ways. This activity is significant because it utilizes a set model.

ACTIVITY 3.13

Group the Counters, Find the Names

Have students set out a specific number of counters in two colors—for example, 24 counters, 16 of them red and 8 yellow. The 24 make up the whole. The task is to group the counters into different fractional parts of the whole and use the parts to create fraction names for the red and the yellow counters. In Figure 3.14, 24 counters are arranged in different array patterns. You might want to suggest arrays or allow students to arrange them in any way they wish. Students should record their different groupings and explain how they found the fraction names. They can simply use Xs and Os for the counters.

In Lamon's version of the last activity, she prompts students with questions such as, "If we make groups of four, what part of the set is red?" (dark in Figure 3.14). With these prompts you can suggest fraction names that students are unlikely to think of. For our example in Figure 3.14, if we make groups of one-half counters, what would the yellow (white) set be called? Suppose we made groups of six? (Groups of six result in a fractional numerator. Why not?)

A challenging exploration about finding equivalent fractions arises from *Gator Pie* (Mathews, 1979), a delightful book about Alice, Alvin, and other alligators sharing a pie they found in the woods. At first glance this book seems too juvenile for students in the upper grades. However, students can enjoy this story when it is a springboard to a challenging task.

FIGURE 3.14 • • • • • • •

Set models for equivalent fractions.

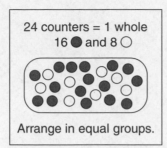

24 counters = 1 whole
16 ● and 8 ○

Arrange in equal groups.

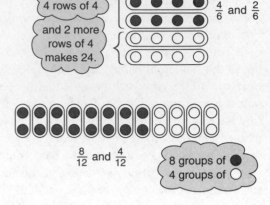

Make the 16 ● into 4 rows of 4

and 2 more rows of 4 makes 24.

$\frac{4}{6}$ and $\frac{2}{6}$

16 is 2 groups of 8.

$\frac{2}{3}$ and $\frac{1}{3}$

$\frac{8}{12}$ and $\frac{4}{12}$

8 groups of ●
4 groups of ○

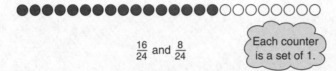

$\frac{16}{24}$ and $\frac{8}{24}$

Each counter is a set of 1.

ACTIVITY 3.14

Divide and Divide Again

In the story, Alvin and Alice find a pie in the woods. However, before they can cut it, another gator appears and demands a share of the pie. As the story continues, more and more gators arrive until there are 100 gators that want a piece of the pie. Finally, Alice painstakingly cuts the pie into hundredths. In the story, Alvin and Alice are prevented from cutting the pie each time because more gators show up. An interesting twist is to change the story so that the pie is cut before more gators appear. The problem is how to share it among a larger number once it is already cut. To illustrate, cut a circle (or rectangle) into halves or thirds, and then ask students to decide how to share it among a larger number once it is already cut. You may want to start going from halves to sixths. This is reasonably easy but may surprise you. After students have shared their approaches, progress into more difficult divisions. For example, what if the pie is cut in thirds and we want to share it in tenths? Students should be expected to identify the fractional parts they used and explain how and why they used those particular fractional parts. (This can also provide an informal look at fraction computation.)

As students work through "Divide and Divide Again," they have to think about the part-whole meaning of fractions: how to divide an amount into equal-sized portions or fair shares. What is challenging is that often the equal-sized portions may not be the same shape or must be pieced together from smaller pieces.

In the activities so far, there has only been a hint of a rule for finding equivalent fractions. The following activity moves a bit closer but should still be done before development of a rule.

Missing-Number Equivalencies

Give students an equation expressing an equivalence between two fractions but with one of the numbers missing. Here are four different examples:

$$\frac{2}{3} = \frac{6}{\square} \qquad \frac{8}{12} = \frac{\square}{3} \qquad \frac{9}{12} = \frac{3}{\square} \qquad \frac{3}{9} = \frac{\square}{6}$$

The missing number can be either a numerator or a denominator. Furthermore, the missing number can either be larger or smaller than the corresponding part of the equivalent fraction. (All four of these possibilities are represented in the examples.) The task is to find the missing number and to explain your solution.

When doing "Missing-Number Equivalencies" you may want to specify a particular model, such as sets or pie pieces. Alternatively, you can allow students to select whatever methods they wish to solve these problems. One or two equivalencies followed by a discussion is sufficient for a good lesson. This activity is surprisingly challenging, especially if students are required to use a set model.

Before continuing with development of an algorithm for equivalent fractions with your class, you should revisit the comparison tasks as children begin to realize that they can change the names of fractions in order to help reason about which fraction is greater.

Developing an Equivalent-Fraction Algorithm

Kamii and Clark (1995) argue that undue reliance on physical models does not help children construct equivalence schemes. When children understand that fractions can have different names, they should be challenged to develop a method for finding equivalent names. It might also be argued that students who are experienced at looking for patterns and developing schemes for doing things can invent an algorithm for equivalent fractions without further assistance. However, the following approach will certainly improve the chances of that happening.

An Area Model Approach

Your goal is to help students see that if they multiply both the top and bottom numbers by the same number, they will always get an equivalent fraction—one with the same value. The approach suggested here is to look for a pattern in the way that the fractional parts in both the part as well as the whole are counted. Activity 3.16 is a good beginning, but a good class discussion following the activity will also be required.

Slicing Squares

Give students a worksheet with four squares in a row, each approximately 3 cm on a side. Have them shade in the same fraction in each square using vertical dividing lines. For example, slice each square in fourths and shade three-fourths as in Figure 3.15. Next, tell students to slice each square into an

(continued)

Start with each square showing $\frac{3}{4}$.

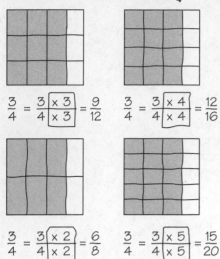

$$\frac{3}{4} = \frac{3 \boxed{\times 3}}{4 \boxed{\times 3}} = \frac{9}{12} \qquad \frac{3}{4} = \frac{3 \boxed{\times 4}}{4 \boxed{\times 4}} = \frac{12}{16}$$

$$\frac{3}{4} = \frac{3 \boxed{\times 2}}{4 \boxed{\times 2}} = \frac{6}{8} \qquad \frac{3}{4} = \frac{3 \boxed{\times 5}}{4 \boxed{\times 5}} = \frac{15}{20}$$

What <u>product</u> tells how many parts are shaded?

What <u>product</u> tells how many parts in the whole?

Notice that the same factor is used for both part and whole.

FIGURE 3.15 •

A model for the equivalent-fraction algorithm.

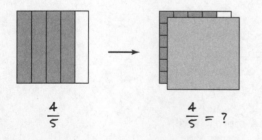

$$\frac{4}{5} \qquad\qquad \frac{4}{5} = ?$$

FIGURE 3.16 •

How can you count the fractional parts if you cannot see them all?

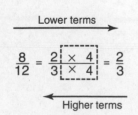

Lower terms →

$$\frac{8}{12} = \frac{2 \,\overline{|\times 4|}}{3 \,\underline{|\times 4|}} = \frac{2}{3}$$

← Higher terms

FIGURE 3.17 • • • • • • •

Using the equivalent-fraction algorithm to write fractions in simplest terms.

equal number of horizontal slices. Each square is sliced with a different number of slices, using anywhere from one to eight slices. For each sliced square, they should write an equation showing the equivalent fraction. Have them examine their four equations and the drawings and challenge them to discover any patterns in what they have done. You may want them to repeat this with four more squares and a different fraction.

Following this activity, write on the board the equations for four or five different fraction names found by the students. Discuss any patterns they found. To focus the discussion, show on the overhead a square illustrating $\frac{4}{5}$ made with vertical slices as in Figure 3.16. Turn off the overhead and slice the square into six parts in the opposite direction. Cover all but two edges of the square as shown in the figure. Ask, "What is the new name for my $\frac{4}{5}$?"

The reason for this exercise is that many students simply count the small regions and never think to use multiplication. With the covered square, students can see that there are four columns and six rows to the shaded part, so there must be 4×6 parts shaded. Similarly, there must be 5×6 parts in the whole. Therefore, the new name for $\frac{4}{5}$ is $\frac{4\times6}{5\times6}$.

Using this idea, have students return to the fractions on their worksheet to see if the pattern works for other fractions.

Examine examples of equivalent fractions that have been generated with other models, and see if the rule of multiplying top and bottom numbers by the same number holds there also. If the rule is correct, how can $\frac{6}{8}$ and $\frac{9}{12}$ be equivalent? What about fractions like $2\frac{1}{4}$? How could it be demonstrated that $\frac{9}{4}$ is the same as $2\frac{2}{12}$?

Writing Fractions in Simplest Terms

The multiplication scheme for equivalent fractions produces fractions with larger denominators. To write a fraction in *simplest terms* means to write it so that numerator and denominator have no common whole number factors. (Some texts use the name *lowest terms* instead of *simplest terms*.) One meaningful approach to this task of finding simplest terms is to reverse the earlier process, as illustrated in Figure 3.17. Try to devise a problem-based task that will help students develop this reverse idea.

Of course, finding and eliminating a common factor is the same as dividing both top and bottom by the same number. The search for a common factor keeps the process of writing an equivalent fraction to one rule: Top and bottom numbers of a fraction can be multiplied by the same nonzero number. There is no need for a different rule for rewriting fractions in lowest terms.

Two additional notes:

1. Notice that the phrase *reducing fractions* was not used. This unfortunate terminology implies making a fraction smaller and is rarely used anymore in textbooks.

2. Many teachers seem to believe that fraction answers are incorrect if not in simplest or lowest terms. This is also unfortunate. When students add $\frac{1}{6} + \frac{1}{2}$ and get $\frac{4}{6}$, they have added correctly and have found the answer. Rewriting $\frac{4}{6}$ as $\frac{2}{3}$ is a separate issue.

Multiplying by One

Many middle school textbooks use a strictly symbolic approach to equivalent fractions. It is based on the multiplicative property that says that any number multiplied by 1 remains unchanged. Any fraction of the form $\frac{n}{n}$ can be used as the identity element. Therefore, $\frac{3}{4} = \frac{3}{4} \times 1 = \frac{3}{4} \times \frac{2}{2} = \frac{6}{8}$. Furthermore, the numerator and denominator of the identity element can also be fractions. In this way, $\frac{6}{12} = \frac{6}{12} \times (\frac{1/6}{1/6}) = \frac{1}{2}$.

This explanation relies on an understanding of the multiplicative identity property, which most students in grades 4 to 6 do not fully appreciate. It also relies on the procedure for multiplying two fractions. Finally, the argument uses solely deductive reasoning based on an axiom of the rational number system. It does not lend itself to intuitive modeling. A reasonable conclusion is to delay this important explanation until at least seventh or eighth grade in an appropriate prealgebra context and not as a method or a rationale for producing equivalent fractions.

Technology Note

In the NCTM e-examples (www.nctm.org), there is a very nice fraction game for two players (*Applet 5.1, Communicating About Mathematics Using Games*). The game uses a number-line model, and knowledge of equivalent fractions plays a significant role.

Number Sense and Fraction Algorithms

A fifth-grade student asks, "Why is it when we times 29 times two-ninths that the answer goes down?" (Taber, 2002, p. 67). Although generalizations from whole numbers can confuse students, you should realize that their ideas about the operations were developed with whole numbers. Students need to build on their ideas of whole-number operations. This is where students are. We can use their understanding of what the operations mean to give meaning to fraction computation.

However, as you will discover in this chapter, a firm understanding of fractions is the most critical foundation for fraction computation. Without this foundation, your students will almost certainly be learning rules without reasons, an unacceptable goal.

Today it is important to be able to compute with fractions, primarily for the purpose of making estimates, for understanding computations done with technology, and for relatively simple calculations. Even standardized testing reflects an emphasis on less tedious computations with fractions.

The Dangerous Rush to Rules

It is important to give students ample opportunity to develop fraction number sense and not immediately to start talking about common denominators and other rules of computation. Even if you are teaching in grade 6, 7, or 8, and you find that your students have not developed both an understanding of fraction concepts and number sense with fractions, it is a mistake to move forward with fraction computation. Invest some time with the ideas discussed earlier in this chapter.

Premature attention to rules for fraction computation has a number of serious drawbacks. None of the rules helps students think about the operations and what they mean. Armed only with rules, students have no means of assessing their results to see if they make sense. Surface mastery of rules in the short term is quickly lost. When mixed together, the myriad rules of fraction computation soon become a meaningless jumble. Students ask, "Do I need a common denominator, or do you just add the bottom numbers like in multiplication?" "Which one do you invert, the first or the second number?" The algorithm rules do not immediately apply to mixed numbers. More rules! And perhaps most important is that this approach to mathematics is immensely defeating to the child.

A Problem-Based, Number Sense Approach

Even if your curriculum guidelines call for teaching all four of the operations with fractions in the fifth grade, you are still advised to delay a rush to algorithmic procedures until it becomes clear that students are ready. (Very few states call for multiplication and division of fractions before the fifth grade.) Students can become adequately proficient using informal, student-invented methods that they understand.

The following guidelines should be kept in mind when developing computational strategies for fractions:

1. *Begin with simple contextual tasks.* Huinker (1998) makes an excellent case for the use of contextual problems and for letting students develop their own methods of computation with fractions. Problems or contexts need not be elaborate. What you want is a context for both the meaning of the operation and the fractions involved.
2. *Connect the meaning of fraction computation with whole-number computation.* To consider what $2\frac{1}{2} \times \frac{3}{4}$ might mean, we should ask, "What does 2×3 mean?" The concepts of each operation are the same, and benefits can be had by connecting these ideas.
3. *Let estimation and informal methods play a big role in the development of strategies.* "Should $2\frac{1}{2} \times \frac{3}{4}$ be more or less than 1? More or less than 3?" Estimation keeps the focus on the meanings of the numbers and the operations, encourages reflective thinking, and helps build informal number sense with fractions.
4. *Explore each of the operations using models.* Use a variety of models. Have students defend their solutions using the models. You will find that sometimes it is possible to get answers with models that do not seem to help with pencil-and-paper approaches. That's fine! The ideas will help children learn to think about the fractions and the operations, contribute to mental methods, and provide a useful background when you eventually do get to the standard algorithms.

In the discussions that follow, informal exploration is encouraged for each operation. There is also a guided development of each traditional algorithm.

Addition and Subtraction

The idea of developing invented strategies for fractions beginning with contextual problems is similar to the approach described in Chapter 2 for whole-number computation. As with whole numbers, expect that students will use a variety of methods and that the methods will vary widely with the fractions encountered in the problems.

No attempt is made in this chapter to describe all of the solution strategies that students might develop. Students will continue to find ways to solve problems with fractions, and their informal approaches will contribute to the development of more standard methods.

Informal Exploration

Consider the following simple context:

> Paul and his brother were each eating the same kind of candy bar. Paul had $\frac{3}{4}$ of his candy bar. His brother still had $\frac{7}{8}$ of a candy bar. How much candy did the two boys have together?

This is an example of the type of task you can pose to students from the very beginning of their exploration with fraction computation.

 Using nothing other than simple drawings, how would you solve this problem without setting it up in the usual manner and finding common denominators? Can you think of two different methods?

Most students will draw a simple rectangle for the two candy bars as in Figure 3.18. The drawing of $\frac{7}{8}$ suggests that if you had one more eighth it would be a whole. So it is the same as $1\frac{3}{4}$ with $\frac{1}{8}$ taken off. Or, the drawing might suggest taking a fourth from the $\frac{7}{8}$ and putting it with the $\frac{3}{4}$ to make a whole. That would leave $\frac{5}{8}$.

3/4   7/8

FIGURE 3.18 • • • • • • • • • • • • • • • •

How could you combine these two quantities to determine the sum?

Students should always be encouraged to use drawings to help with their thinking in mathematics. However, when it comes to fraction drawings, it is easy for students to make incorrect conclusions based on inaccurate drawings. Fractional parts of regions, especially circles, are often difficult to draw. Sometimes you may want to specify that students use a particular physical model instead of a drawing. For example, suppose that you ask students to solve the following problem using fraction strips or Cuisenaire rods.

> Jack and Jill ordered two identical-sized pizzas, one cheese and one pepperoni. Jack ate $\frac{5}{6}$ of a pizza and Jill ate $\frac{1}{2}$ of a pizza. How much pizza did they eat together?

Find a strip for a whole that allows both fractions to be modeled.

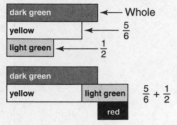

The sum is 1 whole and a red rod more than a whole. A red is $\frac{1}{3}$ of a dark green.

So $\frac{5}{6} + \frac{1}{2} = 1\frac{1}{3}$.

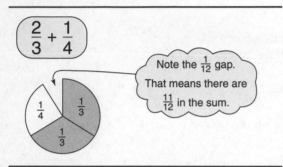

Note the $\frac{1}{12}$ gap. That means there are $\frac{11}{12}$ in the sum.

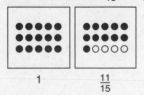

What set size can be used for the whole? The smallest is a set of 15.

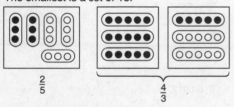

Combine (add) the fractions.
$\frac{2}{5}$ is 6 counters, and $\frac{4}{3}$ is 20 counters.
In sets of 15, that is $\frac{26}{15}$, or $1\frac{11}{15}$.

FIGURE 3.19 •

Using models to add fractions.

The first decision that must be made is what strip (or rod) to use as the whole. That decision is not required with a circular model. The whole must be the same for both fractions although there is a tendency to use the easiest whole for each fraction. Again, this issue does not arise with circles. In this case, the smallest strip that will work is the 6 strip or the dark green strip. Figure 3.19 illustrates a solution. The thinking required in this task helps pave the way for a common denominator approach.

Subtraction of two fractions with models is a similar process, as shown in Figure 3.20. Notice that it is sometimes possible to find the sum or difference of two fractions without splitting pieces into smaller parts. Often the answer is determined by looking at the part left over.

Most of your problems should involve simple fractions with "friendly" denominators no greater than 12. There is no need to add fifths and sevenths or even fifths and twelfths. The results involve numbers that cannot be handled with any model or drawing. Those numbers are rarely found in real problems. At the same time, do not be afraid of including mixed numbers and unlike denominators.

The Myth of Common Denominators

Teachers commonly tell students, "In order to add or subtract fractions, you must first get common denominators." The explanation usually goes something like, "After all, you can't add apples and oranges." This well-intentioned statement is essentially false. A correct statement might be, "In order *to use the standard algorithm* to add or subtract fractions, you must first get common denominators." And the explanation is then, "The algorithm is designed to work only with common denominators."

Using their own invented strategies, students will see that many correct solutions are found without ever getting a common denominator. Consider these sums and differences:

$$\frac{3}{4} + \frac{1}{8} \qquad \frac{1}{2} - \frac{1}{8} \qquad \frac{2}{3} + \frac{1}{2} \qquad 1\frac{1}{2} - \frac{3}{4} \qquad 1\frac{2}{3} + \frac{3}{4}$$

Working with the ways different fractional parts are related one to another often provides solutions without common denominators. For example, halves, fourths, and eighths are easily related. Also, picture three-thirds making up a whole in a circle. Have you ever noticed that one-half of the whole is a third and a half of a third or a sixth? Similarly, the difference between a third and a fourth is a twelfth. With relationships such as these, many fraction computations can be solved without first getting common denominators.

Chapter 3 FRACTION CONCEPTS AND COMPUTATION

Developing the Algorithm

It is important to develop an algorithm for addition and subtraction, and students will likely need some guidance in doing so. At the same time, they can easily build on their informal explorations and see that the common-denominator approach is meaningful.

Like Denominators

Most lists of objectives first specify addition and subtraction with like denominators. This is both unfortunate and unnecessary! If students have a good foundation with fraction concepts, they should be able to add or subtract like fractions immediately. Students who are not confident solving problems such as $\frac{3}{4} + \frac{2}{4}$ or $3\frac{7}{8} - 1\frac{3}{8}$ almost certainly do not have good fraction concepts and will be lost in any further development. The idea that the top number counts and the bottom number tells what is counted makes addition and subtraction of like fractions the same as adding and subtracting whole numbers.

Unlike Denominators

To get students to move to common denominators, consider a task such as $\frac{5}{8} + \frac{2}{4}$. Let students use pie pieces to get the result of $1\frac{1}{8}$ using any approach. Many will note that the models for the two fractions make one whole and there is $\frac{1}{8}$ extra. The key question to ask at this point is, "How can we change this problem into one that is just like the easy ones where the parts are the same?" For this example, it is relatively easy to see that fourths could be changed into eighths. Have students use models to show the original problem and also the converted problem. The main idea is to see that $\frac{5}{8} + \frac{2}{4}$ is exactly the same problem as $\frac{5}{8} + \frac{4}{8}$.

Next try some examples where both fractions need to be changed—for example, $\frac{2}{3} + \frac{1}{4}$. Again, focus attention on *rewriting the problem* in a form that is like "adding apples and apples," where the parts of both fractions are the same. As students discuss solutions, be sure they understand clearly that the new form of the problem is the same problem. This can and should be demonstrated with models. However, if your students express any doubt about the equivalence of the two problems ("Is $\frac{11}{12}$ really the answer to $\frac{2}{3} + \frac{1}{4}$?"), that should be a clue that the concept of equivalent fractions is not well understood.

As a result of modeling and rewriting fractions to make the problems easy, students will come to understand that the process of getting a common denominator is really one of looking for a way to change the *statement* of the problem without changing the problem itself. These ideas are illustrated in Figure 3.21.

Subtraction of two simple fractions follows exactly the same approach.

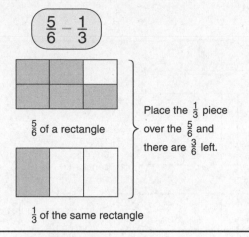

$\frac{5}{6}$ of a rectangle

$\frac{1}{3}$ of the same rectangle

Place the $\frac{1}{3}$ piece over the $\frac{5}{6}$ and there are $\frac{3}{6}$ left.

$\dfrac{7}{8} - \dfrac{1}{2}$

Find a rod that can be broken into eighths and halves: brown.

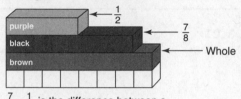

$\frac{7}{8} - \frac{1}{2}$ is the difference between a magenta and a black rod. That is three whites, or $\frac{3}{8}$. So $\frac{7}{8} - \frac{1}{2} = \frac{3}{8}$.

$1\dfrac{1}{3} - \dfrac{1}{2}$

Get a set that can be divided into both halves and thirds. Use sets of 6.

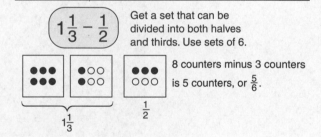

8 counters minus 3 counters is 5 counters, or $\frac{5}{6}$.

$1\frac{1}{3}$ $\frac{1}{2}$

FIGURE 3.20 •

Using models to subtract fractions.

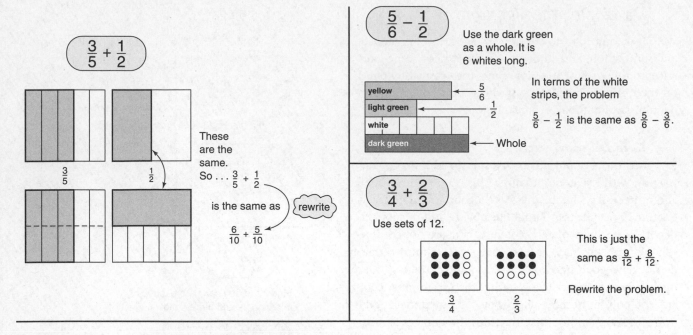

FIGURE 3.21 •

Rewriting addition and subtraction problems involving fractions.

Assessment Note

It is not unusual for a student to provide the following argument when adding fractions with unlike denominators. The drawing supports the incorrect algorithm of adding both the numerators and denominators.

In this and in most cases where this error occurs, the answer is usually not close to the correct one. Rather than correct the student, suggest that he estimate the answer. In this example, an estimate must be greater than $\frac{1}{2}$ and is very close to 1 whole. The answer of $\frac{2}{5}$ is clearly impossible. Suggest that students do two things: First, use a circular pie-piece model to solve the same problem and then provide a short explanation of why the $\frac{2}{5}$ solution is flawed. This puts the responsibility for finding the logical error on the student. It tells the student that while he has made a mistake, you have confidence that he can find the error. In contrast, an appeal to the rule for adding fractions will give the student the idea that mathematics is all about memorizing the correct rule. As discussed earlier (see Figure 3.9, p. 78), the fallacy here is failure to keep the whole fixed for all parts of the problem.

Using common denominators to add fractions can be done both with and without understanding. The key is an understanding of equivalent fractions as simply other names for the same quantities. Try the following task to check on whether students are really using this idea. Begin by having students add $\frac{2}{3}$ and $\frac{1}{2}$ by any method. Have them confirm the result using a model such as circular pie pieces. Once they are convinced that the correct answer is $1\frac{1}{6}$, substitute $\frac{16}{24}$ for the $\frac{2}{3}$ and $\frac{7}{14}$ for the $\frac{1}{2}$. Now have them solve the "new" problem, $\frac{16}{24} + \frac{7}{14}$. Students who understand the use of equivalent fractions in the addition algorithm should immediately know that the answer remains the same, $1\frac{1}{6}$, because they are adding the same fractions. There is no need to solve the problem again. If not all students see the trick you have played on them, the discussion that ensues should be beneficial in correcting the problem.

Mixed Numbers

A separate algorithm for mixed numbers in addition and subtraction is not necessary even though mixed numbers are often treated as separate topics in traditional textbooks and in some lists of objectives. Avoid layering fractions with yet another rule. Include mixed numbers in all of your activities with addition and subtraction and let students solve these problems in ways that make sense to them. Furthermore, it is almost certain that students will add the whole numbers first and then deal with the fractions using the algorithm or whatever method makes sense.

For subtraction, dealing with the whole numbers first still makes sense. Consider this problem: $5\frac{1}{8} - 3\frac{5}{8}$. After subtracting 3 from 5, students will need to deal with the $\frac{5}{8}$. Some will take $\frac{5}{8}$ from the whole part, 2, leaving $1\frac{3}{8}$, and then $\frac{1}{8}$ more is $1\frac{4}{8}$. Others may take away the $\frac{1}{8}$ that is there and then $\frac{4}{8}$ from the remaining 2. A third but unlikely method is to trade one of the wholes for $\frac{8}{8}$, add it to the $\frac{1}{8}$, and then take $\frac{5}{8}$ from the resulting $\frac{9}{8}$. This last method is the same as the traditional algorithm.

Estimation and Simple Methods

With denominators of 16 or less, estimation using "nice" fractions like halves and fourths is usually possible and should be encouraged. Estimation also leads to informal methods that are often easier than traditional algorithms for getting exact answers.

Consider $7\frac{1}{8} - 2\frac{3}{4}$. A first estimate might be 5, ignoring the fractions. Will it be more or less than 5? Others may begin by thinking $7\frac{1}{8}$ is close to 7 and $2\frac{3}{4}$ is close to 3 $\longrightarrow$ about 4, maybe a little more. Once students begin to think in these terms, a meaningful method for an exact answer is often possible without using an algorithm.

Examine the fraction exercises for addition and subtraction in a middle grades textbook. See how many of them you can do without pencil and paper. Challenge students to do the same.

Multiplication

When working with whole numbers, we would say that 3 × 5 means "3 sets of 5." The first factor tells how much of the second factor you have or want. This is a good place to begin. Simple story problems are a significant help in this development.

Informal Exploration

The story problems that you use to pose multiplication tasks to students need not be elaborate, but it is important to think about the numbers that you use in the problems. A possible progression of problem difficulty is developed in the sections that follow.

Beginning Concepts

Consider these two problems as good starting tasks:

> There are 15 cars in Michael's toy car collection. Two-thirds of the cars are red. How many red cars does Michael have?

> Suzanne has 11 cookies. She wants to share them with her three friends. How many cookies will Suzanne and each of her friends get?

Finding the fractional part of a whole number, which is the task in both problems, is not unlike the task of finding a fractional part of a whole. In Michael's car problem, think of the 15 cars as the whole and you want $\frac{2}{3}$ of the whole. First, find thirds by dividing 15 by 3. Multiplying by thirds, regardless of how many thirds, involves dividing by 3. The denominator is a divisor.

Suzanne's cookie problem is a sharing problem. Dividing by 4 is the same as multiplication by $\frac{1}{4}$. Or think of the 11 cookies as the whole. How many in one-fourth? Cookies are used so that the items can be subdivided.

Problems in which the first factor or multiplier is a whole number are also important.

> Wayne filled 5 glasses with $\frac{2}{3}$ liter of soda in each glass. How much soda did Wayne use?

This problem may be solved in different ways. Some students will put the thirds together, making wholes as they go. Others will count all of the thirds and then find out how many whole liters are in 10 thirds.

Unit Parts Without Subdivisions

To expand on the ideas just presented, consider these three problems:

> You have $\frac{3}{4}$ of a pizza left. If you give $\frac{1}{3}$ of the leftover pizza to your brother, how much of a whole pizza will your brother get?

> Someone ate $\frac{1}{10}$ of the cake, leaving only $\frac{9}{10}$. If you eat $\frac{2}{3}$ of the cake that is left, how much of a whole cake will you have eaten?

> Gloria used $2\frac{1}{2}$ tubes of blue paint to paint the sky in her picture. Each tube holds $\frac{4}{5}$ ounce of paint. How many ounces of blue paint did Gloria use?

Chapter **3** FRACTION CONCEPTS AND COMPUTATION

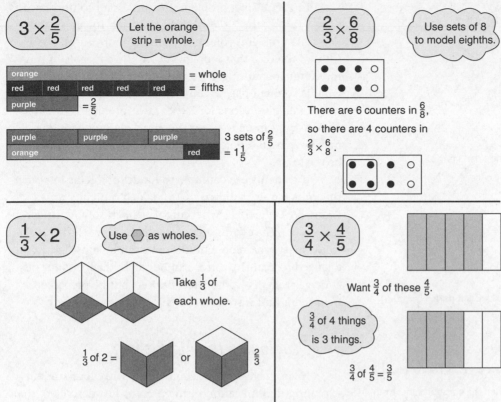

FIGURE 3.22 •••••••

Modeling multiplication problems in which the unit pieces do not require further subdivision.

Notice that the units or fractional parts in these problems do not need to be subdivided further. The first problem is $\frac{1}{3}$ of three things, the second is $\frac{2}{3}$ of nine things, and the last is $2\frac{1}{2}$ of four things. The focus remains on the number of unit parts in all, and then the size of the parts determines the number of wholes. Figure 3.22 shows how problems of this type might be modeled. However, it is very important to let students model and solve these problems in their own way, using whatever models or drawings they choose. Require only that they be able to explain their reasoning.

Subdividing the Unit Parts

When the pieces must be subdivided into smaller unit parts, the problems become more challenging.

••

Zack had $\frac{2}{3}$ of the lawn left to cut. After lunch, he cut $\frac{3}{4}$ of the grass he had left. How much of the whole lawn did Zack cut after lunch?

••

••

The zookeeper had a huge bottle of the animals' favorite liquid treat, Zoo Cola. The monkey drank $\frac{1}{5}$ of the bottle. The zebra drank $\frac{2}{3}$ of what was left. How much of the bottle of Zoo Cola did the zebra drink?

••

 Stop for a moment and figure out how you would solve each of these problems. Draw pictures to help you but do not use a computational algorithm.

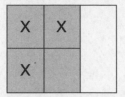

How much is $\frac{3}{4}$ of $\frac{2}{3}$?

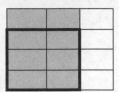

Cut each third in half, and take 3 parts.
Half of a third is a sixth, so it's $\frac{3}{6}$.

Cut all 3 thirds into 4 parts. Each part is $\frac{1}{12}$.
Three-fourths of the 8 twelfths of the grass
left to cut is $\frac{6}{12}$.

FIGURE 3.23 •

Solutions to fraction products when the unit parts must be subdivided.

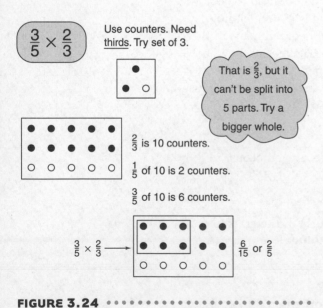

FIGURE 3.24 •

Modeling multiplication of fractions with counters.

In Zack's lawn problem, it is necessary to find fourths of two things, the 2 *thirds* of the grass left to cut. In the Zoo Cola problem, you need thirds of four things, the 4 *fifths* of the cola that remain. Again, the concepts of the top number counting and the bottom number naming what is counted play an important role. Figure 3.23 shows two possible solutions for Zack's lawn problem. Similar approaches can be used for the Zoo Cola problem. You may have used different drawings, but the ideas should be the same.

If students use counters to model problems in which the units require subdivision, an added difficulty arises. Figure 3.24 illustrates what might happen solving the problem $\frac{3}{5} \times \frac{2}{3}$. (*Three-fifths of $\frac{2}{3}$ of a whole is how much of a whole?*) Here the representation of a whole must be changed so that the thirds can be subdivided. Do not discourage students from using counters but be prepared to help them find ways to show thirds using larger sets.

Developing the Algorithm

If you have spent adequate time with your students exploring multiplication of fractions as just described, the traditional multiplication algorithm will be relatively simple to develop. Shift from contextual problems to a straight computation. Have students use a square or a rectangle as the model.

A Beginning Task

To make the development problem based for students, provide them with a drawing of $\frac{3}{4}$ of a square as shown in Figure 3.25. The task is to use the drawing to determine the product $\frac{3}{5} \times \frac{3}{4}$ (three-fifths of three-fourths of a whole) and explain the result. Remember, you want to find a fractional part of the shaded part. The *unit*, however, the way the parts are measured, must remain the whole.

Drawn as shown, the easiest way to get $\frac{3}{4}$ of the shaded region is to divide it into fourths using lines in the opposite direction. Then the problem is to determine what types of unit pieces these are. Although students may not think of it, an easy method of doing this is to extend the lines, subdividing the entire whole into fourths. Then the product of the denominators tells how many pieces are in the whole (the kind of unit), and the product of the numerators tells the number of pieces in the product.

Avoid pushing students to formalize the rule or algorithm of multiplying tops and bottoms. Many students will simply count each small part in the drawings and not notice that the numbers of rows and columns are actually the two numerators and the two denominators, respectively. You might steer students in this direction by posing a

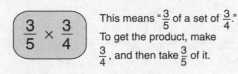

This means "$\frac{3}{5}$ of a set of $\frac{3}{4}$."
To get the product, make $\frac{3}{4}$, and then take $\frac{3}{5}$ of it.

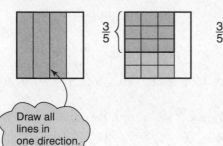

If you extend the dividing lines all the way across the square, you can tell what fractional part each little piece is.

Draw all lines in one direction.

This region is the PRODUCT. It is $\frac{3}{5}$ of $\frac{3}{4}$.

There are three rows and three columns in the PRODUCT, or 3×3 parts.

The WHOLE is now five rows and four columns, so there are 5×4 parts in the whole.

$$\text{PRODUCT} = \frac{3}{5} \times \frac{3}{4} = \frac{\boxed{\text{Number}} \text{ of parts in product}}{\boxed{\text{Kind}} \text{ of parts}} = \frac{3 \times 3}{5 \times 4} = \frac{9}{20}$$

problem with the initial sketch but asking them to determine the product without additional drawing. Try this with $\frac{7}{8} \times \frac{4}{5}$, where the numbers make it almost mandatory that you multiply.

A cautionary note: Many texts make this sliced-square approach so mechanical that it actually becomes a meaningless algorithm in itself. Students are told to shade a square one way for the first factor and the opposite way for the second factor. Without rationale, they are told that the product is the region that is double-shaded. You might as well give students the rule and forget about explanations.

Factors Greater Than One

Once students have explored products with both factors less than 1, it may be challenging to have them see if they can use a similar type of drawing to explain products with either or both factors greater than 1. Figure 3.26 shows how this might look when both factors are mixed numbers. Keep the task problem based. This can be a significant and worthwhile challenge. There is no need to explain how to do this.

Mental Techniques and Estimation

In the real world, there are many instances when the product of a whole number times a fraction occurs, and a mental estimate or even an exact answer is quite useful. For example, sale items are frequently listed as "$\frac{1}{4}$ off," or we read of a "$\frac{1}{3}$ increase" in the number of registered voters. Fractions are excellent substitutes for percents. To get an estimate of 60 percent of $36.69, it is useful to think of 60 percent as $\frac{3}{5}$ or as a little less than $\frac{2}{3}$.

$3\frac{2}{3} \times 2\frac{1}{4}$

Whole

1

$2\frac{1}{4} = \frac{9}{4}$

$3\frac{2}{3}$ or $\frac{11}{3}$

The PRODUCT is $3\frac{2}{3}$ sets of $2\frac{1}{4}$.

There are 11 rows and 9 columns, or 11×9 parts, in the PRODUCT.

The WHOLE now has three rows and four columns, or 3×4 parts.

$$3\frac{2}{3} \times 2\frac{1}{4} = \frac{11}{3} \times \frac{9}{4} = \text{PRODUCT} =$$

$$\frac{\boxed{\text{Number}} \text{ of parts}}{\boxed{\text{Kind}} \text{ of parts}} = \frac{11 \times 9}{3 \times 4} = \frac{99}{12} = 8\frac{1}{4}$$

FIGURE 3.26 •

The same approach used to develop the algorithm for fractions less than 1 can be expanded to mixed numbers.

These products of fractions with large whole numbers can be calculated mentally by thinking of the meanings of the top and bottom numbers. For example, $\frac{3}{5}$ is 3 *one*-fifths. So if you want $\frac{3}{5}$ of 350, for example, first think about *one*-fifth of 350, or 70. If *one*-fifth is 70, then *three*-fifths is 3×70, or 210. Although this example has very accommodating numbers, it illustrates a process for mentally multiplying a large number by a fraction: First determine the unit fractional part and then multiply by the number of parts you want.

When numbers are not so nice, encourage students to use compatible numbers. To estimate $\frac{3}{5}$ of \$36.69, a useful compatible is \$35. One-fifth of 35 is 7, so three-fifths is 3×7, or 21. Now adjust a bit—perhaps add an additional 50 cents, for an estimate of \$21.50.

Students should practice estimating fractions times whole numbers in lots of real contexts: $3\frac{1}{4}$ gallons of paint at \$14.95 per gallon or $\frac{7}{8}$ of the 476 students who attended Friday's football game. When working with decimals and percents, these skills will be revisited, and once again mathematics will seem more connected than disconnected.

Division

Invert the divisor and multiply is probably one of the most mysterious rules in elementary mathematics. We want to avoid this mystery at all costs. However, first it makes sense to examine division with fractions from a more familiar perspective.

As with the other operations, go back to the meaning of division with whole numbers. Recall that there are two meanings of division: partition and measurement. We will review each briefly and look at some story problems that involve fractions. (Can you make up a word problem right now that would go with the computation $2\frac{1}{2} \div \frac{1}{4}$?)

You should have students explore both measurement and partition problems. Here we will discuss each type of problem separately for the purpose of clarity. In the classroom, the types of problems should probably be mixed. As with multiplication, how the numbers relate to each other in the problems tends to affect the difficulty.

Informal Exploration: Partition Concept

Too often we think of the partition problems strictly as sharing problems: 24 apples to be shared with 4 friends. How many will each friend get? However, this same sharing structure applies to rate problems: If you walk 12 miles in 3 hours, how many miles do you walk per hour? Both of these problems, in fact, all partition problems, ask the questions, "How much for one?" "How much is the amount for one friend?" "How many miles are walked in one hour?" The 24 is the amount for the 4 friends. The 12 miles is the amount for the 3 hours.

Whole-Number Divisors

Having the total amount be a fraction with the divisor a whole number is not really a big leap. These problems still are easy to think of as sharing situations. However, as you work through these questions, notice that you are answering the question, "How much is the whole?" or "How much for one?"

> Cassie has $5\frac{1}{4}$ yards of ribbon to make three bows for birthday packages. How much ribbon should she use for each bow if she wants to use the same length of ribbon for each?

When the $5\frac{1}{4}$ is thought of as fractional parts, there are 21 fourths to share, or 7 fourths for each ribbon. Alternatively, one might think of first allotting 1 yard per bow, leaving $2\frac{1}{4}$ yards, or 9 fourths. These 9 fourths are then shared, 3 fourths per bow, for a total of $1\frac{3}{4}$ yards for each bow. Regardless of the particular process, the unit parts required no further subdivision in order to do the division. In the following problem, the parts must be split into smaller parts.

> Mark has $1\frac{1}{4}$ hours to finish his three household chores. If he divides his time evenly, how many hours can he give to each?

Note that the question is, "How much for one chore?" The 5 fourths of an hour that Mark has do not split neatly into three parts. So some or all of the parts must be subdivided. Figure 3.27 shows three different models for figuring this out. In each case, all of the fourths are subdivided into three equal parts, producing twelfths. There are a total of 15 twelfths, or $\frac{5}{12}$ hour for each chore. (Test this answer against the solution in minutes: $1\frac{1}{4}$ hours is 75 minutes, which divided among 3 chores is 25 minutes per chore.)

Fractional Divisors

The sharing concept appears to break down when the divisor is a fraction. However, it is enormously helpful to keep in mind that for partition and rate problems the fundamental question is, "How much is one?" Interestingly, this is exactly the second

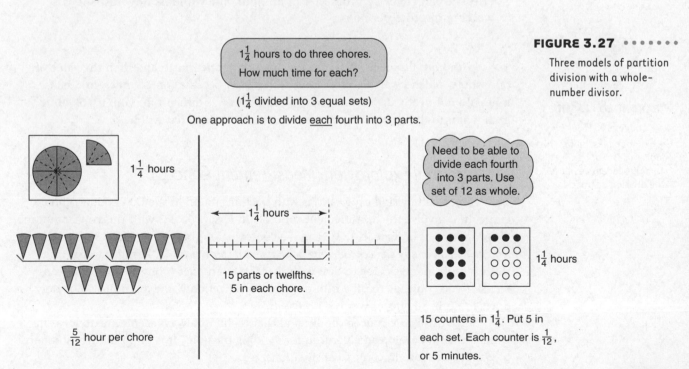

FIGURE 3.27

Three models of partition division with a whole-number divisor.

type of question in the parts-and-whole tasks we discussed earlier in the chapter. (See Figure 3.3.) Given the part, find the whole—how much is one? For example, if a set of 18 counters is $2\frac{1}{4}$, how much is a whole set? In solving these problems, the first task is to find the number in *one*-fourth and then multiply by 4 to get four-fourths or one. Let's see if we can see the same process in the following problem:

> Elizabeth bought $3\frac{1}{3}$ pounds of tomatoes for $2.50. How much did she pay per pound?

 The given amount of $2.50 is *distributed across* $3\frac{1}{3}$ pounds. How much is (distributed across) 1 pound? Solve the problem the same way as you would a parts-and-whole problem. Try it now before reading on.

In $3\frac{1}{3}$ there are 10 thirds. Since the $2.50 covers (or is distributed across) ten-thirds, one-third is covered by one-tenth of the $2.50 or 25 cents. There are three-thirds in one. Therefore, 75 cents must cover 1 pound, or 75 cents per pound.

Try the following problems using a similar strategy. In these problems, the *part of* the whole is known. The task is to find the whole.

> Dan paid $2.40 for a $\frac{3}{4}$-pound box of candy. How much is that per pound?

> Grace found out that if she walks really fast during her morning exercise, she can cover $2\frac{1}{2}$ miles in $\frac{3}{4}$ of an hour. She wonders how fast she is walking in miles per hour.

EXPANDED LESSON

(pages 105–106)

The expanded lesson for this chapter uses story problems to help students explore the division of fractions.

With both problems, first find the amount of one-fourth and then the value of one whole. Aidan's walking problem is a bit harder because the $2\frac{1}{2}$ miles, or 5 half-miles, do not neatly divide into three parts. If this was difficult for you, try dividing each half into three parts. Draw pictures or use models if that will help.

Informal Exploration: Measurement Concept

Almost all division explorations with fractions found in the U.S. middle school curriculum involve the measurement concept. To review, $13 \div 3$ with this concept means "How many sets of 3 are in 13?" Here is a contextual setting: *If you have 13 quarts of lemonade, how many canteens holding 3 quarts each can you fill?* A key idea to get from this example involves how to deal with that last quart after filling the first four canteens. If you continue to fill a fifth canteen, it will get only one quart. It will be only one-third full. So one answer is $4\frac{1}{3}$ *canteens*.

Since this is the concept of division that is almost always seen in textbooks and will be used to develop an algorithm for dividing fractions, it is important for students to explore this idea in contextual situations.

Whole-Number Results

Students readily understand problems such as the following:

> You are going to a birthday party. From Ben and Jerry's ice cream factory, you order 6 pints of ice cream. If you serve $\frac{3}{4}$ of a pint of ice cream to each guest, how many guests can be served? (Schifter, Bastable, & Russell, 1999b, p. 120)

Students typically draw pictures of six things divided into fourths and count out how many sets of $\frac{3}{4}$ can be found. The difficulty is in seeing this as $6 \div \frac{3}{4}$, and that part will require some direct guidance on your part. One idea is to compare the problem to one involving whole numbers (6 pints, 2 per guest) and make a comparison.

Here is a slightly more complex problem:

> Farmer Brown found that he had $2\frac{1}{4}$ gallons of liquid fertilizer concentrate. It takes $\frac{3}{4}$ gallon to make a tank of mixed fertilizer. How many tankfuls can he mix?

Try solving this problem yourself. Use any model or drawing you wish to help explain what you are doing. Notice that you are trying to find out *How many sets of 3 fourths are in a set of 9 fourths?* Your answer should be 3 tankfuls (not 3 fourths). Here is another problem to try:

> Linda has $4\frac{2}{3}$ yards of material. She is making baby clothes for the bazaar. Each dress pattern requires $1\frac{1}{6}$ yards of material. How many dresses will she be able to make from the material she has?

What makes this problem a bit different is that the given quantity is in thirds and the divisor is in sixths. Since you want to measure off "sets" of $1\frac{1}{6}$, someplace in the solution, sixths will need to be used. Two ideas are shown in Figure 3.28.

Answers That Are Not Whole Numbers

If Linda had 5 yards of material, she could still make only four dresses because a part of a dress does not make sense. But suppose that Farmer Brown began with 4 gallons of concentrate. After making five tanks of mix, he would have used $\frac{15}{4}$, or $3\frac{3}{4}$ gallons, of the concentrate. With the $\frac{1}{4}$ gallon remaining he could make a *partial* tank of mix. He could make $\frac{1}{3}$ of a tank of mix, since it takes 3 fourths to make a whole, and he has 1 fourth of a gallon.

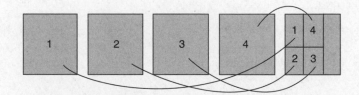

I broke the 2 thirds into 4 sixths. Then I used 1 whole and 1 sixth for each piece. There were four pieces.

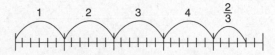

I broke it all up into sixths. That made 24 (from the 4) and 4 more from the $\frac{2}{3}$. That's 28 in all. Then $1\frac{1}{6}$ is $\frac{7}{6}$, so I divided the 28 by 7 and got 4.

FIGURE 3.28 •

Two solutions to the problem: *How many lengths of $1\frac{1}{6}$ yards can be cut from $4\frac{2}{3}$ yards of cloth?*

Here is another problem to try:

John is building a patio. Each section requires $\frac{2}{3}$ of a cubic yard of concrete. The concrete truck holds $2\frac{1}{4}$ cubic yards of concrete. If there is not enough for a full section at the end, John can put in a divider and make a partial section. How many sections can John make with the concrete in the truck?

 You should first try to solve this problem in some way that makes sense to *you*. Stop and do this now.

After you have solved it your way, try this method. Change all of the numbers to the same unit (twelfths). Then the problem becomes: *How many sets of 8 twelfths are in a set of 27 twelfths?* Figure 3.29 shows two noncontextual problems solved in this same way, each with a different model. That is, both the dividend or given quantity and the divisor are expressed in the same type of fractional parts. This results in a whole-number division problem. (In the concrete problem, the answer is the same as 27 ÷ 8.) In the classroom, after students have solved problems such as this using their own methods, suggest this common-unit approach.

Developing the Algorithms

There are two different algorithms for division of fractions. Methods of teaching both algorithms are discussed here.

FIGURE 3.29

Models for the measurement concept of fraction division.

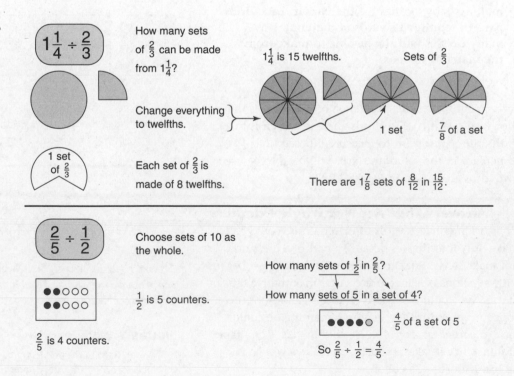

Chapter 3 FRACTION CONCEPTS AND COMPUTATION

The Common-Denominator Algorithm

The common-denominator algorithm relies on the measurement or repeated subtraction concept of division. Consider the problem $\frac{5}{3} \div \frac{1}{2}$. As shown in Figure 3.30, once each number is expressed in terms of the same fractional part, the answer is exactly the same as the whole-number problem $10 \div 3$. The name of the fractional part (the denominator) is no longer important, and the problem is one of dividing the numerators. The resulting rule or algorithm, therefore, is as follows: *To divide fractions, first get common denominators and then divide numerators.* For example, $\frac{5}{3} \div \frac{1}{4} = \frac{20}{12} \div \frac{3}{12} = 20 \div 3 = \frac{20}{3} = 6\frac{2}{3}$.

Try using pie pieces, fraction strips, and then sets of counters to model $1\frac{2}{3} \div \frac{3}{4}$ and $\frac{5}{8} \div \frac{1}{2}$ to help yourself develop this algorithm.

The Invert-and-Multiply Algorithm

To invert the divisor and multiply may be one of the most poorly understood procedures in the K–8 curriculum. (Do you know why invert-and-multiply works?) Interestingly, in a much discussed study of Chinese and U.S. teachers, Liping Ma (1999) found that most Chinese teachers not only use and teach this algorithm, but they also understand why it works. U.S. teachers were found to be sadly lacking in their understanding of fraction division.

If you return to the few partition problems that were discussed, you will find that solving these problems almost immediately gives rise to the invert-and-multiply algorithm. Let's look at one more example in which both the dividend and the divisor are proper fractions.

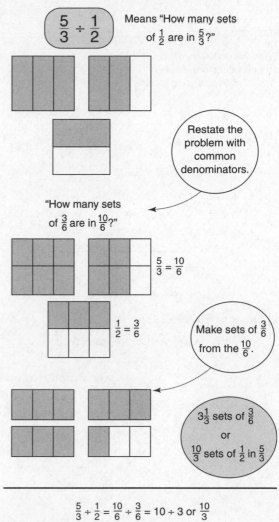

$$\frac{5}{3} \div \frac{1}{2} = \frac{10}{6} \div \frac{3}{6} = 10 \div 3 \text{ or } \frac{10}{3}$$

FIGURE 3.30

Models for the common-denominator method for fraction division.

> A small pail can be filled to $\frac{7}{8}$ full using $\frac{2}{3}$ of a gallon of water. How much will the pail hold if filled completely?

Ignore temporarily that the amount is $\frac{2}{3}$ of a gallon of water. Draw a simple picture like the one in Figure 3.31. Again, recall the parts-and-whole problems in which the task was to find how much in one whole. That is what is done here—find the *whole* pail if the given water is $\frac{7}{8}$ of the whole. A full pail is $\frac{8}{8}$. Because the water in the pail is seven of the eight parts needed to fill the pail, dividing the water by 7 and multiplying that amount by 8 solves the problem. Therefore, take the $\frac{2}{3}$, divide by 7, and multiply by 8.

Now recall the meanings of the denominator and numerator. The denominator in a fraction divides the whole into parts, thus indicating the type of part. The denominator is a divisor. The numerator tells us the number of those parts. The numerator is a multiplier. In the problem we divided the $\frac{2}{3}$ by 7 and multiplied by 8. Therefore, we multiplied the $\frac{2}{3}$ by $\frac{8}{7}$.

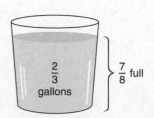

FIGURE 3.31

The pail is $\frac{7}{8}$ full. One-eighth of the water times 8 will be how much it takes to fill the entire pail.

$$\frac{3}{4} \div \frac{5}{6} = \square$$

Write the equation in an equivalent form as a product with a missing factor.

$$\frac{3}{4} = \square \times \frac{5}{6}$$

Multiply both sides by $\frac{6}{5}$. ($\frac{6}{5}$ is the inverse of $\frac{5}{6}$.)

$$\frac{3}{4} \times \frac{6}{5} = \square \times \left(\frac{5}{6} \times \frac{6}{5}\right)$$

$$\frac{3}{4} \times \frac{6}{5} = \square \times 1$$

$$\frac{3}{4} \times \frac{6}{5} = \square$$

But $\frac{3}{4} \div \frac{5}{6} = \square$ also.

Therefore,

$$\frac{3}{4} \div \frac{5}{6} = \frac{3}{4} \times \frac{6}{5} = \square$$

In general,

$$\frac{a}{b} \div \frac{c}{d} = \frac{a}{b} \times \frac{d}{c}$$

FIGURE 3.32 •

To divide, invert the divisor and multiply.

In many middle school textbooks, a more symbolic justification for the invert-and-multiply procedure is offered. That explanation goes something like the one shown in Figure 3.32.

Read through the explanation in Figure 3.32. Is that rationale more or less meaningful to you than the one based on the problem with the pail of water? Given your choice, which algorithm— common denominator or invert-and-multiply— would you select to teach to your students?

Curricular Decisions

Your answers to the questions just posed may have an influence on how you teach division of fractions. It matters very little *how* students do operations, only that they can do them meaningfully and accurately in a reasonably efficient manner. Each of the algorithms has value. Regardless of which algorithm is your goal, you are strongly advised to build on informal work with story problems. Most textbook story problems for fraction division seem to be measurement problems. This is not the case in China. In the United States, very little work has been done to explore the partition approach to invert-and-multiply.

EXPANDED LESSON

Division of Fractions Using the Partition Concept

GRADE LEVEL: Fifth or sixth grade.

MATHEMATICS GOALS
- To develop the partitive meaning of division with fractions through informal explorations.
- To reinforce the partitive meaning of division.

THINKING ABOUT THE STUDENTS
Students solved both partition and measurement problems with whole numbers. They understand the symbolic nota-tion of fractions (i.e., they know what the top number in the fraction means—the number of parts—and what the bottom number in the fraction means—the kind of parts we are counting). The students can add fractions and find equivalent fractions.

MATERIALS AND PREPARATION
- Prepare a transparency with the problems in the lesson.

lesson

BEFORE

Begin with a simpler version of the task:
- Ask students how they would solve the following story problem if they did not know their multiplication facts:

    Marie bought 24 pieces of bubble gum to share among herself and her 3 friends. How many pieces of gum will each person get?

- Have them draw a picture or think about how they would act out the story to determine the answer. Listen to students' ideas. Capitalize on ideas that emphasize the sharing action in the problem.

The Task
- Students are to solve the following problems:

    Cassie has $5\frac{1}{4}$ yards of ribbon to make three bows for birthday packages. How much ribbon should she use for each bow if she wants to use the same length of ribbon for each?

    Mark has $1\frac{1}{4}$ hours to finish his three household chores. If he divides his time evenly, how many hours can he spend on each?

Establish Expectations
- Students should draw pictures and have a written explanation for their solutions. They should also be prepared to explain their thinking. Before you come together as a class, have students explain their ideas to a partner.

DURING
- Be sure that students are drawing pictures to help them think about how to do the problems and explain their thinking.
- Look for students who use different representations to think about the problems. Highlight those different ways in the "after" portion of the lesson.
- For students who finish early, pose another problem to them in which the parts must be split into smaller parts (like the second problem in the task). For example, *Ryan has $6\frac{2}{3}$ yards of rope to hang 4 bird feeders. How much rope will he use for each feeder if he wants to use the same length of rope for each?*

AFTER

- For each problem, first get answers from the class. If more than one answer is offered, simply record them and offer no evaluation.
- Have students come to the board to explain their strategies for thinking about the problem. You may need to ask questions about drawings or explanations to make sure everyone in the class follows the rationale. Encourage the class to comment or ask questions about the student's representation or thinking. Ask if others used a different representation or solved the problem in a different way. If so, have the students come forward to share their solutions. If there are different answers, the class should evaluate the solution strategies and decide which answer is correct and why.
- Discuss the different representations students use (e.g., some students use circles or rectangles, whereas others may use a number line) and how the action in the story is one of sharing.
- For problems that require the parts to be split into smaller parts, students will likely use different approaches. For example, for the second problem in the given task, some students will first divide the hour into thirds and then the quarter hour into twelfths, whereas other students will divide the $1\frac{1}{4}$ hours into twelfths and share the twelfths between the 3 hours. It is important to have students compare and contrast the different approaches. Some solutions that at first appear to be different are actually equivalent in many ways. Through questioning, help students make these connections.
- Help students notice that while they are answering these questions, they are also asking, "How much is in the whole?" or "How much for one?" This mode of thinking will help students when the divisor is a fraction because the sharing concept seems to break down at that point.

ASSESSMENT NOTES

- Are students using their understanding of the meaning of fractions to help them draw a representation or solve the problem in another way? Using the meaning of the fraction is imperative when the problem requires splitting the part into smaller parts.
- Look for students who struggle with identifying the whole. They need more experience working with part-and-whole tasks as described earlier in the chapter. (See Figure 3.3, p. 71.)

next steps

- The next step is to have students explore division when the divisor is a fraction. Begin with a problem in which the divisor is a unit fraction such as $\frac{1}{4}$ or $\frac{1}{3}$. In this exploratory phase, it is still a good idea to pose the problems as story problems.

- The partition concept of division with fractions can be used to develop the invert-and-multiply algorithm if desired. (See p. 103.)

DECIMAL AND PERCENT CONCEPTS AND DECIMAL COMPUTATION

In the U.S. curriculum, decimals are typically introduced in the fourth grade and most of the computation work with decimals occurs in the fifth grade and is repeated later in grades 6 and 7. This fractions-first, decimals-later sequence is arguably the best approach. However, the unfortunate fact is that the topics of fractions and decimals are too often developed separately. Linking the ideas of fractions to decimals can be extremely useful, both from a pedagogical view as well as a practical, social view. Most of this chapter focuses on that connection.

Connecting Two Different Representational Systems

The symbols 3.75 and $3\frac{3}{4}$ represent the same quantity, yet on the surface the two appear quite different. For children especially, the world of fractions and the world of decimals are very distinct. Even adults tend to think of fractions as sets or regions (three-fourths *of* something), whereas we think of decimals as being more like numbers. When we tell children that 0.75 is the same as $\frac{3}{4}$, this can be especially confusing. Even though different

big ideas

1 Decimal numbers are simply another way of writing fractions. Both notations have value. Maximum flexibility is gained by understanding how the two symbol systems are related.

2 The base-ten place-value system extends infinitely in two directions: to tiny values as well as to large values. Between any two place values, the ten-to-one ratio remains the same.

3 The decimal point is a convention that has been developed to indicate the units position. The position to the left of the decimal point is the unit that is being counted as singles or ones.

4 Percents are simply hundredths and as such are a third way of writing both fractions and decimals.

5 Addition and subtraction with decimals are based on the fundamental concept of adding and subtracting the numbers in like position values—a simple extension from whole numbers.

6 Multiplication and division of two numbers will produce the same digits, regardless of the positions of the decimal point. As a result, for most practical purposes, there is no reason to develop new rules for decimal multiplication and division. Rather, the computations can be performed as whole numbers with the decimal placed by way of estimation.

ways of writing the numbers have been invented, the numbers themselves are not different. A significant goal of instruction in decimal and fraction numeration should be to help students see that both systems represent the same concepts.

To help students see the connection between fractions and decimals, we can do three things. First, we can use familiar fraction concepts and models to explore rational numbers that are easily represented by decimals: tenths, hundredths, and thousandths. Second, we can help them see how the base-ten system can be extended to include numbers less than 1 as well as large numbers. Third, we can help children use models to make meaningful translations between fractions and decimals. These three components are discussed in turn.

Base-Ten Fractions

Fractions that have denominators of 10, 100, 1000, and so on will be referred to in this chapter as *base-ten fractions*. This is simply a convenient label and is not one commonly found in the literature. Fractions such as $\frac{7}{10}$ or $\frac{6}{100}$ are examples of base-ten fractions.

Base-Ten Fraction Models

BLMs 2–4

Most of the common models for fractions are somewhat limited for the purpose of depicting base-ten fractions. Generally, the familiar fraction models cannot show hundredths or thousandths. It is important to provide models for these fractions using the same conceptual approaches that were used for fractions such as thirds and fourths.

Two very important region models can be used to model base-ten fractions. First, to model tenths and hundredths, circular disks such as the one shown in Figure 4.1 can be printed on tagboard (see Blackline Masters). Each disk is marked with 100 equal intervals around the edge and is cut along one radius. Two disks of different colors, slipped together as shown, can be used to model any fraction less than 1. Fractions modeled on this hundredths disk can be read as base-ten fractions by noting the spaces around the edge but are still reminiscent of the traditional pie model.

The most common model for base-ten fractions is a 10 × 10 square. These squares can be run off on paper for students to shade in various fractions (see Figure 4.2 and Blackline Masters). Another important variation is to use base-ten place-value strips and squares. As a fraction model, the 10-cm square that was used as the hundreds model for whole numbers is taken as the whole or 1. Each strip is then 1 tenth, and each small square is 1 hundredth. In the Blackline Masters you will find a large square that is subdivided into 10,000 tiny squares. When shown on an overhead projector, individual squares or ten-thousandths can easily be identified and shaded in with a pen on the transparency.

FIGURE 4.1 • • • • • • • •

A hundredths disk for modeling base-ten fractions.

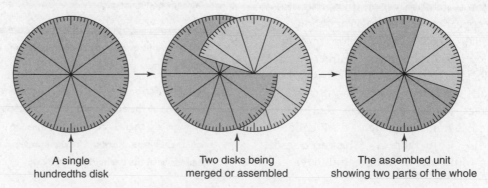

| A single hundredths disk | Two disks being merged or assembled | The assembled unit showing two parts of the whole |

One of the best length models is a meter stick. Each decimeter is one-tenth of the whole stick, each centimeter is one-hundredth, and each millimeter is one-thousandth. Any number-line model broken into 100 subparts is likewise a useful model for hundredths.

Many teachers use money as a model for decimals, and to some extent this is helpful. However, for children, money is almost exclusively a two-place system: Numbers like 3.2 or 12.1389 do not relate to money. Children's initial contact with decimals should be more flexible, and so money is not recommended as a decimal model. However, money is certainly an important *application* of decimal numeration.

Multiple Names and Formats

Early work with base-ten fractions is designed primarily to acquaint students with the models, to help them begin to think of quantities in terms of tenths and hundredths, and to learn to read and write base-ten fractions in different ways.

Have students show a base-ten fraction using any base-ten fraction model. Once a fraction, say, $\frac{65}{100}$, is modeled, the following things can be explored:

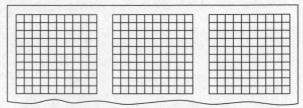

10 × 10 squares on paper. Each square is one whole. Students shade fractional parts.

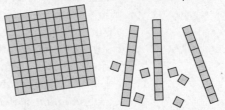

Base-ten strips and squares can be used to model base-ten fractions. Instead of shading in the large square, strips and small squares are placed on it to show a fractional part.

FIGURE 4.2 ●

10 × 10 squares model base-ten fractions.

- Is this fraction more or less than $\frac{1}{2}$? Than $\frac{2}{3}$? Than $\frac{3}{4}$? Some familiarity with these fractions can be developed by comparison with fractions that are easy to think about.
- What are some different ways to say this fraction using tenths and hundredths? ("6 tenths and 5 hundredths," "65 hundredths") Include thousandths when appropriate.
- Show two ways to write this fraction ($\frac{65}{100}$ or $\frac{6}{10} + \frac{5}{100}$).

The last two questions are very important. When base-ten fractions are later written as decimals, they are usually read as a single fraction. That is, 0.65 is read "sixty-five hundredths." But to understand them in terms of place value, the same number must be thought of as 6 tenths and 5 hundredths. A mixed number such as $5\frac{13}{100}$ is usually read the same way as a decimal: 5.13 is "five and thirteen-hundredths." For purposes of place value, it should also be understood as $5 + \frac{1}{10} + \frac{3}{100}$.

The expanded forms will be helpful in translating these fractions to decimals. Exercises at this introductory level should include all possible connections between models, various oral forms, and various written forms. Given a model or a written or oral fraction, students should be able to give the other two forms of the fraction, including equivalent forms where appropriate.

Extending the Place-Value System

Before considering decimal numerals with students, it is advisable to review some ideas of whole-number place value. One of the most basic of these ideas is the 10-to-1 relationship between the value of any two adjacent positions. In terms of a base-ten model such as strips and squares, 10 of any one piece will make 1 of the next larger, and vice versa.

CONNECTING TWO DIFFERENT REPRESENTATIONAL SYSTEMS

A Two-Way Relationship

The 10-makes-1 rule continues indefinitely to larger and larger pieces or positional values. This concept is fun to explore in terms of how large the strips and squares will actually be if you move six or eight places out.

If you are using the strip-and-square model, for example, the strip and square shapes alternate in an infinite progression as they get larger and larger. Having established the progression to larger pieces, focus on the idea that each piece to the right in this string gets smaller by one-tenth. The critical question becomes "Is there ever a smallest piece?" In the students' experience, the smallest piece is the centimeter square. But couldn't even that piece be divided into 10 small strips? And couldn't these small strips be divided into 10 very small squares, and so on? In the mind's eye, there is no smallest strip or smallest square.

The goal of this discussion is to help students see that a 10-to-1 relationship can extend *infinitely in two directions*. There is no smallest piece and no largest piece. The relationship between adjacent pieces is the same regardless of which two adjacent pieces are being considered. Figure 4.3 illustrates this idea.

The Role of the Decimal Point

An important idea to be realized in this discussion is that there is no built-in reason why any one piece should naturally be chosen to be the unit or ones position. In terms of strips and squares, for example, which piece is the ones piece? The small centimeter square? Why? Why not a larger or a smaller square? Why not a strip? *Any piece could effectively be chosen as the ones piece.*

FIGURE 4.3 • • • • • •

Theoretically, the strips and squares extend infinitely in both directions.

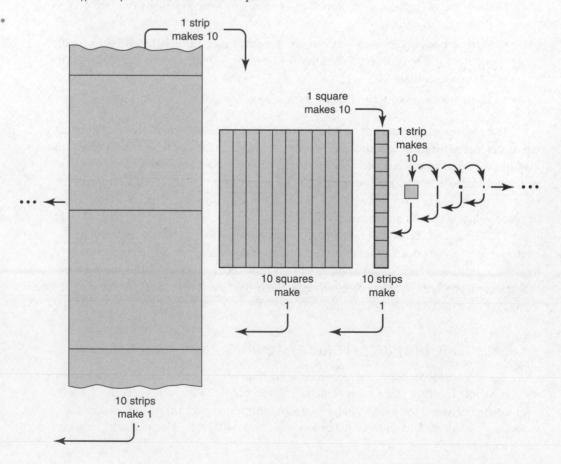

Chapter **4**　DECIMAL AND PERCENT CONCEPTS AND DECIMAL COMPUTATION

As shown in Figure 4.4, a given quantity can be written in different ways, depending on the choice of the unit or what piece is used to count the entire collection. The decimal point is placed between two positions with the convention that the position to the left of the decimal is the units or ones position. Thus, the role of the decimal point is *to designate the units position,* and it does so by sitting just to the right of that position.

A fitting caricature of the decimal is shown in Figure 4.5. The "eyes" of the decimal always focus up toward the name of the units or ones. A tagboard disk of this decimal-point face can be used between adjacent base-ten models or on a place-value chart (found with the hundredths disk in the Blackline Masters). If such a decimal point were placed between the squares and strips in Figure 4.4, the squares would then be designated as the units, and 16.24 would be the correct written form for the model.

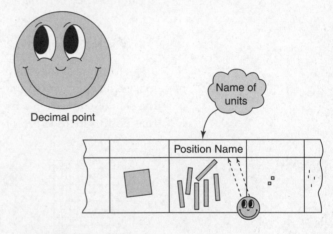

| Super Strips | Squares | Strips | Tinies |

1624 tinies
16.24 squares
1.624 super strips
162.4 strips
0.1624 super squares

Each expression represents the amount shown.

FIGURE 4.4
The decimal point indicates which position is the units.

ACTIVITY 4.1

The Decimal Names the Unit

Have students display a certain number of base-ten pieces on their desks. For example, put out 3 squares, 7 strips, and 4 tinies. Refer to the pieces as "squares," "strips," and "tinies," and reach an agreement on names for the theoretical pieces both smaller and larger. To the right of tinies can be "tiny strips" and "tiny squares." To the left of squares can be "super strips" and "super squares." Each student should also have a tagboard smiley decimal point. Now ask students to write and say how many squares they have, how many super strips, and so on, as in Figure 4.4. The students position their decimal point accordingly and both write and say the amounts.

Decimal point

Name of units

Position Name

FIGURE 4.5
The decimal point always "looks up at" the name of the units position.

Activity 4.1 illustrates vividly that the decimal indicates the named unit and that the unit can change without changing the quantity.

The Decimal with Measurement and Monetary Units

The notion that the decimal "looks at the units place" is useful in a variety of contexts. For example, in the metric system, seven place values have names. As shown in Figure 4.6, the decimal can be used to designate any of these places as the unit without changing the actual measure. Our monetary system is also a decimal system. In the amount $172.95, the decimal point designates the dollars position as the unit. There are 1 hundred (of dollars), 7 tens, 2 singles, 9 dimes, and 5 pennies or cents in this

CONNECTING TWO DIFFERENT REPRESENTATIONAL SYSTEMS

FIGURE 4.6 • • • • • • • •

In the metric system, each place-value position has a name. The decimal point can be placed to designate which length is the unit length.

kilometer	hectometer	dekameter	meter	decimeter	centimeter	millimeter	
		4	**3**	**8**	**5**		

4 dekameters, 3 meters, 8 decimeters, and 5 centimeters =

43.85	meters
43850	millimeters
0.04385	kilometers
4385	centimeters

Unit names

amount of money regardless of how it is written. If pennies were the designated unit, the same amount would be written as 17,295 cents or 17,295.0 cents. It could just as correctly be 0.17295 thousands of dollars or 1729.5 dimes.

In the case of actual measures such as metric lengths or weights or the U.S. monetary system, the name of the unit is written after the number rather than above the digit as on a place-value chart. You may be 1.62 meters tall, but it does not make sense to say you are "1.62 tall." In the paper, we may read about Congress spending $7.3 billion. Here the units are billions of dollars, not dollars. A city may have a population of 2.4 million people. That is the same as 2,400,000 individuals.

Making the Fraction–Decimal Connection

To connect the two numeration systems, fractions and decimals, students should make concept-oriented translations. The purpose of such activities has less to do with the skill of converting a fraction to a decimal than with construction of the concept that both systems express the same ideas.

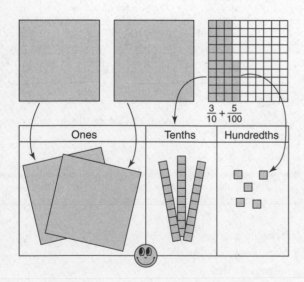

$\frac{3}{10} + \frac{5}{100}$

$2\frac{35}{100} = 2.35 =$ "two and thirty-five hundredths"

FIGURE 4.7 •

Translation of a base-ten fraction to a decimal.

> ## ACTIVITY 4.2
>
> ### Base-Ten Fractions to Decimals
>
> For this activity, have students use their place-value strips and squares. Agree that the large square represents one. Have students cover a base-ten fractional amount of the square using their strips and tinies. For example, have them cover $2\frac{35}{100}$ of the square. Whole numbers require additional squares. The task is to decide how to write this fraction as a decimal and demonstrate the connection using their physical models.

For the last activity, a typical (and correct) reason why $2\frac{35}{100}$ is the same as 2.35 is that there are 2 wholes, 3 tenths, and 5 hundredths. It is important to see this physically. The exact same materials that are used to represent $2\frac{35}{100}$ of the square can be rearranged or placed on an imaginary place-value chart with a paper decimal point used to designate the units position as shown in Figure 4.7.

The reverse of this activity is also worthwhile. Give students a decimal number such as 1.68 and have them show it with base-ten pieces. Their task is to write it as a fraction and show it as a fractional part of a square.

Although these translations between decimals and base-ten fractions are rather simple, the main agenda is for students to learn from the beginning that decimals are simply fractions.

The calculator can also play a significant role in decimal concept development.

ACTIVITY 4.3

Calculator Decimal Counting

Recall how to make the calculator "count" by pressing + 1 = = ... Now have students press + 0.1 = = ... When the display shows 0.9, stop and discuss what this means and what the display will look like with the next press. Many students will predict 0.10 (thinking that 10 comes after 9). This prediction is even more interesting if, with each press, the students have been accumulating base-ten strips as models for tenths. One more press would mean one more strip, or 10 strips. Why should the calculator not show 0.10? When the tenth press produces a display of 1 (calculators never display trailing zeros to the right of the decimal), the discussion should revolve around trading 10 strips for a square. Continue to count to 4 or 5 by tenths. How many presses to get from one whole number to the next? Try counting by 0.01 or by 0.001. These counts illustrate dramatically how small one-hundredth and one-thousandth really are. It requires 10 counts by 0.001 to get to 0.01 and 1000 counts to reach 1.

The fact that the calculator counts 0.8, 0.9, 1, 1.1 instead of 0.8, 0.9, 0.10, 0.11 should give rise to the question "Does this make sense? If so, why?"

Calculators that permit entry of fractions also have a fraction–decimal conversion key. On some calculators a decimal such as 0.25 will convert to the base-ten fraction $\frac{25}{100}$ and allow for either manual or automatic simplification. Graphing calculators can be set so that the conversion is either with or without simplification. The ability of fraction calculators to go back and forth between fractions and decimals makes them a valuable tool as students begin to connect fraction and decimal symbolism.

Developing Decimal Number Sense

So far, the discussion has revolved around the connection of decimals with base-ten fractions. Number sense implies more. It means having intuition about or a flexible understanding of numbers. To this end, it is useful to connect decimals to the fractions with which children are familiar, to be able to compare and order decimals readily, and to approximate decimals with useful familiar numbers.

Familiar Fractions Connected to Decimals

The following two activities help students think of decimals in terms of familiar fraction equivalents and to make this connection in a conceptual manner.

EXPANDED LESSON

(pages 129–130)

A complete lesson plan based on "Friendly Fractions to Decimals" can be found at the end of this chapter.

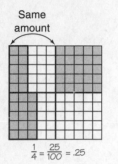

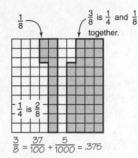

$$\frac{1}{4} = \frac{25}{100} = .25 \qquad \frac{3}{8} = \frac{37}{100} + \frac{5}{1000} = .375$$

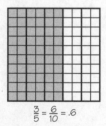

$$\frac{3}{5} = \frac{6}{10} = .6$$

FIGURE 4.8 • • • • • • • • • • • • • • • • • •

Familiar fractions converted to decimals using a 10 × 10 square.

ACTIVITY 4.4

Friendly Fractions to Decimals

Students are given a "friendly" fraction to convert to a decimal. They first model the fraction using either a 10 × 10 grid or the base-ten strips and squares. With the model as a guide, they then write and draw an explanation for the decimal equivalent. If strips and squares are used, be sure that students draw pictures as part of their explanations.

A good sequence is to start with halves and fifths, then fourths, and possibly eighths. Thirds are best done as a special activity.

Figure 4.8 shows how translations in the last activity might go with a 10 × 10 grid. For fourths, students will often shade a 5 × 5 section (half of a half). The question then becomes how to translate this to decimals. Ask these students how they would cover $\frac{1}{4}$ with strips and squares if they were only permitted to use nine or fewer tinies. The fraction $\frac{3}{8}$ represents a wonderful challenge. A hint might be to find $\frac{1}{4}$ first and then notice that $\frac{1}{8}$ is half of a fourth. Remember that the next smaller pieces are tenths of the little squares. Therefore, a half of a square is $\frac{5}{1000}$.

Because the circular model carries such a strong mental link to fractions, it is well worth the time to do some fraction-to-decimal conversions with the hundredths disk.

ACTIVITY 4.5

Estimate, Then Verify

With the blank side of the disk facing them, have students adjust the disk to show a particular friendly fraction, for example, $\frac{3}{4}$. Next they turn the disk over and record how many hundredths were in the section they estimated (note that the color reverses when the disk is turned over). Finally, they should make an argument for the correct number of hundredths and the corresponding decimal equivalent.

The estimation component of the last activity adds interest, and the visual "feeling" for fractions is greater than with strips and squares. In one fifth-grade class that was having difficulty finding a decimal equivalent for their hundredths disk fraction, the teacher cut up some extra disks into tenths and hundredths so that these parts of the fraction could be placed on a chart. (See Figure 4.9.)

The exploration of modeling $\frac{1}{3}$ as a decimal is a good introduction to the concept of an infinitely repeating decimal. Try to partition the whole square into 3 parts using strips and squares. Each part receives 3 strips with 1 left over. To divide the leftover strip, each part gets 3 small squares with 1 left over. To divide the small square, each part gets 3 tiny strips with 1 left over. (Recall that with base-ten pieces, each smaller piece must be $\frac{1}{10}$ of the preceding size piece.) Each of the 3 parts will get 3 tiny strips with 1 left over. It becomes obvious that this process is never-ending. As a result, $\frac{1}{3}$ is the same as 0.333333 . . . or 0.$\overline{3}$. For practical purposes, $\frac{1}{3}$ is about 0.333. Similarly, $\frac{2}{3}$ is a repeating string of sixes, or about 0.667. Later, students will discover that many fractions cannot be represented by a finite decimal.

The number line is another good connecting model. Students are more apt to think of decimals as numbers that appear on the number line than they are to think of fractions in that way. The following activity continues the development of fraction–decimal equivalences.

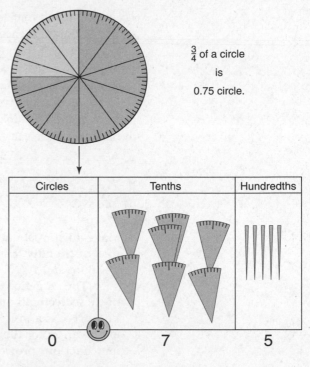

$\frac{3}{4}$ of a circle
is
0.75 circle.

Circles	Tenths	Hundredths
0	7	5

FIGURE 4.9 •

Fraction models could be decimal models.

ACTIVITY 4.6

Decimals on a Friendly Fraction Line

Give students five decimal numbers that have friendly fraction equivalents. Keep the numbers between two consecutive whole numbers. For example, use 3.5, 3.125, 3.4, 3.75, and 3.66. On a worksheet, show a number line encompassing the same whole numbers. The subdivisions on the number line should be only fourths, only thirds, or only fifths but without labels. The students' task is to locate each of the decimal numbers on the number line and to provide the fraction equivalent for each.

Results of National Assessment of Educational Progress (NAEP) examinations consistently reveal that students have difficulties with the fraction–decimal relationship. Kouba et al. (1988a) note that students could express proper fractions as decimals but only 40 percent of seventh graders could give a decimal equivalent for a mixed number. In the sixth NAEP, students had difficulty placing decimals on a number line where the subdivisions were fractions (Kouba, Zawojewski, & Strutchens, 1997). In the seventh NAEP, only 39 percent of eighth graders correctly placed decimal numbers on a number line when the increments were multiples of 0.1—not even in fraction increments (Wearne & Kouba, 2000). Division of the numerator by the denominator may be a means of converting fractions to decimals, but it contributes nothing to understanding the resulting equivalence. Note that this method has not been and will not be suggested in this chapter.

Approximation with a Nice Fraction

In the real world, decimal numbers are rarely those with exact equivalents to nice fractions. What fraction would you say approximates the decimal 0.52? In the sixth NAEP exam, only 51 percent of eighth graders selected $\frac{1}{2}$. The other choices were $\frac{1}{50}$ (29 percent), $\frac{1}{5}$ (11 percent), $\frac{1}{4}$ (6 percent), and $\frac{1}{3}$ (4 percent) (Kouba et al., 1997). Again, the most plausible explanation for this performance is a reliance on rules. Students need to wrestle with the size of decimal numbers and begin to develop a sense of familiarity with them.

As with fractions, the first benchmarks that should be developed are 0, $\frac{1}{2}$, and 1. For example, is 7.3962 closer to 7 or 8? Why? (Would you accept this response: "Closer to 7 because 3 is less than 5"?) Is it closer to 7 or $7\frac{1}{2}$? Often the 0, $\frac{1}{2}$, or 1 benchmarks are good enough to make sense of a situation. If a closer approximation is required, students should be encouraged to consider the other friendly fractions (thirds, fourths, fifths, and eighths). In this example, 7.3962 is close to 7.4, which is $7\frac{2}{5}$. A good number sense with decimals would imply the ability to think quickly of a meaningful fraction that is a close substitute for almost any number.

To develop this type of familiarity with decimals, students do not need new concepts or skills. They do need the opportunity to apply and discuss the related concepts of fractions, place value, and decimals in activities such as the following.

ACTIVITY 4.7

Close to a Friendly Fraction

Make a list of about five decimals that are close to but not exactly equal to a nice or friendly fraction equivalent. For example, use 24.8025, 6.59, 0.9003, 124.356, and 7.7.

The students' task is to decide on a decimal number that is close to each of these decimals and that also has a friendly fraction equivalent that they know. For example, 6.59 is close to 6.6, which is $6\frac{3}{5}$. They should write an explanation for their choices. Different students may select different equivalent fractions providing for a discussion of which is closer.

ACTIVITY 4.8

Best Match

On the board, list a scattered arrangement of five familiar fractions and at least five decimals that are close to the fractions but not exact. Students are to pair each fraction with the decimal that best matches it. Figure 4.10 is an example. The difficulty is determined by how close the various fractions are to one another.

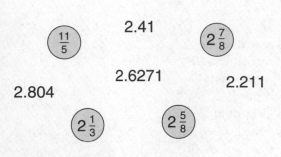

FIGURE 4.10

Match the decimal numbers with the closest fraction expression.

In Activities 4.7 and 4.8, students will have a variety of reasons for their answers. Sharing their thinking with the class provides a valuable opportunity for all to learn. Do not focus on the answers but on the rationales.

Assessment Note

The connections between models and the two symbol systems for rational numbers—fractions and decimals—provide a good schema for assessment. Provide students with a number represented in any one of these three ways and have them provide the other two along with an explanation. Here are a few examples:

- Write the fraction $\frac{5}{8}$ as a decimal. Use a drawing or a physical model (meter stick or 10 × 10 grid) and explain why your decimal equivalent is correct.
- What fraction is also represented by the decimal 2.6? Use words, pictures, and numbers to explain your answer.

- Use both a fraction and a decimal to tell what point is indicated on this number line. Explain your reasoning.

Notice that in the last example, an exact number is not indicated although it could have been. In the example here, you may also be able to get some information about students' ability to estimate fraction and decimal quantities.

Ordering Decimal Numbers

Putting a list of decimal numbers in order from least to most is a skill closely related to the one just discussed. In the fourth NAEP (Kouba et al., 1988a), only about 50 percent of seventh graders could identify the largest number in the following list: 0.36, 0.058, 0.375, and 0.4. The most common error is to select the number with more digits, which is an incorrect application of whole-number ideas. Some students later pick up the idea that digits far to the right represent very small numbers. They then incorrectly identify numbers with more digits as smaller. Both errors reflect a lack of conceptual understanding of how decimal numbers are constructed. The following activities can help promote discussion about the relative size of decimal numbers.

ACTIVITY 4.9

Line 'Em Up

Prepare a list of four or five decimal numbers that students might have difficulty putting in order. They should all be between the same two consecutive whole numbers. Have students first predict the order of the numbers, from least to most. Next have them place each number on a number line with 100 subdivisions, as in Figure 4.11. As an alternative, have students shade in the fractional part of each number on a separate 10 × 10 grid using estimates for the thousandths and ten-thousandths. In either case, it quickly becomes obvious which digits contribute the most to the size of a decimal.

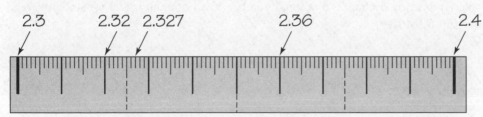

Cut four strips of poster board measuring 6 × 28 inches. Tape end to end. Place on chalk tray.

Write on board above. Endpoints can be any interval of 1, $\frac{1}{10}$, $\frac{1}{100}$.

FIGURE 4.11 • • • • • • • • • • •

A decimal number line.

DEVELOPING DECIMAL NUMBER SENSE

Close "Nice" Numbers

Write a four-digit decimal on the board—3.0917, for example. Start with the whole numbers: "Is it closer to 3 or 4?" Then go to the tenths: "Is it closer to 3.0 or 3.1?" Repeat with hundredths and thousandths. At each answer, challenge students to defend their choices with the use of a model or other conceptual explanation. A large number line without numerals, shown in Figure 4.11, is useful.

Too often, the process of rounding numbers is taught as an algorithm without any reflection on why the algorithm makes sense. Students come to believe that to "round" a number means to do something to it or change it in some way. In reality, to *round* a number means that you *substitute* a "nice" number as an approximation for the cumbersome original number. In this sense, we can also round decimal numbers to "nice fractions" and not just to tenths and hundredths. For example, instead of rounding 6.73 to the nearest tenth, a number sense perspective might suggest rounding it to the nearest quarter (6.75 or $6\frac{3}{4}$) or to the nearest third (6.67 or $6\frac{2}{3}$).

Other Fraction–Decimal Equivalents

Recall that the denominator is a divisor and the numerator is a multiplier. For example, $\frac{3}{4}$, therefore, means the same as $3 \times (1 \div 4) = 3 \div 4$. So how would you express $\frac{3}{4}$ on a simple four-function calculator? Simply enter $3 \div 4$. The display will read 0.75.

Too often students think that dividing the denominator into the numerator is simply an algorithm for converting fractions to decimals, and they have no understanding of why this might work. Use the opportunity to help students develop the idea that in general $\frac{a}{b} = a \div b$. (See Chapter 3, p. 68, and Chapter 5, p. 147.)

Finding the decimal equivalents with a calculator can produce some interesting patterns and observations. For example, here are some questions to explore:

* Which fractions have decimal equivalents that terminate? Is the answer based on the numerator, the denominator, or both?

* For a given fraction, how can you tell the maximum length of the repeating part of the decimal? Try dividing by 7 and 11 and 13 to reach an answer.

* Explore all of the ninths—$\frac{1}{9}$, $\frac{2}{9}$, $\frac{3}{9}$, . . . $\frac{8}{9}$. Remember that $\frac{1}{3}$ is $\frac{3}{9}$ and $\frac{2}{3}$ is $\frac{6}{9}$. Use only the pattern you discover to predict what $\frac{9}{9}$ should be. But doesn't $\frac{9}{9} = 1$?

* How can you find what fraction produced this repeating decimal: 3.454545 . . . ?

The final task in this list can be generalized for any repeating decimal, illustrating that every repeating decimal is a rational number. It is not at all useful for students to become skillful at this.

Percents

Textbooks have traditionally treated percents as a separate topic from fractions and decimals or stuck them in a chapter on ratios. The connection of percents to fraction and decimal concepts is so strong that it also makes sense to discuss percents as students begin to have a good grasp of the fraction–decimal relationship.

A Third Operator System

The results of the NAEP tests and numerous other studies have consistently shown that students have difficulty with problems involving percents (Wearne & Kouba, 2000). For example, on the seventh NAEP, only 35 percent of eighth graders could determine an amount following a given percent of increase. Almost half selected the answer obtained by adding the percent itself to the original amount. That is, for a 7 percent increase, they selected the answer that was 7 more than the original amount. A good reason for this continual dismal performance is a failure to develop percent concepts meaningfully. In this book we explore percentages twice. Here we will connect them to fractions and decimals. In Chapter 6 we will revisit percent as a ratio as part of the study of proportional reasoning. It can be argued that the connection to fractions is more important for daily understanding.

Another Name for Hundredths

The term *percent* is simply another name for *hundredths*. If students can express common fractions and simple decimals as hundredths, the term *percent* can be substituted for the term *hundredth*. Consider the fraction $\frac{3}{4}$. As a fraction expressed in hundredths, it is $\frac{75}{100}$. When $\frac{3}{4}$ is written in decimal form, it is 0.75. Both 0.75 and $\frac{75}{100}$ are read in exactly the same way, "seventy-five hundredths." When used as operators, $\frac{3}{4}$ of something is the same as 0.75 or 75 percent of that same thing. Thus, percent is merely a new notation and terminology, not a new concept.

Models provide the main link among fractions, decimals, and percents, as shown in Figure 4.12. Base-ten fraction models are suitable for fractions, decimals, and percents, since they all represent the same idea.

Another helpful approach to the terminology of percent is through the role of the decimal point. Recall that the decimal identifies the units. When the unit is ones, a number such as 0.659 means a little more than 6 tenths of 1. The word *ones* is understood (6 tenths of 1 *one*). But 0.659 is also 6.59 tenths and 65.9 hundredths and 659 thousandths. In each case, the name of the unit must be explicitly identified, or else the unit ones would be assumed. Since *percent* is another name for *hundredths,* when the decimal identifies the hundredths position as the units, the word *percent* can be specified as a synonym for *hundredths*. Thus, 0.659 (of some whole or 1) is 65.9 hundredths or 65.9 percent of that same whole. As illustrated in Figure 4.13, the notion of placing the decimal point *to identify the percent position* is conceptually more meaningful than the

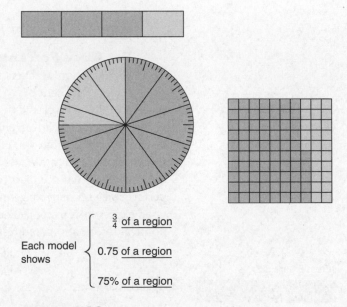

Each model shows
$\left\{ \begin{array}{l} \frac{3}{4} \text{ of a region} \\ 0.75 \text{ of a region} \\ 75\% \text{ of a region} \end{array} \right.$

FIGURE 4.12 • • • • • • • • • • • • • • • •

Models connect three different notations.

Ones	Tenths	Percent	
		Hundredths	Thousandths
	3	6	5

0.365 (of 1) = 36.5 percent (of 1)

FIGURE 4.13 • • • • • • • • • • • • • • • •

Hundredths are also known as percents.

apparently arbitrary rule: "To change a decimal to a percent, move the decimal two places to the right." A better idea is to equate hundredths with percent both orally and in notation.

Using Percent with Familiar Fractions

Students should use base-ten models for percents in much the same way as for decimals. The disk with 100 markings around the edge is now a model for percents as well as a fraction model for hundredths. The same is true of a 10 × 10 square. Each tiny square inside is 1 percent of the square. Each row or strip of 10 squares is not only a tenth but also 10 percent of the square.

Similarly, the familiar fractions (halves, thirds, fourths, fifths, and eighths) should become familiar in terms of percents as well as decimals. Three-fifths, for example, is 60 percent as well as 0.6. One-third of an amount is frequently expressed as $33\frac{1}{3}$ percent instead of 33.3333 . . . percent. Likewise, $\frac{1}{8}$ of a quantity is $12\frac{1}{2}$ percent or 12.5 percent of the quantity. These ideas should be explored with base-ten models and not as rules about moving decimal points.

Realistic Percent Problems

The Three Percent Problems

Middle school teachers talk about "the three percent problems." The sentence "_____ is _____ percent of _____" has three spaces for numbers; for example, "20 is 25 percent of 80." The classic three percent problems come from this sterile expression; two of the numbers are given, and the students are asked to produce the third. Students learn very quickly that you either multiply or divide the two given numbers, and sometimes you have to move a decimal point. But they have no way of determining when to do what, which numbers to divide, or which way to shift the decimal. As a result, performance on percentage problems is very poor. Furthermore, commonly encountered expressions using percent terminology, such as sales figures, taxes, census data, political information, and trends in economics, are almost never in the "_____ is _____ percent of _____" format. So when asked to solve a realistic percent problem, students are frequently at a loss.

Chapter 3 explored three types of exercises with fractions, in which one element—part, whole, or fraction—was unknown. Students used models and simple fraction relationships in those exercises. Those three types of exercises are precisely the same as the three percent problems. Developmentally, then, it makes sense to help students make the connection between the exercises done with fractions and those done with percents. How? Use the same types of models and the same terminology of parts, wholes, and fractions. The only thing that is different is that the word *percent* is used instead of *fraction*. In Figure 4.14, three exercises from Chapter 3 have been changed to the corresponding percent terminology. A good idea for early work with percents would be to review (or explore for the first time) all three types of exercises in terms of percents. The same three types of models can be used (refer to Figures 3.2, 3.3, and 3.4 on pp. 71–72).

(From Figure 3.2)

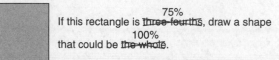

100%
If this strip is ~~one whole~~,
66⅔%
what strip is ~~two-thirds~~?
150%
What strip is ~~three-halves~~?

(From Figure 3.3)

75%
If this rectangle is ~~three-fourths~~, draw a shape
100%
that could be ~~the whole~~.

(From Figure 3.4)

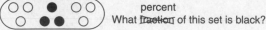

percent
What ~~fraction~~ of this set is black?

FIGURE 4.14 •

Part-whole-fraction exercises can be translated into percent exercises.

Chapter **4** DECIMAL AND PERCENT CONCEPTS AND DECIMAL COMPUTATION

Realistic Percent Problems and Nice Numbers

Though students must have some experience with the noncontextual situations in Figure 4.14, it is important to have them explore these relationships in real contexts. Find or make up percent problems, and present them in the same way that they appear in newspapers, on television, and in other real contexts. In addition to realistic problems and formats, follow these maxims for your unit on percents:

- Limit the percents to familiar fractions (halves, thirds, fourths, fifths, and eighths) or easy percents ($\frac{1}{10}$, $\frac{1}{100}$), and use numbers compatible with these fractions. The focus of these exercises is the relationships involved, not complex computational skills.

- Do not suggest any rules or procedures for different types of problems. Do not categorize or label problem types.

- Use the terms *part, whole,* and *percent* (or *fraction*). *Fraction* and *percent* are interchangeable. Help students see these percent exercises as the same types of exercises they did with simple fractions.

- Require students to use models or drawings to explain their solutions. It is better to assign three problems requiring a drawing and an explanation than to give 15 problems requiring only computation and answers. Remember that the purpose is the exploration of relationships, not computational skill.

- Encourage mental computation.

The following sample problems meet these criteria for easy fractions and numbers. Try working each problem, identifying each number as a part, a whole, or a fraction. Draw length or area models to explain or work through your thought process. Examples of this informal reasoning are illustrated with additional problems in Figure 4.15.

1. The PTA reported that 75 percent of the total number of families were represented at the meeting last night. If children from 320 families go to the school, how many were represented at the meeting?
2. The baseball team won 80 percent of the 25 games it played this year. How many games were lost?
3. In Mrs. Carter's class, 20 students, or $66\frac{2}{3}$ percent, were on the honor roll. How many students are in her class?
4. George bought his new computer at a $12\frac{1}{2}$ percent discount. He paid $700. How many dollars did he save by buying it at a discount?
5. If Joyce has read 60 of the 180 pages in her library book, what percent of the book has she read so far?
6. The hardware store bought widgets at 80 cents each and sold them for $1 each. What percent did the store mark up the price of each widget?

 Examine the examples in Figure 4.15. Notice how each problem is solved with simple fractions and mental math. Then try each of the six problems just listed. Each can be done easily and mentally using friendly fraction equivalents.

FIGURE 4.15 ●●●●●●●●

Real percent problems with nice numbers. Simple drawings help with reasoning.

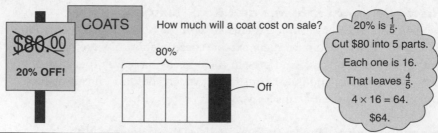

COATS

How much will a coat cost on sale?

~~$80.00~~

20% OFF!

80%

Off

20% is $\frac{1}{5}$.
Cut $80 into 5 parts.
Each one is 16.
That leaves $\frac{4}{5}$.
$4 \times 16 = 64$.
$64.

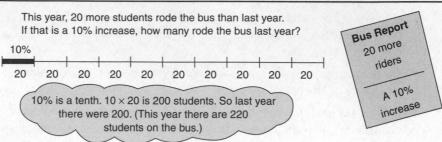

This year, 20 more students rode the bus than last year. If that is a 10% increase, how many rode the bus last year?

10%

20 20 20 20 20 20 20 20 20 20

Bus Report
20 more riders

A 10% increase

10% is a tenth. 10×20 is 200 students. So last year there were 200. (This year there are 220 students on the bus.)

Roads
600 miles: 2-lane
300 miles: 4-lane

The highway department is responsible for 600 miles of two-lane roads and 300 miles of four-lane roads. What percent of the roads are two-lane?

600 2-lane	300 4-lane

That's 900 miles in all.
6 is $\frac{2}{3}$ of 9. So 600 is $\frac{2}{3}$ of 900, or $66\frac{2}{3}$%.

Assessment Note

Realistic percent problems are still the best way to assess a student's understanding of percent. Assign one or two and have students explain why they think their answer makes sense. You might take a realistic percent problem and substitute fractions for percents (e.g., use $\frac{1}{8}$ instead of 12.5 percent) to see how students handle these problems with fractions compared to decimal numbers.

If your focus is on reasons and justifications rather than number of problems correct, you will be able to collect all the information you need.

Estimation in Percent Problems

Of course, not all real percent problems have nice numbers. Frequently in real life an approximation or estimate in percent situations is all that is required or is enough to help one think through the situation. Even if a calculator will be used to get an exact answer, an estimate based on an understanding of the relationship can confirm that a correct operation was performed or that the decimal was positioned correctly.

To help students with estimation in percent situations, two ideas that have already been discussed can be applied. First, when the percent is not a "nice" one, substitute a close percent that is easy to work with. Second, select numbers that are compatible with the percent involved, to make the calculation easy to do mentally. In essence, convert the not-nice percent problem into one that is nice. Here are some examples.

1. The 83,000-seat stadium was 73 percent full. How many people were at the game?
2. The treasurer reported that 68.3 percent of the dues had been collected, for a total of $385. How much more money could the club expect to collect if all dues are paid?
3. Max McStrike had 217 hits in 842 at-bats. What was his batting average?

 Use friendly fractions and compatible numbers to solve each of these last three problems. Do this before reading on.

Possible Estimates

1. (Use $\frac{3}{4}$ and 80,000) $\longrightarrow$ about 60,000
2. (Use $\frac{2}{3}$ and $380; will collect $\frac{1}{3}$ more) $\longrightarrow$ about $190
3. ($4 \times 217 > 842$; $\frac{1}{4}$ is 25 percent, or 0.250) $\longrightarrow$ a bit more than 0.250

The following activity is also useful in helping students with estimation in percent situations.

ACTIVITY 4.11

Estimate with Nice Fractions

Provide students with realistically stated percent problems. For percentages in the problems, use values that are close to but not the same as the nice percents or friendly fractions. Choose the other numbers in the problems so that they are compatible with the close friendly fraction. The students' task is to make estimates of the answers using easy computations or mental mathematics. As always, they should write down their procedures and rationale. Do not expect that every student will estimate in the same manner.

Here are three percent problems with two sets of numbers. The first set involves nice numbers that allow the problem to be worked mentally using fraction equivalents. The second set of numbers requires that the numbers be substituted with approximations allowing for an estimate as in the last activity.

1. The school enrolls {480, 547} students. Yesterday {$12\frac{1}{2}$ percent, 13 percent} of the students were absent. How many came to school?
2. Mr. Carver sold his lawn mower for {$45, $89}. This was {60 percent, 62 percent} of the price he paid for it new. What did the mower cost when it was new?
3. When the box fell off the shelf {90, 63} of the {720, 500} widgets broke. What percentage was lost in the breakage?

The first problem asks for a part (whole and fraction given), the second asks for a whole (part and fraction given), and the third asks for a fraction (part and whole given). Notice again that these are exactly the same as the three parts-and-whole questions found in Chapter 3.

It is also convenient at times to use simple base-ten equivalents: 1 percent and 10 percent and multiples of these (including halves). For example, we often use 10 percent plus half of that much to compute a 15 percent tip at a restaurant. To find 0.5 percent we can think of half of 1 percent. Some adults (and also students) get so used to the strategies related to these base-ten fractions that they never think to use other fraction equivalents that might produce more accurate results. A focus on these base-ten percentages is not as likely to help students conceive of percents as fractions.

Computation with Decimals

Certainly, students should develop some computational fluency with decimal numbers. In the past, decimal computation was dominated by the following rules: Line up the decimal points (addition and subtraction), count the decimal places (multiplication), and shift the decimal point in the divisor and dividend so that the divisor is a whole number (division). Traditional textbooks continue to emphasize these rules. The position taken in this book and in some of the reform curricula is that specific rules for decimal computation are not really necessary, especially if computation is built on a firm understanding of place value and a connection between decimals and fractions.

The Role of Estimation

Contrary to the traditional curriculum, students should become adept at estimating decimal computations well before they learn to compute with pencil and paper. For many decimal computations, rough estimates can be made easily by rounding the numbers to nice whole numbers or simple base-ten fractions. A minimum goal for your students should be to have the estimate contain the correct number of digits to the left of the decimal—the whole-number part. Select problems for which estimates are not terribly difficult.

 Before going on, try making easy whole-number estimates of the following computations. Do not spend time with fine adjustments in your estimates.

1. $4.907 + 123.01 + 56.1234$
2. $459.8 - 12.345$
3. 24.67×1.84
4. $514.67 \div 3.59$

Your estimates might be similar to the following:

1. Between 175 and 200
2. More than 400, or about 425 to 450
3. More than 25, closer to 50 (1.84 is more than 1 and close to 2)
4. More than 125, less than 200 ($500 \div 4 = 125$ and $600 \div 3 = 200$)

In these examples, an understanding of decimal numeration and some simple whole-number estimation skills can produce rough estimates. When estimating, thinking focuses on the meaning of the numbers and the operations and not on counting decimal places. However, students who are taught to focus on the pencil-and-paper rules for decimal computation do not even consider the actual values of the number much less estimate.

Therefore, a good *place* to begin decimal computation is with estimation. Not only is it a highly practical skill, but it also helps children look at answers in ballpark terms and can form a check on calculator computation.

A good *time* to begin computation with decimals is as soon as a conceptual background in decimal numeration has been developed. Learning the rules for decimal computation will do little or nothing to help students understand decimal numeration and will interfere with a more robust development of number sense. Even for students in seventh and eighth grades who have been exposed to decimal computation rules, an emphasis on estimation is very important. Many students who are totally reliant on rules for decimals make mistakes without being aware. For middle school students, estimation with multiplication and division is especially important.

Addition and Subtraction

Consider this problem:

....

Max and Moe each timed his own quarter-mile run with a stopwatch. Max says that he ran the quarter in 74.5 seconds. Moe was more accurate. He reported his run as 81.34 seconds. How many seconds faster did Max run than Moe?

....

Students who understand decimal numeration should first of all be able to tell approximately what the difference is—close to 7 seconds. With an estimate as a beginning, students should then be challenged to figure out the exact difference. The estimate will help them avoid the common error of lining up the 5 under the 4. A variety of student strategies are possible. For example, students might note that 74.5 and 7 is 81.5 and then figure out how much extra that is. Others may count on from 74.5 by adding 0.5 and then 6 more seconds to get to 81 seconds and then add on the remaining 0.34 second. These and other strategies will eventually confront the difference between the one-place decimal (.5) and the two-place decimal (.34). Students can resolve this issue by returning to their understanding of place value. Similar story problems for addition and subtraction, some involving different numbers of decimal places, will help develop students' understanding of these two operations. Always request an estimate prior to computation.

After students have had several opportunities to solve addition and subtraction story problems, the following activity is reasonable.

ACTIVITY 4.12

Exact Sums and Differences

Give students a sum involving different numbers of decimal places. For example: 73.46 + 6.2 + 0.582. The first task is to make an estimate and explain the way the estimate was made. The second task is to compute the

(continued)

exact answer and explain how that was done (no calculators). In the third and final task students devise a method for adding and subtracting decimal numbers that they can use with any two numbers.

When students have completed these three tasks, have students share their strategies for computation and test them on a new computation that you provide.

The same task can be repeated for subtraction.

The earlier estimation practice will focus students' attention on the meanings of the numbers. It is reasonable to expect that students will develop an algorithm that is essentially the same as aligning the decimal points. Students who already know the line-up-the-decimals rule should still be challenged to explain why this rule makes sense.

Multiplication

Estimation should play a significant role in developing an algorithm for multiplication. As a beginning point, consider this problem:

The farmer fills each jug with 3.7 liters of cider. If you buy 4 jugs, how many liters of cider is that?

Begin with an estimate. It is more than 12 liters. What is the most it could be? Could it be 16 liters? Once an estimate of the result is decided on, let students use their own methods for determining an exact answer. Many will use repeated addition: 3.7 + 3.7 + 3.7 + 3.7. Others may begin by multiplying 3 × 4 and then adding up 0.7 four times. Eventually, students will agree on the exact result of 14.8 liters. Explore other problems involving whole-number multipliers. Multipliers such as 3.5 or 8.25 that involve nice fractional parts—here, one-half and one-fourth—are also reasonable.

As a next step, have students compare a decimal product with one involving the same digits but no decimal. For example, how are 23.4 × 6.5 and 234 × 65 alike? Interestingly, both products have exactly the same digits: 15210. (The zero may be missing from the decimal product.) Using a calculator, have students explore other products that are alike except for the decimals involved. The digits in the answer are always alike.

ACTIVITY 4.13

Where Does the Decimal Go? Multiplication

Have students compute the following product: 24 × 63. Using only the result of this computation and estimation, have them give the exact answer to each of the following:

$$0.24 \times 6.3 \qquad 24 \times 0.63 \qquad 2.4 \times 63 \qquad 0.24 \times 0.63$$

For each computation they should write a rationale for their answers. They can check their results with a calculator. Any errors must be acknowledged and the rationale that produced the error adjusted.

The product of 24 × 63 is 1512. Use this information to give the answer to each of the products in the previous activity. Do *not* count decimal places. Remember your fractional equivalents.

The method of placing the decimal point in a product by way of estimation is more difficult as the product gets smaller. For example, knowing that 54 × 83 is 4482 does not make it easy to place the decimal in the product 0.0054 × 0.00083. Even the product 0.054 × 0.83 is hard. The practical question is this: Can you think of any situation outside of school in which someone might require an exact answer to a product such as one of these but would not have access to a calculator? When precision is important, technology makes sense and is always available. Yes, there is a conceptual rationale for counting the decimal places. Even if learned, it focuses attention on the smallest part of the product and provides absolutely no practice with estimation. It is a non-number-sense method that need not be used today.

Division

Division can be approached in a manner exactly parallel to multiplication. In fact, the best approach to a division estimate generally comes from thinking about multiplication rather than division. Consider the following problem:

The trip to Washington was 282.5 miles. It took exactly $4\frac{1}{2}$ hours or 4.5 hours to drive. What was the average miles per hour?

To make an estimate of this quotient, think about what times 4 or 5 is close to 280. You might think 60 × 4.5 = 240 + 30 = 270. So maybe about 61 or 62 miles per hour.

Here is a second example without context. Make an estimate of 45.7 ÷ 1.83. Think only of what times $1\frac{8}{10}$ is close to 45.

Will the answer be more or less than 45? Why? Will it be more or less than 20? Now think about 1.8 being close to 2. What times 2 is close to 46? Use this to produce an estimate.

Since 1.83 is close to 2, the estimate is near 22. And since 1.83 is less than 2 the answer must be greater than 22—say, 25 or 26. (The actual answer is 24.972677.)

Okay, so estimation can produce a reasonable result, but you may still require a pencil-and-paper algorithm to produce the digits the way it was done for multiplication. Figure 4.16 shows division by a whole number and how that can be carried out to as many places as you wish. (The explicit-trade

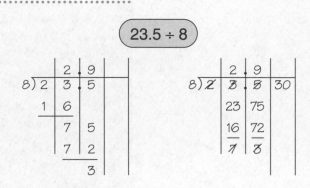

Trade 2 tens for 20 ones, making 23 ones.
Put 2 ones in each group, or 16 in all.
That leaves 7 ones.

Trade 7 ones for 70 tenths, making 75 tenths.
Put 9 tenths in each group, or 72 in all.

Trade the 3 tenths for 30 hundredths.

(Continue trading for smaller pieces as long as you wish.)

FIGURE 4.16 •

Extension of the division algorithm.

method described in Chapter 2 is shown on the right.) It is not necessary to move the decimal point up into the quotient. Leave that to estimation.

ACTIVITY 4.14

Where Does the Decimal Go? Division

Provide a quotient such as 146 ÷ 7 = 20857 correct to five digits but without the decimal point. The task is to use only this information and estimation to give a fairly precise answer to each of the following:

146 ÷ 0.7   1.46 ÷ 7   14.6 ÷ 0.7   1460 ÷ 70

For each computation students should write a rationale for their answers and then check their results with a calculator. Any errors should be acknowledged and the rationale that produced the error adjusted.

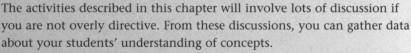 **STOP** **Give the answer to each of the products in the previous activity.**

A reasonable algorithm for division is parallel to that for multiplication: *Ignore the decimal points, and do the computation as if all numbers were whole numbers. When finished, place the decimal by estimation.* This is reasonable for divisors with no more than two significant digits. If students have a method for dividing by 45, they can divide by 0.45 and 4.5 and even 0.045.

Assessment Note ——————————

The activities described in this chapter will involve lots of discussion if you are not overly directive. From these discussions, you can gather data about your students' understanding of concepts.

So as not to rely totally on listening to discussions, you can and should have students write out explanations and draw pictures to support their answers to many of the activities. Here are two questions that could serve as assessments or as instructional tasks:

1. Consider these two computations: $3\frac{1}{2} \times 2\frac{1}{4}$ and 2.276 × 3.18. Without doing the calculations, which do you think is larger? Provide a reason for your answer that can be understood by someone else in this class.
2. How much larger is 0.76 × 5 than 0.75 × 5? How can you tell without doing the computation? (Kulm, 1994)

EXPANDED LESSON

Friendly Fractions to Decimals

Based on Activity 4.4, p. 114

GRADE LEVEL: Fifth or sixth grade.

MATHEMATICS GOALS

- To help students connect decimals and familiar fraction equivalents in a conceptual manner.
- To reinforce the notion of the 10-to-1 relationship between adjacent digits in our numeration system.

THINKING ABOUT THE STUDENTS

Students are familiar with the 10-to-1 relationship between adjacent digits in our numeration system. They have worked with decimals and can add and subtract decimals somewhat successfully, but they appear to have at best a procedural understanding of the process. Students also understand the part-whole meaning of fractional parts and the meaning of the numerator and denominator in a fraction.

MATERIALS AND PREPARATION

- Provide each student at least two sheets of 10 × 10 grids (see Blackline Master 2).
- Make a transparency of the 10 × 10 grid sheet to use in the "before" and "after" portions of the lesson.

lesson

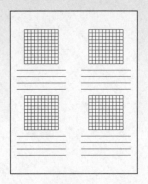

BLM 2

BEFORE

Begin with a simpler version of the task:

- Write the number 34 on the board. Remind students that 34 is 3 tens and 4 ones. Ask students to describe 34 with tens and ones in other ways. As students suggest names such as 2 tens and 14 ones, focus on the 10-to-1 relationship between adjacent digits: A larger unit can be exchanged for 10 of the next smaller unit and vice versa.
- Ask students what it means to have $\frac{1}{10}$ of something. Highlight the idea that the whole is divided into 10 *equal* parts and $\frac{1}{10}$ means you have one of those parts. Showing students the 10 × 10 grid, ask them to shade $\frac{1}{10}$ of the grid. Ask students to share different ways to shade $\frac{1}{10}$ of the grid. It might be helpful to illustrate using base-ten materials as one way to think about this task (i.e., the flat hundreds piece is used as the whole and the long ten stick is then used as a tenth). Explain to students how you could represent 1.3 with the base-ten materials if the flat piece is the whole (e.g., one flat piece and three long pieces).

The Task

- For each of the following fractions, use a 10 × 10 grid to determine the decimal equivalent and explain your reasoning.

$$\frac{3}{4} \qquad \frac{2}{5} \qquad \frac{3}{8}$$

Establish Expectations

- Using the 10 × 10 grids, students should:
  - Shade the fractional amount.
  - Identify the decimal number that also represents this amount.
  - Be prepared to explain their reasoning.

DURING

- Look for students who are shading their 10 × 10 grids differently. Highlight those different ways in the "after" portion of the lesson.
- If students have shaded their grid in a way that does not use long rows of ten, ask students how they would cover the area using strips and squares if they could use no more than nine tinies.
- The $\frac{3}{8}$ task is the most challenging. A useful hint is to ask students how they would find $\frac{1}{8}$ if they had $\frac{1}{4}$.

- You may need to remind students as they need something smaller than the smallest square on the grid that the next smaller pieces are tenths of the little squares. Since a small square is $\frac{1}{100}$, one-tenth of it would be $\frac{1}{1000}$ and half of it would be $\frac{5}{1000}$.

AFTER

- Students are likely to shade their grids differently. It is important to compare and contrast between different shadings so that students see that they have shaded an equivalent amount. For example, for fourths, students might shade a 5 × 5 section (half of a half). Others may shade two and a half rows of ten. Ask students to determine how these both show one-fourth.
- For some shadings, it may be difficult for students to see the decimal equivalent. For example, when students shade a 5 × 5 section to show a fourth, it can be difficult for them to translate that representation into a decimal. You might focus students' attention to finding tenths within the 10 × 10 grid by looking at rows of 10. One way to help them think about this is to ask how they would cover the area using strips and squares if they could use no more than nine tinies.

ASSESSMENT NOTES

- Some students will be very successful with shading equal parts but have difficulty connecting this to the decimal representation. As you suggest to them to use strips and tinies, make sure they can explain why they are using these groupings rather than, say, strips of 5.
- Students able to move quickly between the equal parts for fractions and the decimal equivalents in this task are ready to think about the decimal equivalent for one-third.

next steps

- For students who have difficulty with these tasks, provide a base-ten flat to use as the whole and have them cover this with strips and tinies to represent the fraction. Have them use this representation before moving back to the 10 × 10 grid.
- To continue to help students build connections between fractions and decimals, have them engage in tasks that use the hundredths disk (see Blackline Master 3), such as Activity 4.5, "Estimate, Then Verify."

EXTENDING THE NUMBER SYSTEM

Early in their education students begin to develop an understanding of our number system, in particular the notion of place value and the ten-to-one relationship between digits. Fraction and decimal concepts extend whole-number ideas beginning in the third and fourth grades. The ideas discussed in this chapter represent an even further expansion or enhancement of the ways in which we represent numbers. Specifically, students in the middle grades need to develop a more complete understanding of the number system, extend whole numbers to integers, start to think of fractions as rational numbers (both positive and negative), and begin to appreciate the completeness of the real number system.

big ideas

1 Exponential notation is a powerful way to express repeated products of the same number. Specifically, powers of 10 express very large and very small numbers in an economical manner.

2 Integers add to number the idea of opposite, so that every number has both size and a positive or negative relationship to other numbers. A negative number is the opposite of the positive number of the same size.

3 Every fraction, both positive and negative, is a rational number. Furthermore, every rational number can be expressed as a fraction.

4 Many numbers are not rational and can be expressed only symbolically or approximately using a close rational number. Examples include $\sqrt{2} \approx 1.41421\ldots$ and $\pi \approx 3.14159\ldots.$

Large Numbers, Small Numbers, and Exponents

As numbers in our technological world get very small or very large, expressing them in standard form is cumbersome. Exponential notation is much more efficient for conveying numeric or quantitative information.

Exponents

In algebra classes, students get confused trying to remember the rules of exponents. For example, when you raise numbers to powers, do you add or multiply the exponents? Here is an example of procedural knowledge that is often learned without supporting conceptual knowledge. Before algebra, students should have ample opportunity to explore working with exponents on whole numbers rather than with letters or variables. By doing so, they are able to deal directly with the concept and actually generate the rules themselves.

A *whole-number exponent* is simply shorthand for repeated multiplication of a number times itself; for example, $3^4 = 3 \times 3 \times 3 \times 3$. That is the only conceptual knowledge required.

Conventions of symbolism must also be learned. These are arbitrary rules with no conceptual basis. The first is that *an exponent applies to its immediate base*. For example, in the expression $2 + 5^3$, the exponent 3 applies only to the 5, so the expression is equal to $2 + (5 \times 5 \times 5)$. However, in the expression $(2 + 5)^3$, the 3 is an exponent of the quantity $2 + 5$ and is evaluated as $(2 + 5) \times (2 + 5) \times (2 + 5)$, or $7 \times 7 \times 7$.

The other convention involves the *order of operations:* Multiplication and division are always done before addition and subtraction. Since exponentiation is repeated multiplication, it also is done before addition and subtraction. In the expression $5 + 4 \times 2 - 6 \div 3$, 4×2 and $6 \div 3$ are done first. Therefore, the expression is evaluated as $5 + 8 - 2 = 13 - 2 = 11$.

> **STOP** **Try evaluating the same expression in left-to-right order. Do you get 4?**

Parentheses are used to group operations that are to be done first. Therefore, in $(5 + 4) \times 2 - 6 \div 3$, the addition can be done inside the parentheses first, or the distributive property can be used, and the final result is 16. The phrase "*Please excuse my dear Aunt Sally*" is sometimes used to help students recall that operations inside *p*arentheses are done first, then *e*xponentiation, and then *m*ultiplication and *d*ivision before *a*ddition and *s*ubtraction.

Calculators and Notation

Most scientific calculators employ "algebraic logic" that will evaluate expressions correctly and also allow grouping with parentheses. However, with the exception of the TI-MathMate, simple four-function calculators generally do not use algebraic logic. Operations are processed as they are entered. On calculators without algebraic logic, the following two keying sequences produce the same results:

Key: →	3 $\boxed{+}$	2 $\boxed{\times}$	7 $\boxed{=}$
Display → 3	2	5 7	35

Key: →	3 $\boxed{+}$ 2 $\boxed{=}$ $\boxed{\times}$ 7 $\boxed{=}$
Display → 3	2 5 7 35

Whenever an operation sign is pressed, the effect is the same as pressing $\boxed{=}$ and then the operation. Of course, neither result is correct for the expressions $3 + 2 \times 7$, which should be evaluated as $3 + 14$, or 17. Calculators designed for middle grades do use algebraic logic and include parenthesis keys so that both $3 + 2 \times 7$ and $(3 + 2) \times 7$ can be keyed in to generate the desired result. Now all of the major manufacturers offer calculators that show an entire expression in the window, including parentheses, as do graphing calculators. Results are shown only after pressing the [Enter] or the [=] key. With the Explorer Plus and most scientific calculators, the display shows only one number at a time, as illustrated here.

Key: →   3 [+] 2 [×] 7 [=]
Display →   3   2 █ 7 17

Notice that the display does not change when [×] is pressed. When using parentheses, note that a right parenthesis is never displayed. Instead, the expression that the right parenthesis encloses is calculated and that result displayed.

Key: →   [(] 3 [+] 2 [)] [×] 7 [=]
Display → [3   2 [5] 7 35

The graphing calculator offers the best solution to these problems. When the expression $3 + 2 \times (6^2 - 4)$ is keyed in, the display shows the full expression. Nothing is evaluated until you press [Enter] or [EXE]. Then the result appears on the next line to the right of the screen:

$$3 + 2 * (6^2 - 4)$$
$$67$$

Moreover, the last expression entered can be recalled and edited so that students can see how different expressions are evaluated. Only minimum key presses are required.

$3 + 2 * (6^2 - 4)$	
	67
$(3 + 2) * (6^2 - 4)$	
	160
$(3 + 2) * 6^2 - 4$	
	176
$3 + 2 * 6^2 - 4$	
	71

Nevertheless, the simple four-function calculator remains a powerful tool regardless of its limitations. For example, to evaluate 3^8, press 3 [×] [=] [=] [=] [=] [=] [=] [=]. (The first press of [=] will result in 9, or 3×3.) Students will be fascinated by how quickly numbers grow. Enter any number, press [×], and then repeatedly press [=]. Try two-digit numbers. Try 0.2.

Give students ample opportunity to explore expressions involving mixed operations and exponents with only the conventions and the meaning of exponents to guide them. No rules for exponents should be promoted. When experience has provided a firm background, the rules of exponents will make sense and should not require rote memorization.

ACTIVITY 5.1

What's in an Expression?

Provide students with numeric expressions to evaluate with simple four-function calculators. At the top of the next page are some examples of the types of expressions that can be valuable:

(continued)

$3 + 4 \times 8$	$3^6 + 2^6$	$3^4 \times 7 - 5^2$	$3^4 \times 5^2$
$4 \times 8 + 3$	$(3 + 2)^6$	$(3 \times 7)^4 - 5 \times 2$	$(3 \times 5)^6$

$\dfrac{5^3 \times 5^2}{5^6}$	$4 \times 3 - 2^3 \times 5 + 23 \times 9$	$\dfrac{4 \times 3^5}{2}$ $\quad 4 + \dfrac{3^5}{2}$

When experiencing difficulty, students should write equivalent expressions without exponents or include parentheses to indicate explicit groupings. For example:

$$
\begin{aligned}
(7 \times 2^3 - 5)^3 &= (7 \times (2 \times 2 \times 2) - 5) \times \\
&\quad (7 \times (2 \times 2 \times 2) - 5) \times \\
&\quad (7 \times (2 \times 2 \times 2) - 5) \\
&= ((7 \times 8) - 5) \times ((7 \times 8) - 5) \times ((7 \times 8) - 5) \\
&= (56 - 5) \times (56 - 5) \times (56 - 5) \\
&= 51 \times 51 \times 51
\end{aligned}
$$

When discussing results, place all of the emphasis on the procedures rather than the answer. The fact that two groups got the same result does not help a group that got a different result. For many expressions, there is more than one way to proceed, and one may be easier to do or to understand than another.

Of course, calculators with algebraic logic will automatically produce correct results. Yet it remains important for students to know the correct order of operations. The calculator should not replace an understanding of the rules. The order-of-operation rules apply to symbolic manipulation in algebra and must also be understood if a calculator without algebraic logic is used.

Many books emphasize rules and exercises at the expense of opportunities for explorations. Activities like "What's in an Expression?" provide good opportunities to see how students reason, communicate ideas, go beyond the answer to generate their own ideas, and generally do mathematics. Once students have learned the relatively simple definition of what an exponent is, the search for easy tricks for multiplying and dividing should be left to students' discovery and their own reasoning. The discussions that ensue will be better than drilling rules about adding exponents when you multiply numbers with like bases. These are good opportunities to assess mathematical power.

Very Large Numbers

The real world is full of very large quantities and measures. We see references to huge numbers in the media all the time. Unfortunately, most of us have not developed an appreciation for extremely large numbers. Here are a few examples:

- A state lottery with 44 numbers from which to pick 6 has over 7 million possible combinations of 6 different numbers. There are $44 \times 43 \times 42 \times 41 \times 40 \times 39$ possible ways that the balls could come out of the hopper (5,082,517,440). But generally the order in which they are picked is not important. Since there are $6 \times 5 \times 4 \times 3 \times 2 \times 1 = 720$ different arrangements of 6 numbers, each collection appears 720 times. Therefore, there are *only* 5,082,517,440 ÷ 720 possible lottery numbers, or in other words, 1 out of 7,059,052 chances to win.

- An estimate of the size of the universe is 40 billion light-years. One light-year is the number of miles light travels in *one year.* The speed of light is 186,281.7 miles per *second,* or 16,094,738,880 miles in a single day.
- The human body has about 100 billion cells.
- The distance to the sun is about 150 million kilometers.
- The population of the world has surpassed 6 billion.

Connecting these large numbers to meaningful points of reference can help students get a handle on the size of these large numbers. For example, suppose students determine the population in their city or town is about 500,000 people. They can then figure that it would take about 12,000 cities of the same population size to generate the population of the world. Or suppose students determine that it is about 4600 km between San Francisco, California, and Washington, DC. This would mean that it would take over 32,000 trips back and forth between these two cities to equal the distance between the earth and the sun. Building from such familiar or meaningful reference points can help students develop benchmarks to work with and make sense of large numbers.

Representation of Large Numbers: Scientific Notation

The more common it becomes to find very large numbers in our daily lives, the more important it is to have convenient ways to represent them. One option is to say and write numbers in their common form. However, this practice can at times be cumbersome. Another option is to use exponential notation and our base-ten place-value system.

Students in elementary school learn how to multiply by 10, by 100, and by 1000 by simply adding the appropriate number of zeros. Help students expand this idea by examining powers of 10 on a calculator that handles exponents. A graphing calculator is best but not the only option.

ACTIVITY 5.2

Exploring Powers of 10

Have students use any calculator that permits entering exponents to explore some of the following:

a. Explore 10^N for various values of N. What patterns do you notice? What does 1E15 mean? (1E15 is the typical calculator form of 1×10^{15}.)

b. Find different expressions for numbers such as one thousand, one million, one billion, one trillion. What patterns are there in the different expressions of the different expressions of these numbers?

c. Enter 45 followed by a string of zeros. How many will your calculator permit? What happens when you press Enter ? What does 4.5E10 mean?

d. What does 5.689E6 mean? Can you enter this another way?

e. Try sums like $(4.5 \times 10^N) + (27 \times 10^K)$ for different values of N and K. Try N > K, N < K, N = K. What can you find out?

f. What happens with products of numbers like those in item (e)?

It is useful to become comfortable with the power-of-10 expressions in Activity 5.2. Students should eventually discover that when scientific or graphing calculators display numbers with more digits than the display will hold, they use *scientific notation*—a decimal number between 1 and 10 times a power of 10. For example, on a TI-73, the product of 45,000,000 × 8,000,000 is displayed as 3.6E14, meaning 3.6×10^{14}, or 360,000,000,000,000 (360 trillion).

Ask students why there are only 13 zeros. What happens when the numbers in the computation do not involve a lot of zeros?

 With each factor in the product expressed in scientific notation: $(4.5 \times 10^7) \times (8 \times 10^6)$, or 4.5E7 × 8.0E6, can you compute the result mentally?

Notice the advantages of scientific notation, especially for multiplication and division. Here the significant digits can be multiplied mentally ($4.5 \times 8 = 36$) and the exponents added to produce almost instantly 36×10^{13} or 3.6×10^{14}.

Different notations have different purposes and values. Consider this fact: In 1990, the population of the world was more than 5,050,700,000 persons, about 1 billion fewer than in the year 2000. This can be expressed in various ways:

- 5 billion 50 million 700 thousand
- 5,050,700,000
- 5.0507×10^9
- Less than 5.1 billion
- A little more than 5 billion

Each way of stating the number has value and purpose in different contexts. Rather than spend time with exercises converting numbers from standard form to scientific notation, consider large numbers found in newspapers, magazines, and atlases. How are they written? How are they said aloud? When are they rounded? When not and why? What forms of the numbers seem best for the purposes?

Negative Exponents

When students begin to explore exponents and have also experienced negative integers, it is interesting to consider what it might mean to raise a number to a negative power. For example, what does 2^{-4} mean? Two related options for exploring the possibilities of negative exponents seem reasonable. First, in the spirit of patterns in mathematics, examine a pattern of numbers, and see how it might best be expanded. As with large numbers, the powers of 10 seem the most profitable to explore because they are directly related to place value. Have students consider 10^N as follows:

$10^4 = 10,000$
$10^3 = 1000$
$10^2 = 100$
$10^1 = 10$
$10^0 = ?$
$10^{-1} = ?$

In this sequence, the most obvious entry for 10^0 is 1, and that is the *definition* of 10^0. That is, it is a convention that 10 or any other nonzero number raised to the power 0 is 1. So what is 10^{-1}? If the pattern is to continue, the 1 should move to the right of the decimal:

$$10^0 = 1$$
$$10^{-1} = 0.1$$
$$10^{-2} = 0.01$$
$$10^{-3} = 0.001$$

and so on. Notice how each of these numbers is written as a fraction:

$$10^{-3} = 0.001 = \frac{1}{1000} = \frac{1}{10^3}$$

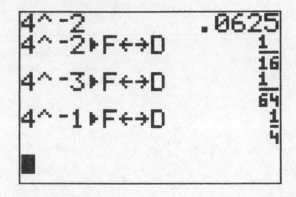

FIGURE 5.1 •

Graphing calculators routinely evaluate expressions as decimals. However, some also provide a way to convert decimals to fractions. This figure shows the screen of a TI-73 calculator. The [F↔D] key converts fractions to decimals and also decimals to fractions as shown here.

Students should be encouraged to explore these numbers on a calculator. That leads to the second way to explore negative exponents: Use a calculator to see if you can figure out what things like 4^{-3} or 2^{-5} mean. The calculator should, of course, never be seen as the *reason* for anything in mathematics, but here you are searching for a notation convention. Assuming that one exists, it is reasonable to believe that the calculator will have the correct convention incorporated. If the calculator has decimal-to-fraction conversion, suggest that students use that feature to help develop the meaning of negative exponents. Figure 5.1 gives an example of how this might look on a graphing calculator.

Very Small Numbers

As with large numbers, it is extremely important to use real examples of very small numbers. Without real contexts, you may be tempted to resort to drill exercises that have little meaning for students. As with large numbers, connecting these small numbers to meaningful points of reference can help students conceptualize how very tiny these numbers really are. Here are a few examples of real-world values to explore:

- The length of a DNA strand in a cell is about 10^{-7} m. This is also measured as 1000 *angstroms*. (Based on this information, how long is an angstrom?) To put things in perspective, the diameter of a human hair is about 2.54×10^{-5} m.

- Human hair grows at the rate of 10^{-8} miles per hour. Garden snails have been clocked moving at about 3×10^{-2} mph.

- The chances of winning the Virginia lottery, based on selecting six numbers from 1 to 44, is 1 in 7.059 million. That is a probability of less than 1.4×10^{-10}.

- The mass of one atom of hydrogen is 0.000 000 000 000 000 000 001 675 g, while the mass of one paper clip is about 1 gram.

- It takes sound 0.28 second (2.8×10^{-1}) to travel the length of a football field. In contrast, a TV signal travels a full mile in about 0.000005368 second, or 5.3×10^{-6} second. A TV viewer at home hears the football being kicked before the receiver on the field does.

Integer Concepts

Students almost daily have some interaction with negative numbers or experience phenomena that negative numbers can model. Some examples:

- A loss of money is a negative cash flow.
- Slowing down the car is negative acceleration, and driving in reverse is negative velocity.
- Below-zero temperature and below-ground level are negatives relative to a scale.

In fact, almost any concept that is quantified and has direction probably has both a positive and a negative value.

Generally, negative values are introduced with *integers*—the whole numbers and their negatives or opposites—instead of with fractions or decimals.

Intuitive Models of Signed Quantities

As with any new types of numbers that students encounter, real models or examples are useful. Negative numbers or situations that model them do exist. It is a good idea to discuss some of these with your class before jumping directly into computation with signed numbers.

Debits and Credits

Suppose that you are the bookkeeper for a small business. At any time, your records show how many dollars the company has in its account. There are always so many dollars in cash (credits or receipts) and so many dollars in accounts payable (debits). The difference between the debit and credit totals tells the value of the account. If there are more credits than debits, the account is positive, or "in the black." If there are more debits than credits, the account is in debt, shows a negative cash value, or is "in the red." Suppose further that all transactions are handled by mail. The mail carrier can bring mail, a positive action, or take mail away, a negative action.

With this scenario, it is easy to discuss addition and subtraction of signed quantities. An example is illustrated in Figure 5.2.

Integer Football

An integer football field might have the center as the 0-yard line with one goal the +50 goal and the other the –50 goal. Any position on the field is determined by a signed number between +50 and –50. Gains or losses are like positive and negative quantities. A positive team moves toward the positive goal, and a negative team toward the negative goal. If the negative team starts on the –15-yard line and has a loss of 20 yards, it will be on the +5-yard line. As this example illustrates, "loss" does not necessarily mean that

Credits		Debits		Balance
In	Out	In	Out	Begin 0
50				+50
		30		+20
	10			+10
		50		–40
25				–15
			20	+5

FIGURE 5.2 •

A ledger sheet model for integers.

you subtract. Loss is defined based on the context. In this case, loss is defined as the direction opposite that which the team is moving.

 You should sketch a picture of this example and convince yourself that it is numerically the same as the one in Figure 5.2 using the debit-credit model.

Contrived situations such as mailing debits and credits and the football field are suggested as introductory discussion models. They can help students think intuitively about what happens to quantities when an action causes them to be less than 0. They also provide examples of a joining or positive action and a removal or negative action of both positive and negative quantities.

The calculator is another model that might be explored early in the discussion of signed numbers. It gives correct and immediate results that students seem to believe. The major drawback is that no rationale for the result is provided.

Have students explore subtraction problems such as $5 - 8 = ?$, and discuss the results. (Be aware that the negative sign appears in different places on different calculators.)

Students can benefit by using the calculator along with the intuitive models and questions mentioned earlier. For example, how can you get from -5 to -17 by addition? 13 minus *what* is 15?

Mathematical Definition of Negative Numbers

Although ancient civilizations used distinct symbols to indicate a debt owed (i.e., negatives), Western mathematicians did not recognize and use negative numbers in their theoretical work until the Renaissance. In their studies of polynomial equations, mathematicians found that the degree of the polynomial equation was often equal to the number of solutions to the equation. For example, a polynomial of degree 2, such as $x^2 - 5x + 6 = 0$, has two solutions ($(x - 2)(x - 3) = 0 \longrightarrow x = 2$ or $x = 3$). However, for some equations, such as $x^2 + x - 6 = 0$, they assumed only one solution ($(x - 2)(x + 3) = 0 \longrightarrow x = 2$) since there was no number to which they could add to 3 to get 0. In an effort to maintain the pattern that they had found, mathematicians defined negative numbers as numbers that were solutions to equations such as $x + 3 = 0$.

Therefore, the mathematician defines a negative number in terms of whole numbers. The definition of negative 3 is the solution to the equation $3 + ? = 0$. In general, the *opposite of n* is the solution to $n + ? = 0$. If n is a positive number, the *opposite of n* is a negative number. The set of integers, therefore, consists of the positive whole numbers, the opposites of the whole numbers, or negative numbers, and 0, which is neither positive nor negative. This is the definition found in student textbooks. Like many things in mathematics, abstract or symbolic definitions are best when there is some intuitive or conceptual framework with which to link the idea.

Operations with Integers

Until students encounter integers, the plus and minus signs are used only for the operations of addition and subtraction. Notation for signed numbers represents a real

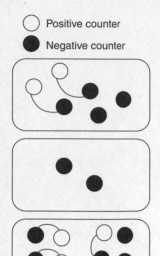

○ Positive counter

● Negative counter

FIGURE 5.3

Each collection is a model of negative 2.

problem for many students. For example, the sum of 3 and negative 7 can be written as 3 + (–7) or as 3 + ⁻7. The latter form might be clear in a printed book but may be obscure in handwritten form. The use of parentheses is awkward, especially in expressions already involving parentheses. On graphing calculators, the distinction is forced on the user: One key is used for subtraction and another for negatives. They do not work interchangeably.

Two Models for Integer Operations

Two models are popular for helping students understand how the four operations (+, –, ×, and ÷) work with the integers. One model consists of counters in two different colors, one for positive counts and one for negative counts. Two counters, one of each type, cancel each other out. Thus, if yellows are positive and reds are negative, 5 yellows and 7 reds is the same as 2 reds, each representing ⁻1 for a total of ⁻2 (see Figure 5.3). It is important with this model that students understand that it is always possible to add to or remove from a pile any number of pairs consisting of one positive and one negative counter without changing the value of the pile. (Intuitively, this is like adding equal quantities of debits and credits.) The actions of addition and subtraction are the same as for whole numbers; addition is joining or adding counters, and subtraction is removing or taking away counters.

The other commonly used model is the number line. It is a bit more traditional and mathematical, yet many students find it confusing. The football field model provides an intuitive background. Positive and negative numbers are measured distances to the right and left of 0. It is important to remember that signed values are *directed distances* and not points on a line. The points on the number line are not models of integers; the directed distances are. To emphasize this for students, represent all integers with arrows, and avoid referring to the number line coordinates as "numbers." Poster board arrows of different whole-number lengths can be made in two colors, yellow pointing to the right for positive quantities and red to the left for negative quantities (see Figure 5.4). The arrows help students think of integer quantities as directed distances. A positive arrow never points left, and a negative arrow never points right. Furthermore, each arrow is a quantity with both length (magnitude or absolute value) and direction (sign). These properties remain for each arrow regardless of its position on the number line. Small versions of the arrows can easily be cut from poster board for individual students to work with.

It is no doubt easier simply to give students the rules for integers than to develop them with arrows and counters. The conceptual explanations do not make the rules easier to use, and it is never intended that students continue to think in terms of these models as they practice integer arithmetic. Rather, it is important that students not view the procedural rules for manipulating integers as arbitrary and mysterious. Here is a case where we must make students responsible for the conceptual knowledge. If we emphasize only the procedural rules, there is little reason for students to attend to the conceptual justifications. Do not be content with right answers; always demand explanations.

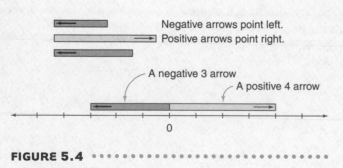

Negative arrows point left.
Positive arrows point right.

A negative 3 arrow
A positive 4 arrow

0

FIGURE 5.4

Number-line model for integers.

Which Model to Use

Although the two models appear quite different, they are alike mathematically. Integers involve two concepts—*quantity* and *opposite*. Quantity is modeled by the number of counters or the length of the arrows. Opposite is represented as different colors or different directions.

Many teachers who have tried both models with their students report that students find one model easy and the other hard. (The counter model seems to be the favorite.) As a result, they decide to use only the model that students like or understand better. This is a mistake! Remember that the dual concepts of integers are not in the models but rather must be constructed by the students and imposed on the models. It may be that students find the operations easier when they use counters. This is not the same thing as understanding integer operations. Students should experience both models and, perhaps even more important, discuss how the two are alike. A parallel development using both models at the same time may be the most conceptual approach.

A Problem-Solving Approach for Integers

The following discussion is more a quick explanation of how counters and arrows can be used to model operations with integers than a suggested pedagogical approach. Once your students understand how integers are represented by each of the models, you can present the operations for the integers in the form of problems. In other words, rather than explaining how addition of integers works and showing students how to solve exercises with the models, you pose an integer computation and let students use their models to find a solution. It may be useful to assign half of the class the arrow model and the other half the counters. When solutions have been reached, the groups can compare and justify their results. Many incorrect ideas will surface, but the learning that will come from the discussion and clarification will be far superior to an expository approach.

Addition and Subtraction

Since middle school students may not have used counters or number lines for some time, it would be good to begin work with either of these models using positive whole numbers. After a few examples to help students become familiar with the model for addition or subtraction with whole numbers, have them work through an example with integers using exactly the same reasoning. Remember, the emphasis should be on the rationale and not on how quickly students can get correct answers.

Several examples of addition are modeled in Figure 5.5, each in two ways: with positive and negative counters and with the number-line-and-arrow model. First examine the counter model. After the two quantities are joined, any pairs of positive and negative counters cancel each other out, and students can remove these, making it easier to see the result.

To add using the arrow model, note that each added arrow begins at the point end of the previous arrow. Help students with the analogy between these arrows and

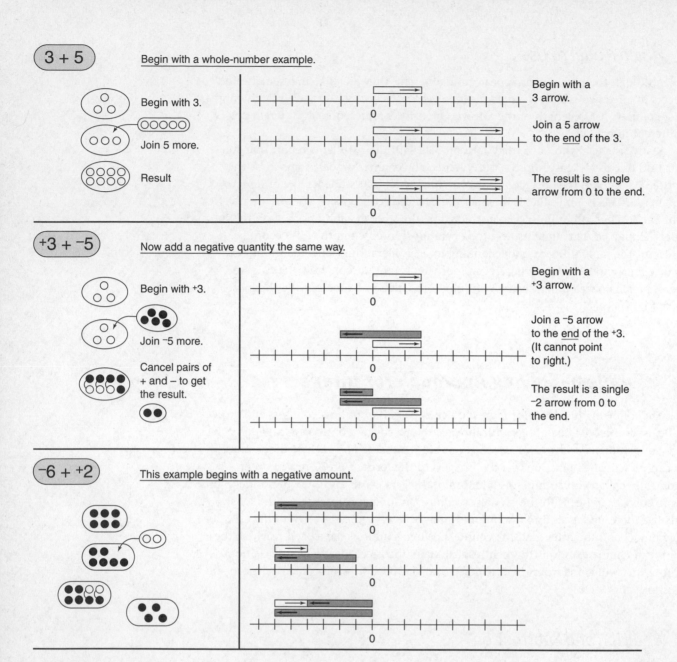

FIGURE 5.5 • • • • • • • • •

Relate integer addition to whole-number addition.

the football situation: Players always face their own goal. They may go forward or backward, but they never face the opponents' goal. Addition is the advance of a team from the previous position. In the ⁺3 + ⁻5 example, the positive arrow (+ team) starts at 0 and ends at positive 3. From that point, the negative arrow begins (the negative team takes over and *advances* in the negative direction). The result, then, is an arrow beginning at 0 and ending where the second arrow ended.

Subtraction is represented as "remove" in terms of the counter model and "back up" in terms of the arrow model. In Figure 5.6, for ⁻5 – ⁺2, both models begin with a representation of ⁻5. To remove two positive counters from a set that has none, a different representation of ⁻5 must first be made. Since any number of neutral pairs (one pos-

Chapter 5 **EXTENDING THE NUMBER SYSTEM**

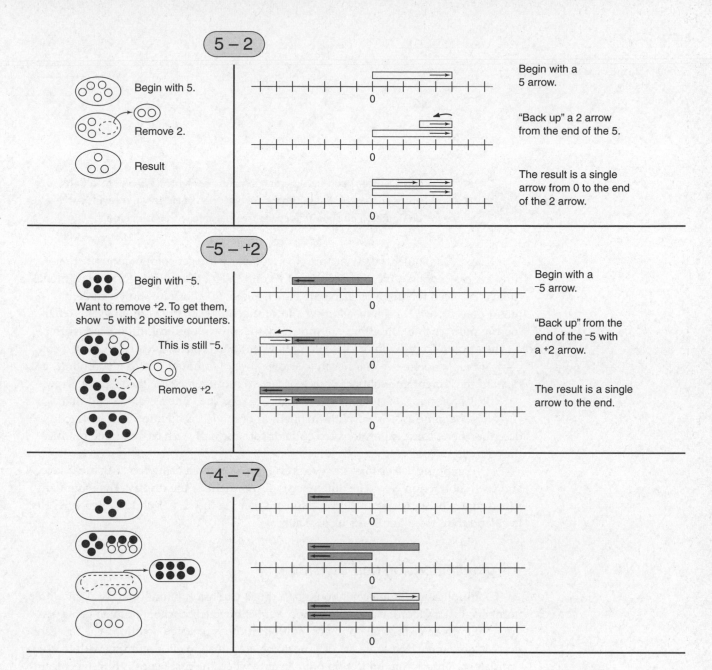

FIGURE 5.6 • • • • • • • •

Integer subtraction is also related to whole numbers.

itive, one negative) can be added without changing the value of the set, two pairs are added so that two positive counters can be removed. The net effect is to have more negative counters.

With the number-line-and-arrow model, subtraction means to back up or to move in the opposite direction. Using the football field analogy, teams move backward when penalized or they lose yardage. In the example of ⁻5 – ⁺2, the first arrow ends at ⁻5. Since a positive quantity is subtracted, use a positive arrow. To subtract it, move it in its opposite direction (left). The forward movement ends at ⁻7. The result of the operation is an arrow from 0 to the back end of the ⁺2 arrow.

A PROBLEM-SOLVING APPROACH FOR INTEGERS

FIGURE 5.7 •••••••

Students do not need
elaborate drawings to
think through the
number-line model.

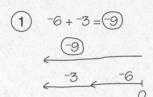

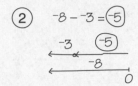

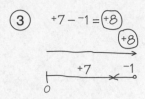

> **STOP** Before reading further, go through each example in Figures 5.5 and 5.6. Solve
> the problems without examining the figure and then compare your results with
> those in the figures. You should become comfortable with both models.

Have your students draw pictures to accompany integer computations. Set pictures are easy enough; they may consist of Xs and Os, for example. For the arrow model, there is no need for anything elaborate either. Figure 5.7 illustrates how a student might draw arrows for simple addition and subtraction exercises without even sketching the number line. Directions are shown by the arrows, and magnitudes are written on the arrows. For your initial modeling, however, the poster board arrows in two colors will help students see that negative arrows always point left and that addition is a forward movement and subtraction is a backward movement for either type of arrow.

It is important for students to see that $^+3 + {}^-5$ is the same as $^+3 - {}^+5$ and that $^+2 - {}^-6$ is the same as $^+2 + {}^+6$. With the method of modeling addition and subtraction described here, these expressions are quite discernible and yet have the same result as they should have.

On graphing calculators, these expressions are entered using the "negative" key and the "subtraction" key. The difference is also evident in the display. The redundant superscript plus signs are not shown. Students can see that $3 + {}^-5$ and $3 - 5$ each results in $^-2$ and that $3 - {}^-5$ and $3 + 5$ are also alike.

Multiplication and Division

Multiplication of integers should be a direct extension of multiplication for whole numbers, just as addition and subtraction were connected to whole-number concepts. We frequently refer to whole-number multiplication as repeated addition. The first factor tells how many sets there are or how many are added in all, beginning with 0. This translates to integer multiplication quite readily when the first factor is positive, regardless of the sign of the second factor. The first example in Figure 5.8 illustrates a positive first factor and a negative second factor.

What could the meaning be when the first factor is negative, as in $^-2 \times {}^-3$? If a positive first factor means repeated addition (how many times added to 0), a negative first factor should mean repeated subtraction (how many times subtracted from 0). The second example in Figure 5.8 illustrates how multiplication with the first factor negative can be modeled.

The deceptively simple rules of "like signs yield positive products" and "unlike signs yield negative products" are quickly established. However, once more, it is just as important that your students be able to produce answers correctly and skillfully as that they be able to supply a rationale.

"Positive 3 sets" of ⁻4 means "make" 3 sets of ⁻4 or <u>add</u> them to zero.

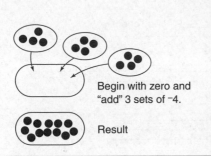

Begin with zero and "add" 3 sets of ⁻4.

Result

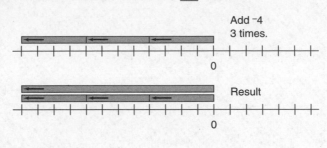

Add ⁻4 3 times.

Result

⁻2 × ⁻3

"Negative 2 sets" of ⁻3 means 2 sets of ⁻3 <u>less</u> than 0 — or to "remove" 2 sets of ⁻3 from 0.

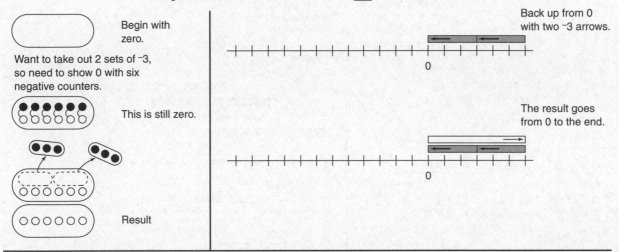

Begin with zero.

Want to take out 2 sets of ⁻3, so need to show 0 with six negative counters.

This is still zero.

Result

Back up from 0 with two ⁻3 arrows.

The result goes from 0 to the end.

FIGURE 5.8 • • • • • • • •

Multiplication by a positive first factor is repeated addition. Multiplication by a negative first factor is repeated subtraction.

With division of integers, again explore the whole-number case first. Recall that 8 ÷ 4 with whole numbers has two possible meanings corresponding to two missing-factor expressions: 4 × ? = 8 asks, "Four sets of *what* make eight?" whereas ? × 4 = 8 asks, "How many fours make eight?" Generally, the measurement approach (? × 4) is the one used with integers, although both concepts can be exhibited with either model. It is helpful to think of building the dividend with the divisor from 0, or repeated addition—to find the missing factor.

The first example in Figure 5.9 illustrates how the two models work for whole numbers. Following that is an example where the divisor is positive but the dividend is negative.

Try using both models to compute ⁻8 ÷ ⁺2. Draw pictures using Xs and Os and also arrows. Check your understanding with the examples in Figure 5.9. Once you understand that example, try ⁺9 ÷ ⁻3 and also ⁻12 ÷ ⁻4.

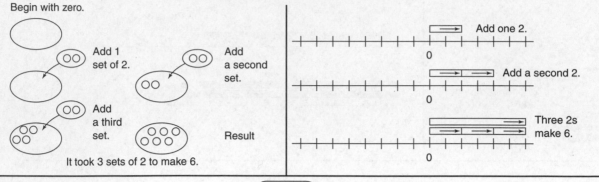

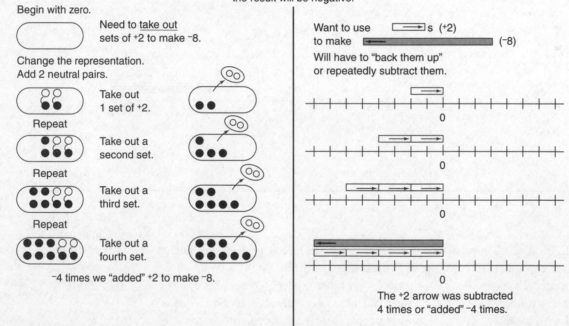

FIGURE 5.9 ● ● ● ● ● ● ● ●

Division integers following
a measurement approach.

The entire understanding of integer division rests on a good concept of a negative
first factor for multiplication and a knowledge of the relationship between multiplication and division.

There is no need to rush your students on to some mastery of use of the models.
It is much better that they first think about how to model the whole-number situation
and then figure out, with some guidance from you, how to deal with integers.

Rational Numbers

Several number ideas that students have been exposed to in earlier grades, coupled with the ideas of the integers, need to come together in the middle grades. A complete understanding of the rational numbers as positive and negative decimals and equivalently as positive and negative fractions is an important development.

Fractions as Indicated Division

If four people were to share three pizzas, the amount that each would get can be expressed as $3 \div 4$; that is, three things divided four ways. Each person would receive three-fourths of a pizza. So $\frac{3}{4}$ and $3 \div 4$ are both expressions for the same idea: 3 things divided by 4.

In Chapter 3, we saw that this sharing idea is in fact compatible with the part-whole meaning of fractions. With $\frac{3}{4}$ of a pizza, each pizza can be divided into four parts (the denominator) and then each person gets 3 of these $\frac{1}{4}$ pieces (the numerator). And so any fraction $\frac{k}{n}$ can be thought of as $k \div n$ or as k parts of $\frac{1}{n}$ pieces. These ideas appear quite different but in fact are not.

Students will likely find this division interpretation meaning of fractions unusual. Fractions are commonly thought of as parts of wholes, not as operations. Similarly, expressions such as $7 \div 3$ are thought of as operations (things to be done), not numbers. However, 4, $2 + 2$, $12 \div 3$, and $\frac{8}{2}$ are all symbolic expressions for the same number: $12 \div 3$ is not the question and 4 the answer; both are expressions for 4.

Here is one possible way to help students develop the idea that a fraction is another way of expressing division.

ACTIVITY 5.3

How Do You Write It?

Present students with a simple word problem similar to the following: *Zach has 18 meters of rope. He cuts off one-fifth of the rope to make a leash for his dog, Sam. How much rope did he use for the leash?* Three students have solved this problem.

Student A: Zach cut off 3.6 meters because $18 \div 5 = 3.6$.
Student B: I did $\frac{1}{5} \times 18$ like this: $\frac{1}{5} \times \frac{18}{1} = \frac{18}{5} = 3\frac{3}{5}$. So the answer is 3 and $\frac{3}{5}$ meters.
Student C: I did the same thing, but I just said the answer was $\frac{18}{5}$ meters.

Which student is correct? Which one has the "best" answer?

 How would you respond to the questions in Activity 5.3?

In the discussion of a problem situation like the one in Activity 5.3, you can lead students to see that $18 \div 5$ and $\frac{18}{5}$ mean exactly the same thing. All three students are correct. However, the discussion of which answer is "best" can help students see that different expressions can be more meaningful given a context. For example, the expressions $3\frac{3}{5}$ and 3.6 m as opposed to $\frac{18}{5}$ m give a person a better sense of how much rope was used to make the leash.

Similarly, discuss the difference between these three expressions:

$$\tfrac{1}{4} \text{ of } 24 \qquad \tfrac{24}{4} \qquad 24 \div 4$$

This discussion can lead to a general development of the idea that a fraction can be thought of as division of the numerator by the denominator or that $\frac{a}{b}$ is the same as $a \div b$.

Fractions as Rational Numbers

Because students tend to think of fractions as parts of sets or objects, they remain, in the minds of students, more physical object than number. This is one reason that students can have such a difficult time placing fractions on a number line. A significant leap toward thinking about fractions as numbers is made when students begin to understand that a decimal is a representation of a fraction. In Chapter 4, we explored the idea of the "friendly" fractions (halves, thirds, fourths, fifths, eighths) in terms of their decimal equivalents.

In the middle grades, it is time to combine all of these ideas:

- $4\frac{3}{5}$ is 4.6 because $\frac{3}{5}$ is six-tenths of a whole, so 4 wholes and six-tenths is 4.6.
- $4\frac{3}{5}$ is $\frac{23}{5}$, and that is the same as $23 \div 5$, or 4.6 if I use decimals.
- 4.6 is read "four and six-tenths," so I can write that as $4\frac{6}{10} = 4\frac{3}{5}$.

What becomes clear in a discussion building on students' existing ideas is that any number, positive or negative, that can be written as a fraction can also be written as a decimal number. You can also reverse this idea and convert decimal numbers to fractions. Keep in mind that the purpose is to see that there are different symbolic notations for the same quantities—not to become skilled at conversions.

The result of this discussion is a reasonable definition of rational numbers: A *rational number* is any number that can be expressed as a fraction. Equivalently, a *rational number* is any number that can be written as either a terminating or repeating decimal number.

The following activity investigates the types of rational numbers that have terminating or repeating decimal forms.

ACTIVITY 5.4

The Repeater or the Terminator

Students are to generate a table as follows for the first 20 unit fractions. (This can be done easily with a spreadsheet.) Students should already be familiar with the meaning of prime and composite numbers and prime factorization.

Unit Fraction	Prime Factorization of Denominator	Decimal Form
$\frac{1}{2}$	2 (2 is prime)	0.5
$\frac{1}{3}$	3 (3 is prime)	0.333 . . .
$\frac{1}{4}$	$4 = 2 \times 2$	0.25

After students complete the table for the first 20 unit fractions, have them use their calculator to find the decimal forms of the fractions. Students should begin to generate hypotheses about what types of rational numbers have terminating decimal forms and what types have repeating decimal forms and check their hypotheses by continuing to add unit fractions to the list, keeping denominators between 21 and 100. As a class, discuss the patterns they notice and why these patterns occur. Use these patterns to determine what types of rational numbers have decimal forms that terminate and what types of rational numbers have decimal forms that repeat.

 Before reading further, try Activity 5.4. What patterns do you notice? Use these patterns to determine what types of rational numbers have decimal forms that terminate or repeat. Why do these patterns occur?

You probably did not have to get beyond denominators of 20 or so to find out that the only fractions with terminating decimal equivalents factor into all 2s and/or 5s. The next question to ask is: Why is this so? Here is one explanation. Every terminating decimal can be written as a fraction with a denominator that is a power of 10. For example, $\frac{1}{8}$, which is 0.125, can be written as $\frac{125}{1000}$. That means that the denominator (in this case 8) must be a factor of a power of 10 (in this case 1000). Note that $\frac{125}{1000} = \frac{1 \times 125}{8 \times 125}$. Two and 5 are the only factors of 10 and, therefore, the only factors of any power of 10. If any other prime is involved in the denominator, no multiple of it will be a power of 10.

Once students have discovered the characteristics of rational numbers that cause them to terminate or repeat, the next activity helps them develop a better understanding of the structure of the rational number system.

ACTIVITY 5.5

How Close Is Close?

Have students select any two fractions or any two decimals that they think are "really close." It makes no difference what numbers students pick or even how close together they really are. Now challenge them to find at least ten more numbers (fractions or decimals) that are between these two numbers. Do not be tempted to show students any clever methods for finding the numbers.

EXPANDED LESSON

(pages 152–153)
A complete lesson plan based on "How Close Is Close?" can be found at the end of this chapter.

"How Close Is Close?" is an opportunity to find out how your students understand fractions and decimals. (The activity should be done in both forms eventually.) If students haven't been told a method, they must rely on their own ideas to come up with a solution. The activity offers a great opportunity for discussion, assessment of individual students' fraction and decimal concepts, and the introduction of perhaps the most interesting feature of the rational number system: density. The rational numbers are said to be *dense* because between any two rational numbers there exists an *infinite* number of other rational numbers.

The density of the rationals makes the irrationals even more amazing.

Real Numbers

Irrational numbers are numbers that are not rational. The irrationals together with the rational numbers make up the *real* numbers. The real numbers fill in all the holes on the number line even though the holes are infinitesimally small. Students' first experience with irrational numbers typically occurs when exploring roots of whole numbers.

Introducing the Concept of Roots

The following activity provides a good introduction to square roots and cube roots. From this beginning, the notion of roots of any degree is easily developed.

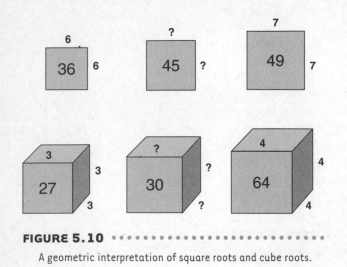

FIGURE 5.10 •
A geometric interpretation of square roots and cube roots.

ACTIVITY 5.6

Edges of Squares and Cubes

Show students pictures of three squares (or three cubes) as in Figure 5.10. The edges of the first and last figures are consecutive whole numbers. The areas (volumes) of all three figures are provided. The students' task is to use a calculator to find the edge of the figure in the center. Use of the square root key is not permitted. Solutions will satisfy these equations:

$\square \times \square = 45$,   or $\square^2 = 45$

and

$\square \times \square \times \square = 30$,   or $\square^3 = 30$

In "Edges of Squares and Cubes," the calculator permits students to test a possible edge length to see if it is too long or too short. For example, to solve the cube problem, students might start with 3.5 and find that 3.5^3 is 42.875, much too large. Quickly, they will find that the solution is between 3.1 and 3.2. But where?

 Use a calculator to continue getting a better approximation of the cube root of 30 to two decimal places.

From this simple introduction, students can be challenged to find solutions to equations such as $\square^6 = 8$. These students are now prepared to understand the general definition of the *nth root* of a number *N* as the number that when raised to the *n*th power equals *N*. The *square* and *cube roots* are simply other names for the second and third roots. The notational convention of the radical sign comes last. It should then be clear that $\sqrt{6}$ is a number and not an exercise to be done. The cube root of eight is the same as $\sqrt[3]{8}$, which is just another way of writing 2.

Discussing Real Numbers

Eighth-grade students probably do not need a very sophisticated knowledge of the real number system. A few powerful ideas, however, deserve to be explored informally.

Irrational Numbers

One characterization of a rational number is that it can be written as a decimal where the decimal part is either finite or repeats infinitely. Thus, both 3.45 and 87.19363636 . . . are rational numbers and can each be converted to fractional form. But what about a decimal number that just goes on and on, with no repetition? Or what about the number 3.101001000100001000001 . . . ? These never repeat and are not finite and, therefore, are not rational. A real number that is not rational is called *irrational*.

The numbers π and $\sqrt{2}$ are both irrational numbers. The number π is a ratio of two measures in a circle, the circumference and the diameter. Although it is not possible to prove the irrationality of π at this level, the fact that it is irrational implies that it is impossible to have a circle with the lengths of both the circumference and the diameter rational. (Why?) A proof that $\sqrt{2}$ is irrational usually assumes that $\sqrt{2}$ *is* rational, which then leads to a contradiction. However, such a proof is generally too difficult for middle school students.

Density of the Real Numbers

If the density of the rationals is impressive, even more astounding is that the irrationals are also dense. And the irrationals and the rationals are all mixed up together. The density of the irrationals is not as easy to demonstrate and is not within the scope of the middle school.

Rational Roots

One reason it is difficult to comprehend irrational numbers is that we have very little firsthand experience with them. The ones we are most familiar with are roots of numbers. For example, we just noted that students are frequently shown a proof for the irrationality of $\sqrt{2}$. An intuitive notion of that fact is difficult to come by. Most calculators will show only eight to ten digits, requiring a leap of faith to accept that the decimal representation is infinitely long and nonrepeating.

Unfortunately, what can happen is that whenever students see the radical sign, they think the number is irrational. A possible approach is to consider roots from the opposite direction. Rather than ask what is the square root of 64 or the cube root of 27, we might suggest that *every* number is the square root, the cube root, the fourth root, and so on, of some number (3 is the second root of 9, the third root of 27, etc.). From this vantage point, students can see that "square root" is just a way of indicating a relationship between two numbers. That the cube root of 27 is 3 indicates a special relationship between 3 and 27.

EXPANDED LESSON

How Close Is Close?

Based on Activity 5.5, p. 149

GRADE LEVEL: Seventh or eighth grade.

MATHEMATICS GOALS
- To develop the concept of density of the rational numbers.
- To reinforce the idea that fractions and decimal numbers are different symbolic notations for the same quantities.

THINKING ABOUT THE STUDENTS
Students are skilled at finding equivalent fractions and at converting fractions to decimals.

MATERIALS AND PREPARATION
- Have available copies of 10×10 grids (see Blackline Master 2) for students who need them.
- Have a transparency of the 10×10 grid sheet available for the "after" portion of the lesson.

lesson

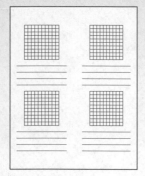

BLM 2

BEFORE

Begin with a simpler version of the task:
- Ask students to list four fractions between $\frac{1}{9}$ and $\frac{8}{9}$. This should be an easy task and should not require much, if any, discussion. Now ask students to find four fractions between $\frac{1}{2}$ and $\frac{9}{10}$. Have students share the fractions that they have identified and the strategies they used to find them. Resist telling students any method to use. The fractions $\frac{6}{10}$, $\frac{7}{10}$, and $\frac{8}{10}$ are easy to find; a fourth fraction may be a challenge if students are looking for fractions with common denominators. However, $\frac{2}{3}$, $\frac{3}{4}$, $\frac{5}{6}$, and $\frac{7}{8}$ are among the many other possible solutions. Listen to and encourage the class to discuss students' ideas about approaches to finding the fourth fraction.

The Task
- As a class, select two fractions that students believe are "really close." The task is to find 10 fractions that are between the two that the class decides on.

Establish Expectations
- Students can use any method they wish to find their fractions, but they have to be able to explain their methods and defend their results.

DURING
- Look for students who are identifying fractions using various strategies. Possible strategies include:
  - Trying different fractions without a system (often leading to fractions not in the desired interval).
  - Getting a large common denominator and then using consecutive numerators.
  - Converting the given fractions to decimals and using decimal representations instead of fractions.
- Resist telling students how to find the fractions. They will have to rely on their own understanding of fractions to come up with a solution.
- Think about what information you can glean from students' strategies about their understanding of fractions.

AFTER
- Have students share the fractions they have identified and the strategies they used to find them. Listen to, but do not judge, students' ideas. Instead, encourage the class to discuss students' ideas about approaches to finding the fractions.

- If students convert the fractions to decimals, see if they can convert one or more of the decimal numbers to fractions. Use this strategy to highlight that these are different symbolic notations for the same quantities. If you suspect that students are not convinced that the fraction and decimal number represent equivalent quantities, give them a copy of the 10 × 10 grids and ask them to represent the fraction quantity on one grid and the decimal quantity on another grid and compare the amounts.
- Ask students if they think they could find 10 more fractions between two of the closest fractions they found in this activity. Encourage students to discuss their conjectures. If there is any doubt, have the class work together to find 10 more fractions.
- At the conclusion of this lesson, explain that what they have been exploring is the concept of the *density of the rational numbers*. Students may be able to come up with their own definition of what it means to say that the rational numbers are *dense*.

ASSESSMENT NOTES

- Do students have a systematic way to determine fractions between the given fractions or are they haphazardly identifying possibilities?
- If students convert the fractions to decimals, do they only identify decimals in between the two given quantities? Can they also solve the problem using fractions? If they struggle with using fractions, this may indicate a weak understanding of equivalent fractions.
- How do students respond to finding more fractions between two of the closest fractions identified in the activity? Are they hesitant or do they seem to understand the concept of density?

next steps

- For students who are experiencing difficulty with the task, use as the "bookend" fractions one fraction whose denominator is a multiple of the other fraction (e.g., $\frac{2}{5}$ and $\frac{11}{25}$).
- Have students repeat the same activity, but now they are to identify two decimal numbers that they believe are "really close" and find at least 10 decimals between the two identified decimals.

Do students see that the exercise with decimals is equivalent to the one with fraction?

EXPANDED LESSON

DEVELOPING CONCEPTS OF RATIO AND PROPORTION

Proportional reasoning has been referred to as the capstone of the elementary curriculum and the cornerstone of algebra and beyond (Lesh, Post, & Behr, 1987). The ability to reason proportionally was a hallmark of Piaget's distinction between concrete levels of thought and formal operational thought. It represents the ability to begin to understand multiplicative relationships where most arithmetic concepts are additive in nature.

big ideas

1 A ratio is a comparison of any two quantities. A key developmental milestone is the ability of a student to begin to think of a ratio as a distinct entity, different from the two measures that made it up.

2 Proportions involve multiplicative rather than additive comparisons. Equal ratios result from multiplication or division, not from addition or subtraction.

3 Proportional thinking is developed through activities involving comparing and determining the equivalence of ratios and solving proportions in a wide variety of problem-based contexts and situations without recourse to rules or formulas.

Proportional Reasoning

Proportional reasoning is difficult to define. It is not something that you either can or cannot do but is developed over time through reasoning. One way to describe proportional reasoning is to say it is the ability to think about and compare multiplicative relationships between quantities. These relationships are represented symbolically as ratios.

Examples of Ratios in Different Contexts

A *ratio* is a comparison of two quantities or measures. Students may perceive ratios in different settings or contexts as very different ideas and, thus, different difficulties may arise as the setting or context changes.

Part-to-Whole Ratios
Ratios can express comparisons of a part to a whole, for example, the ratio of girls to all students in the class. Because fractions are also part-whole ratios, it follows that

every fraction is also a ratio. In the same way, percentages are ratios, and in fact, percentages are sometimes used to express ratios. Probabilities are ratios of a part of the sample space to the whole sample space.

Part-to-Part Ratios

A ratio can also compare one part of a whole to another part of the same whole. For example, the number of girls in the class can be compared to the number of boys. For other examples, consider Democrats to Republicans or peanuts to cashews. Although the probability of an event is a part-to-whole ratio, the *odds* of an event happening is a ratio of the number of ways an event can happen to the number of ways it cannot happen—a part-to-part ratio.

Rates as Ratios

Both part-to-whole and part-to-part ratios compare two measures of the same type. A ratio that compares measures of two different types is called a rate (see Figure 6.1). Miles per gallon, miles per hour, dollars per item, cents per pound, passengers per busload, and roses per bouquet are all rates. Relationships between two units of measure are also rates, for example, inches per foot, milliliters per liter, and centimeters per inch.

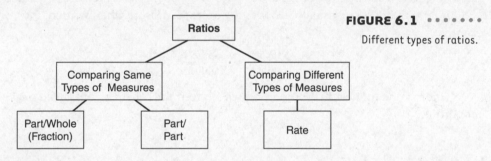

FIGURE 6.1 • • • • • • •

Different types of ratios.

Examples

Number of red roses to number of flowers in bouquet	$\frac{6}{24}$	Number of red roses to number of yellow roses	6 to18	Number of roses per bouquet	12 to 1
Number of footballs to number of balls in gym supply	$\frac{5}{25}$	Number of footballs to number of soccer balls	5 to 8	Number of footballs per class	5 : 5 or 1 : 1
Number of points earned to number of possible points	$\frac{80}{100}$	Number of points earned to number of points not earned	80 : 20	Number of points earned per pupil	$\frac{1140}{15}$ or $\frac{76}{1}$
Probability of getting a head with one coin toss	$\frac{1}{2}$	Odds of getting a head with one coin toss	1 to 1	Number of heads in 10 tosses	6 to 10

Other Examples of Ratio

In geometry, the ratios of corresponding parts of similar geometric figures are always the same. The ratio of the diagonal of any square to its side is always $\sqrt{2}$. π (pi) is the ratio of the circumference of a circle to the diameter. The trigonometric functions can be developed from ratios of sides of right triangles. The slope of a line or of a roof is a ratio of rise for each unit of horizontal distance or run.

In nature, the ratio known as the *golden ratio* is found in many spirals, from nautilus shells to the swirls of a pinecone or a pineapple. Artists and architects have used the same ratio in creating shapes that are naturally pleasing to the eye.

Proportions

The comparison of ratios forms an important category of tasks for students in developing proportional reasoning.

A *proportion* is a statement of equality between two ratios. Different notations for proportions can be used, for example:

$$3 : 9 = 4 : 12 \qquad \text{or} \qquad \tfrac{3}{9} = \tfrac{4}{12}$$

These might be read "3 is to 9 as 4 is to 12" or "3 and 9 are in the same ratio as 4 and 12."

A ratio that is a rate usually includes the units of measure when written, for example:

$$\frac{\$12.50}{1 \text{ gallon}} = \frac{\$37.50}{3 \text{ gallons}}$$

Finding one number in a proportion when given the other three is called *solving* a proportion.

Proportional Reasoning and Children

While *proportional reasoning* is difficult to define, you can gain a sense of what is involved by considering some of the characteristics of proportional thinkers (Lamon, 1999):

- Proportional thinkers understand ratios as distinct entities representing a relationship different from the quantities they compare.

- Proportional thinkers have a sense of covariation. That is, they understand relationships in which two quantities vary together and are able to see how the variation in one coincides with the variation in another.

- Proportional thinkers recognize proportional relationships as distinct from nonproportional relationships in real-world contexts.

- Proportional thinkers develop a wide variety of strategies for solving proportions or comparing ratios, most of which are based on informal strategies rather than prescribed algorithms.

It is estimated that more than half of the adult population cannot be viewed as proportional thinkers (Lamon, 1999). We do not acquire the habits and skills of proportional reasoning simply by getting older. Thus, instruction in proportional reasoning is a must. Research provides direction for how to help young students develop proportional thought processes (for example, see Karplus, Pulos, & Stage, 1983; Lamon, 1993; Lo & Watanabe, 1997; Noelting, 1980; Post, Behr, & Lesh, 1988). Some of these ideas are outlined here.

1. Provide ratio and proportion tasks in a wide range of contexts. These might include situations involving measurements, prices, geometric and other visual contexts, and rates such as miles per hour, pizza slices per person, or inches per foot.
2. Encourage discussion and experimentation in predicting and comparing ratios. Help children distinguish between proportional and nonproportional comparisons by providing examples of each and discussing the differences.
3. Help students relate proportional reasoning to existing processes. The concept of unit fractions is very similar to unit rates. Research indicates that the use of a unit rate for comparing ratios and solving proportions is the most common approach among middle school students even when cross-product methods have been taught. (This approach is explained later in this chapter.)
4. Recognize that symbolic or mechanical methods, such as the cross-product algorithm, for solving proportions do not develop proportional reasoning and should not be introduced until students have had many experiences with intuitive and conceptual methods.

In general, the research indicates that instruction can have an effect, especially if rules and algorithms for fraction computation, for comparing ratios, and for solving proportions are delayed. Students may need as much as three years' worth of opportunities to reason in multiplicative situations in order to adequately develop proportional reasoning skills. Premature use of rules encourages students to apply rules without thinking and, thus, the ability to reason proportionally often does not develop.

Informal Activities to Develop Proportional Reasoning

Five categories of informal activities are suggested here: identifying multiplicative situations, selection of equivalent ratios, comparison of ratios, scaling with ratio tables, and construction and measurement activities. Each provides a different opportunity for the development of proportional reasoning. The first category includes activities that can provide you with information about whether your students readily distinguish between proportional situations and additive or nonproportional ones. The remaining categories are not in any definitive sequence, nor are they designed to teach specific methods for solving proportions. Note that these are informal, exploratory activities. They do not directly produce algorithmic skills or procedures. However, it is critical that students spend ample time with these and similar activities to properly develop proportional reasoning.

Identifying Multiplicative Situations

Proportional reasoning develops slowly over the middle school years. An introductory unit of two or three weeks' duration in the sixth grade is not enough for most children to develop *true* proportional thought. Posing problems such as the following can provide you with information about the type of reasoning your students tend to use or can understand. The problem is adapted from the book *Adding It Up* (National Research Council, 2001).

> **Two weeks ago, two flowers were measured at 8 inches and 12 inches, respectively. Today they are 11 inches and 15 inches tall. Did the 8-inch or 12-inch flower grow more?**

 Before reading further, find and defend two different answers to this problem.

One answer is that they both grew the same amount—3 inches. This correct response is based on additive reasoning, which is one way to think about the situation. With additive reasoning, the same amount is added to each measure to result in two new measures. A second way to think about the problem is to compare the amount of growth to the original height of the flower. The first flower grew $\frac{3}{8}$ of its height while the second grew $\frac{3}{12}$. Based on this multiplicative view ($\frac{3}{8}$ *times as much* more), the first flower grew more. This is a proportional view of this change situation. An ability to understand the difference between these situations is an indication of proportional reasoning.

The following activity provides you with an opportunity to explore this distinction with your students.

ACTIVITY 6.1

Which Has More?

Provide students with the situations found in Figure 6.2. Whether students work individually or in groups, a follow-up class discussion is imperative. This discussion can provide you with insights into how students are thinking and can also provide opportunities for students to help others see the situations from different perspectives.

Do not prompt students by telling them to look for a multiplicative relationship but wait to see what sort of answers the students provide.

The problems in Figure 6.2 can be interpreted either additively or multiplicatively. The ambiguity is the key: If students recognize and understand the difference between the additive and multiplicative approaches, this is an indication of proportional reasoning. Clearly, the additive approach is correct, but do students suggest that there is another way to look at the situation (i.e., relatively or multiplicatively)? If at first they do not voluntarily suggest another way, you can always modify your question to suggest the relative or multiplicative perspective (e.g., Which class team has a larger proportion of girls?). If students are able to explain their reasoning from this perspective, they are thinking multiplicatively.

Watch for students who mindlessly set up proportions to attempt to solve these problems. For example, in responding to the dog problem, students may write $\frac{4}{8} = \frac{4}{11}$ or $\frac{4}{4} = \frac{4}{7}$ (growth to either final or beginning weights) because during their previous ratio and proportion instruction, this is what they remember they are "supposed to do."

FIGURE 6.2 • • • • • • • • •

Additive and multiplicative
situations.

Situation 1: Which class team has more girls?

The Stars

The Comets

Situation 2: Which fish tank has more goldfish?

Tank A

Tank B

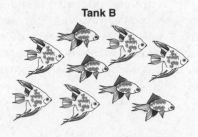

Situation 3: Which figure has more circles?

Figure A

Figure B

Situation 4: Shelley has two dogs, Ollie and Sandy. When she brought them home as puppies, Ollie weighed 4 pounds and Sandy weighed 7 pounds. Now Ollie weighs 8 pounds and Sandy weighs 11 pounds. Did Ollie or Sandy grow more?

You cannot predict in which context students will begin to think multiplicatively, and it may take time for students to do so. Consequently, students need continued opportunities to consider the additive versus multiplicative approach across varied contexts. Forcing the issue by requiring ahead of time that students solve these comparison problems by comparing ratios will only mask the true thinking of your students.

Equivalent-Ratio Selections

In selection activities, a ratio is presented, and students select an equivalent ratio from others presented. The focus should be on an intuitive rationale for why the pairs selected are in the same ratio. Sometimes numeric values will play a part to help students develop numeric methods to explain their reasoning. In later activities, students will be asked to construct an equivalent ratio without choices being provided.

In the activities it is extremely informative to include pairs of ratios that are not proportional but have a common difference. For example, $\frac{5}{8}$ and $\frac{9}{12}$ are not equivalent ratios, but the corresponding differences are the same: $8 - 5 = 12 - 9$. Students who focus on this additive relationship are not seeing the multiplicative relationship of proportionality.

BLM 5, 6

ACTIVITY 6.2

Look-Alike Rectangles

Provide groups of students with a copy of Blackline Master 5 and have them cut out the 10 rectangles. Three of the rectangles (A, I, and D) have sides in the ratio of 3 to 4. Rectangles C, F, and H have sides in the ratio of 5 to 8. J, E, and G have sides in the ratio of 1 to 3. Rectangle B is a square, so its sides are in the ratio of 1 to 1.

The students' task is to group the rectangles into three sets of three that "look alike" with one "oddball." If your students know the word *similar* from geometry, you can use that instead of "look alike." To explain what "look alike" means, draw three rectangles on the board with two that are similar and one that is clearly dissimilar to the other two, as in the following example. Have students use their language to explain why rectangles 1 and 3 are alike.

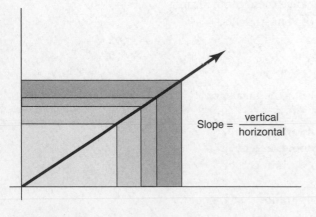

When students have decided on their groupings, stop and discuss reasons they classified the rectangles as they did. Be prepared for some students to try to match sides or look for rectangles that have the same amount of difference between them. Do not evaluate any rationale offered. Next have them measure and record the sides of each rectangle to the nearest half-centimeter and calculate the ratios of the short to long sides for each. Blackline Master 6 can be used to record the data. Discuss these results and ask students to offer explanations. If the groups are formed of proportional (similar) rectangles, the ratios within each group will all be the same.

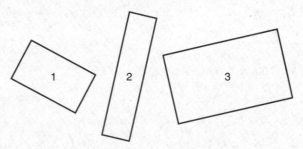

$$\text{Slope} = \frac{\text{vertical}}{\text{horizontal}}$$

FIGURE 6.3 •

The slope of a line through a stack of proportional rectangles is equal to the ratio of the two sides.

From a geometric standpoint, "Look-Alike Rectangles" is an activity about similarity. The two concepts—proportionality and similarity—are closely connected. However, if the activity were done with figures other than rectangles, the congruent angles of similar figures would defeat the purpose because students could simply find congruent corresponding angles without thinking proportionally.

Another characteristic of proportional rectangles can be observed by stacking like rectangles aligned at one corner, as in Figure 6.3. Placing a straightedge across the diagonals, you will see that opposite corners also line up. If the rectangles are placed on a coordinate axis with the common corner at the origin, the slope of the line connecting the corners is the ratio of the sides. Here is a connection between proportional reasoning and algebra (i.e., slope).

ACTIVITY 6.3

Different Objects, Same Ratios

Prepare cards with distinctly different objects, as shown in Figure 6.4. Given one card, students are to select a card on which the ratio of the two types of objects is the same. This task moves students to a numeric approach rather than a visual one and introduces the notion of ratios as rates. A unit rate is depicted on a card that shows exactly one of either of the two types of objects. For example, the card with three boxes and one truck provides one unit rate. A unit rate for the other ratio is not shown. What would it be? Objects paired with coins or bills is a way to introduce price as a ratio.

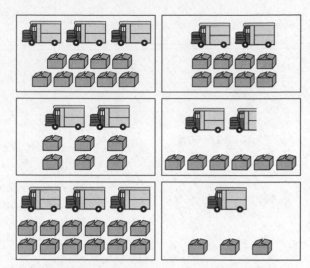

On which cards is the ratio of trucks to boxes the same? Also, compare trucks to trucks and boxes to boxes.

FIGURE 6.4 •

Rate cards: Match cards with the same rate of boxes per truck.

Comparing Ratios

An understanding of proportional situations includes being able to compare ratios. Consider the following problem:

Two camps of Scouts are having pizza parties. The Bear Camp ordered enough so that every 3 campers will have 2 pizzas. The leader of the Raccoons ordered enough so that there would be 3 pizzas for every 5 campers. Did the Bear campers or the Raccoon campers have more pizza to eat?

 Get some scrap paper and solve this problem without using any numeric algorithms such as cross-products. You may want to draw pictures or use counters, but there is no prescribed method to use.

Here are two different possibilities for informal methods. When the pizzas are sliced into fractional parts (Figure 6.5a), the approach is to look for a unit rate—pizzas per camper. This is accomplished by sharing equal amounts of pizza among the campers. But notice that this problem does not say that the camps have only 3 and 5 campers, respectively. Thus, any multiples of 2 to 3 and 3 to 5 can be used to make the comparison. Suppose three "clones" of the 2-to-3 ratio and two clones of the 3-to-5 ratio are made so that the number of campers getting a like number of pizzas can be compared (Figure 6.5b). From a fraction perspective, this is like getting common numerators. Because there are more campers in the Raccoon ratio (larger denominator), there is less pizza for each camper.

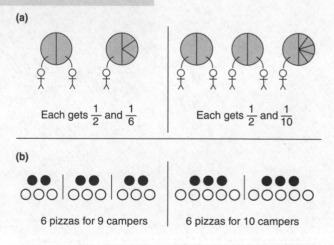

(a)

Each gets $\frac{1}{2}$ and $\frac{1}{6}$ | Each gets $\frac{1}{2}$ and $\frac{1}{10}$

(b)

6 pizzas for 9 campers | 6 pizzas for 10 campers

FIGURE 6.5 •

Two informal methods for comparing two ratios.

The following activity suggests some similar comparison tasks.

EXPANDED LESSON

(pages 177–178)

A complete lesson plan
based on "Comparing Ratios"
can be found at the end
of this chapter.

ACTIVITY 6.4

Comparing Ratios

Pose problems to students that are similar to the following. Allow them to solve the problems in any manner they wish as long as they can explain why their answers make sense. Do not allow any algorithms that the students cannot defend in the context of the problem.

a. Terry can run 4 laps in 12 minutes. Susan can run 2 laps in 5 minutes. Who is the faster runner, or are they equally fast?

b. Jack and Jill were picking strawberries at the Pick Your Own Berry Patch. Jack "sampled" 5 berries every 25 minutes. Jill ate 3 berries every 10 minutes. If they both pick at about the same speed, who will bring home more berries, or will they each take home the same?

c. Some of the hens in Farmer Brown's chicken farm lay brown eggs and the others lay white eggs. Farmer Brown noticed that in the large hen house he collected about 4 brown eggs for every 10 white ones. In the smaller hen house the ratio of brown to white was 1 to 3. In which hen house do the hens lay more brown eggs, or is it the same in each?

d. Talks-A-Lot phone company charges 70¢ for every 15 minutes. Reaching Out phone company charges $1.00 for 20 minutes. Which company is offering the cheaper rate, or are the rates the same?

e. Which rectangle is "fatter": a 3×5 rectangle or an 8×14 rectangle, or are they equally "fat"—similar?

The suggested problems in Activity 6.4 are simply to provide you with some ideas. You can easily create your own. You can also change the numbers to make the tasks easier or harder.

Assessment Note

How do your students approach these problems? Do they use a variety of means, or do they always use the same approach? Many middle school students tend to use unit rates to compare ratios, even when a "cloning" approach may be easier. If students always use the unit rate approach, encourage them to consider different approaches. A nonflexible or algorithmic approach, even if correct, may signal that a student is simply following rules.

Scaling with Ratio Tables

Ratio tables or charts that show how two variable quantities are related are often good ways to organize information. Consider the following table:

Acres	5	10	15	20	25		
Pine trees	75	150	225				

If the task were to find the number of trees for 65 acres of land or the number of acres needed for 750 trees, students can easily proceed by using addition. That is, they can add 5's along the top row and 75's along the bottom row until the problems are solved. Although this is efficient and orderly, it is an additive procedure and does little as a task to promote proportional reasoning. As illustrated in the next activity, the instructional "trick" is to select numbers that require some form of multiplicative reasoning.

ACTIVITY 6.5

Using Ratio Tables

Given a situation like one of the following, the task is to build a ratio table and use it to answer the question. Tasks are adapted from Lamon (1999, p. 183).

a. A person who weighs 160 pounds on Earth will weigh 416 pounds on the planet Jupiter. How much will a person weigh on Jupiter who weighs 120 pounds on Earth?

b. At the local college, 5 out of every 8 seniors live in apartments. How many of the 30 senior math majors are likely to live in an apartment?

c. The tax on a purchase of $20 is $1.12. How much tax will there be on a purchase of $45.50?

d. When in Australia you can exchange $4.50 in U.S. dollars for $6 Australian. How much is $17.50 Australian in U.S. dollars?

Note that in no case is it easy to simply add or subtract to get to the desired entry for the tasks in this activity. You may recognize these tasks as typical "solve the proportion" tasks. One ratio and one part of a second are given with the task being to find the fourth number. However, resist showing students a traditional algorithm. The ratio-table approach is not rule oriented but rather focuses on multiplicative reasoning. Tasks such as these should come long before any formal approach is suggested to ensure students rely on reasoning, not rote algorithms, to solve the tasks. You will likely need to model how a ratio-table approach can be used. Nonetheless, keep in mind that ratio tables are ways to record an individual's thought processes and that there are several ways to solve these types of tasks. Figure 6.6 shows three different ways to solve the Jupiter weight task using ratio tables.

Different formats can also be used, but the format of the ratio table is not important. In fact, some students may not use a table format at all but simply draw arrows and explain in words how they went from one ratio to another. The key is to maintain focus on multiplicative *reasoning*. The following problem and the table in Figure 6.7 are from Lamon (1999, p. 233) and show another type of format. Notice that the numbers are not "nice" at all.

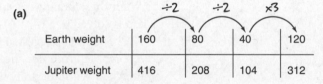

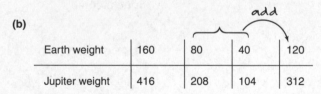

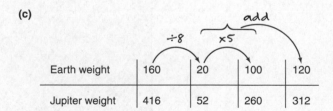

FIGURE 6.6 •

160 pounds on Earth is 416 pounds on Jupiter. If something weighs 120 pounds on Earth, how many pounds would it weigh on Jupiter? Three solutions using ratio tables.

Cheese is $4.25 per pound. How much will 12.13 pounds cost?

INFORMAL ACTIVITIES TO DEVELOP PROPORTIONAL REASONING

	Pounds	Cost	Notes
A	1	4.25	Given
B	10	42.50	A × 10
C	2	8.50	A × 2
D	0.1	0.425	A ÷ 10
E	12.1	51.425	B + C + D
F	0.01	0.0425	D ÷ 10
G	0.03	0.1275	F × 3
H	12.13	51.5525	E + G

FIGURE 6.7 •

A more structured ratio table. The notes column shows what was done in each step. The task is to find the cost of 12.13 pounds.

The format in Figure 6.7 allows for easier tracking of what was done at each step. The format is just that—a format—a way to organize and record one's reasoning. Since there are likely to be several different reasonable ratio tables, the class can discuss similarities and differences between tables. Such discussions can help students realize there are multiple ways to solve these tasks and provide opportunities for students to possibly see more efficient approaches than the ones they are currently using.

With ratio tables, students are using multiplicative relationships to transform a given ratio into an equivalent ratio. As Lamon points out, the process is not random. Students should mentally devise a plan for getting from one number to another. Consider the following problem:

How many pounds of grass seed can be purchased for $18 if you can buy 28 pounds for $35?

 Before reading further, write down a plan for moving from 35 to 18. Then create a ratio table using your plan to solve the problem. Compare your strategy with someone else's, or try to find another one yourself.

One possible plan for getting from 35 to 18 follows: 35 ÷ 5 is 7; 7 × 2 is 14. (Now you need 4 more.) Go back to 7: 7 ÷ 7 is 1; 1 × 4 is 4. Now add 4 and 14 to make 18. When these same steps are applied to 28, you get 14.4 pounds, and the foregoing problem is solved.

The tasks suggested in Activity 6.5 have quite reasonable numbers. However, as you can see from the cheese example, it is quite possible to use this technique with almost any numbers. By using easy multiples and divisors, often the arithmetic can be done mentally.

Assessment Note

Since ratio tables are written records of how a student reasoned through a particular problem, they can serve as a great assessment tool. A lengthy or hit-or-miss approach may signal that the student is merely guessing rather than using good multiplicative reasoning. As students work through various combinations of numbers and operations and are encouraged to share different approaches to the same problem, they can become more skillful at manipulating the numbers, which in turn can reduce the number of steps taken to solve a problem.

It should also be clear to students why the same factor must be used for both parts of the table. For example, in row A of Figure 6.7, we multiply 1 by 10 and also 4.25 by 10. In row G, we multiply both parts by 3. (Each pair of entries comprises a ratio.)

Asking students to explain why they "do the same thing" to both parts of the table can tell you if they are doing it simply because they have seen others do it or because they understand why it is necessary. Ask students to compare the results when they use the same factor for both parts and when they use it for only one of the parts. Do they notice that the ratios are not equivalent when they operate on only one part of the table? Both parts of the ratios must be operated on in the same way or the ratio changes.

Any ratio table provides data that can be graphed. Make each axis correspond to one of the quantities in the table. This idea is developed in the next activity.

ACTIVITY 6.6

Graphs Showing Ratios

Have students make a graph of the data from a collection of equal ratios that they have scaled or discussed. The graph in Figure 6.8 is of the ratios of two sides of similar rectangles. If only a few ratios have actually been computed, the graph can be drawn carefully and then used to determine other equivalent ratios. This is especially interesting when there is a physical model to coincide with the ratio. In the rectangle example, students can draw rectangles with sides determined by the graphs and compare them to the original rectangles. A unit ratio can be found by locating the point on the line that is directly above or to the right of the number 1 on the graph. (There are actually two unit ratios for every ratio. Why?) Students can then use the unit ratio to scale up to other values and check to see that they are on the graph as well. Note that the slope of any line through the origin is a ratio of the y-coordinate of any point on that line to the corresponding x-coordinate.

Graphs provide another way of thinking about proportions, and they connect proportional thought to algebraic interpretations. All graphs of equivalent ratios fall along straight lines that pass through the origin. If the equation of one of these lines is written in the form $y = mx$, the slope m is always one of the equivalent ratios. As an illustration, consider the graph of the prices of widgets in Figure 6.9.

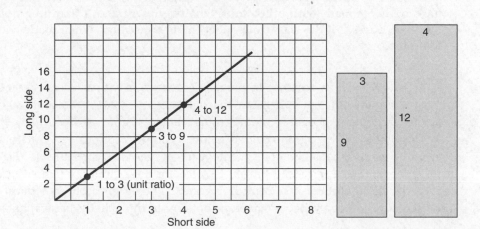

FIGURE 6.8 • • • • • • • •

Graphs show ratios of sides in similar rectangles.

INFORMAL ACTIVITIES TO DEVELOP PROPORTIONAL REASONING

FIGURE 6.9 • • • • • • • • • • •

Graph of price-to-item ratios.

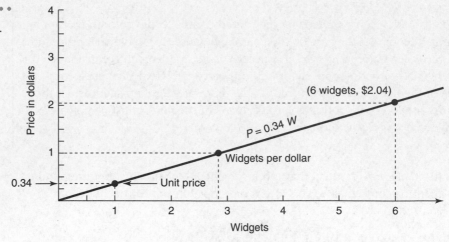

Construction and Measurement Activities

In these activities, students make measurements or construct physical or visual models of equivalent ratios in order to provide a tangible example of a proportion as well as look at numeric relationships.

ACTIVITY 6.7

Different Units, Equal Ratios

Cut strips of adding machine tape all the same length, and give one strip to each group in your class. Each group is to measure the strip using a different unit. Possible units include different Cuisenaire rods, a piece of chalk, a pencil, the edge of a book or index card, or standard units such as inches or centimeters. When every group has measured the strip, ask for the measure of one of the groups, and display the unit of measure. Next, hold up the unit of measure used by another group, and have the class compare it with the first unit. See if the class can estimate the measurement that the second group found. The ratio of the measuring units should be the inverse of the measurements made with those units. For example, if two units are in a ratio of 2 to 3, the respective measures will be in a ratio of 3 to 2. Examine measurements made with other units. Finally, present a unit that no group has used, and see if the class can predict the measurement when made with that unit.

Activity 6.7 can be extended by providing each group with an identical set of four strips of quite different lengths. Good lengths might be 20, 50, 80, and 120 cm. As before, each group measures the strips using a different unit.

This time, have each group enter data into a common spreadsheet. (Alternatively, share group data so that all groups can enter data on their own spreadsheets.) Figure 6.10 shows what a spreadsheet might look like for three groups. A template can be prepared ahead of time, or students can create their own spreadsheets. Almost all spreadsheets will offer a variety of graphing options. In this activity, bar graphs show

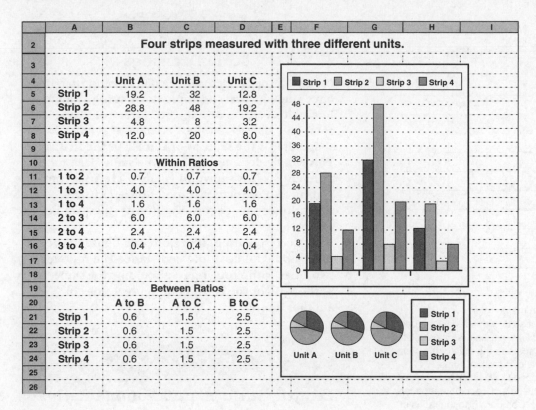

FIGURE 6.10 · · · · · · ·

A spreadsheet can be used to record data, create tables of interesting ratios, and produce bar and circle graphs.

Source: Screen reprinted with permission from Apple Computer, Inc.

Four strips measured with three different units.

	Unit A	Unit B	Unit C
Strip 1	19.2	32	12.8
Strip 2	28.8	48	19.2
Strip 3	4.8	8	3.2
Strip 4	12.0	20	8.0

Within Ratios

	Unit A	Unit B	Unit C
1 to 2	0.7	0.7	0.7
1 to 3	4.0	4.0	4.0
1 to 4	1.6	1.6	1.6
2 to 3	6.0	6.0	6.0
2 to 4	2.4	2.4	2.4
3 to 4	0.4	0.4	0.4

Between Ratios

	A to B	A to C	B to C
Strip 1	0.6	1.5	2.5
Strip 2	0.6	1.5	2.5
Strip 3	0.6	1.5	2.5
Strip 4	0.6	1.5	2.5

the actual measurements for each group and circle graphs show each measure in ratio to the sum of the measures (i.e., a percentage of total measures).

Once the graphs are completed, there are numerous opportunities to observe and explore proportions. The bar graphs, though different, all look "alike." Since the circle graphs illustrate the ratios rather than the actual measurements, they will be identical or nearly so. Within ratios (for a set of strips) and between ratios (one unit to another) are easily calculated with the spreadsheet. (Within and between ratios are discussed later in the chapter.)

Continue the exploration by introducing a new strip. If you know its measure with any one of the units, what will its measure be with the other units? Similarly, if a new unit of measure is introduced, how can the measures of the strips be determined? Can this be done by comparing the new unit with an old one? If a known strip is measured with the new unit, can all other measures and ratios be determined?

Bar graphs and circle plots are also easily made with a TI-73 graphing calculator. If technology is not available, this same activity can be done by hand. To make circle graphs, use the hundredths disk in the Blackline Masters.

The connection between proportional reasoning and the geometric concept of similarity is very important. Similar figures provide a visual representation of proportions, and proportional thinking enhances the understanding of similarity. Whenever similarity is discussed, ratios in the figures should almost certainly be explored. The next two activities are aimed at this connection.

BLM 3

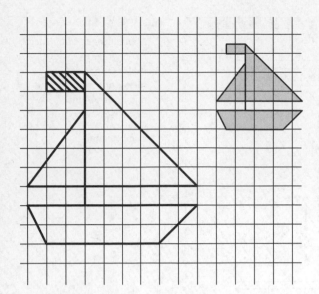

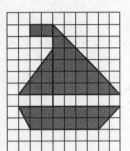

Use a metric ruler
• Choose two lengths on one boat and form a ratio (use a calculator). Compare to the ratio of the same parts of the other boats.
• Choose two boats. Measure the same part of each boat, and form a ratio. Compare with the ratios of another part.
• Compare the areas of the big sails with the lengths of the bottom sides.

FIGURE 6.11 ••••••••••••••••••••••••••••••

Comparing similar figures drawn on grids.

ACTIVITY 6.8

Scale Drawings

On grid or dot paper (see the Blackline Masters), have students draw a simple shape using straight lines with vertices on the dots. After one shape is complete, have them draw a larger or smaller shape that is the same as or similar to the first. This can be done on a grid of the same size or a different size, as shown in Figure 6.11. After completing two or three pictures of different sizes, the ratios of the lengths of different sides can be compared.

Corresponding sides from one figure to the next should all be in the same ratio. The ratio of two sides within one figure should be the same as the ratio of the corresponding two sides in another figure.

ACTIVITY 6.9

Length, Surface, and Volume Ratios

A three-dimensional version of Activity 6.8 can be done with blocks, as shown in Figure 6.12. Using 1-inch or 2-cm wooden cubes, make a simple "building." Then make a similar but larger building and compare measures. A different size can also be made using different-sized blocks. To measure buildings made with different blocks, use a common unit such as centimeters.

Activities 6.8 and 6.9 involve area and volume as well as length. Comparisons of corresponding lengths, areas, and volumes in proportional figures lead to some interesting ratios. If two figures are proportional (similar), any two linear dimensions you measure will be in the same ratio on each, say, 1 to k. Corresponding areas, however, will be in the ratio of 1 to k^2, and corresponding volumes in the ratio of 1 to k^3. Try this with some constructions of your own.

As a means of contrasting proportional situations with additive ones, start with a figure on a grid or a building made with blocks and add two units to every dimension in the figure. The result will be larger but will not look at all the same. Try this with a simple rectangle that is 1 cm by 15 cm. The new rectangle is twice as "thick" (2 cm) but only a bit longer. It will not appear to be the same shape as the original.

Dynamic geometry software such as *The Geometer's Sketchpad* (Key Curriculum Press) offers a very effective method of exploring the idea of ratio. In Figure 6.13, two lengths are drawn on a grid using the "snap-to-grid" option. The lengths are measured, and two ratios are computed. As the length of either line segment is changed, the measures and ratios are updated instantly. In this example, notice that the second pair of lines has the same difference but that the ratios are not the same. A similar drawing could be prepared for the overhead on a transparency of a centimeter dot grid if software was not available.

Solving Proportions and Percent Problems

The activities to this point have been designed to lead students to an intuitive concept of ratio and proportion to help in the development of proportional reasoning.

One practical value of proportional reasoning is to use observed proportions to find unknown values. Knowledge of one ratio can often be used to find a value in the other. Comparison pricing, using scales on maps, and solving percentage problems are just a few everyday instances where solving proportions is required. Students need to learn to set up proportions symbolically and to solve them.

Within and Between Ratios

When examining two ratios, it is sometimes useful to think of them as being either *within* ratios or *between* ratios. A ratio of two measures in the same setting is a *within* ratio. For example, in the case of similar rectangles, the ratio of length to width for any one rectangle is a within ratio, that is, it is "within" the context of that rectangle. For all similar rectangles, corresponding within ratios will be equal.

A *between* ratio is a ratio of two corresponding measures in different situations. In the case of similar rectangles, the ratio of the length of one rectangle to the length of another is a between ratio; that is, it is "between" the two rectangles. For two similar rectangles, all of the between ratios will be equal. However, the between ratios for each pair of similar rectangles will be different.

 Consider three rectangles A, B, and C. A measures 2 × 6, B measures 3 × 9, and C measures 8 × 24. Find the within ratio for each rectangle. This should convince you that the rectangles are similar. Now examine the between ratios for A and B, and for A and C. Why are these ratios different?

Figure 6.4 (p. 161) shows six pictures of trucks and boxes. The within ratios are trucks to boxes (within one picture). The between ratios are from trucks to trucks and boxes to boxes. Be sure that you can distinguish within and between ratios in that figure.

The simple drawing in Figure 6.14 is a nice generic way of looking at two ratios and determining if a ratio is between or within. A drawing similar to this will be very helpful to students in setting up

Similar "buildings" can be made by changing the number of blocks in each dimension (factor of change) or by using different-sized blocks.

FIGURE 6.12 • • • • • • • • • • • • • • • • • •

Similar constructions.

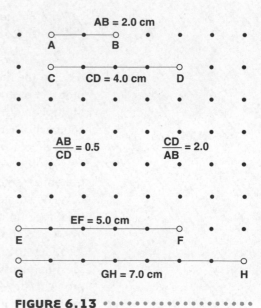

FIGURE 6.13 • • • • • • • • • • • • • • • • • •

Dynamic geometry software or just a centimeter grid can be used to discuss ratios of two lengths.

169

SOLVING PROPORTIONS AND PERCENT PROBLEMS

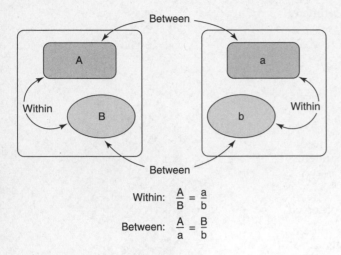

Within: $\dfrac{A}{B} = \dfrac{a}{b}$

Between: $\dfrac{A}{a} = \dfrac{B}{b}$

FIGURE 6.14 •

Given a proportional situation, the two between ratios and the two within ratios will be the same.

proportions. Pick any two equivalent truck and box pictures and place the numbers in this figure.

An Informal Approach

Traditional textbooks show students how to set up an equation of two ratios involving an unknown, "cross-multiply," and solve for the unknown. This can be a very mechanical approach and will almost certainly lead to confusion and error. Although you may wish eventually to cover the cross-product algorithm, it is well worth the time for students to find ways to solve proportions using their own ideas first. If you have been exploring proportions informally, students will have a good foundation on which to build their own approaches.

To illustrate some intuitive approaches for solving proportions, consider the following tasks:

Tammy bought 3 widgets for $2.40. At the same price, how much would 10 widgets cost?

Tammy bought 4 widgets for $3.75. How much would a dozen widgets cost?

 Before reading further, solve these two problems using an approach for each that seems most reasonable to you.

In the first situation, it is perhaps easiest to determine the cost of one widget—the unit rate or unit price. This can be found by dividing the price of three widgets by 3. Multiplying this unit rate of $0.80 per widget by 10 will produce the answer. This approach is referred to as a *unit-rate* method of solving proportions. Notice that the unit rate is a within ratio.

In the second problem, a unit-rate approach could be used, but the division does not appear to be easy. Since 12 is a multiple of 4, it is easier to notice that the cost of a dozen is 3 times the cost of 4. This is called a *factor-of-change* method. It could have been used on the first problem but would have been awkward. The factor of change between 3 and 10 is $3\frac{1}{3}$. Multiplying $2.40 by $3\frac{1}{3}$ will produce the correct answer. Although the factor-of-change method is a useful way to think about proportions, it is most frequently used when the numbers are compatible. Students should be given problems in which the numbers lend themselves to both approaches so that they will explore both methods. The factor of change is a between ratio.

For each of the following two problems, place the numbers in a little drawing of two ratios like Figure 6.14. Solve each problem. Think about within or between ratios matching up. Do not use cross-multiplication.

Chapter 6 **DEVELOPING CONCEPTS OF RATIO AND PROPORTION**

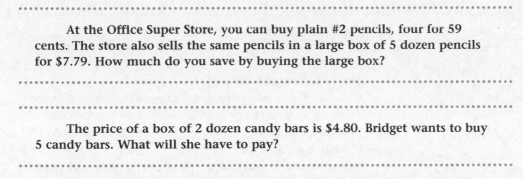

At the Office Super Store, you can buy plain #2 pencils, four for 59 cents. The store also sells the same pencils in a large box of 5 dozen pencils for $7.79. How much do you save by buying the large box?

The price of a box of 2 dozen candy bars is $4.80. Bridget wants to buy 5 candy bars. What will she have to pay?

To solve the pencil problem, you might notice that the between ratio of pencils to pencils is 4 to 60, or 1 to 15. If you multiply the 59 cents by 15, the factor of change, you will get the price of the box of 60 if the pencils were sold at the same price. In the candy problem, the within ratio of 24 to $4.80 is easy to use to get the unit rate of 20 cents per candy bar. But what do you do if the numbers don't "come out nicely" like they do in these problems?

Try solving the same problems with new numbers that do not work out so easily. If you are having difficulty with the new problems, discuss them with a friend.

 Try the following problem. Make a little sketch as before and use a technique you have figured out yourself. (Do this now before reading on.)

Brian can run 5 km in 18.4 minutes. If he keeps on running at the same speed, how far can he run in 23 minutes?

The first situation for your sketch is Brian's 5-km run (5 km and 18.4 minutes). The second situation is the unknown distance and 23 minutes. There are at least two things you might consider, and one is no easier than the other. You could look at the between ratios of minutes to minutes in order to find a factor of change. That is, what do you multiply 18.4 by to get 23? On the calculator, compute 23 ÷ 18.4 to get 1.25, the factor of change. Now 5 km × 1.25 is 6.25 km.

The second possibility is to get a unit rate for the 5 km and multiply by 23. That would mean divide both the 5 and the 18.4 by 18.4 (like simplifying a fraction to a denominator of 1). The calculator yields 0.2717391, or about 0.27 km per minute. Multiply this unit rate by 23 minutes and you get 6.2499993 km. In both cases, the longer distance is 6.25 km.

What is important here is to see how to use multiplication to solve the proportional situation. Furthermore, notice that the calculations are based on ideas already developed. The sketch of the two ratios helps keep things straight and avoids any ambiguous cross-multiplying.

The Cross-Product Algorithm

The methods just described come close to being well-defined algorithms, though they are a bit more flexible than cross-product methods. The reality is that

SOLVING PROPORTIONS AND PERCENT PROBLEMS

Apples are 3 pounds for 89 cents. How much should you pay for 5 pounds?

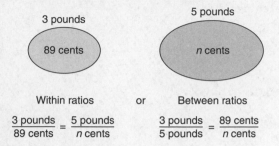

Within ratios   or   Between ratios

$$\frac{3 \text{ pounds}}{89 \text{ cents}} = \frac{5 \text{ pounds}}{n \text{ cents}} \qquad \frac{3 \text{ pounds}}{5 \text{ pounds}} = \frac{89 \text{ cents}}{n \text{ cents}}$$

FIGURE 6.15 •

A simple drawing helps in a price-to-ratio problem.

the computations involved are exactly the same as in cross-multiplication. Yet some teachers may still want to teach cross-multiplication.

Draw a Simple Model

Given a ratio word problem, the greatest difficulty students have is setting up a correct proportion or equation of two ratios, one of which includes the missing value. "Which fractions do I make? Where does the *x* go?"

Rather than drill and drill in the hope that they will somehow eventually get it, show students how to sketch a simple picture that will help them determine what parts are related. In Figure 6.15, a simple model is drawn for a typical rate or price problem. The two equations in the figure come from setting up within and between ratios.

Solve the Proportion

Examine the left (within) ratios in the same way as we did for Brian's 5-km race: Find out what to multiply the left fraction by to get the right. To do this, we would divide 5 by 3 and then multiply that result by 89:

$$\frac{5}{3} \times 89$$

Looking at the same left equation in Figure 6.15, we could also determine the unit price or the price for 1 pound by dividing the 89 cents by 3 and then multiplying this result by 5 to determine the price of 5 pounds:

$$\frac{89}{3} \times 5$$

Now look what happens if we cross-multiply in the original equation:

$$3n = 5 \times 89$$

$$n = \frac{5 \times 89}{3}$$

This equation can be solved by dividing the 5 by 3 and multiplying by 89 or dividing 89 by 3 and multiplying by 5. These are exactly the two devices we employed in our more intuitive approach. If you cross-multiply the between ratios, you get exactly the same result. Furthermore, you get the same result if you had written the two ratios inverted, that is, with the reciprocals of each fraction. Try it!

So if you want to develop a cross-product algorithm, it is not unreasonable to do problems like these while encouraging students to use their own methods. If you write out the computations involved, a very small amount of direct teaching can develop the cross-product approach. But why hurry?

In Figure 6.16, a problem involving rates of speed is modeled with simple lines representing the two distances.

Jack can run an 8-km race in 37 minutes. If he runs at the same rate, how long should it take him to run a 5-km race?

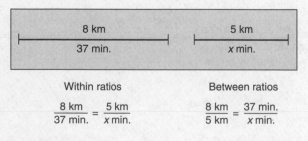

Within ratios   Between ratios

$$\frac{8 \text{ km}}{37 \text{ min.}} = \frac{5 \text{ km}}{x \text{ min.}} \qquad \frac{8 \text{ km}}{5 \text{ km}} = \frac{37 \text{ min.}}{x \text{ min.}}$$

FIGURE 6.16 •

Line segments can be used to model both time and distance.

• •

Chapter 6 **DEVELOPING CONCEPTS OF RATIO AND PROPORTION**

The distance and the time for each run are modeled with the same line. You cannot see time, but it fits into the distance covered. All equal-rates-of-speed problems can be modeled this way. There really is no significant difference from the drawing used for the apples. Again, it is just as acceptable to write between ratios as within ratios, and students need not worry about which one goes on top as long as the ratios are written in the same order. The model helps with this difficulty.

Activities Leading to Proportions

In the preceding discussion, simple rate problems were used to help students develop a technique for solving proportions. The next two activities illustrate other common uses of proportional reasoning.

ACTIVITY 6.10

Scale Drawings

Provide students with a drawing of a simple geometric figure, including its dimensions. The task is to create a new drawing that is either larger or smaller than the given one. One dimension of the new drawing is specified (see Figure 6.17 for an example). Students can set up between or within ratios and determine the other dimensions by solving the proportion.

This scale drawing activity is somewhat simplistic, but it provides students with the essential ideas for setting up proportions. Here are some more interesting situations to consider:

• If you wanted to make a scale model of the solar system and use a Ping-Pong ball for the earth, how far away should the sun be? How large a ball would you need?

• What scale should be used to draw a scale map of your city (or some interesting region) so that it will nicely fit onto a standard piece of poster board?

• Use the scale on a map to estimate the distance and travel time between two points of interest.

• Roll a toy car down a ramp, timing the trip with a stopwatch. How fast was the car traveling in miles per hour? If the speed is proportional to the size of the car, how fast would this have been for a real car?

• Your little sister wants a table and chair for her doll. Her doll is 14 inches tall. How big should you make the table?

• Determine the various distances that a ten-speed bike travels in one turn of the pedals. You will need to count the sprocket teeth on the front and back gears.

Have you ever wondered how scientists estimate the number of bass in a lake or the number of monarch

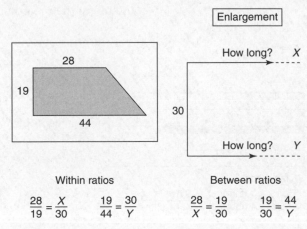

Within ratios

$$\frac{28}{19} = \frac{X}{30} \qquad \frac{19}{44} = \frac{30}{Y}$$

Between ratios

$$\frac{28}{X} = \frac{19}{30} \qquad \frac{19}{30} = \frac{44}{Y}$$

FIGURE 6.17 • • • • • • • • • • • • • • • • • •

Pictures help in establishing equal ratios.

butterflies that migrate each year to Mexico? One method often used is a capture-recapture technique modeled in the next activity.

ACTIVITY 6.11

Capture-Recapture

Prepare a shoebox full of some uniform small object such as centicubes or plastic chips. You could also use a larger box filled with Styrofoam packing "peanuts." If the box is your lake and the objects are the fish you want to count, how can you estimate the number without actually counting them? Remember, if they were fish, you couldn't even see them! Have a student reach into the box and "capture" a representative sample of the "fish." For a large box, you may want to capture more than a handful. "Tag" each fish by marking it in some way—marking pen or sticky dot. Count and record the number tagged, and then return them to the box. The assumption of the scientist is that tagged animals will mix uniformly with the larger population, so mix them thoroughly. Next, have five to ten students make a recapture of fish from the box. Each counts the total captured and the number in the capture that are tagged. Accumulate these data.

Now the task is to use all of the information to estimate the number of fish in the lake. The recapture data provide an estimated ratio of tagged to untagged fish. The number tagged to the total population should be in the same ratio. After solving the proportion, have students count the actual items in the box to see how close their estimate is.

Percent Problems as Proportions

Percent has traditionally been included as a topic with ratio and proportion because percent is one form of ratio, a part-to-whole ratio. In Chapter 4, it was shown that percent problems can be connected to fraction concepts. Here the same part-to-whole fraction concept of percent will be extended to ratio and proportion concepts. Ideally, all of these ideas (fractions, decimals, ratio, proportion, and percent) should be conceptually integrated. The better that students connect these ideas, the more flexible and useful their reasoning and problem-solving skills will be.

Equivalent Fractions as Proportions

First consider how equivalent fractions can be interpreted as a proportion using the same simple models already used. In Figure 6.18, a line segment is partitioned in two different ways: in fourths on one side and in twelfths on the other. In the previous examples, proportions were established based on two amounts of apples, two different distances or runs, and two different sizes of drawings. Here only one thing is measured—the part of a whole—but it is measured or partitioned two ways: in fourths and in twelfths.

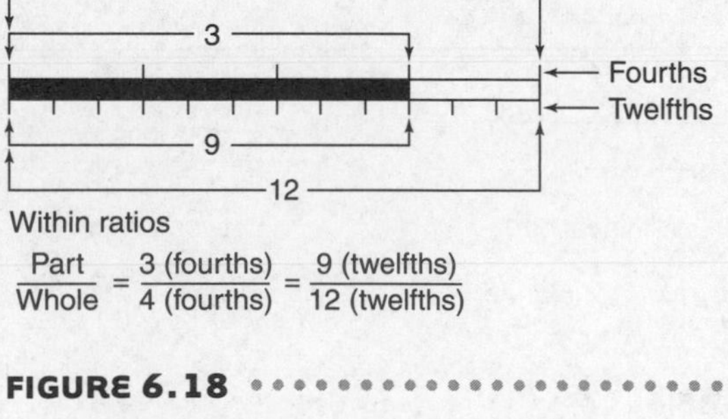

The within ratios are ratios of part to whole within each measurement. Within ratios result in the usual equivalent fraction equation, $\frac{3}{4} = \frac{9}{12}$ (3 fourths are to 4 fourths as 9 twelfths are

Within ratios

$$\frac{\text{Part}}{\text{Whole}} = \frac{3 \text{ (fourths)}}{4 \text{ (fourths)}} = \frac{9 \text{ (twelfths)}}{12 \text{ (twelfths)}}$$

FIGURE 6.18 •

Equivalent fractions as proportions.

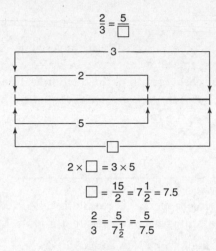

$$\frac{2}{3} = \frac{5}{\square}$$

$$2 \times \square = 3 \times 5$$

$$\square = \frac{15}{2} = 7\frac{1}{2} = 7.5$$

$$\frac{2}{3} = \frac{5}{7\frac{1}{2}} = \frac{5}{7.5}$$

Can you interpret these fractions?

FIGURE 6.19 •

Solving equivalent-fraction problems as equivalent ratios using cross-products.

to 12 twelfths). The between proportion equates a part-to-part ratio with a whole-to-whole ratio, or $\frac{3}{9} = \frac{4}{12}$ (3 fourths are to 9 twelfths as 4 fourths are to 12 twelfths).

A simple line segment drawing similar to the one in Figure 6.18 could be drawn to set up a proportion to solve any equivalent-fraction problem, even ones that do not result in whole-number numerators or denominators. An example is shown in Figure 6.19.

Percent Problems

All percent problems are exactly the same as the equivalent-fraction examples. They involve a part and a whole measured in some unit and the same part and whole measured in hundredths—that is, in percents. A simple line segment drawing can be used for each of the three types of percent problems. Using this model as a guide, a proportion can be written and solved by the cross-product algorithm. Examples of each type of problem are shown in Figure 6.20.

It is tempting to teach all percent problems in this one way. Developmentally, such an approach is not recommended. Even though the approach is conceptual, it does not translate easily to intuitive ideas, mental arithmetic, or estimation as discussed in Chapter 4. The modeling and proportion approach of Figure 6.20 is suggested only as a way to help students analyze problems that may verbally present some difficulty. The approach of Chapter 4, which relates percent to part-whole fraction concepts, should probably receive more emphasis.

In 1960, U.S. railroads carried 327 million passengers. Over the next 20 years, there was a 14 percent decrease in passengers. How many passengers rode the railroads in 1980?

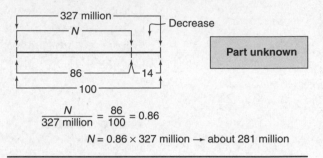

$$\frac{N}{327 \text{ million}} = \frac{86}{100} = 0.86$$

$N = 0.86 \times 327$ million → about 281 million

Sylvia's new boat cost $8950. She made a down payment of $2000. What percent of the sales price was Sylvia's down payment?

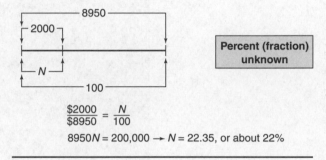

$$\frac{\$2000}{\$8950} = \frac{N}{100}$$

$8950N = 200{,}000$ → $N = 22.35$, or about 22%

The average dressed weight of a beef steer is 62.5 percent of its weight before being slaughtered. If a dressed steer weighs 592 pounds, how much did it weigh "on the hoof"?

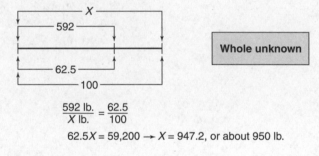

$$\frac{592 \text{ lb.}}{X \text{ lb.}} = \frac{62.5}{100}$$

$62.5X = 59{,}200$ → $X = 947.2$, or about 950 lb.

FIGURE 6.20 •

The three percentage problems solved by setting up a proportion using a simple line segment model.

SOLVING PROPORTIONS AND PERCENT PROBLEMS

Technology Note

You have already seen how spreadsheets can be used to create tables and compute ratios. Dynamic geometry programs allow figures to be scaled to larger or smaller sizes by using either a specified ratio or the dilation feature. This provides an excellent connection between the concepts of similarity and proportion.

Assessment Note

As you work with your students in solving proportional reasoning tasks, continue to think about the type of reasoning that students are using.

- Do they distinguish between proportional situations and additive or nonproportional ones?
- Are they flexible in the way that they attempt to solve proportions? A nonflexible or algorithmic approach, even if correct, may signal that a student is simply following rules.
- Are there differences in thinking about different types of proportional situations? For example, discrete (countable) items in a proportion are sometimes easier to deal with than continuous quantities such as time, distance, or volume.
- Do students seem to understand rates (miles per hour, inches per yard, dollars per pound) as ratios? How students deal with these ideas reflects the development of their proportional thinking.

If most of your students seem to be at the beginning levels of proportional thought, activities involving selection of equal ratios, constructions, and scaling will be more useful than harder proportion problems. Using numbers that lend themselves to easy relationships will also make it easier for students to describe different methods for solving proportion tasks.

EXPANDED LESSON

Comparing Ratios

Based on Activity 6.4, p. 162

GRADE LEVEL: Seventh or eighth grade.

MATHEMATICS GOALS
- To develop proportional reasoning (multiplicative as opposed to additive).
- To develop conceptual strategies for comparing ratios.

THINKING ABOUT THE STUDENTS
Students understand equivalent fractions. They are also familiar with the term *unit fraction* (e.g., $\frac{1}{3}$, $\frac{1}{4}$, $\frac{1}{9}$). Students have had experiences with ratios, but some may still not be able to distinguish between additive and multiplicative relationships. Some students may have also used symbolic or mechanical methods for solving proportions in a prior year, but the assumption is that these methods are not understood.

MATERIALS AND PREPARATION
- Prepare copies of Blackline Master L-1 and also make a transparency.

lesson

BLM L-1

BEFORE

Brainstorm
- Show the first problem on the Blackline Master and read it together. Ask students to simply make a guess at which of the two runners they think is faster. Get a show of hands for Terry and then for Susan.
- Next, have students think for a moment about how they could decide which of the two runners is actually faster. Students should share their ideas with a partner.
- Accept student ideas without evaluating them. Do not pursue any of the proposed strategies.

The Task
- Pass out the worksheet with the four problems. Students should solve any three of the problems in any manner they wish and be prepared to explain why their answers make sense.

Establish Expectations
- Students must be able to explain their reasoning. Simply doing a series of calculations is not sufficient.

DURING

- For students who are having difficulty, look at one ratio in a problem and ask what the unit rate is. For example, *How fast can Terry run in one minute? How often does Jack eat one berry?* In all four of these problems, one or both of the ratios can be converted to a unit rate.
- For students who are ready for a challenge, change the numbers so that neither rate is easily reducible to a unit rate.
- Do not give students an algorithm. Instead, encourage them to make sense of the numbers in the given context.

AFTER

- For each problem, ask students to share their strategies. Do not evaluate students' approaches but allow the class to discuss and question the different strategies. Through questioning, help the students compare and contrast the different approaches.
- If students use unit rates in their strategies, help the class relate unit rates to the concept of unit fractions.

- Change the numbers in one or more problems so that unit rates are not easy to use. For example, suppose that Terry runs 5 laps in 12 minutes and Susan runs 2 laps in 5 minutes. How students respond to this problem will give you insight into problems for the next lesson.

ASSESSMENT NOTES

- Look for students who focus on additive relationships. They are not seeing the multiplicative relationship of proportionality.
- Which students are using a unit rate approach? Which are not? Another possible approach, a "building up" approach, uses the idea that a ratio does not represent absolute values but represents instead a multiplicative relationship between the two numbers forming the ratio. Therefore, multiples of the two numbers forming the ratio can be used to solve the problems by finding a common element in each of the ratios.
- Watch for students who are using a mechanical method (such as the cross-product algorithm). These methods do not develop proportional reasoning and should not be encouraged (or introduced) until students have had many experiences with intuitive and conceptual methods. If students are using such methods, insist they also come up with another way to find a solution.

- For students who have difficulty seeing the multiplicative relationships, provide examples of additive and multiplicative relationships and discuss the differences.
- Repeat this lesson with more difficult comparisons. Ratios that can be compared using a factor-of-change method is one possibility. For example, $3 for 7 pounds and $24 for 60 pounds.
- Because proportional reasoning develops over time, continue to provide ratio and proportion tasks in a variety of contexts. These might include situations involving measurements, prices, geometric and other visual contexts, and rates of all sorts. Look-Alike Rectangles (Activity 6.2), Using Ratio Tables (Activity 6.5), and Different Units, Equal Ratios (Activity 6.7) are examples of activities that provide different paths to the development of proportional reasoning.

next steps

GEOMETRIC THINKING AND GEOMETRIC CONCEPTS

Geometry in K–8 is finally being taken seriously. Geometry used to be the chapter that was skipped or put off until late in the year. Many teachers were not comfortable with geometry, associating it with high school and proofs. Nor was geometry seen as important because it was only minimally tested on standardized tests. Now geometry is a strand of the curriculum in nearly every state and district.

This change is due in large part to the influence of the NCTM standards movement beginning in 1989. A second significant influence is an attention to a theoretical perspective that has helped us understand how students reason about spatial concepts.

Geometry Goals for Your Students

It is useful to think about your geometry objectives in terms of two quite different yet related frameworks: spatial reasoning, or spatial sense, and the specific content such as that most likely found in your state or district objectives. The first of these frameworks has to do with the way students think and reason about shape and space. There is a well-researched theoretical basis for organizing the development of geometric thought that guides this framework. The second framework is content in the more traditional sense—knowing about

big ideas

1 What makes shapes alike and different can be determined by an array of geometric properties. For example, shapes have sides that are parallel, perpendicular, or neither; they have line symmetry, rotational symmetry, or neither; they are similar, congruent, or neither.

2 Shapes can be moved in a plane or in space. These changes can be described in terms of translations (slides), reflections (flips), and rotations (turns).

3 Shapes can be described in terms of their location in a plane or in space. Coordinate systems can be used to describe these locations precisely. In turn, the coordinate view of shape offers another way to understand certain properties of shapes, changes in position (transformations), and how they appear or change size (visualization).

4 Shapes can be seen from different perspectives. The ability to perceive shapes from different viewpoints helps us understand relationships between two- and three-dimensional figures and mentally change the position and size of shapes.

symmetry, triangles, parallel lines, and so forth. The NCTM *Principles and Standards for School Mathematics* authors have helped describe content goals across the grades. We need to understand both of these aspects of geometry—thought and content—so that we can best help students grow.

Spatial Sense

Spatial sense can be defined as an intuition about shapes and the relationships among shapes. Individuals with spatial sense have a feel for the geometric aspects of their surroundings and the shapes formed by objects in the environment.

Spatial sense includes the ability to mentally visualize objects and spatial relationships—to turn things around in your mind. It includes a comfort with geometric descriptions of objects and position. People with spatial sense appreciate geometric form in art, nature, and architecture. They are able to use geometric ideas to describe and analyze their world.

Many people say they aren't very good with shape or that they have poor spatial sense. The typical belief is that you are either born with spatial sense or not. This simply is not true! We now know that rich experiences with shape and spatial relationships, when provided consistently over time, can and do develop spatial sense. Without geometric experiences, most people do not grow in their spatial sense or spatial reasoning. Between 1990 and 1996, NAEP data indicated a steady, continuing improvement in students' geometric reasoning at all three grades tested, 4, 8, and 12 (Martin & Strutchens, 2000). Students did not just get smarter. More likely there has been an increasing emphasis on geometry at all grades. Still, much more needs to be done if U.S. children are to rise to the same level as their European and Asian counterparts.

Geometric Content

For too long, the geometry curriculum in the United States has been somewhat of an eclectic mix of activities and lists of "bold print words"—too much emphasis has been placed on learning terminology. At the same time, the growing emphasis placed on geometry has spawned a huge assortment of wonderful tasks for students. Fortunately, the authors of *Principles and Standards for School Mathematics* have provided a content framework for the pre-K–12 curriculum. As with each of the content standards, the geometry standard has a number of goals that apply to all grade levels. The four goals for geometry can be loosely summarized with these headings: *Shapes and Properties, Transformation, Location,* and *Visualization*. A very brief description of these headings is offered next.

- *Shapes and Properties* includes a study of the properties of shapes in both two and three dimensions, as well as a study of the relationships built on properties.
- *Transformation* includes a study of translations, reflections, and rotations (slides, flips, and turns) and the study of symmetries.
- *Location* refers primarily to coordinate geometry or other ways of specifying how objects are located in the plane or in space.
- *Visualization* includes the recognition of shapes in the environment, developing relationships between two- and three-dimensional objects, and the ability to draw and recognize objects from different perspectives.

The value of these content goals is that a content framework finally exists that cuts across grades so that both teachers and curriculum planners can examine growth from year to year.

You are strongly encouraged to read the geometry goals for grades pre-K–2 and 3–5 in *Principles and Standards* (NCTM, 2000).

Geometric Thought: Reasoning About Shapes and Relationships

Not all people think about geometric ideas in the same manner. Certainly, we are not all alike, but we are all capable of growing and developing in our ability to think and reason in geometric contexts. The research of two Dutch educators, Pierre van Hiele and Dina van Hiele-Geldof, has provided insight into the differences in geometric thinking and how the differences came to be. The van Hieles' work began in 1959 and immediately attracted a lot of attention in the Soviet Union but for nearly two decades received little notice in this country (Hoffer, 1983; Hoffer & Hoffer, 1992). But today the van Hiele theory has become the most influential factor in the American geometry curriculum.

The van Hiele Levels of Geometric Thought

The most prominent feature of the model is a five-level hierarchy of ways of understanding spatial ideas. Each of the five levels describes the thinking processes used in geometric contexts. The levels describe how we think, and what types of geometric ideas we think about, rather than how much knowledge we have. A significant difference from one level to the next is the objects of thought—what we are able to think about geometrically.

Level 0: Visualization

The objects of thought at level 0 are shapes and what they "look like."

Students recognize and name figures based on the global, visual characteristics of the figure—a gestaltlike approach to shape. Students operating at this level are able to make measurements and even talk about properties of shapes, but these properties are not abstracted from the shapes at hand. It is the appearance of the shape that defines it for the student. A square is a square "because it looks like a square." Because appearance is dominant at this level, appearances can overpower properties of a shape. For example, a square that has been rotated so that all sides are at a 45-degree angle to the vertical may now be a diamond and no longer a square. Students at this level will sort and classify shapes based on their appearances—"I put these together because they are all pointy" (or "fat," or "look like a house," or are "dented in sort of," and so on). With a focus on the appearances of shapes, students are able to see how shapes are alike and different. As a result, students at this level can create and begin to understand classifications of shapes.

The products of thought at level 0 are classes or groupings of shapes that seem to be "alike."

Level 1: Analysis

The objects of thought at level 1 are classes of shapes rather than individual shapes.

Students at the analysis level are able to consider all shapes within a class rather than a single shape. Instead of talking about *this* rectangle, it is possible to talk about *all* rectangles. By focusing on a class of shapes, students are able to think about what makes a rectangle a rectangle (four sides, opposite sides parallel, opposite sides same length, four right angles, congruent diagonals, etc.). The irrelevant features (e.g., size or orientation) fade into the background. At this level, students begin to appreciate that a collection of shapes goes together because of properties. Ideas about an individual shape can now be generalized to all shapes that fit that class. If a shape belongs to a particular class such as cubes, it has the corresponding properties of that class. "All cubes have six congruent faces, and each of those faces is a square." These properties were only implicit at level 0. Students operating at level 1 may be able to list all the properties of squares, rectangles, and parallelograms but not see that these are sub-classes of one another, that all squares are rectangles and all rectangles are parallelograms. In defining a shape, level 1 thinkers are likely to list as many properties of a shape as they know.

The products of thought at level 1 are the properties of shapes.

Level 2: Informal Deduction

The objects of thought at level 2 are the properties of shapes.

As students begin to be able to think about properties of geometric objects without the constraints of a particular object, they are able to develop relationships between and among these properties. "If all four angles are right angles, the shape must be a rectangle. If it is a square, all angles are right angles. If it is a square, it must be a rectangle." It is at this level that students can appreciate the nature of a definition. With greater ability to engage in "if–then" reasoning, shapes can be classified using only minimum characteristics. For example, four congruent sides and at least one right angle can be sufficient to define a square. Rectangles are parallelograms with a right angle. Observations go beyond properties themselves and begin to focus on logical arguments *about* the properties. Students at level 2 will be able to follow and appreciate an informal deductive argument about shapes and their properties. Proofs may be more intuitive than rigorously deductive. However, there is an appreciation that a logical argument is compelling. An appreciation of the axiomatic structure of a formal deductive system, however, remains under the surface.

The products of thought at level 2 are relationships among properties of geometric objects.

Level 3: Deduction

The objects of thought at level 3 are relationships among properties of geometric objects.

At level 3, students are able to examine more than just the properties of shapes. Their earlier thinking has produced conjectures concerning relationships among properties. Are these conjectures correct? Are they "true"? As this analysis of the informal arguments takes place, the structure of a system complete with axioms, definitions, theorems, corollaries, and postulates begins to develop and can be appreciated as the necessary means of establishing geometric truth. The student at this level is able to work with abstract statements about geometric properties and make conclusions based more on logic than intuition. This is the level of the traditional high school geometry course.

The products of thought at level 3 are deductive axiomatic systems for geometry.

Level 4: Rigor

The objects of thought at level 4 are deductive axiomatic systems for geometry.

At the highest level of the van Hiele hierarchy, the objects of attention are axiomatic systems themselves, not just the deductions within a system. This is generally the level of a college mathematics major who is studying geometry as a branch of mathematical science.

The products of thought at level 4 are comparisons and contrasts among different axiomatic systems of geometry.

We have given brief descriptions of all five levels to illustrate the scope of the van Hiele theory. In every grade from 5 to 8, you will certainly see students at levels 0, 1, and 2.

Characteristics of the van Hiele Levels

You no doubt noticed that the products of thought at each level are the same as the objects of thought at the next. This object–product relationship between levels of the van Hiele theory is illustrated in Figure 7.1. The objects (ideas) must be created at one level so that relationships among these objects can become the focus of the next level. In addition to this key concept of the theory, four related characteristics of the levels of thought merit special attention.

1. The levels are sequential. To arrive at any level above level 0, students must move through all prior levels. To move through a level means that one has experienced geometric thinking appropriate for that level and has created in one's own mind the types of objects or relationships that are the focus of thought at the next level.

The van Hiele Theory of Geometric Thought

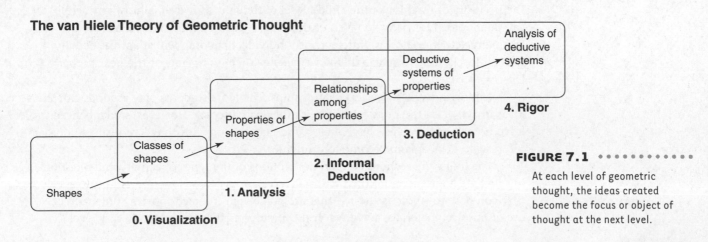

FIGURE 7.1

At each level of geometric thought, the ideas created become the focus or object of thought at the next level.

GEOMETRIC THOUGHT: REASONING ABOUT SHAPES AND RELATIONSHIPS

2. The levels are not age dependent in the sense of the developmental stages of Piaget. A third grader or a high school student could be at level 0. Indeed, some students and adults remain forever at level 0, and a significant number of adults never reach level 2. But age is certainly related to the amount and types of geometric experiences that we have. Therefore, it is reasonable to assume that most children in the K–2 range as well as many children in grades 3 and 4 are at level 0.

3. Geometric experience is the greatest single factor influencing advancement through the levels. Activities that permit children to explore, talk about, and interact with content at the next level, while increasing their experiences at their current level, have the best chance of advancing the level of thought for those children. Some researchers believe that it is possible to be at one level with respect to a familiar area of content and at a lower level with less familiar ideas (Clements & Battista, 1992).

4. When instruction or language is at a level higher than that of the student, there will be a lack of communication. Students required to wrestle with objects of thought that have not been constructed at the earlier level may be forced into rote learning and achieve only temporary and superficial success. A student can, for example, memorize that all squares are rectangles without having constructed that relationship. A student may memorize a geometric proof but fail to create the steps or understand the rationale involved (Fuys, Geddes, & Tischler, 1988; Geddes & Fortunato, 1993).

Implications for Instruction

If the van Hiele theory is correct—and there is much evidence to support it—then a major goal of the K–8 curriculum must be to advance students' level of geometric thought. If students are to be adequately prepared for the deductive geometry curriculum of high school, then it is important for their thinking to have grown to level 2 by the end of the eighth grade.

Not every teacher will be able to move children to the next level. However, all teachers should be aware that the experiences they provide are the single most important factor in moving children up this developmental ladder. Every teacher should be able to see some growth in geometric thinking over the course of the year.

The van Hiele theory and the developmental perspective of this book highlight the necessity of teaching at the child's level of thought. However, almost any activity can be modified to span two levels of thinking, even within the same classroom. For many activities, how we interact with individual children will adapt the activity to their levels and encourage them or challenge them to operate at the next higher level.

Explorations help develop relationships. The more students play around with the ideas in activities, the more relationships they will discover. However, students need to learn how to explore ideas in geometry and play around with the relationships in order for ideas to develop and become meaningful.

The following sections contain descriptions of the types of activity and questioning that are appropriate for the first three levels. Apply these descriptors to the tasks that you pose to students and use them to guide your interaction with students. The use of physical materials, drawings, and computer models is a must at every level.

Instruction at Level 0

Instructional activities in geometry appropriate for level 0 should:

- Involve lots of sorting and classifying. Seeing how shapes are alike and different is the primary focus of level 0. As students learn more content, the types of things that they notice will become more sophisticated. At an early stage they may talk about very nongeometric-sounding attributes of shape such as "fat" or even the color of the pieces. When properties such as symmetry and numbers of sides and corners are introduced, students should be challenged to use these features to classify shapes.

- Include a sufficient variety of examples of shapes so that irrelevant features do not become important. Students need ample opportunities to draw, build, make, put together, and take apart shapes in both two and three dimensions. These activities should be built around specific characteristics or properties so that students develop an understanding of geometric properties and begin to use them naturally.

To help students move from level 0 to level 1, students should be challenged to test ideas about shapes for a variety of examples from a particular category. Say to them, "Let's see if that is true for other rectangles," or "Can you draw a triangle that does *not* have a right angle?" In general, students should be challenged to see if observations made about a particular shape apply to other shapes of a similar kind.

Instruction at Level 1

Instructional activities in geometry appropriate for level 1 should:

- Focus more on the properties of figures rather than on simple identification. As new geometric concepts are learned, the number of properties that figures have can be expanded.

- Apply ideas to entire classes of figures (e.g., *all* rectangles, *all* prisms) rather than individual models. Analyze classes of figures to determine new properties. For example, find ways to sort all possible triangles into groups. From these groups, define types of triangles. Dynamic geometry software such as *The Geometer's Sketchpad* (Key Curriculum Press) is especially useful for exploring many examples of a class of shapes. This software is essential for exploring geometric ideas in grades 5 to 8.

To assist students in moving from level 1 to level 2, challenge them with questions such as "Why?" and those that involve some reasoning. For example, ask "If the sides of a four-sided shape are all congruent, will you always have a square?" and "Can you find a counterexample?"

Instruction at Level 2

Instructional activities in geometry appropriate for level 2 should:

- Encourage the making and testing of hypotheses or conjectures. "Do you think that will work all the time?" "Is that true for all triangles or just equilateral ones?"

GEOMETRIC THOUGHT: REASONING ABOUT SHAPES AND RELATIONSHIPS

- Examine properties of shapes to determine necessary and sufficient conditions for different shapes or concepts. "What properties of diagonals do you think will guarantee that you will have a square?"

- Use the language of informal deduction: *all, some, none, if–then, what if,* and so on.

- Encourage students to attempt informal proofs. As an alternative, require them to make sense of informal proofs that other students or you have suggested.

Assessment Note

Nearly all students in grades K–3 will be at level 0. However, by at least grade 3 teachers certainly want to begin to challenge students who seem able to engage in level 1 thinking. Teachers in the upper grades may have children at two or even all three levels within the same classroom. How do you discover the level of each student? Once you know, how will you select the right activities to match your students' levels?

No simple test exists to pigeonhole students at a certain level. However, examine the descriptors for the first two levels. As you conduct an activity, listen to the types of observations that students make. Can they talk about shapes as classes? Do they refer, for example, to "rectangles" rather than basing discussion around a particular rectangle? Do they generalize that certain properties are attributable to a type of shape or simply the shape at hand? Do they understand that shapes do not change when the orientation changes? With simple observations such as these, you will soon be able to distinguish between levels 0 and 1.

At the upper grades, attempt to push students from level 1 to level 2. If students are not able to follow or appreciate logical arguments and are not comfortable with conjectures and if–then reasoning, these students are likely still at level 1 or below.

Content and the Levels of Thinking

This chapter offers a sample of activities organized around the four content areas: Shapes and Properties, Transformations, Location, and Visualization. A section of the chapter is devoted to each of these areas. The van Hiele theory applies to all geometric activity regardless of content. However, it is within the content area of shapes and properties that the theory is most clearly seen. For that reason the activities in that section are subdivided into those appropriate for level 0, level 1, and level 2 thinkers. You will find this subdivision helpful for matching activities to your students and encouraging student development of thinking to higher levels. The three remaining sections focus on activities for developing spatial sense through location, transformation, and visualization. Each of these sections is organized in a progression of difficulty and sophistication.

Understand that all of these subdivisions are quite fluid; that is, the content areas overlap and build on each other. Activities in one section may help develop geometric thinking in another area. For example, developing spatial sense through an investigation of symmetry can help students move from level 0 to level 1. A more sophisticated analysis of symmetry can continue to help students move to level 2. In most instances, an activity described for one level of thinking can easily be adapted to an adjacent level simply by the way it is presented to students.

Shapes and Properties Activities

Children need experiences with a rich variety of both two- and three-dimensional shapes. It is useful for students to be able to identify common shapes, notice likenesses and differences among shapes, become aware of the properties that different shapes have, and eventually use these properties to further define and understand their geometric world. As students find out more about shapes over time, they can begin to appreciate how definitions of special shapes come to be.

This gradual development of student understanding of shapes and their properties clearly reflects the van Hiele theory of geometric thought. Within this aspect of geometric content, an awareness and application of the theory to your instruction are most important.

Activities for Level 0 Thinkers

The emphasis at level 0 is on the shapes that students can observe, feel, build, take apart, and perceive in many ways. The general goal is to explore how shapes are alike and different and use these ideas to create classes of shapes (both physically and mentally). Some of these classes of shapes have names—rectangles, triangles, prisms, cylinders, and so on. Properties of shapes, such as parallel sides, symmetry, right angles, and so on, are included at this level but only in an informal, observational manner.

Children need experience with a rich variety of both two- and three-dimensional shapes. Triangles should be more than just equilateral. Shapes should have curved sides, straight sides, and combinations of these. Along the way, the names of shapes and their properties can be introduced casually but only after students have described the shape or property.

Remember that *level 0* is not a synonym for *primary*. If you teach in the upper grades, you will almost certainly have students who need to begin with activities similar to these.

Sorting and Classifying

As students work at classification of shapes, be prepared for them to notice features that you do not consider to be "real" geometric attributes, such as "curvy" or "looks like a rocket." Students at this level will also attribute to shapes ideas that are not part of the shape, such as "points up" or "has a side that is the same as the edge of the board."

For variety in two-dimensional shapes, create your own materials. A good set found in the Blackline Masters is called 2-D Shapes. Make multiple copies so that groups of students can all work with the same shapes. The shapes in Figure 7.2 are similar to those in the Blackline Masters, but you will want many more. Once you have your sets constructed, the following activities provide several ideas.

FIGURE 7.2

An assortment of shapes for sorting.

BLMs 12–18

Shape Sorts

Have students work in groups of four with a set of 2-D Shapes similar to those in Figure 7.2. Here are several related activities that might be done in order:

- Each student randomly selects a shape. In turn, students tell one or two things they find interesting about their shape. There are no right or wrong responses.
- Students each randomly select two shapes. The task is to find something that is alike about their two shapes and something that is different. (Have them select their shapes before they know the task.)
- The group selects one shape at random and places it in the center of the workspace. Their task is to find all other shapes that are like the target shape, but all according to the same rule. For example, if they say, "This one is like our shape because it has a curved side and a straight side," then all other shapes that they put in the collection must have these properties. Challenge them to do a second sort with the same target shape but using a different property.
- Have students share their sorting rules with the class and show examples. All students then draw a new shape that will also fit in the group according to the same rule. They should write about their new shape and why it fits the rule.
- Do a "secret sort." You or one of the students creates a small collection of about five shapes that fit a secret rule. Leave others that belong in your group in the pile. The other students try to find additional pieces that belong to the set and/or guess the secret rule.

 Why do you think that the teacher should not say things such as, "Find all the pieces with straight sides," or "Find the triangles," and instead let students choose how to sort?

In any sorting activity, the students should decide how to sort, not the teacher. This allows the students to do the activity using ideas *they* own and understand. By listening to the kinds of attributes that they use in their sorting, you will be able to tell what properties they know and use and how they think about shapes. At level 0, students will likely make groups such as "has a curved side" or will sort by the number of sides a shape has. They will use expressions such as "has sides that go the same way" for parallel, "dented in" for concave, and "square corners" for right angles.

The secret sorting activity is one option for introducing a new property. For example, sort the shapes so that all have at least one right angle or "square corner." When students discover your rule, you have an opportunity to talk more about that property.

The following activity is also done with the 2-D Assorted Shapes.

What's My Shape?

From the Blackline Masters, make a set of 2-D Shapes on paper. Cut out about a third of the shapes and paste each inside a folded half-sheet of construction paper to make "secret shape" folders.

In a group, one student is designated the leader and given a secret-shape folder. The other students are to find the shape that matches the shape in the folder. To this end, they ask questions to which the leader can answer only "yes" or "no." The students can sort the shapes as they ask questions to help narrow down the possibilities. They are not allowed to point to a piece and ask, "Is it this one?" Rather, they must continue to ask questions that reduce the choices to one shape. The final piece is tested against the one in the leader's folder.

The difficulty of Activity 7.2 largely depends on the shape in the folder. The more shapes in the collection that resemble the secret shape, the more difficult the task.

Most of the activities in "Shape Sorts" can and should be done with three-dimensional shapes as well. The difficulty is finding or making a collection that has sufficient variability. Geoblocks are a large set of wooden blocks available through various distributors. The variety is good, but no blocks have curved surfaces. Check catalogs for other collections. Consider combining several different sets to get variation. Another option is to collect real objects such as cans, boxes, balls, and Styrofoam shapes. Again, the types of categories that students use will be quite revealing.

BLM 19

Assessment Note

The way that children describe shapes in "Shape Sorts" and similar activities with three-dimensional shapes is a good clue to their level of thinking. The classifications made by level 0 thinkers will generally be restricted to the shapes that they can actually put into a group. As they begin to think in terms of the properties of shapes, they will create categories based on properties, and their language will indicate that there are many more shapes in the group than those that are physically present. For example, students may say, "These shapes have square corners sort of like rectangles," or "These look like boxes. All the boxes have square (rectangular) sides."

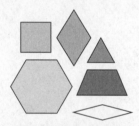

Pattern blocks

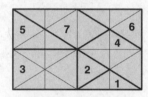

The 7-piece mosaic puzzle is built on an isometric grid (van Hiele, 1999).

Tangrams

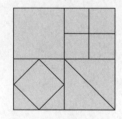

Try cutting up squares or rectangles in other ways to get pieces that are related (Lindquist, 1987b).

Constructing and Dissecting Shapes

Students need to freely explore how shapes fit together to form larger shapes and how larger shapes can be made of smaller shapes. Among two-dimensional shapes for these activities, pattern blocks and tangrams are the best known. In a 1999 article, Pierre van Hiele describes an interesting set of tiles he calls the mosaic puzzle (see Figure 7.3). Another excellent tile set for building is a set of triangles cut from squares (isosceles right triangles). Patterns for the mosaic puzzle and tangrams can be found in the Blackline Masters.

Although tangrams are extremely popular, their value begins to diminish in the intermediate grades. (An

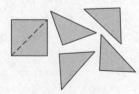

Triangles cut from squares

FIGURE 7.3 •

Activities with tiles can involve an assortment of shapes or can be designed with just one shape.

SHAPES AND PROPERTIES ACTIVITIES

(a)

Harder

Full-sized
outlines

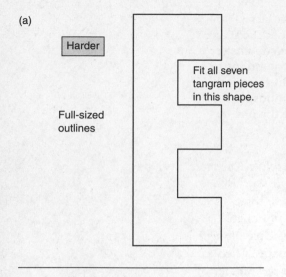

Fit all seven
tangram pieces
in this shape.

(b)

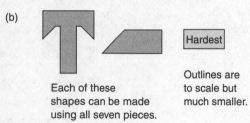

Hardest

Each of these
shapes can be made
using all seven pieces.

Outlines are
to scale but
much smaller.

FIGURE 7.4 •

Two types of tangram puzzles that are different
in difficulty.

exception is their use in measuring area. See Chapter 8.) Nonetheless, level 0 students do gain experiences with the way that shapes fit together when they solve tangram puzzles. A full-sized outline that will contain exactly all seven tangram pieces can be quite challenging. The most difficult tangram puzzle is a shape that can be made of all seven pieces but shown to the student in reduced form. (See Figure 7.4.) This latter puzzle format involves proportional reasoning because the student must mentally enlarge the shape in order to create it with the tangrams.

The value of van Hiele's mosaic puzzle is partly due to the fact that the set contains five different angles (see Figure 7.5). If appropriate, you can use the pieces to talk about square corners (*right* angles) and angles that are more and less than a right angle (*obtuse* and *acute* angles).

Building three-dimensional shapes is a little more difficult compared with two-dimensional shapes. A variety of commercial materials permits fairly creative construction of geometric solids (for example, 3D Geoshapes, Polydron, and the Zome System). The 3D Geoshapes and Polydron are examples of materials consisting of plastic polygons that snap together to make three-dimensional models. The Zome System is a stick and connector set; skeletal models can be created with a great deal of variation. The following are three highly recommended homemade approaches to skeletal models.

- *Plastic coffee stirrers with pipe cleaners.* Plastic stirrers can be easily cut to different lengths. To connect the corners, cut pipe cleaners into 2-inch lengths. These are inserted into the ends of the stirrers.

- *Plastic drinking straws with flexible joints.* Cut the straws lengthwise with scissors from the top down to the flexible joint. These slit ends can then be inserted into the uncut bottom ends of other straws, making a strong but flexible joint. Three or more straws are joined in this fashion to form two-dimensional polygons. To make skeletal solids, use tape or wire twist ties to join polygons side to side.

- *Rolled newspaper rods.* Fantastic superlarge skeletons can be built using newspaper and masking tape. Roll three large sheets of newspaper on the diagonal to form a rod. The more tightly the paper is rolled, the less likely the rod is to bend. Secure the roll at the center with a bit of masking tape. The ends of the rods are thin and flexible for about 6 inches where there is less paper. Connect the rods by bunching this thin part together and fastening with tape. Use masking tape freely, wrapping it several times around each joint. Additional rods can be joined after two or three are already taped (see Figure 7.6).

With these homemade models, students should compare the rigidity of a triangle with the lack of rigidity of polygons with more than three sides. Point out that triangles are used in many bridges, in the long booms of construction cranes, in gates, and in the structural parts of buildings. Discuss why this may be so. As students build large skeleton structures, they will find that they need to add diagonal members to form triangles. The more triangles, the less likely their structure will collapse.

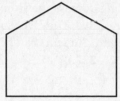
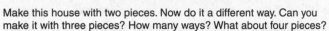

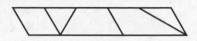

Make this house with two pieces. Now do it a different way. Can you make it with three pieces? How many ways? What about four pieces?

This is a long parallelogram. What other parallelograms can you make?

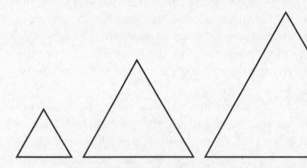

Build enlargements of the equilateral triangle.

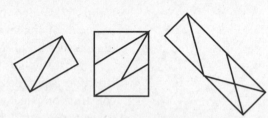

How many different rectangles can you make? Can you make any in more than one way?

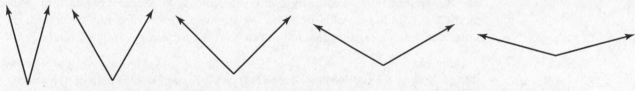

How many different-sized angles can you find in the set of pieces? Put them in order from smallest to largest.

FIGURE 7.5 ••

A sample of activities with the mosaic puzzle.

Based on van Hiele, P. M. (1999). Developing geometric thinking through activities that begin with play. *Teaching Children Mathematics, 5,* 310–316.

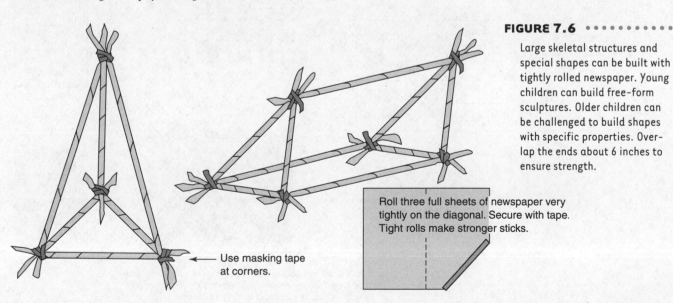

FIGURE 7.6 ••••••••••••

Large skeletal structures and special shapes can be built with tightly rolled newspaper. Young children can build free-form sculptures. Older children can be challenged to build shapes with specific properties. Overlap the ends about 6 inches to ensure strength.

Roll three full sheets of newspaper very tightly on the diagonal. Secure with tape. Tight rolls make stronger sticks.

← Use masking tape at corners.

SHAPES AND PROPERTIES ACTIVITIES

The newspaper rod method is exciting because the structures quickly become large. Let students work in groups of four or five. They will soon discover what makes a structure rigid and ideas of balance and form. Students can be challenged to make shapes with specific properties. (See pp. 226–227.)

Tessellations

A *tessellation* is a tiling of the plane using one or more shapes in a repeated pattern with no holes or gaps. Making tessellations is an artistic way for level 0 and level 1 students from first grade to eighth grades to explore patterns in shapes and to see how shapes combine to form other shapes. One-shape or two-shape tessellation activities can vary considerably in difficulty. Some shapes are easier to tessellate than others (see Figure 7.7). When the shapes can be put together in more than one pattern, both the problem-solving level and the creativity increase. Literally hundreds of shapes can be used as tiles for tessellations.

Most students will benefit from using actual tiles to create patterns. Simple construction paper tiles can be cut quickly on a paper cutter. Other tiles can be traced onto construction paper and several thicknesses cut at once with scissors. When the tile shape fits in a grid, students can use dot or line grids and plan their tessellations with pencil and paper. To plan a tessellation, use only one color so that the focus is on the spatial relationships. To complete an artistic-looking tessellation, add a color design. Color designs are also repeated regularly all over the tessellation.

Tessellations can be made by gluing paper tiles to large sheets of paper, by drawing them on dot or line grids, or by tracing around a poster board tile. Work from the center out, leaving ragged edges to indicate that the pattern goes on and on.

 STOP **Look at the top-left tessellation in Figure 7.7. What single tile (a combination of squares and half squares) made this pattern?**

FIGURE 7.7 • • • • • • • •

Tessellations.

Tessellations can be drawn on grids or made of construction paper tiles. They are challenging and provide an opportunity for both artistic creativity and spatial reasoning.

Chapter 7 GEOMETRIC THINKING AND GEOMETRIC CONCEPTS

Activities for Level 1 Thinkers

A significant difference between level 1 and level 0 is the object of students' thought. While students will continue to use models and drawings of shapes, they begin to see these as representatives of classes of shapes. Their understanding of the properties of shapes—such as symmetry, perpendicular and parallel lines, and so on—continues to be refined.

For the sake of clarity, the important definitions of two- and three-dimensional shapes are provided here. You will notice that shape definitions include relationships between and among shapes.

Special Categories of Two-Dimensional Shapes

Table 7.1 lists some important categories of two-dimensional shapes. Examples of these shapes can be found in Figure 7.8.

In the classification of quadrilaterals and parallelograms, the subsets are not all disjoint. For example, a square is a rectangle and a rhombus. All parallelograms are trapezoids, but not all trapezoids are parallelograms.* Children at level 1 have difficulty seeing this type of subrelationship. They may quite correctly list all the properties of a square, a rhombus, and a rectangle and still identify a square as a "nonrhombus" or a "nonrectangle." Is it wrong for students to refer to subgroups as disjoint sets? By fourth or fifth grade, it is only wrong to encourage such thinking. Burger (1985) points out that upper elementary students correctly use such classification schemes in other contexts. For example, individual students in a class can belong to more than one club. A square is an example of a quadrilateral that belongs to two other clubs.

Special Categories of Three-Dimensional Shapes

Important and interesting shapes and relationships also exist in three dimensions. Table 7.2 describes classifications of solids. Figure 7.9 on p. 196 shows examples of cylinders and prisms.

---

*Some definitions of trapezoid specify *only one* pair of parallel sides, in which case parallelograms would not be trapezoids. The University of Chicago School Mathematics Project (UCSMP) uses the "at least one pair" definition, meaning that parallelograms and rectangles are trapezoids.

TABLE 7.1
Categories of Two-Dimensional Shapes

Shape	Description
Simple Closed Curves	
Concave, convex	An intuitive definition of *concave* might be "having a dent in it." If a simple closed curve is not concave, it is *convex*. A more precise definition of *concave* may be interesting to explore with older students.
Symmetrical, nonsymmetrical	Shapes may have one or more lines of symmetry and may or may not have rotational symmetry. These concepts will require more detailed investigation.

Polygons
  Concave, convex
  Symmetrical, nonsymmetrical
	Simple closed curves with all straight sides.

Regular	All sides and all angles are congruent.
Triangles	
Triangles	Polygons with exactly three sides.
Classified by sides	
Equilateral	All sides are congruent.
Isosceles	At least two sides are congruent.
Scalene	No two sides are congruent.
Classified by angles	
Right	Has a right angle.
Acute	All angles are smaller than a right angle.
Obtuse	One angle is larger than a right angle.
Convex Quadrilaterals	
Convex quadrilaterals	Convex polygons with exactly four sides.
Kite	Two opposing pairs of congruent adjacent sides.
Trapezoid	At least one pair of parallel sides.
Isosceles trapezoid	A pair of opposite sides is congruent.
Parallelogram	Two pairs of parallel sides.
Rectangle	Parallelogram with a right angle.
Rhombus	Parallelogram with all sides congruent.
Square	Parallelogram with a right angle and all sides congruent.

SHAPES AND PROPERTIES ACTIVITIES

FIGURE 7.8 ••••••••

Classification of two-dimensional shapes.

Simple Closed Curves

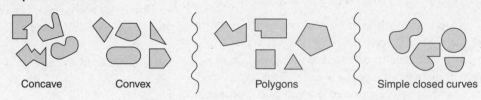

Triangles

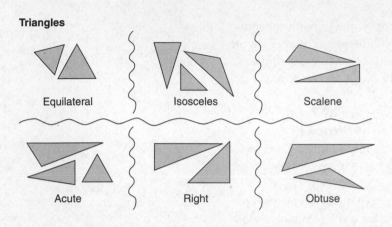

Convex Quadrilaterals

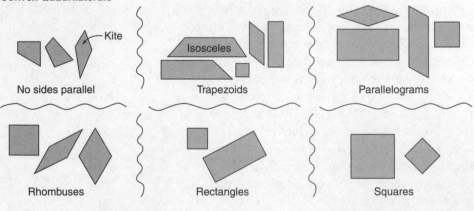

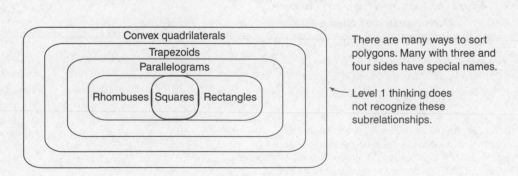

There are many ways to sort polygons. Many with three and four sides have special names.

Level 1 thinking does not recognize these subrelationships.

TABLE 7.2 •
Categories of Three-Dimensional Shapes

Shape	Description
Sorted by Edges and Vertices	
Sphere and "egglike" shapes	Shapes with no *edges* and no *vertices* (corners). Shapes with *edges* but no *vertices* (e.g., a flying saucer). Shapes with *vertices* but no *edges* (e.g., a football).
Sorted by Faces and Surfaces	
Polyhedron	Shapes made of all faces (a *face* is a flat surface of a solid). If all surfaces are faces, all the edges will be straight lines. Some combination of faces and rounded surfaces (cylinders are examples, but this is not a definition of a cylinder). Shapes with curved surfaces. Shapes with and without edges and with and without vertices. Faces can be parallel. Parallel faces lie in places that never intersect.
Cylinders	
Cylinder	Two congruent, parallel faces called *bases*. Lines joining corresponding points on the two bases are always parallel. These parallel lines are called *elements* of the cylinder.
Right cylinder	A cylinder with elements perpendicular to the bases. A cylinder that is not a right cylinder is an *oblique cylinder*.
Prism	A cylinder with polygons for bases. All prisms are special cases of cylinders.
Rectangular prism	A cylinder with rectangles for bases.
Cube	A square prism with square sides.
Cones	
Cone	A solid with exactly one face and a vertex that is not on the face. Straight lines (elements) can be drawn from any point on the edge of the base to the vertex. The base may be any shape at all. The vertex need not be directly over the base.
Circular cone	Cone with a circular base.
Pyramid	Cone with a polygon for a base. All faces joining the vertex are triangles. Pyramids are named by the shape of the base: *triangular* pyramid, *square* pyramid, *octagonal* pyramid, and so on. All pyramids are special cases of cones.

Note that prisms are defined here as a special category of cylinder—a cylinder with a polygon for a base. Figure 7.10 shows a similar grouping of cones and pyramids.

 Explain the following: Prisms are to cylinders as pyramids are to cones. How is this relationship helpful in learning volume formulas?

FIGURE 7.9 • • • • • • • •

Cylinders and prisms.

Cylinders

Not Cylinders

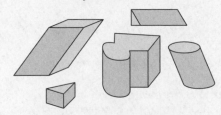
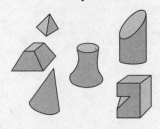

Special Cylinders

Cylinders have two parallel faces, and parallel lines join corresponding points on these faces. If the parallel faces are polygons, the cylinder can be called a prism.

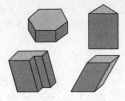 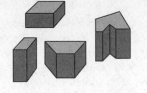 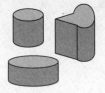

Prisms   Right prisms   Right cylinders (*not* prisms)

FIGURE 7.10 • • • • • • •

Cones and pyramids.

 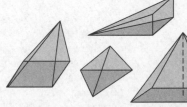

Cones   Special cones—pyramids

Cones and cones with a polygon base (pyramids) all have straight-line elements joining every point of the base with the vertex. (Yes, a pyramid is just a special type of cone.)

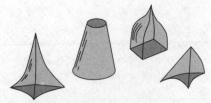 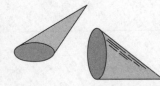

Not cones   Cones—not pyramids

Many textbooks define cylinders strictly as circular cylinders. These books do not have special names for other cylinders. Under that definition, the prism is not a special case of a cylinder. This points to the fact that definitions are conventions, and not all conventions are universally agreed upon. If you look at the development of the volume formulas in Chapter 8, you will see that the more inclusive definition of cylinders and cones given there allows one formula for any type of cylinder—hence, prisms—with a similar statement that is true for cones and pyramids.

Sorting and Classifying Activities

The next activity provides a good method when you want to introduce a category of shapes that you plan to define formally later.

ACTIVITY 7.3

Mystery Definition

Use the overhead or chalkboard to conduct activities such as the example in Figure 7.11. For your first collection be certain that you have allowed for all possible variables. In Figure 7.11, for example, a square is included in the set of rhombi. Similarly, choose nonexamples to be as close to the positive examples as is necessary to help with an accurate definition. The third or mixed set should also include those nonexamples with which students are most likely to be confused.

Rather than confirm the choice of shapes in the third set, students should write an explanation for their choice.

The value of the "Mystery Definition" approach is that students develop ideas and definitions based on their own concept development. After their definitions have been discussed and compared, you can offer the usual "book" definition for the sake of clarity.

For defining types or categories of triangles, the next activity is especially good and uses a different approach.

All of these have something in common.

None of these has it.

Which of these have it?

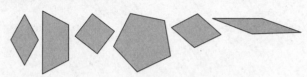

The name of a property is not necessary for it to be understood. It requires more careful observation of properties to discover what shapes have in common.

FIGURE 7.11 •

All of these, none of these: a mystery definition.

ACTIVITY 7.4

Triangle Sort

Make copies of the Assorted Triangles sheet found in the Blackline Masters. Note the examples of right, acute, and obtuse triangles; examples of equilateral, isosceles, and scalene triangles; and triangles that represent every possible combination of these categories. Have students cut them out. The task is to sort the entire collection into three groups so that no triangle belongs to two groups. When this is done and descriptions of the groupings have been written, students should then find a second criterion for creating three different groupings. Students may need a hint to look only at angle sizes or only at the issue of congruent sides, but hold these hints if you can.

BLM 20

"Triangle Sort" results in definitions of the six different types of triangles without having to list these definitions on the board and have students memorize them. As a follow-up activity, make a chart such as the one shown here. Challenge students to sketch a triangle in each of the nine cells.

	Equilateral	Isosceles	Scalene
Right			
Acute			
Obtuse			

 Of the nine cells in the chart, two of them are impossible to fill. Can you tell which ones and why?

Quadrilaterals (polygons with four sides) are an especially rich source of investigations. For the following activity, students should be familiar with the concepts of

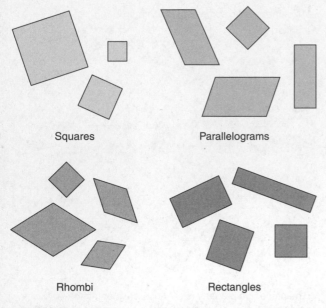

Squares

Parallelograms

Rhombi

Rectangles

FIGURE 7.12 •

Shapes for "Property Lists for Quadrilaterals" worksheets can be found in the Blackline Masters.

BLMs 21–24

right, obtuse, and acute angles, congruence of line segments, and symmetry (line and rotational).

ACTIVITY 7.5

Property Lists for Quadrilaterals

Prepare worksheets for parallelograms, rhombi, rectangles, and squares. (See the Blackline Masters.) On each sheet are three or four examples of that category of shape. Examples are illustrated in Figure 7.12. Assign students working in groups of three or four to one type of quadrilateral. Their task is to list as many properties as they can. Each property listed must be applicable to all of the shapes on their sheet. They will need a simple index card to check right angles, to compare side lengths, and to draw straight lines. Mirrors (to check line symmetry) and tracing paper (for angle congruence and rotational symmetry) are also useful tools. Encourage students to use the words "at least" when describing how many of something: for example, "rectangles have at least two lines of symmetry," since squares—included in the rectangles—have four.

Have students prepare their property lists under these headings: Sides, Angles, Diagonals, and Symmetries. Groups then share their lists with the class and eventually a class list for each shape will be developed.

This last activity may take two or three periods. Share lists beginning with parallelograms, then rhombi, then rectangles, and finally squares. Have one group present its list. Then others who worked on the same shape should add to or subtract from it. The class must agree with everything that is put on the list. As new relationships come up in this presentation-and-discussion period, you can introduce proper terminology. For example, if two diagonals intersect in a square corner, then they are *perpendicular.* Other terms such as *parallel, congruent, bisect, midpoint,* and so on can be clarified as you help students write their descriptions. This is also a good time to introduce symbols such as ≅ for "congruent" or ‖ for "parallel."

As an extension, repeat Activity 7.5 using kites and trapezoids. "Property Lists for Quadrilaterals" has some important follow-ups that are described in the section on level 2 activities (see p. 203). Furthermore, similar activities can be used to introduce three-dimensional shape definitions.

Construction Activities

Students building or drawing shapes continues to be important at level 1. Dynamic geometry software (*Geometer's Sketchpad, The Geometry Inventor,* and *Cabri*) dramatically enhances the exploration of shapes at this level.

In the "Property Lists for Quadrilaterals" activity (Activity 7.5), students examine the diagonals of various classes of quadrilaterals. If that activity has not been done already, the following exploration is very interesting. Rather than beginning with the shapes, it begins with the diagonals.

Every type of quadrilateral can be uniquely described in terms of its diagonals using only the conditions of length, ratio of parts, and whether or not they are perpendicular. Some students will work with the diagonal relationships to see what shapes can be made. Others will begin with examples of the shapes and observe the diagonal relationships. A dynamic geometry program such as *The Geometer's Sketchpad* is an excellent vehicle for this investigation.

Similar Figures and Proportional Reasoning

A good first definition of similar figures is shapes that "look alike but are different sizes." More precisely, two figures are *similar* if all of their corresponding angles are congruent and the corresponding sides are proportional. Many proportional reasoning activities are good connections to geometry. Activities 6.8, 6.9, and 6.10 involve scale drawings and proportional relationships in three-dimensional figures that are similar.

FIGURE 7.13 • • • • • • • • • • • • • •

Diagonals of quadrilaterals.

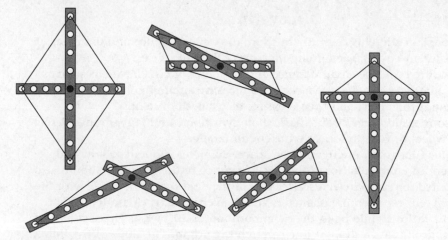

Quadrilaterals can be determined by their diagonals. Consider the length of each, where they cross, and the angles between them. What conditions will produce parallelograms? Rectangles? Rhombi? Challenge: What properties will produce a nonisosceles trapezoid?

FIGURE 7.14 •• •• •• •

Begin with figure ABCDE and place point P anywhere at all. Draw lines from P through each vertex. Place point A' twice as far from P as A is from P (scale factor of 2). Do similarly for the other points. In this drawing, ABCDE is the same in both figures and the images are congruent.

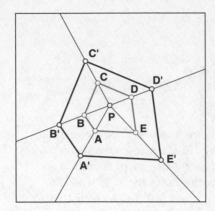

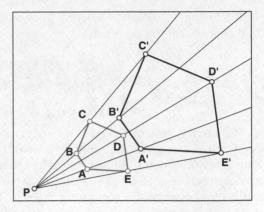

A *dilation* is a nonrigid transformation that produces similar figures. Figure 7.14 shows how a given figure can be *dilated* to make larger or smaller figures. If groups of students using different dilation points dilate the same figure using the same scale factor, they will find that the resulting figures are all congruent. Dynamic geometry software makes the results of this exercise quite dramatic. The software allows for the scale factors to be set at any value. Once a dilation is made, the dilation point can be dragged around the screen and the size and shape of the image clearly stay unchanged. Scale factors less than 1 produce smaller figures.

Circles

Many interesting relationships can be observed between measures of different parts of the circle. Among the most astounding and important is the ratio between measures of the circumference and the diameter.

STOP   **True or False: All circles are similar. Explain.**

ACTIVITY 7.7

Discovering Pi

Have groups of students carefully measure the circumference and diameter of many different circles. Each group measures different circles.

Measure both the circumference and diameter of circular items such as jar lids, tubes, cans, and wastebaskets. To measure circumference, wrap string once around the object and then measure that length of string.

Also measure large circles marked on gym floors and playgrounds. Use a trundle wheel or rope to measure the circumference.

Collect measures of circumference and diameter from all groups and enter them in a table. Ratios of the circumference to the diameter should also be computed for each circle. A scatter plot of the data should be made with the horizontal axis representing diameters and the vertical axis circumferences.

Most ratios should be in the neighborhood of 3.1 or 3.2. The scatter plot should approximate a straight line through the origin. The slope of the line should be close to 3.1. (Recall from Chapter 6 that graphs of equivalent ratios are always straight lines through the origin. The exact ratio is an irrational number, about 3.14159, represented by the Greek letter π, pi.)

What is most important in Activity 7.7 is that students develop a clear under-standing of π as the ratio of circumference to diameter in any circle. The quantity π is not some strange number that appears in math formulas; it is a naturally occurring and universal ratio.

Technology Note

As students begin to do more than build with geometric "blocks" (tan-grams, pattern blocks, grid drawing, etc.), the computer begins to offer powerful tools for explorations. Dynamic geometry software is especially powerful.

Dynamic Geometry Software

In a dynamic geometry program, points, lines, and geometric figures are easily constructed on the computer using only the mouse. Once drawn, the geometric objects can be moved about and manipulated in endless variety. Distances, lengths, areas, angles, slopes, and perimeters can be measured. As the figures are changed, the mea-surements update instantly.

Lines can be drawn perpendicular or parallel to other lines or segments. Angles and segments can be drawn congruent to other angles and segments. A point can be placed at the midpoint of a segment. A figure can be produced that is a reflection, rota-tion, or dilation of another figure. The most significant thing is that when a geometric object is created with a particular relationship to another object, that relationship is maintained no matter how either object is moved or changed.

Three of the best-known dynamic geometry programs are *The Geometer's Sketchpad* (Key Curriculum Press, 2001), *Geometry Inventor* (Riverdeep, 1996), and *Cabri Geometry II* (Texas Instruments, 1998). Although each operates somewhat differently, they are suffi-ciently alike that separate descriptions are not required here. Originally designed for high school students, all can be used profitably and should be used starting about grade 4.

Dynamic Geometry Examples

To appreciate the potential (and the fun) of dynamic geometry software, you really need to experience it on a computer. In the meantime, an example is offered here in an attempt to illustrate how these programs work.

In Figure 7.15, the midpoints of a freely drawn quadrilateral ABCD have been joined. The diagonals of the resulting quadrilateral (EFGH) are also drawn and measured. No matter how the points A, B, C, and D are dragged around the screen, even inverting the quadrilateral, the other lines will maintain the same relationships (joining midpoints and diagonals), and the measurements will be instantly updated on the screen.

Remember that at level 1, the objects of thought are *classes* of shapes. In a dynamic geometry program, if a quadrilateral is drawn, only one shape is observed, as would be the case on paper or on a geoboard. But now that quadrilateral can be stretched and altered in endless ways. Students actually explore not one shape but an enormous number of examples from that class of shapes. If a property does not change when the figure changes, the property is attributable to the *class* of shapes rather than any particular shape.

Another example in Figure 7.16 shows how *Sketchpad* can be used to investigate quadrilaterals starting with the diagonals. The directions for creating the sketch are

SHAPES AND PROPERTIES ACTIVITIES

FIGURE 7.15 •••••••

A *Sketchpad* construction
illustrating an interesting
property of quadrilaterals.

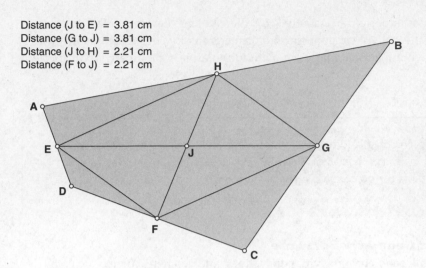

Distance (J to E) = 3.81 cm
Distance (G to J) = 3.81 cm
Distance (J to H) = 2.21 cm
Distance (F to J) = 2.21 cm

FIGURE 7.16 •••••••

With *The Geometer's
Sketchpad* students can
construct two line seg-
ments that will always
bisect each other. When
the endpoints are joined,
the resulting quadrilateral
will always be of the same
class, regardless of how
points A, B, C, and D are
moved around.

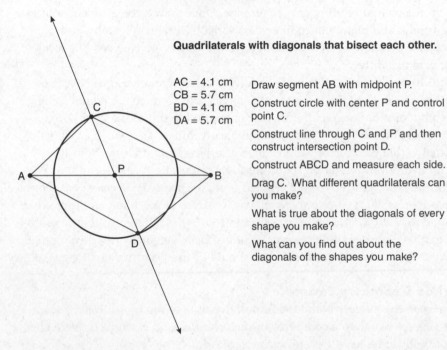

Quadrilaterals with diagonals that bisect each other.

AC = 4.1 cm
CB = 5.7 cm
BD = 4.1 cm
DA = 5.7 cm

Draw segment AB with midpoint P.

Construct circle with center P and control
point C.

Construct line through C and P and then
construct intersection point D.

Construct ABCD and measure each side.

Drag C. What different quadrilaterals can
you make?

What is true about the diagonals of every
shape you make?

What can you find out about the
diagonals of the shapes you make?

included and can be done quite simply with minimal experience with the software. By
creating the drawing in this manner, the diagonals of ABCD will always bisect each other
no matter how the drawing is altered. By dragging point C around, ABCD can be made
into a parallelogram, rectangle, rhombus, and square. But for each of these figures, additional information about the diagonals can be determined by looking at the drawing.

Dynamic geometry programs are also powerful for investigating concepts of symmetry and transformations (slides, flips, and turns). The publishers of these programs
provide excellent activities that are appropriate for level 1 investigations. Many activities are included with the software, and others are found in supplemental publications.

 **Why can't the drawing in Figure 7.16 be transformed into a kite or a trapezoid
that is not also a parallelogram?**

The symmetry investigations (both line symmetry and rotational symmetry), "Diagonal Strips" (Activity 7.6), investigations of similarity, and "Discovering Pi" (Activity 7.7) can all be explored profitably with dynamic geometry programs. The publishers of these programs provide excellent activities that are appropriate for level 1 investigations. Many activities are included with the software, and others are found in supplementary publications.

Activities for Level 2 Thinkers

The hallmark of level 2 activities is the inclusion of informal logical reasoning. Most fifth- to eighth-grade students will still be at level 1 at best. However, as students develop an understanding of various geometric properties and attach these properties to important categories of shapes, it is essential to begin to encourage conjecture and to explore informal deductive arguments. Do not be afraid to explore some of the activities at this level just because you may be teaching fifth or sixth grade.

Definitions and Proofs

To really understand the difference between levels 1 and 2 of the van Hiele theory, contrast the required thinking in the level 1 activity "Property Lists for Quadrilaterals" (Activity 7.5) and the following activity that is designed as a follow-up to that one.

ACTIVITY 7.8

Minimal Defining Lists

(This activity must be done as a follow-up to the "Property Lists for Quadrilaterals" activity on p. 198.) Once property lists for the parallelogram, rhombus, rectangle, and square (and possibly the kite and trapezoid) have been agreed on by the class, have these lists posted or type them up and duplicate them. In groups, the task is to find "minimal defining lists," or MDLs, for each shape. An MDL is a subset of the properties for a shape that is "defining" and "minimal." "Defining" here means that any shape that has all the properties on the MDL *must* be that shape. Thus, an MDL for a square will guarantee that you have a square. "Minimal" means that if any single property is removed from the list it is no longer defining. For example, one MDL for a square is a quadrilateral with four congruent sides and one right angle. Students should attempt to find at least two or three MDLs for their shape. A proposed list can be challenged as either not minimal or not defining. A list is not minimal if a property can be removed yet the list still defines the shape. A list is not defining if a counterexample—a shape other than one being described—can be produced using only the properties on the list.

The parallelogram, rhombus, rectangle, and square each have at least four MDLs. One of the most interesting MDLs for each shape consists only of the properties of its diagonals. For example, a quadrilateral with diagonals that bisect each other and are perpendicular (intersect at right angles) is a rhombus. Several MDLs have only one property. For example, a parallelogram is a quadrilateral with rotational symmetry of at least order 2.

The MDL activity is worth some further discussion. First, notice the logic component. "*If* a quadrilateral has these properties, *then* it must be a square." Logic is also involved in disproving a faulty list. A second feature is the opportunity to discuss what constitutes a definition. In fact, any MDL could be the definition of the shape. The definitions we usually use are MDLs that have been chosen probably due to the ease with which we can understand them. A quadrilateral with diagonals that bisect each other does not immediately call to mind a parallelogram. Recall that when students created their property lists, no definition was given, only a collection of shapes and a label. Theoretically, the lists could have been created without ever having heard of these shapes. Finally, notice that the object of students' thinking in this activity is clearly on properties, not on shapes. The products of the activity are relationships among the properties.

The next activity is also a good follow-up to the "Property Lists for Quadrilaterals" activity, although it is not restricted to quadrilaterals and can include three-dimensional shapes as well. Notice again the logic involved.

ACTIVITY 7.9

True or False?

Prepare statements of the following forms: "If it is a _____, then it is also a _____." "All _____ are _____." "Some _____ are _____."
A few examples are suggested here but numerous possibilities exist.

- If it is a square, then it is a rhombus.
- All squares are rectangles.
- Some parallelograms are rectangles.
- All parallelograms have congruent diagonals.
- If it has exactly two lines of symmetry, it must be a quadrilateral.
- If it is a cylinder, then it is a prism.
- All prisms have a plane of symmetry.
- All pyramids have square bases.
- If a prism has a plane of symmetry, then it is a right prism.

The task is to decide if the statements are true or false and to present an argument to support the decision. Four or five true-or-false statements will make a good lesson. Once this format is understood, let students challenge their classmates by making their own lists of five statements. Each list should have at least one true statement and one false statement. Use the students' lists in subsequent lessons.

 Use the property list for squares and rectangles to prove "All squares are rectangles." Notice that you must use logical reasoning to understand this statement. It does little good to simply force it on students who are not ready to develop the relationship.

Although logic has been involved in the previous activities, you may have difficulty understanding how middle school students can actually do proofs. The following activity was designed by Sconyers (1995) to demonstrate that students can create proofs in geometry well before high school.

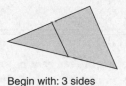

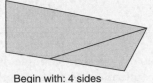

FIGURE 7.17 • • • • • • • • • • • • •

Start with a polygon and draw a segment to divide it into two polygons. How many sides will the two new polygons have?

Begin with: 3 sides
Two new shapes: 7 sides

Begin with: 4 sides
Two new shapes: 7 sides

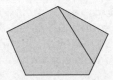

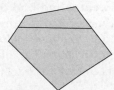

Begin with: 6 sides
Two new shapes: 8 sides

Begin with: 5 sides
Two new shapes: 8 sides

Begin with: 5 sides
Two new shapes: 9 sides

ACTIVITY 7.10

Two Polygons from One

Pose the following problem:

> Begin with a convex polygon with a given number of sides. Connect two points on the polygon with a line segment forming two new polygons. How many sides do the two resulting polygons have together?

Demonstrate with a few examples (see Figure 7.17). Have students explore by drawing polygons and slicing them. Encourage students to make a table showing sides in original and resulting sides. Students should first make conjectures about a general rule. When groups are comfortable with their conjectures, they should try to reason why their statement is correct—that is, prove their conjectures.

Obviously, the number of resulting sides depends on where the slice is made. With the exception of triangles, there are three possibilities. For each case, a clear argument can be made. The appropriate conjecture and proof are left to you, but trust that students working together can do this task.

Notice that in this task, as in others we have explored, the statements to be proved come from students. If you write a theorem on the board and ask students to prove it, you have already told them that it is true. If, by contrast, a student makes a statement about a geometric situation the class is exploring, it can be written on the board with a question mark as a *conjecture,* a statement whose truth has not yet been determined. You can ask, "Is it true? Always? Can we prove it? Can we find a counterexample?" Reasonable deductive arguments can be forged out of discussions.

The Pythagorean Relationship

The *Pythagorean relationship* is so important that it deserves special attention. In geometric terms, this relationship states that if a square is constructed on each side of a right triangle, the areas of the two smaller squares will together equal the area of the square on the longest side, the hypotenuse. To discover this relationship, consider the following activity.

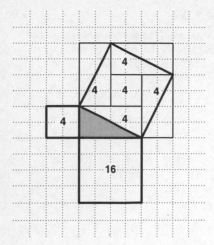

FIGURE 7.18 • • • • • • • • • • • • •

The Pythagorean relationship. Note that if drawn on a grid, the area of all squares is easily determined. Here 4 + 16 = area of the square on the hypotenuse.

The Pythagorean Relationship

Have students draw a right triangle on half-centimeter grid paper. Assign each student a different triangle by specifying the lengths of the two legs. Students are to draw a square on each leg and the hypotenuse and find the area of all three squares. (For the square on the hypotenuse, the exact area can be found by making each of the sides the diagonal of a rectangle. See Figure 7.18.) Make a table of the area data (Sq. on leg 1, Sq. on leg 2, Sq. on hyp.) and ask students to look for a relationship between the squares.

As an extension to the last activity, students can explore drawing other figures on the legs of right triangles and computing areas. For example, they can draw semicircles or equilateral triangles instead of squares. The areas of any regular polygons drawn on the three sides of right triangles will have the same relationship.

Activity 7.11 establishes the Pythagorean relationship. What about a proof? Figure 7.19 shows two proofs that students can follow. The first consists of only the two drawings. It is taken from the book *Proofs without Words* (Nelson, 1993). An algebraic proof is shown below the drawings, based on the second square.

 Use the two drawings in Figure 7.19 to create a proof of the Pythagorean relationship.

Technology Note ———————————

The *e-Standards* includes a dynamic proof without words of the Pythagorean relationship that is worth sharing with your students (Applet 6.5). Because it requires knowing that parallelograms and rectangles with the same base and height have the same area (see Chapter 8), it is also a good review.

Finding Versus Explaining Relationships

Dynamic geometry software such as *The Geometer's Sketchpad* allows students to explore an entire class of figures and observe properties or relationships that are attributable to that class. At level 2, however, the focus is on reasoning or deductive thinking. Can these computer programs help students develop deductive arguments to support the relationships they come to believe through inductive reasoning? Consider the following situation.

Suppose that you have students use a dynamic geometry program to draw a triangle, measure all of the angles, and add them up. As the triangle vertices are dragged around, the sum of the angles would remain steadfast at 180 degrees. Students can conjecture that the sum of the interior angles of a triangle is always 180 degrees, and they would be completely convinced of the truth of this conjecture based on this inductive experience. (Several noncomputer activities lead to the same conclusion.)

As Michael de Villiers notes in his excellent book *Rethinking Proof with the Geometer's Sketchpad* (1999), "The observation that the sun rises every morning does not explain why this is true" (p. 24). De Villiers points out that the experience leading to the conjecture or truth should also help students develop a rationale for the result. In the case of interior angles of a triangle, the experience just described fails to explain *why it is so*. Consider the following activity, which can be done easily with paper and scissors or quite dramatically with a dynamic geometry program.

ACTIVITY 7.12

Angle Sum in a Triangle

Have all students cut out three congruent triangles. (Stack three sheets of paper and cut three shapes at one time.) Place one triangle on a line and the second directly next to it in the same orientation. Place the third triangle in the space between the triangles as shown in Figure 7.20(a). Based on this experience, what conjecture can you make about the sum of the angles in a triangle?

In a dynamic geometry program, the three triangles in Figure 7.20(a) can be drawn by starting with one triangle, translating it to the right the length of AC, and then rotating the same triangle about the midpoint of side BC. When vertices of the original triangle are dragged, the other triangles will change accordingly and remain congruent. We still do not know why the angle sum is always a straight angle, but this exploration allows students to see why it might be so. In the figure, there are lines parallel to each side of the original triangle. By using properties of angles formed by cutting parallel lines with a transverse line, it is easy to argue that the sum of the angles will always be a straight line (see Figure 7.20(b); the proof is left to you).

Dynamic geometry software can be enormously powerful for helping students observe geometric relationships and make conjectures. The truth of the conjectures will often be obvious. At level 2, however, we must begin to ask why. The following activity further illustrates the point.

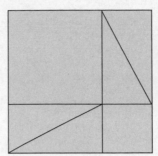
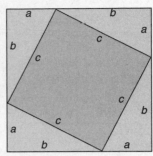

The area of the large square is $(a + b)^2 = a^2 + 2ab + b^2$

The same area is also c^2 plus 4 times the area of one triangle.
$$c^2 + 4\left(\frac{1}{2}ab\right) = c^2 + 2ab$$

So $c^2 + 2ab = a^2 + 2ab + b^2$
$$c^2 = a^2 + b^2$$

FIGURE 7.19 •

Two proofs of the Pythagorean relationship. The two squares together are a "proof without words." Can you supply the words? The second proof is the algebraic proof based on the right-hand figure.

FIGURE 7.20 • • • • • • •

Deductive, logical reasoning is necessary to *prove* relationships that appear true from observations.

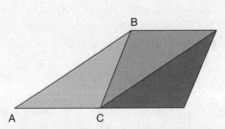

(a)
Three congruent triangles can be arranged to show that the sum of the interior angles will always be a straight angle or 180 degrees.

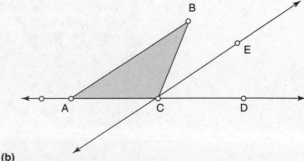

(b)
Draw CE parallel to AB. Why is angle BAC congruent to angle ECD? Why is angle ABC congruent to angle BCE?

SHAPES AND PROPERTIES ACTIVITIES

FIGURE 7.21 ••••••••

The midsegment of a tri-
angle is always parallel to
the base and half as long.

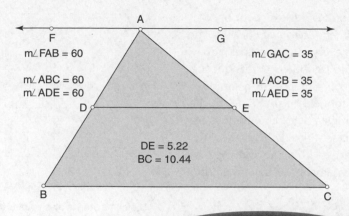

A

F
m∠FAB = 60

G
m∠GAC = 35

m∠ABC = 60
m∠ADE = 60

m∠ACB = 35
m∠AED = 35

D

E

DE = 5.22
BC = 10.44

B

C

EXPANDED LESSON

(pages 228–229)

A complete lesson plan
based on "Triangle Midsegments" can be found at
the end of this chapter.

ACTIVITY 7.13

Triangle Midsegments

Using a dynamic geometry program, draw a triangle, and label the vertices A,
B, and C. Draw the segment joining the midpoints of AB and AC, and label
this segment DE, as in Figure 7.21. Measure the length of DE and BC. Also
measure angles ADE and ABC. Drag points A, B, and C. What conjectures can
you make about the relationships between segment DE, the *midsegment* of
ABC, and BC, the base of ABC?

It is very clear that the midsegment is half the length of the base and parallel to
it, but why is this so? Students will need a bit more guidance, but you should not necessarily have to provide the argument for them. Suggest that they draw a line through
A parallel to BC. List all pairs of angles that they know are congruent. Why are they
congruent? Note that triangle ABC is similar to triangle ADE. Why is it similar? With
hints such as these, many middle grade students can begin to make logical arguments
for why the things they observe to be true are in fact true.

Assessment Note

With a greater focus on explaining *why* something is true, we need to
consider how students may approach this endeavor. Researchers hypoth-
esize that students' abilities to justify and prove follow a developmental
path that progresses from inductive to deductive approaches.

Stage 0: Students are ignorant of the need for, or existence of, proof.

Stage 1: Students are aware of the notion of proof but consider checking a
few cases as sufficient.

Stage 2: Students are aware that checking a few cases is not sufficient but are
satisfied that either (a) checking extreme cases or random cases is
proof, or (b) use of a generic example forms a proof for a class of
objects.

Stage 3: Students are aware of the need for a general argument but are
unable to produce such arguments themselves; however, they are
likely to be able to understand the generation of such an argument
(for example, by a classmate). This also includes the ability to follow

a short chain of deductive reasoning. At this stage, students are able to apply a definition without allowing intuitive and familiar notions of a concept to interfere with the application of the definition. They are also able to understand necessary and sufficient conditions.

Stage 4: Students are aware of the need for a general argument, are able to understand the generation of such an argument, and are able to produce such arguments themselves in a limited number of (familiar) contexts.

Stage 5: Students are aware of the need for a general argument, are able to understand the generation of such an argument (including more formal arguments), and are able to produce such arguments themselves in a variety of contexts (both familiar and unfamiliar) (Knuth, Choppin, Slaughter, & Sutherland, 2002, pp. 1694–1695).

Knuth et al.(2002) suggest that middle school students overwhelmingly rely on the use of examples as a method of demonstrating and/or confirming the truth of a statement (Stage 1/Stage 2). It is very likely that most students in grades 5 to 8 will be functioning between stages 0 and 3. As you work with students to help them generate logical arguments for why things are true, keep in mind these stages of proof concept development to help you make sense of students' approaches.

Transformation Activities

Transformations are also called "rigid motions"—movements that do not change the size or shape of the object moved. Usually, three transformations are discussed in grades 5–8: *translations* or slides, *reflections* or flips, and *rotations* or turns. The goal of instruction is to help students recognize and apply these transformations. You can use a nonsymmetrical shape on the overhead to introduce these terms (see Figure 7.22). Most elementary school textbooks only use the center of the figure as the point of rotation and a vertical or horizontal line as the line of reflection. These restrictions are for simplicity. In general, the center of rotation can be anywhere on or off the figure. Lines of reflection can also be anywhere.

Interestingly, the study of symmetry is also included under the study of transformations. Do you know why?

If a shape can be folded on a line so that the two halves match, then it is said to have *line symmetry* (or mirror symmetry). Notice that the fold line is actually a line of reflection—the portion of the shape on one side of the line is reflected onto the other side. That is the connection between line symmetry and transformations.

To explain line symmetry to students, you can show examples and nonexamples. Another approach is to have students fold a sheet of paper in half and cut out a shape of their choosing. When they open the paper, the fold line will be a line of symmetry. A third way is to use mirrors. When you place a mirror on a picture or design so that

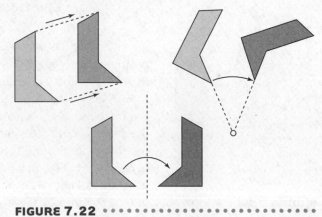

FIGURE 7.22 •
Translation (slide), reflection (flip), rotation (turn).

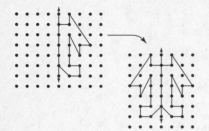

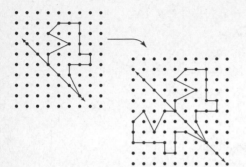

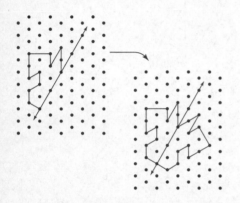

the mirror is perpendicular to the table, you see a shape with symmetry when you look in the mirror.

Here is an activity with line symmetry.

ACTIVITY 7.14

Dot Grid Line Symmetry

For this activity, students need to use either isometric or rectangular dot grid paper. Students should draw a line through several dots. This line can be horizontal, vertical, or skewed. Students should make a design completely on one side of the drawn line that touches the line in some way (see the left-hand drawings in Figure 7.23). Now the task is to make the mirror image of their design on the other side of the line. (Students can exchange designs and make the mirror image of a classmate's design.) When finished, they can use a mirror to check their work. They place the mirror on the line and look into it from the side of the original design. With the mirror in place, they should see exactly the same image as they see when they lift the mirror. You can also challenge them to make designs with more than one line of symmetry.

A plane of symmetry in three dimensions is analogous to a line of symmetry in two dimensions. Figure 7.24 illustrates a shape built with cubes that has a plane of symmetry.

ACTIVITY 7.15

Plane Symmetry Buildings

With cubes, build a building that has a plane of symmetry. If the plane of symmetry goes between cubes, slice the shape by separating the building into two symmetrical parts. Try making buildings with two or three planes of symmetry. Build various prisms. Do not forget that a plane can slice diagonally through the blocks.

FIGURE 7.23

Exploring symmetry on dot grids.

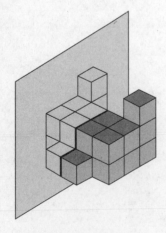

FIGURE 7.24

A block building with one plane of symmetry.

A shape has *rotational symmetry* if it can be rotated about a point and land in a position exactly matching the one in which it began. A square has rotational symmetry as does an equilateral triangle.

A good way to understand rotational symmetry is to take a shape with rotational symmetry, such as a square, and trace around it on a piece of paper. Call this tracing the shape's "box." The order of rotational symmetry will be the number of ways that the shape can fit into its box without flipping it over. A square has rotational symmetry of *order* 4, whereas an equilateral triangle has rotational symmetry of *order* 3. The parallelogram in Figure 7.25 has rotational symmetry of *order* 2. Some books would call order 2 symmetry "180-degree symmetry." The number of degrees refers to the smallest angle of rotation required before the shape matches itself or fits into its box. A square has 90-degree rotational symmetry.

ACTIVITY 7.16

Pattern Block Rotational Symmetry

Have students construct designs with pattern blocks with different rotational symmetries. They should be able to make designs with order 2, 3, 4, 6, or 12 rotational symmetry. Which of the designs have mirror symmetry as well?

FIGURE 7.25 • • • • • • • • • • • • • • •

This parallelogram fits in its box two ways without flipping it over. Therefore, it has rotational symmetry of order 2.

Rotational symmetry in the plane (also referred to as *point symmetry*) has an analogous counterpart in three dimensions. Whereas a figure in a plane is rotated about a point, a three-dimensional figure is rotated about a line. This line is called an *axis of symmetry*. As a solid with rotational symmetry revolves around an axis of symmetry, it will occupy the same position in space (its "box") but in different orientations. A solid can have more than one axis of rotation. For each axis of symmetry, there is a corresponding order of rotational symmetry. A regular square pyramid has only one axis of symmetry that runs through the tip of the pyramid and the center of the square. A cube, by contrast, has a total of 13 axes of symmetry: three (through opposite faces) of order 4, four (through diagonally opposite vertices) of order 3, and six (through midpoints of diagonally opposite edges) of order 2.

ACTIVITY 7.17

Find the Spin Lines

Give students a solid shape that has one or more axes of rotational symmetry. Color or label each face of the solid to help keep track. The task is to find all axes of rotational symmetry (spin lines) and determine the order of rotational symmetry for each. Suggest that students use one finger of each hand to hold the solid at the two points where the axis of symmetry emerges. A partner can then slowly turn the solid, and both can decide when the solid is again "in its box"—that is, in the same space it was in originally (see Figure 7.26).

FIGURE 7.26 • • • • • • •

Rotations of a cube.

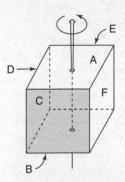

With A on top, the cube fits in its "box" four ways. Through this axis, the order of rotational symmetry is order 4.

These two axes also have rotational symmetry of order 4.

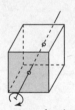

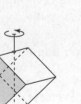

Edge-to-edge axes each have symmetry of order 2. How many are there?

If the axis is corner to opposite corner, what is the order of symmetry? How many of these axes are there?

Composition of Transformations

One transformation can be followed by another. For example, a figure can be reflected over a line, and then that figure can be rotated about a point. A combination of two or more transformations is called a *composition*.

Have students experiment with compositions of two or even three transformations using a simple shape on a rectangular dot grid. For example, have students draw an L-shape on a dot grid and label it L_1. (Refer to Figure 7.27.) Reflect it through a line, and then rotate the image $\frac{1}{4}$ turn clockwise about a point not on the shape. Call this image L_2, the image of a composition of a reflection followed by a rotation. Notice that if L_1 is rotated $\frac{1}{4}$ turn clockwise about the same point used before to L_3 there is a relationship between L_2 and L_3. (How could you get L_3 from L_2?)

>
> A composite transformation can involve more than two individual transformations, just as multiplication can involve more than one factor (e.g., 3 × 8 × 2). Can you describe a composite transformation to get from L_1 to L_3 that is the same as the single transformation of a quarter turn about A?

Continue to explore different combinations of transformations. Don't forget to include translations (slides) in the compositions. Compositions do not have to involve different types of transformations. For example, a reflection can be followed by another reflection. When your students understand compositions of transformations on a grid, challenge them with the next task.

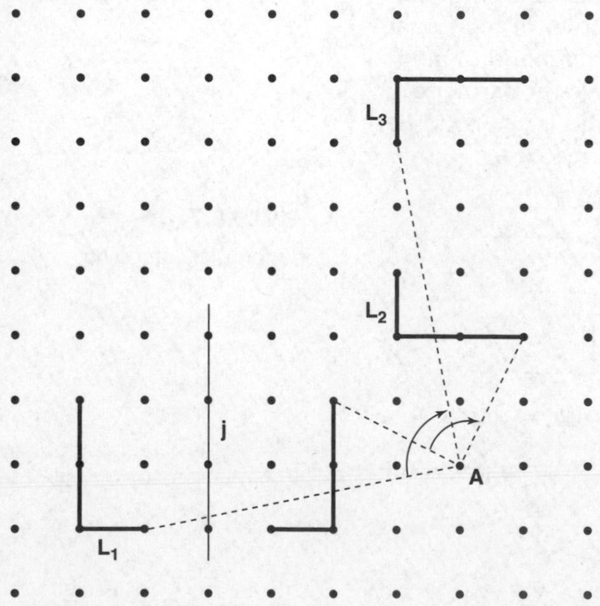

FIGURE 7.27

Shape L_1 was reflected across line j and rotated $\frac{1}{4}$ turn about point A resulting in L_2. L_1 was also rotated $\frac{1}{4}$ turn about point A. How are L_2 and L_3 related? Will this always work?

ACTIVITY 7.18

Mystery Transformations

Draw a small L-shaped figure near one corner of a rectangular dot grid. On this page, students draw a congruent L-shape somewhere near the center of the page. The second L can be flipped or turned in any orientation they wish. Then students trade papers with a partner. The task is to find some combination of slides, flips, and $\frac{1}{4}$ or $\frac{1}{2}$ turns that will take the shape in the corner onto the shape drawn by the students.

This is a challenging activity. To help students, ask if the L has been flipped over. If it is flipped over, then there will have to be one or three reflections. Regardless of how the two shapes are oriented, it can always be done in three or fewer transformations.

Technology Note

In NCTM's *e-Standards*, "Understanding Congruence, Similarity, and Symmetry" (Applet 6.4)

is one of the best examples of a simple yet valuable interactive applet. In the first part of the applet, students develop an understanding of all three rigid motions. In the second part, a transformation is complete and the student uses a guess-and-check procedure to determine which exact transformation was done. In the last two parts, students can explore compositions of reflections and then other compositions up to three transformations. This applet is strongly recommended.

Tessellations Revisited

Either by using transformations or by combining compatible polygons, students can create tessellations that are artistic and quite complex.

The Dutch artist M. C. Escher is well known for his tessellations, where the tiles are very intricate and often take the shape of things like birds, horses, angels, or lizards. Escher took a simple shape, such as a triangle, parallelogram, or hexagon, and performed transformations on the sides. For example, a curve drawn along one side might be translated (slid) to the opposite side. Another idea was to draw a curve from the midpoint of a side to the adjoining vertex. This curve was then rotated about the midpoint to form a totally new side of the tile. These two ideas are illustrated in part (a) of Figure 7.28. Dot paper is used to help draw the lines. *Escher-type tessellations,* as these have come to be called, are quite popular projects for students in grades 5 and up. Once a tile has been designed, it can be cut from two different colors of construction paper instead of drawing the tessellation on a dot grid.

A *regular tessellation* is made of a single tile that is a regular polygon (all sides and angles congruent). Each vertex of a regular tessellation has the same number of tiles meeting at that point. A checkerboard is a simple example of a regular tessellation. A *semiregular tessellation* is made of two or more tiles, each of which is a regular polygon. At each vertex of a semiregular tessellation, the same collection of regular polygons comes together in the same order. A vertex (and, therefore, the complete semiregular tessellation) can be described by the series of shapes meeting at a vertex. Under each example of these tessellations in part (b) of Figure 7.28, the vertex numbers are given. Students can figure out what polygons are possible at a vertex and design their own semiregular tessellations.

Tessellations like these are very popular with teachers. A number of excellent resource books can be found in catalogs such as ETA/Cuisenaire.

Technology Note

Several computer programs make it easy to create Escher-type tessellations. One example is *TesselMania!* (The Learning Company, 1994).

Although exciting to use, these programs should be used with care. It is so easy to create intricate results with almost no understanding of the transformations being used. Planning on paper before using the computer is strongly recommended. Then the computer can be used to do the tedious work of creating a finished product complete with color and embellishments.

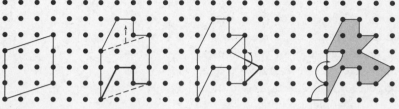

1. Start with a simple shape.

2. Draw the same curve on two opposite sides. This tile will stack up in columns.

3. Rotate a curve on the midpoint of one side.

4. Rotate a curve on the midpoint of the other side. Use this tile for tessellation (below).

A column of this tile will now match a like column that is rotated one complete turn. Find these rotated columns in the tessellation below.

(a)

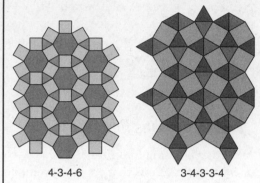

4-3-4-6   3-4-3-3-4

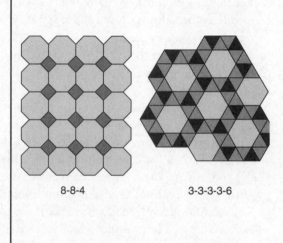

8-8-4   3-3-3-3-6

(b)

FIGURE 7.28 • • • • • • •

(a) One of many ways to create an Escher-type tessellation. (b) Examples of semiregular tessellations.

The following activity is a challenge to establish an interesting relationship between symmetries and transformations. The activity utilizes the 12 pentomino shapes, the set of all shapes made from five squares joined at matching edges. Many students in the upper grades will have done pentomino activities in earlier grades. If your students are not familiar with pentominoes, you may want to have them do the "Pentominoes" activity (Activity 7.26, p. 222) in the Visualization section that has students develop them.

ACTIVITY 7.19

Pentomino Positions

Have students cut out a set of 12 pentominoes from 2-cm grid paper. (See Figure 7.29.) Mark one side of each piece to help remember if it has been flipped over. The first part of the task is to determine how many different positions on the grid each piece has. Call positions "different" if a reflection or a turn is required to make them match. Therefore, the cross-shaped piece has only one position. The strip of five squares has two positions. Some pieces have as many as eight positions. The second part of the task is to find a relationship between the line symmetries and rotational symmetries for each piece and the number of positions it can have on the grid.

The first part of this activity was adapted from the classic book *Boxes, Squares, and Other Things* (Walter, 1970), which has many more excellent explorations. The second part of the problem is not hard if students make a table of what they know. The solutions to the task are left to you and your students. A follow-up to this activity can be found in *Boxes, Squares, and Other Things*.

The next task challenges students to develop generalizations about certain compositions of transformations.

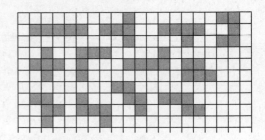

There are 12 pentominoes.

Finding all possible shapes made with five squares—or six squares (called "hexominoes") or six equilateral triangles and so on—is a good exercise in spatial problem solving.

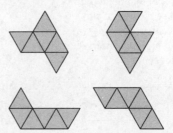

Four of the different shapes that six equilateral triangles will make.

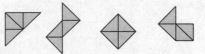

Four of the different shapes that four "half-square" triangles will make.

FIGURE 7.29 • • • • • • • • • • • • • • • •

Pentominoes and related shape challenges.

ACTIVITY 7.20

Double Reflections

There are two similar tasks in this activity:

1. Verify that the composition of two reflections across parallel lines (first across one and then the other) is the same as a translation. Make a drawing on a dot grid to illustrate. Challenge: If you know the distance between the two parallel lines, what can you say about the translation—both its direction and its distance? Does it matter where the shape begins (between the lines or outside) or which line is used as the first reflection? Explain your conclusions.

2. Verify that the composition of two reflections across intersecting lines is the same as a rotation about the point of intersection of the lines. Make a drawing on a dot grid to illustrate. Challenge: How is the angle of rotation related to the angle between the lines? Explain your conclusions.

In the first problem, the translation distance is always double the distance between the lines and is perpendicular to them. The direction is determined by which line is used for the first reflection in relation to the preimage. In the second problem, the angle of rotation is double the angle between the lines. It is possible to construct reasonable arguments for these conclusions by examining drawings.

Location Activities

Location activities prior to this level should prepare students for coordinates and build on students' position language (*over, under, near, far, between, left,* and *right*). The need for a coordinate system should be developed if it has not been already. Through location activities, students in grades 5–8 should become more familiar with the four

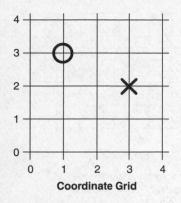

FIGURE 7.30 • • • • • • • • •

A simple coordinate grid. The X is at (3, 2) and the O is at (1, 3). Use the grid to play Three in a Row (like Tic-Tac-Toe). Put marks on intersections, not spaces.

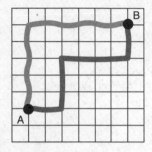

FIGURE 7.31 • • • • • • •

Coloring in different paths on a grid. What is the fewest number of turns needed to get from A to B? The most?

quadrants in the coordinate grid. However, if your students are not familiar with grids and coordinates, begin with activities that use the first quadrant only.

Once a coordinate system has been introduced, students may want to use it in a simple game similar to the commercial game called "Battleship." Each player has a grid similar to the one in Figure 7.30. Players secretly put their initials on five intersections of their own grid. Then, with the grids kept hidden from each other, the players take turns trying to "hit" the other player's targets by naming a point on the grid using coordinates. The other player indicates if the "shot" was a hit or a miss. When a player scores a hit, he or she gets another turn. Each player keeps track of where he or she has taken shots, recording an "X" for a hit and an "O" for a miss. The game ends when one player has hit all of the other player's targets.

At this level, students are simply using coordinates to describe positions. Although this is not very challenging, it provides practice for finding coordinates in a gamelike setting that can be motivating for students.

Taxicab Geometry: A Non-Euclidean Excursion

When determining coordinates, many students become confused about what they are supposed to count—is it the interval between points or is it the points? In taxicab geometry you are allowed to "travel" only on grid lines, as if you are traveling in a taxicab on the streets of a city laid out in grid form. Like taxis, travel is always toward the destination. If moving toward the upper right, all paths are either upward or to the right. Distance between points is determined by counting the intervals (city blocks) between intersections. Figure 7.31 illustrates two of many legitimate paths between points A and B. Either path is a distance of 11 units. Will paths between two points always be the same length?

The next activity is an introduction to this different version of geometry.

ACTIVITY 7.21

Taxicab Geometry Distances

Explain the following scenario to students:

> Katie and Clarissa want to meet at a restaurant that is equidistant from each of their houses and such that the total of the distances they each travel does not exceed 8 miles. Their city is arranged like a grid, and they can either drive or walk along the streets, but they cannot cut diagonally across a block. One block is 1 mile. If Clarissa's house is 4 miles east and 2 miles north of Katie's, draw a map showing where they could look for a restaurant. Explain.

> It may be helpful to suggest that students locate Katie's house at (0, 0), although this is not necessary.

 Before continuing, try "Taxicab Geometry Distances." What patterns do you see? Look both at the coordinates and at the visual image you get.

In solving the problem in Activity 7.21, it is likely that students will first find the points that are 3 miles from each house since the distance between the houses is 6.

Interestingly, there are three such points in this problem. But then you have to look for a longer distance for each to travel. There are lots of points that are 4 miles from each house but only two that are 4 miles from both houses and similarly for 5, 6, 7, and 8 miles away. If Katie's house is placed at (0, 0), the sum of the coordinates forms a pattern. The closest three points have a sum of 3. The points at 4 miles have coordinates of (1, 3) and (3, –1). If you add absolute values, these sums are 4. The sum for the next two points is 5, and so on. If Katie's house is placed at a point other than (0, 0), there will still be a pattern, but it will be a bit different. In your discussion with students, try to get them to see most of these ideas.

When looking for points farther away from each house, say, 5 miles from each, it may be useful to look to find *all* of the points that are 5 miles from each house. In our familiar geometry, called Euclidean geometry, the set of all points 5 units from a point is commonly known as a circle with radius 5. What is the shape of all points 5 miles from a point in taxicab geometry? This shape can be referred to as a "taxicab circle." If you plot the taxicab circles for 3, 4, 5, 6, 7, and 8 miles from each house, the corresponding intersections will be the points that solve the problem. What is interesting is that in Euclidean geometry the solution is exactly the same: The set of all points equidistant from two points is the set of intersections of all circles of like size.

Finally, students may wonder why the set of points in the solution is not quite in a straight path. Suggest that they try other locations for Clarissa's house, beginning first at (3, 3). Keep Katie's house at the origin, (0, 0), for simplicity and to better observe patterns.

Taxicab geometry is an example of *non-Euclidean* geometry. It is fun to explore ideas in Euclidean geometry and see how they turn out in taxicab geometry. Activity 7.21 was one example. Definitions of line, angle, square, and circle can be applied to taxicab geometry with interesting results. Are there parallel lines and perpendicular lines in taxicab geometry? What is the shortest distance between two points? Is that path unique? *Taxi-Cab Geometry: An Adventure in Non-Euclidean Geometry* by Krause (1987) provides an excellent introduction to non-Euclidean geometry through activities that can be used with elementary and middle school students.

So far, the location activities and tasks in this section have used coordinates to identify locations on a grid and to examine distances between points. In grades 5–8, students can also use coordinates to describe transformations on a coordinate grid. This can be done as an alternative method of introducing slides, flips, and turns or as a follow-up to that discussion.

Coordinates and Transformations

In grades 5–8, shapes and properties can be investigated on a full coordinate grid. Even fifth-grade students can use negative integers so that all four quadrants of the plane can be represented. The activities here suggest how coordinates can be used to examine transformations.

ACTIVITY 7.22

Coordinate Reflections

Have students draw a five-sided shape in the first quadrant on coordinate grid paper using grid points for vertices. Label the figure ABCDE and call it Figure 1. Use the *y*-axis as a line of symmetry and draw the reflection of the

(continued)

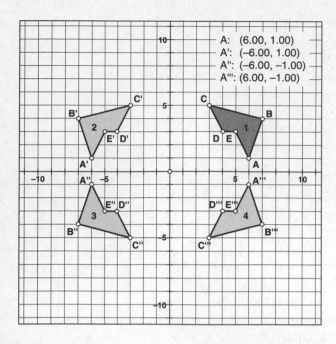

A: (6.00, 1.00)
A': (−6.00, 1.00)
A'': (−6.00, −1.00)
A''': (6.00, −1.00)

FIGURE 7.32 •

Figure 1 (ABCDE) is reflected across the y-axis. Then both Figures 1 and 2 are reflected across the x-axis.

shape in the second quadrant. Call it Figure 2 (for second quadrant) and label the reflected points A'B'C'D'E'. Now use the x-axis as the line of symmetry. Reflect both Figure 2 and Figure 1 into the third and fourth quadrants, respectively, and call these Figures 3 and 4. Label the points of these figures with double and triple primes (A'' and A''', and so on). Write in the coordinates for each vertex of all four figures.

- How is Figure 3 related to Figure 4? How else could you have gotten Figure 3? How else could you have found Figure 4?
- How are the coordinates of Figure 1 related to its image in the y-axis, Figure 2? What can you say about the coordinates of Figure 4?
- Make a conjecture about the coordinates of a shape reflected in the y-axis and a different conjecture about the coordinates of a shape reflected in the x-axis.
- Draw lines from the vertices of Figure 1 to the corresponding vertices of Figure 2. What can you say about these lines? How is the y-axis related to each of these lines?

STOP **Use Figure 7.32 or a drawing of your own to answer the questions in Activity 7.22.**

Rotations can be explored in a similar manner to Activity 7.22. Have students begin with a figure in the first quadrant, rotate it a quarter turn clockwise and a quarter turn counterclockwise into the second and fourth quadrants, using the origin as the center of rotation. Then have students rotate the original figure a half turn into the third quadrant. Similar questions can be asked about the coordinates. An interesting result can be seen in the figure in the third quadrant.

STOP **There is a relationship between a 180-degree turn and reflections through two perpendicular lines. Can you tell what that is?**

In the activities just discussed, students perform a transformation on a figure and observe how the transformation affects the coordinates. In the next two activities, the coordinates will be changed and students observe the resulting change on the figure. Get a coordinate grid and follow along with the next activity.

ACTIVITY 7.23

Coordinate Translations

Students begin with a five-sided shape in the first quadrant. Make a list of the coordinates. Next, students make a new set of coordinates by adding 3 to all of the x-coordinates of the initial figure and then they draw this figure. They then create a third figure by subtracting 4 from each of the y-coordinates of the original figure. What happens? What will happen if you do both: add 3 to the *x*-coordinates and subtract 4 from the *y*-coordinates? Try it. Students now have the original and three image figures on their paper. Now have them draw lines from the vertices of the original figure to the corresponding vertices of the last figure (the one in which both coordinates were changed). What do you notice about these lines? (They are parallel and the same length.) In general, what does adding or subtracting a fixed value to all coordinates do to a figure?

Students who have done the two preceding activities and the variation for rotational symmetry should have a general way to describe translations, reflections across an axis, and 90-degree rotations about the origin all in terms of coordinates. In the following activity, multiplying a constant times the coordinates makes a different type of change.

ACTIVITY 7.24

Coordinate Dilations

Students begin with a four-sided shape in the first quadrant. They then make a list of the coordinates and make a new set of coordinates by multiplying each of the original coordinates by 2. They plot the resulting shape. What is the result? Now have students multiply each of the original coordinates by $\frac{1}{2}$ and plot that shape. What is the result? Next, students draw a line from the origin to a vertex of the largest shape on their paper. Repeat for one or two additional vertices and ask for observations. (An example is shown in Figure 7.33.)

 How do the lengths of the sides and the areas of the shapes compare when the coordinates are multiplied by 2? What if they are multiplied by 3 or by $\frac{1}{2}$?

It is impressive to see how an arithmetic operation can control a figure. Imagine being able to control slides, flips, turns, and dilations, not just in the plane but also for three-dimensional figures. The process is identical to and is the essence of computer animation techniques.

When the coordinates of a shape are multiplied as in the preceding activity, each by the same factor, the shape gets either larger or smaller. The size is changed but not the shape. The new shape is similar to the old shape. This is called a *dilation*, a transformation that is *not* rigid because the shape changes.

Your students may enjoy exploring this phenomenon a bit further because they can get some quite interesting effects. If they start with a line drawing of a simple face, boat, or some other shape drawn with straight lines connecting vertices, they see an interesting effect by multiplying just the first coordinates, just the

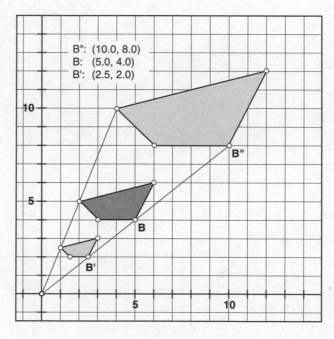

FIGURE 7.33

Dilations with coordinates. Coordinates of the center figure were multiplied by 2 and also by 0.5 to create the other two figures.

second coordinates, or using a different factor for each. For example, students could sketch the cat shown here on a coordinate grid. Then suggest that they add 10 to each first coordinate and multiply each second coordinate by 3.

 Before reading on, predict what you think will happen to the cat if you add 10 to the first coordinates and multiply the second coordinates by 3. What will happen if you do the reverse—multiply the first coordinates by 3 and add 10 to the second coordinates?

Multiplication of both coordinates by a factor greater than one dilates the figure to a similar but larger shape. When only one coordinate is multiplied, the vertical dimensions alone are dilated, so the figure is proportionately stretched in a vertical manner as in Figure 7.34. By adding 10 units to the first coordinates the new stretched figure is moved to the right so as not to interfere with the original. Students will enjoy exploring with variations of stretching and dilating shapes in various ways.

FIGURE 7.34 • • • • • • • • • • • • • • • • • • •

Using coordinates to cause a distortion. The coordinates for the larger cat are based on those of the smaller: $(x + 10, 3y)$.

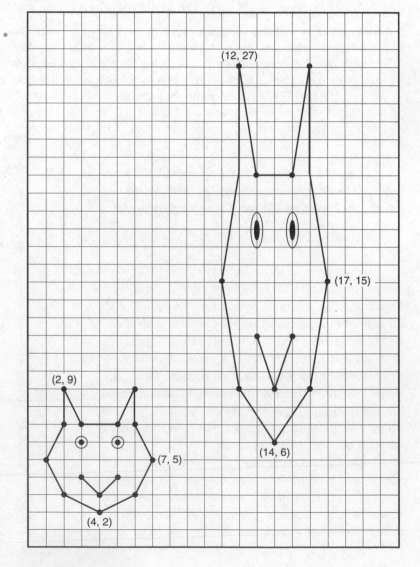

Chapter 7 **GEOMETRIC THINKING AND GEOMETRIC CONCEPTS**

Applying the Pythagorean Relationship

The geometric version of the Pythagorean relationship is about areas. The following activity has students use the coordinate grid and the Pythagorean relationship to develop a formula for the distance between points.

ACTIVITY 7.25

The Distance Formula

Have students draw a line between two points in the first quadrant that are not on the same horizontal or vertical line. The task is to use only the coordinates of the endpoints to calculate the distance between them in terms of the units on the grid. To this end, suggest that they draw a right triangle using the line as the hypotenuse. The vertex at the right angle will share one coordinate from each endpoint. Students can compute the areas of the squares on the legs and add to find the area of the square on the hypotenuse. The length of the original line segment (the distance between the points) is the number whose square is the area of the square on the hypotenuse. (This last sentence is a geometric interpretation of square root.) By computing the areas of these squares students can compute the length of the original line.

Have students look through all of their calculations and see how the coordinates of the two endpoints were used. Challenge students to use the same type of calculations to get the distance between two new points without drawing any pictures.

Although most students in the middle grades are unable to construct proofs, they should be able to follow the rationale if shown proofs. By leading students through the procedure of finding the length of one line (or the distance between the endpoints), you give them sufficient information to compute the lengths of other lines. Students will see that all they need are the coordinates of the two endpoints to compute the areas of all three squares and, hence, the length of the hypotenuse. If you then help them substitute letters for specific coordinates, a general distance formula results.

Slope

The topic of slope is another important connection between geometry and algebra. To begin a discussion of slope, draw several different slanted lines on the board. Discuss how they are different. Some are steeper than others. Some go up, others go down. If you agree that "up" means sloping upward from left to right, then you can agree which ones go up and which go down. This "steepness" of a line is an attribute that can be measured like other measurable attributes. To give slope a number requires a reference line. The coordinate grid provides a reference (the *x*-axis) and the numbers to use in the measurement. Spend some time having students invent their own methods for attaching a number to the concept of steepness.

The convention for measuring the steepness of a line or the *slope* is based on the ideas of the *rise* and *run* between any two points on the line. The *rise* is the vertical change from the left point to the right point—positive if up, negative if down. The *run* is the horizontal distance from the left point to the right point. Slope is then defined as *rise ÷ run* or the ratio of the vertical change to the horizontal change (see Figure 7.35). By agreement, vertical lines have no slope or the slope is said to be "undefined." Horizontal lines have a slope of 0 as a result of the definition.

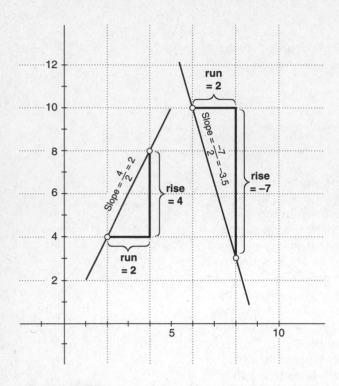

FIGURE 7.35 •

The slope of a line is rise ÷ run.

Once students are given the definition, they should be able to compute the slopes of any nonvertical line drawn on a coordinate grid without further assistance and *without formulas.*

A good problem-based task is to figure out what can be said about the slopes of parallel lines and perpendicular lines. (Is this geometry or algebra? Does it matter?)

Visualization Activities

Visualization activities involve seeing and understanding shapes from different perspectives.

Finding out how many different shapes can be made with a given number of simple tiles demands that students mentally flip and turn shapes in their minds and find ways to decide if they have found them all. Although pentominoes have been around for decades, as a visualization activity they remain superb. If your students are not familiar with pentominoes, the following activity is strongly recommended.

ACTIVITY 7.26

Pentominoes

A pentomino is a shape formed by joining five squares as if cut from a square grid. Each square must have at least one side in common with another. Provide students with five square tiles and a sheet of square grid paper for recording. Challenge them to see how many different pentomino shapes they can find. Shapes that are flips or turns of other shapes are not considered different. Do not tell students how many pentomino shapes there are. Good discussions will come from deciding if some shapes are really different and if all shapes have been found.

Once students have decided that there are just 12 pentominoes (see Figure 7.29, p. 215), the 12 pieces can then be used in a variety of activities. Paste the grids with the students' pentominoes onto tagboard and let them cut out the 12 shapes. These can be used in the next two activities.

It is also fun to explore the number of shapes that can be made from six equilateral triangles or from four 45-degree right triangles (halves of squares). With the right triangles, sides that touch must be the same length. How many of each of these "ominoes" do you think there are? These variations of pentominoes are excellent for a class that has worked previously with pentominoes and still is in need of an early visualization experience.

Lots of activities can be done with pentominoes. For example, try to fit all 12 pieces into a 6 × 10 or 5 × 12 rectangle. Also, each of the 12 shapes can be used as a tessellation tile. Another task is to examine each of the 12 pentominoes and decide which

Chapter 7   GEOMETRIC THINKING AND GEOMETRIC CONCEPTS

will fold up to make an open box. For those that are "box makers," which square is the bottom? Once a "box maker" has been identified, challenge students to write the letters M—A—T—H on the four sides so that the box will spell *MATH* around the sides.

As students work at mentally folding a "box maker" pentomino and attempting to correctly orient the letters of *MATH* on the sides, they are making connections between the two-dimensional world and the three-dimensional world. If a "box maker" had one more square attached at an appropriate place, you could fold it up to make a cube. A flat shape that will fold up to make a solid figure is called a *net* of that solid. The following activity suggests several challenges involving nets.

ACTIVITY 7.27

Net Challenges

The following tasks are only related because each involves nets of solids.

- For each of the pentomino "box makers," see how many different places a sixth square can be attached to create a net for a cube. Are there other nets for a cube that do not begin with a pentomino?
- Begin with a solid, such as a rectangular prism or square pyramid. Sketch as many nets as possible for this shape. Add to the collection some arrangements of the sides of the solid that are not nets. Challenge a friend to decide which are nets of the shape and which are not.
- Use Polydrons or 3D Geoshapes to create a flat figure that you think will fold up into a solid. Test the result. If the number and/or the type of flat shapes is specified, the task can be made more or less difficult. Can you make a net of a solid with 12 regular pentagons or 8 equilateral triangles? (These can be made into a *dodecahedron* and an *octahedron*, respectively, two of the five completely regular polyhedra, also known as the five *Platonic solids*.)

The following activity also provides students with experiences in the three-dimensional world but in a rather different manner. Here students also must mentally move shapes and predict the results. The activity combines ideas of line symmetry and (reflections) as well as visualization and spatial reasoning.

ACTIVITY 7.28

Notches and Holes

Use a half sheet of paper that will easily fit on the overhead. Fold it in half and then half again, making the second fold in the opposite direction from the first. Students make a sketch of the paper when it is opened, showing a line for each fold. With the paper folded, cut notches in one or two sides and/or cut off one or two corners. You can also use a paper punch to make a hole or two. While still folded, place the paper on the overhead showing the notches and holes. The folded edges should be to the left and at the top. (See Figure 7.36.) The task is for students to draw the notches and holes that they think will appear when you open the paper.

To introduce this activity, begin with only one fold and only two cuts. Stay with one fold until students are ready for a more difficult challenge.

VISUALIZATION ACTIVITIES

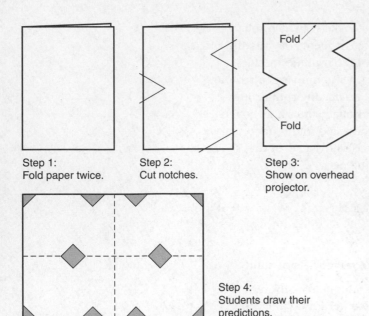

Step 1:
Fold paper twice.

Step 2:
Cut notches.

Step 3:
Show on overhead projector.

Fold

Fold

Step 4:
Students draw their predictions.

FIGURE 7.36 •••

An example showing how the "Notches and Holes" activity is done. Students make two folds and cut notches and/or punch holes in the folded paper. Before unfolding, they draw a sketch predicting the result when the paper is unfolded.

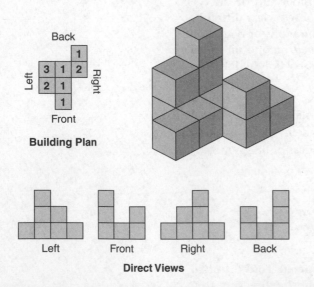

Building Plan

Left

Right

Back

Front

| 3 | 1 | 2 |
| 2 | 1 | |

1

1

Left   Front   Right   Back

Direct Views

FIGURE 7.37 •••

Tasks can begin with the Building Plan, or with the Direct View, or even with the building. Students give the other representations.

In "Notches and Holes" students will eventually learn which cuts create holes and how many and which cuts make notches in the edges or on the corners. Notice how line symmetry, or reflections, plays a major role in the activity. Symmetry determines the position, the shape, and the number of holes created by each cut.

STOP Stop now and try the "Notches and Holes" activity yourself. Try cuts in various places on the folded paper and see what is involved in this well-known activity.

One of the main goals of the Visualization strand of the Geometry Standard is to be able to identify and draw two-dimensional images of three-dimensional figures and to build three-dimensional figures from two-dimensional images. Activities aimed at this goal often involve drawings of small "buildings" made of 1-inch cubes.

ACTIVITY 7.29

Viewpoints

a. In the first version, students begin with a building and draw the left, right, front, and back direct views. In Figure 7.37, the building plan shows a top view of the building and the number of blocks in each position. After students build a building from a plan like this, their task is to draw the front, right, left, and back direct views as shown in the figure.

b. In the reverse version of the task, students are given right and front views. The task is to build the building that has those views. To record their solution, they draw a building plan (top view with numbers).

Notice that front and back direct views are symmetric, as are the left and right views. That is why only one of each is given in part b of the activity.

In "Viewpoints," students made "buildings" out of 1-inch cubes and coordinated these with direct views of the sides and top. A significantly more challenging activity is to draw perspective views of these block buildings or to match perspective drawings with a building. Isometric dot grids are used for the drawings. The next activity provides a glimpse at this form of visualization activity.

Perspective Drawings

a. In the first version, students begin with a perspective drawing of a building. The assumption is that there are no hidden blocks. From the drawing the students build the actual building with their blocks. To record the result, they draw a building plan indicating the number of blocks in each position.

b. In the second version, students are given either a block plan or the five direct views. They build the building accordingly and draw two or more of the perspective views. There are four possible perspectives from above the table: the front left and right, and the back left and right. It is useful to build the building on a sheet of paper with the words *front, back, left,* and *right* written on the edges to keep from getting different viewpoints confused.

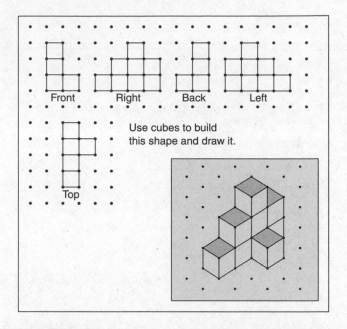

Front　Right　Back　Left

Top

Use cubes to build this shape and draw it.

FIGURE 7.38

Develop perspective and visual perception with cubes and plain views. Draw block "buildings" on isometric grids.

Figure 7.38 shows an example of this last activity. Some excellent resource books exist for this type of activity. It is not necessary to prepare these tasks yourself. Perhaps the best-known book is *Middle Grades Mathematics Project: Spatial Visualization* (Winter, Lappan, Phillips, & Fitzgerald, 1986). NCTM's *Navigating Through Geometry* books have similar activities in both the 3–5 and 6–8 grade books.

Technology Note

An amazing computer tool, the "Isometric Drawing Tool," for drawing perspective views of block buildings such as in Activity 7.30 is available on the *Illuminations* website (www.illuminations.nctm.org/tools/isometric/isometric.asp). This applet requires only mouse clicks to draw either whole cubes, any single face of a cube, or just lines. The drawings, however, are actually "buildings" and can be viewed as three-dimensional objects. They can be rotated in space so that they can be seen from any vantage. Prepared investigations are informative and also lead students through the features of the tool.

Another interesting connection between two and three dimensions is found in slicing solids in different ways. When a solid is sliced into two parts, a two-dimensional figure is formed on the slice faces. Figure 7.39 shows a cube being sliced off at the corner, leaving a triangular face. Slices can be explored with clay sliced with a potter's wire as shown in the figure. A niftier method is to partially fill a plastic solid with water. The surface of the water is the same as the face of a slice coinciding with the surface of the water. By tilting the shape in different ways, every possible "slice" can be observed. Small plastic solids such as *Power Solids* are excellent for this.

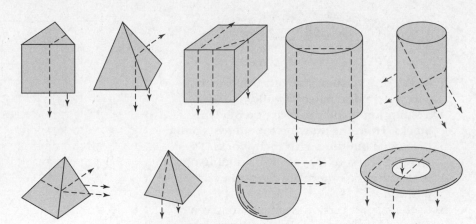

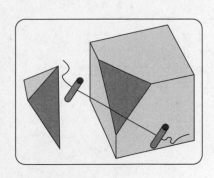

FIGURE 7.39 ●● ●● ●● ●●

Predict the slice face
before you cut a clay
model with a potter's
wire.

ACTIVITY 7.31

Water Slices

Students are given a solid and challenged to find out how to slice it to make a designated slice face. The list of challenges should include some that are impossible. Before water is poured into the solids, students must commit themselves on paper as to whether or not the slice is possible. If they think it is possible, they write and/or draw a description of where the slice must be made. Then water is put into the shape to test their predictions. If there are no plastic shapes available, clay models are the next best option. Here is a list of potential slice faces for a cube:

> Square, nonsquare rectangle, nonrectangular parallelogram, isosceles trapezoid, nonisosceles trapezoid, equilateral triangle, isosceles right triangle, other isosceles triangle, scalene right triangle, other scalene triangle.

A tetrahedron, a square pyramid, and prisms offer similar challenges. For other solids, it may be more interesting to find out how many different types of slice faces can be found and to describe each.

A *polyhedron* is a three-dimensional shape with polygons for all faces. Among the various polyhedra, the Platonic solids are especially interesting. *Platonic solids* is the name given to the set of completely regular polyhedrons. *Completely regular* means that each face is a regular polygon and every vertex has exactly the same number of faces joining at that point. An interesting visualization task appropriate for this level is to find and describe all of the Platonic solids.

ACTIVITY 7.32

Search for the Platonic Solids

Provide students with a supply of equilateral triangles, squares, regular pentagons, and regular hexagons from one of the plastic sets for building solids (e.g., *Polydron* or *Geofix*). Explain what a completely regular solid is. The task is to find as many different completely regular solids as possible.

One approach to conducting this activity is to leave it as stated and allow students to work with no additional guidance. Success will depend on their problem-solving skills. Alternatively, you might suggest a systematic approach as follows. Since the smallest number of sides a face can have is three, begin with triangles, then squares, then pentagons, and so on. Furthermore, since every vertex must have the same number of faces, try three faces at a point, then four, and so on. (It is clearly impossible to have only two faces at a point.)

With this plan, students will find that for triangles they can have three, four, or five triangles coming to a point. For each of these, they can begin with a "tent" of triangles and then add more triangles so that each vertex has the same number. With three at a point you get a four-sided solid called a *tetrahedron* (*tetra* = four). With four at each point you get an eight-sided solid called an *octahedron* (*octa* = eight). It is really exciting to build the shape with five triangles at each point. It will have 20 sides and is called an *icosahedron* (*icosa* = twenty).

In a similar manner, students will find that there is only one solid made of squares—three at each point and six in all—a *hexahedron* (*hex* = six), also called a cube. And there is only one solid with pentagons, three at each point, 12 in all. This is called a *dodecahedron* (*dodeca* = twelve).

STOP Why are there no regular polyhedra with six or more triangles or four or more squares? Why are there no regular polyhedra made with hexagons or with polygons with more than six sides? The best way to answer these questions is to experiment with the polygons and explain the answers in your own words. Students should do the same.

A fantastic skeletal icosahedron can be built out of the newspaper rods described earlier. (See Figure 7.6, p. 191.) Since five triangles converge at each point, there are also five edges emerging at each point. Simply work at bringing five rods to each vertex and remember that each face is a triangle. This icosahedron will be about 4 feet across and will be amazingly sturdy.

Assessment Note

Principles and Standards is extremely helpful for articulating growth in geometric content across the grades. For each of the four goals articulated by the standards (shape and properties, location, transformations, and visualization) examine the 3–5 grade-level expectations as well as those for the 6–8 grade band. (See Appendix A, p. 352.)

Try to include a sense of growth over time in your assessment of content. If you limit your assessment to a mastery of skills or definitions, the spirit of exploration that you want in your geometry program will be lost. We most often teach in a manner that reflects our assessment plans. Although mastery of some ideas is perhaps important, conceptual development is rarely reflected in memorizing definitions. In deciding what to assess and how, it is best to take a long-term view of geometry rather than a more traditional mastery-oriented approach.

EXPANDED LESSON

Triangle Midsegments

Based on Activity 7.13, p. 208

GRADE LEVEL: Eighth grade.

MATHEMATICS GOALS
- To look at the relationship between a triangle's midsegment and its base.
- To develop the rationale for why particular relationships exist in a triangle.
- To develop logical reasoning in a geometric context.

THINKING ABOUT THE STUDENTS
- Most students are beginning to function at the van Hiele level 2, where they are ready to grapple with "why" and "what-if" questions. Students are aware of the properties of angles formed by cutting parallel lines with a transverse line. They also have experience working with similar triangles.

- To do the lesson with a dynamic geometry program, students should be relatively competent with the program tools and be able independently to draw different geometric objects (e.g., triangles, lines, line segments), label vertices, find midpoints, and measure lengths and angles.

MATERIALS AND PREPARATION
- This lesson can be done either with computers or as a paper-and-pencil task. As described, the lesson only assumes a demonstration computer with display screen. Although desirable, a computer is not required.
- The computer used in the lesson requires a dynamic geometry program, such as *The Geometer's Sketchpad.*
- Students will need rulers that measure in centimeters.

lesson

BEFORE

Brainstorm
- Have each student draw a line segment measuring 16 cm near the long edge of a blank sheet of paper. Demonstrate using the computer. Label the segment BC.
- Have students randomly select another point somewhere on their papers but at least a few inches above BC. Illustrate on the computer that you want all students to have very different points. Some might be in the upper left, upper right, near the center, and so on. Have them label this point A and then draw segments AB and AC to create triangle ABC. Do the same on the computer.
- Next, students find the midpoints D and E of AB and AC, respectively, and draw the midsegment DE. Do the same on the computer. You can introduce the term *midsegment* if you wish as the line joining the midpoints of two sides of a triangle. Terminology is not important, however.
- Have students measure their midsegments and report what they find. Amazingly, all students should report a measure of 8 cm. On the computer, measure BC and DE. Move point A all over the screen. The two measures will stay the same, with the length of DE being half of BC. Even if B or C is moved, the ratio of BC to DE will remain 2 to 1.
- Ask students for any conjectures they may have about why this relationship exists. Discuss each idea briefly but without any evaluation.
- On the computer draw a line through A parallel to BC. Have students draw a similar line on their paper. Label points F and G on the line as shown here.

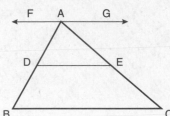

- Ask students what else they know about the figure now that line FG has been added. List all ideas on the board.

The Task

- What conjecture can be made about the midsegment of any triangle?
- What reason can be given for why the conjecture might be true?

Establish Expectations

- Students are to write out a conjecture about the midsegment of a triangle.
- In pairs, students are to continue to explore their sketch, looking for reasons why this particular relationship between the midsegment of a triangle and its base exists. They should record all of their ideas and be ready to share them with the class. If they wish to explore an idea on the computer sketch, they should be allowed to do so.

DURING

- Resist giving too much guidance at first. See what students can do on their own. Notice what they focus on in forming conjectures.
- For students having difficulty, suggest that they focus on angles ADE and ABC as well as angles AED and ACB. (These pairs of angles are congruent.)
- Suggest that they list all pairs of angles that they know are congruent. Why are they congruent?
- If necessary, ask students to compare triangle ABC with triangle ADE. What do they notice? They should note that the triangles are similar. Why are they similar?

AFTER

- Have students discuss their initial arguments for why the midsegment relationship holds. They can use the demonstration computer to share their ideas.
- Using their ideas, help students build arguments so that one can see how one point flows to the next in a logical sequence.

ASSESSMENT NOTES

- Look for students who struggle seeing the connections or relationships between properties. They may not be functioning at level 2 of the van Hiele levels of geometric thought.
- Do students see the difference between simply observing a relationship and considering the reasons the relationship exists?

- If students are not able to follow logical arguments (yours or their peers') in this activity, they may not yet be at the van Hiele level 2. These students need more informal experiences exploring properties of shapes and looking for relationships. Select from the level 1 activities for Shapes and Properties beginning on p. 193.
- If this activity is successful, continue having students grapple with making logical arguments for why the things they observe to be true are in fact true. Activity 7.12, "Angle Sum in a Triangle," provides students another opportunity to consider the reasoning behind a geometric relationship. The arguments there are similar to those in this activity.

next steps

EXPANDED LESSON

DEVELOPING MEASUREMENT CONCEPTS AND FORMULAS

Students begin exploring the meaning and process of measuring in kindergarten. By the time they get to the middle grades, they have had numerous experiences with attributes such as length, area, volume, time, and weight. They should have at least an intuitive feel for these attributes. In the middle grades, they investigate relationships between various attributes as they develop a more sophisticated understanding of measurement and begin to develop and use formulas to find measures.

big ideas

1 Measurement involves a comparison of an attribute of an item or situation with a unit that has the same attribute. Lengths are compared to units of length, areas to units of area, time to units of time, and so on. Before anything can be measured meaningfully, it is necessary to understand the attribute to be measured.

2 Meaningful measurement and estimation of measurements depend on a personal familiarity with the unit of measure being used.

3 Estimation of measures and the development of personal benchmarks for frequently used units of measure help students increase their familiarity with units, prevent errors in measurements, and aid in the meaningful use of measurement.

4 Measurement instruments are devices that replace the need for actual measurement units. It is important to understand how measurement instruments work so that they can be used correctly and meaningfully.

5 Area and volume formulas provide a method of measuring these attributes by using only measures of length.

6 Area, perimeter, and volume are related to each other, although not precisely or by formula. For example, as the shapes of regions or three-dimensional objects change but maintain the same areas or volumes, there is a predictable effect on the perimeters and surface areas.

Developing Measurement Concepts and Skills

Technically, a *measurement* is a number that indicates a comparison between the attribute of the object (or situation, or event) being measured (e.g., length of a shoe) and the same attribute of a given unit of measure (e.g., length of an inch). This may sound simple enough, but it is actually quite complex for students. In learning to measure, students first must understand the attribute being measured. What is meant by area, volume, and angle size? Then students need to learn that to measure that attribute they must use a unit that has that attribute, a notion that many times is not made clear for students—especially if they have been rushed to use formulas.

For most of the attributes that are measured in schools, we can say that *to measure* a given attribute means to compare that attribute (e.g., fill, cover, match) with a unit that has that same attribute. With this understanding, then, we can say that *the measure* of an attribute is a count of how many units are needed to fill, cover, or match the attribute of the object being measured. So, to measure something, one must perform three steps:

1. Decide on the attribute to be measured.
2. Select a unit that has that attribute.
3. Compare the units, by filling, comparing, matching, or some other method, with the attribute of the object being measured.

Measuring instruments such as rulers, scales, protractors, and clocks are devices that make the filling, covering, or matching process easier. A ruler lines up the units of length and numbers them. A protractor lines up the unit angles and numbers them. A clock lines up the units of time and marks them off.

Students have likely engaged in hands-on measurement activities throughout elementary school. However, even in middle school, some "filling" and "covering" activities can be worthwhile tasks to further strengthen students' understanding of various attributes and what it means to measure. In fact, the Measurement Standard in *Principles and Standards of School Mathematics* (NCTM, 2000) stresses that students should have ample opportunities to use informal units and engage in meaningful experiences with measurement *before* focusing on measurement tools and formulas. We share a general plan of instruction for measurement that follows this instructional sequence suggested in *PSSM*.

A General Plan of Instruction

A basic understanding of measurement suggests how to help students develop conceptual knowledge of measuring. These suggestions are summarized in Table 8.1.

Let's briefly discuss each of these three instructional components described in the table.

Making Comparisons

The first and most critical goal is for students to understand the attribute they are going to measure. When students compare objects on the basis of some measurable attribute, that attribute becomes the focus

TABLE 8.1 •
Plan for Measurement Instruction

Step One

Goal: Students will understand the attribute to be measured.

Type of Activity: Make comparisons based on the attribute. For example, longer/shorter, heavier/lighter. Use direct comparisons whenever possible.

Notes: When it is clear that the attribute is understood, there is no further need for comparison activities.

Step Two

Goal: Students will understand how filling, covering, matching, or making other comparisons of an attribute with measuring units produces a number called a measure.

Type of Activity: Use physical models of measuring units to fill, cover, match, or make the desired comparison of the attribute with the unit.

Notes: In most instances it is appropriate to begin with informal units. Progress to the direct use of standard units when appropriate and certainly before using formulas or measuring tools.

Step Three

Goal: Students will use common measuring tools with understanding and flexibility.

Type of Activity: Make measuring instruments and use them in comparison with the actual unit models to see how the measurement tool is performing the same function as the individual units. Be certain to make direct comparisons between the student-made tools and the standard tools.

Notes: Student-made tools are usually best made with informal units. Without a careful comparison with the standard tools, much of the value in making the tools can be lost.

DEVELOPING MEASUREMENT CONCEPTS AND SKILLS

of the activity. For example, is the capacity of one box more than, less than, or about the same as the capacity of another? No measurement is required, but some manner of comparing one volume to the other must be devised. The attribute of "capacity" (how much a container can hold) is inescapable.

Using Models of Units

The second goal is for students to understand what a unit of measure is and how it is used to produce a measurement. Students' initial measurement of any attribute should begin with informal units and progress over time to the use of standard units and standard measuring tools. Informal units make it easier to focus directly on the attribute being measured and can provide a good rationale for standard units. A discussion of the need for a standard unit can have more meaning after groups in your class have measured the same objects with their own units and arrived at different answers. In this chapter, informal units will be used in the development of angle measurement, an attribute with which most middle-grade students have little experience.

For most attributes that are measured in schools, it is possible to have physical models of the units of measure. Time and temperature are exceptions. (Many other attributes not commonly measured in school also do not have physical units of measure. Light intensity, speed, loudness, viscosity, and radioactivity are just a few examples.) Unit models can be found for both informal units and standard units. For length, for example, drinking straws (informal) or tagboard strips 1-foot long (standard) might be used as units.

The most easily understood use of unit models is actually to use as many copies of the unit as are needed to fill or match the attribute measured. To measure the area of the desktop with an index card unit, you can literally cover the entire desk with index cards. Somewhat more difficult is to use a single copy of the unit with an iteration process of moving it from position to position and keeping track of which areas the card has covered.

It is useful to measure the same object with different-sized units. Results should be predicted in advance and discussed afterward. This will help students understand that the unit used is as important as the attribute being measured. The fact that smaller units produce larger numeric measures, and vice versa, can only be constructed by reflecting on measurements with varying-sized units. Predictions and discussions of results add to the reflective nature of the activities.

Making and Using Measuring Instruments

An understanding of the devices we use to measure is the third goal. In the sixth National Assessment of Educational Progress (Kenney & Kouba, 1997), only 24 percent of fourth-grade students and 62 percent of eighth-grade students could give the correct measure of an object not aligned with the end of a ruler, as in Figure 8.1. These results point to the difference between using a measuring device and understanding how it works. Students also experienced difficulty when the increments on a measuring device were other than one unit.

If students actually make simple measuring instruments using unit models with which they are familiar, it is more likely that they will understand how an instrument measures. A ruler is a good example. If students line up physical units along a strip of tagboard and mark them off, they can see that it is the *spaces* on rulers and not the marks

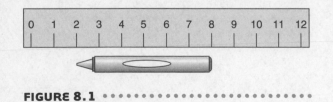

FIGURE 8.1

"How long is this crayon?"

or numbers that are important. Later in the chapter we illustrate how having students make their own protractors helps them focus on what they are measuring to find angle size. It is essential that the measurement with actual unit models be compared with the measurement using an instrument. Without this comparison, students may not understand that these two methods are really two means to the same end. Always have students explain how the ruler, scale, or other device compares to using actual units.

Assessment Note

As students use measuring tools, ask yourself if they are using them meaningfully. Rulers and protractors are often poorly understood. Ask students to find two different ways to measure with a ruler, or have them react to the technique used by another student. ("Monique measured the width of her locker. She lined up the 10-cm mark on one side. The other side of the locker was lined up between the 42- and 43-cm marks. Monique was confused. Without measuring the locker again, how would you help Monique?") Another technique is to have students explain how a ruler or protractor works to make a measurement. To help with their explanations, have them compare a student-made device, such as the waxed-paper protractor, with the standard device.

Estimation

Measurement estimation is the process of using mental and visual information to measure or make comparisons without the use of measuring instruments. It is a practical skill. Almost every day, we make estimates of measures. Do I have enough sugar to make the cookies? Can you throw the ball 50 feet? Is this suitcase over the weight limit? About how long is the fence?

The Role of Estimation in Learning Measurement

In addition to the value of estimation outside the classroom, building estimation into classroom measurement activities improves instruction. There are at least four good reasons for including estimation in measurement activities:

- Estimation helps students focus on the attribute being measured and the measuring process. Think how you would estimate the area of the front of this book with standard playing cards as the unit. To do so, you have to think about what area is and how the units might be fitted into the book cover.

- Estimation provides intrinsic motivation to measurement activities. It is fun to see how close you can come in your estimate or if your team can make a better estimate than the other teams in the room.

- When standard units are used, estimation helps develop familiarity with the unit. If you estimate the height of the door in meters before measuring, you have to devise some way to think about the size of a meter.

- The use of a benchmark to make an estimate promotes multiplicative reasoning. The width of the building is about one-fourth of the length of a football field—perhaps 25 yards.

DEVELOPING MEASUREMENT CONCEPTS AND SKILLS

Techniques of Measurement Estimation

Just as for computational estimation, specific strategies exist for estimating measures. Four strategies can be taught specifically:

1. *Develop and use benchmarks or referents for important units.* (This strategy is also a good way to develop familiarity with units.) Students should have a good referent for single units and also useful multiples of standard units. Referents or benchmarks for 1, 5, 10, and perhaps 100 pounds might be useful. A referent for 500 milliliters is very useful. These benchmarks can then be compared mentally to objects being estimated: "That tree is about as tall as four doorways, or between 8 and 9 meters tall."

2. *Use "chunking" when appropriate.* Figure 8.2 is an example. It may be easier to estimate the shorter chunks along the wall than to estimate the whole length as one. The weight of a stack of books is easier if some estimate is given to an "average" book.

3. *Use subdivisions.* This is a similar strategy to chunking, with the chunks imposed on the object by the estimator. For example, if the wall length to be estimated has no useful chunks, it can be mentally divided in half and then in fourths or even eighths by repeated halving until a more manageable length is arrived at. Length, volume, and area measurements all lend themselves to this technique.

4. *Iterate a unit mentally or physically.* For length, area, and volume, it is sometimes easy to mark off single units visually. You might use your hands or make marks or folds to keep track as you go. For length, it is especially useful to use a body measure as a unit and iterate with that. If you know, for example, that your stride is about $\frac{3}{4}$ meter, you can walk off a length and then multiply to get an estimate. Hand and finger widths are useful for shorter measures.

Tips for Teaching Estimation

Each of the four strategies just listed should be taught directly and discussed with students. But the best approach to improving estimation skills is to have students do a lot of estimating. Keep the following tips in mind:

1. Help students learn strategies by having them use a specified approach. Later activities should permit students to choose whatever techniques they wish.

FIGURE 8.2 • • • • • • • •

Estimating measures by chunking.

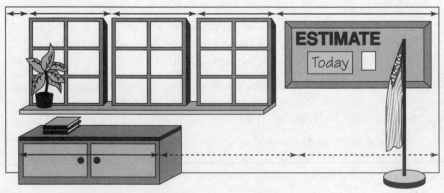

Estimate the room length.
Use: windows, bulletin board, and spaces between as "chunks."
Use: cabinet length—looks like about three cabinets will fit into the room—plus a little bit.

2. Periodically discuss how different students made their estimates. This will help students understand that there is no single right way to estimate and also remind them of different approaches that are useful.

3. Accept a range of estimates. Think in relative terms about what is a good estimate. Within 10 percent for length is quite good. Even 30 percent off may be reasonable for weights or volumes.

4. Sometimes have students give a range of measures that they believe includes the actual measure. This not only is a practical approach in real life but also helps focus on the approximate nature of estimation.

5. Make measurement estimation an ongoing activity. A daily measurement to estimate can be posted on the bulletin board. Students can turn in their estimates on paper and discuss them in a 5-minute period. Students can even be given the task of making up the things to estimate, with a team assigned this task each week.

6. Make an effort to include estimations of all attributes. It is easy to get carried away with length and forget about area, volume, weight, and angles.

Measurement Estimation Activities

Estimation activities need not be elaborate. Any measurement activity can have an "estimate first" component. For more emphasis on the process of estimation itself, simply think of things that can be estimated, and have students estimate. Here are a few suggestions.

ACTIVITY 8.1

Estimation Quickie

Select a single object such as a box, a watermelon, a jar, or even the principal. Each day, select a different attribute or dimension to estimate. For a watermelon, for example, students can estimate its length, girth, weight, volume, and surface area.

ACTIVITY 8.2

Estimation Scavenger Hunt

Conduct measurement scavenger hunts. Give teams a list of measurements and have them find things that are close to having those measurements. Permit no measuring instruments. A list might include the following items:

A length of 3.5 m
Something that weighs more than 1 kg but less than 2 kg
A container that holds about 200 ml
An angle that is less than 45 degrees

Let students suggest how to judge results in terms of accuracy.

ACTIVITY 8.3

E-M-E Sequences

Use estimate-measure-estimate sequences. Select pairs of objects to estimate that are somehow related or close in measure but not the same. Have students

(continued)

DEVELOPING MEASUREMENT CONCEPTS AND SKILLS

estimate the measure of the first and check by measuring. Then have them estimate the second. Here are some examples of pairs:

Width of a window, width of a wall
Volume of a coffee mug, volume of a pitcher
Distance between the eyes, width of the head
Weight of a handful of marbles, weight of a bag of marbles

Activity 8.3 can help students understand how benchmarks are used in estimation.

The Approximate Nature of Measurement

In all measuring activities, emphasize the use of approximate language. The desktop is *about* 6 square feet. The table is *about* $2\frac{1}{2}$ feet tall. The use of approximate language is very useful because it emphasizes that many measurements do not come out evenly. Students can begin to search for smaller units or use fractional units to try to measure exactly. Here is an opportunity to develop the idea that all measurements include some error. Each smaller unit or subdivision produces a greater degree of *precision*.

For example, let's consider measuring the length of a pencil. Suppose that we have a ruler that is marked off only in whole inches (see Figure 8.3(a)). Using this measuring tool, the best that we can say is that the pencil is a little more than 3 inches long. In fact, since it is less than halfway between the 3-inch and the 4-inch marks, we would likely round down and say it is about 3 inches long. With the level of precision offered by this ruler, the best we can say is that it is about 3 inches long. The difference between the actual measure and what we are reporting is less than $\frac{1}{2}$ inch. This difference is the error in measurement.

Now consider a ruler that has a little more precision (i.e., smaller units) so that we can get a more accurate measurement of the same pencil. The ruler in Figure 8.3(b) is marked in half inches. Using this ruler, we can see that the pencil is more than halfway between the 3- and $3\frac{1}{2}$-inch marks, so we would round up to report that the pencil is about $3\frac{1}{2}$ inches long. With the level of precision of this ruler, the best we can say is that the pencil is about $3\frac{1}{2}$ inches long. The error in measurement in this situation is less than $\frac{1}{4}$ inch.

Hence, a length measure can never be more than one-half unit in error because of how we round. And yet, since there is mathematically no "smallest unit," there is always some error involved.

FIGURE 8.3 • • • • • • • •

Measuring the length of a pencil with an inch ruler. The precision with which we can measure depends on the increments marked on the ruler. The same is true of any measuring device.

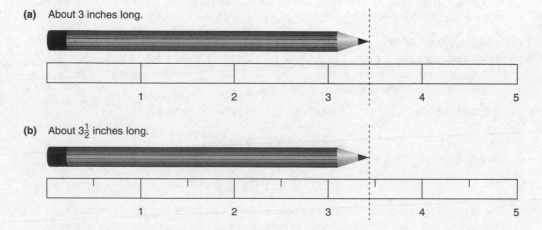

(a) About 3 inches long.

(b) About $3\frac{1}{2}$ inches long.

Measuring Angles

Angle measurement is often mysterious or difficult for students for several reasons: The attribute of angle size is often misunderstood, the idea of using an angle to measure angles is usually poorly developed, and protractors are introduced and used without understanding how they work. In this section we suggest an approach that minimizes these difficulties. The sequence suggested follows the plan of instruction described earlier, progressing from comparison activities to informal units and, finally, to measurement tools.

Comparing Angles: Understanding the Attribute

The attribute of angle size might be called the "spread of the angle's rays." Angles are composed of two rays that are infinite in length with a common vertex. The only difference in their size is how widely or narrowly the two rays are spread apart.

Some students mistakenly believe that they can use a ruler to measure the spread of the angle or the distance between the rays. Other students believe the size of the angle has something to do with the "length" of the rays that form the angle. In an effort to help students understand the attribute of angle size, one approach is to have them think about how much one ray has rotated away from the other. Two rulers held together near the ends can be used to demonstrate this idea. As one ruler is rotated, the size of the angle is seen to get larger. Instead of two rulers, two pencils or straws of different lengths can be used to emphasize that it is not the "length" of the rays that determines the size of the angle but the amount of turning that has occurred. The downfall of this approach is that when we see angles represented, the rays have already been spread—there is no apparent rotation. (Do you think of the angles in a triangle as one side being rotated away from the other?) So, although this rotation approach can help students focus on what is being measured, students should also understand how the notion of rotation is not evident in most representations of angles.

Another idea to help students conceptualize the attribute of the spread of the rays is to directly compare two angles by tracing one and placing it over the other, as in Figure 8.4. Be sure to have students compare angles with sides of different lengths. Again, this helps students realize that the lengths of the sides of the angle do not determine angle size. Plus, a wide angle with short sides may seem smaller than a narrow angle with long sides. This is a common misconception among students. As soon as students can tell the difference between a large angle and a small one, regardless of the length of sides, you can move on to measuring angles.

Using Units of Angular Measure

A unit for measuring an angle must be an angle. Nothing else has the same attribute of spread that we want to measure. (Contrary to popular opinion, you do not need to use degrees to measure angles.)

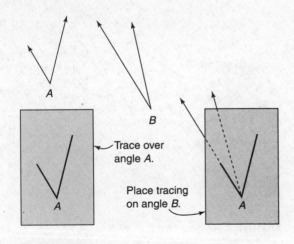

FIGURE 8.4 •••••••••••••••••••

Which angle is larger? Use tracings to compare.

MEASURING ANGLES

A Unit Angle

Give each student an index card or a small piece of tagboard. Have students draw a narrow angle on the tagboard using a straightedge and then cut it out. The resulting wedge can then be used as a unit of angular measure by counting the number that will fit in a given angle. Pass out a worksheet with assorted angles on it, and have students use their unit to measure them. Because students made their own unit angles, the results will differ and can be discussed in terms of unit size.

Activity 8.4 illustrates that measuring an angle is the same as measuring length or area. Unit angles are used to fill or cover the spread of an angle just as unit lengths fill or cover a length. Once this concept is well understood, you can move on to the use of measuring instruments.

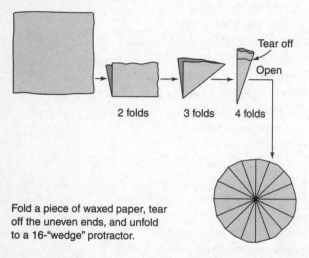

Fold a piece of waxed paper, tear off the uneven ends, and unfold to a 16-"wedge" protractor.

FIGURE 8.5 •

Making a waxed-paper protractor.

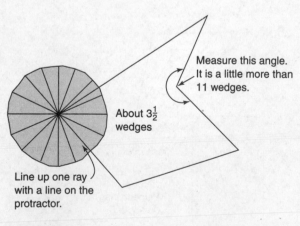

FIGURE 8.6 •

Measuring angles in a polygon using a waxed-paper protractor.

Making a Protractor

The protractor is one of the most poorly understood measuring instruments found in schools. Part of the difficulty arises because the units (degrees) are so very small. It would be physically impossible to cut out a single degree and use it in, say, Activity 8.4. Another problem is that there are no visible angles showing; there are only little marks around the outside edge of the protractor. Finally, the numbering that appears on most protractors runs both clockwise and counterclockwise along the marked edges. "Which numbers do I use?" By making a protractor with a large unit angle, all of these mysterious features can be understood. A careful comparison with a standard protractor will then permit that instrument to be used with understanding.

Tear off about a foot of ordinary waxed paper for each student. Have the students fold the paper in half and crease the fold tightly. Fold in half again so that the folded edges match. Repeat this two more times, each time bringing the folded edges together and creasing tightly. Cut or tear off the resulting wedge shape about 4 or 5 inches from the vertex and unfold. If done correctly, there will be 16 angles surrounding the center, as in Figure 8.5. This serves as an excellent protractor with a unit angle that is one-eighth of a straight angle. It is sufficiently transparent that it can be placed over an angle on paper, on the blackboard, or on the overhead projector to measure angles, as shown in Figure 8.6. Reasonable estimates of angle measures can be made with a waxed-paper protractor as small as the one in Figure 8.6. In that figure, one angle of a free-form polygon is measured for you. Use a waxed-paper protractor to mea-

sure the other four angles in this polygon as carefully as possible. Use fractional estimates. Your sum for all five interior angles should be very close to 24 wedges. There are
two possible ways to get the measure of the angle indicated with the arrow. How would
you measure that angle if your protractor was only a half circle instead of a full circle?

The waxed-paper protractor makes it quite clear how a protractor fits unit angles
into an angle for measurement. When measuring angles, students can easily estimate
halves, thirds, or fourths of a "wedge," a possible name for this informal unit angle.
This is sufficiently accurate to measure, for example, the interior angles of a polygon
and discover the usual relationship between the number of sides and the sum of the
interior angles. For a triangle, the sum is 8 wedges, recorded as 8^w. For a quadrilateral,
the sum is 16^w. And in general, the sum for an n-sided polygon is $(n - 2) \times 8^w$. The
superscript w is a forerunner of the degree symbol (°).

Figure 8.7 illustrates how a tagboard semicircle can be made into a protractor to
measure angles in wedges. This tagboard version is a bit closer to a standard protractor,
since the rays do not extend down to the vertex and the markings are numbered in two
directions. The only difference between this protractor and a standard one is the size of
the unit angle. The standard unit angle is the *degree,* which is simply a very small angle.
A standard protractor is not very helpful in teaching the meaning of a degree. But an
analogy between wedges and degrees and between these two protractors is a very effective approach. (See the Blackline Masters.)

Encourage students to determine and use benchmark angles such as right angles,
straight angles, and 45-degree angles. Familiarity with these angles will make it less
likely that students will misread a protractor. For example, if students have estimated
that an angle is less than 90 degrees, when they see the choices on the protractor of
"30" and "150" degrees, they will be more likely to correctly read its measurement as
30 degrees.

Waxed-paper wedges

Degrees

FIGURE 8.7 • • • • • • • •

Comparisons of protrac-
tors and unit angles.

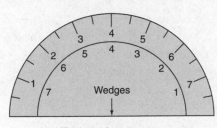

Tagboard protractor

Standard protractor

The marks on the tagboard wedge protractor are the rays on the waxed-paper version.
The marks on a plastic protractor are the rays of <u>degrees</u>. A degree is just a very small angle.
A large picture of 180 degrees can be found in the Blackline Masters.

Measuring Area

Area is a measure of the space inside a region or how much it takes to cover a region. As with other attributes, students must first understand the attribute of area before measuring. Although students have been learning about area since early elementary school, data from the seventh National Assessment of Educational Progress suggest that fourth- and eighth-grade students have an incomplete understanding of the concept (Martin & Strutchens, 2000). Providing some opportunities for middle school students to measure area by covering or physically comparing shapes to further develop their understanding of area will be time well spent.

The following activity is a good starting point to see what ideas your students have about area measurement.

ACTIVITY 8.5

Cover and Compare

Draw two rectangles and a blob shape on a sheet of paper. Make it so that the three areas are not the same but with no area clearly largest or smallest. The students' task is to first make a guess about which is the smallest and the largest of the three shapes. After recording their guesses, they should use a cover of their choice to decide. Provide small units such as circular disks, Color Tiles, lima beans, or any unit that has area as an attribute. They should explain in writing what they found out.

After filling the regions with units of area, students may come up with different measures for the same region, especially if round units are used. Discuss these differences with students. Point to the difficulties involved in making measurements around the edges of regions when the unit used to measure does not fit exactly along the edges or when the unit used to measure does not cover the region entirely. Avoid the idea that there is a "right" answer. Remember that the goal is to reinforce the notion of what measuring area means and to assess where your students are in this understanding.

Assessment Note

In Activity 8.5, as students decide which region is the smallest and largest prior to actually filling the regions, notice how they go about comparing the regions. Think about what their approach tells you about their understanding of area. What part of the region do they focus on? Are they looking at the linear dimensions of the objects and attempting to compare those? If so, are they aware of how these linear dimensions help them measure the region *inside* or are they just attempting to apply the formula $L \times W$? Are they using an imaginary visual "guesstimate" of a unit of area and moving those around the region while they count and then comparing counts? You may have to ask students questions to clarify for yourself exactly how they are reasoning.

The following activity provides an opportunity for students to physically compare areas of given rectangles without using explicit units of area.

ACTIVITY 8.6

Rectangle Comparison—No Units

Provide students with pairs of rectangles as follows.

Pair A: 2×9 and 3×6
Pair B: 1×10 and 3×5
Pair C: 3×8 and 4×5

(These three rectangles can be found in the Blackline Masters.)

BLM 25

The rectangles should be blank except for the labels. The students' task is to decide in each pair which rectangle has the greater area or if the two are the same size. They are allowed to cut or fold the rectangles in any way they wish, but they must include an explanation for their decision in each pair. Pair C will cause the most difficulty, and you may wish to reserve it as a challenge.

 Consider how you would compare each pair of rectangles in the preceding activity without relying on a formula or drawing squares.

In the first two pairs, the skinny rectangle can be folded and cut to either match or be easily compared to the second rectangle. For pair C, one rectangle can be placed on the other and then the extended pieces compared.

Units of Area and "Instruments" for Measuring Area

Although square units are the most convenient units of area (and most commonly used), any tile that adequately fills up a plane region can be used. Even filling a region with uniform circles or lima beans provides a useful idea of what it means to measure areas.

With the exception of computer drafting equipment, there really are no instruments designed for measuring area. However, grids of various types can be thought of as a kind of "area ruler." A grid of squares for area does exactly what a ruler does for length. It lays out the units for you. Square grids are available in the Blackline Masters. Note that triangular grids can also be used. Make transparencies of any grid paper. Have students place the grid over the region to be measured and count the units inside. An alternative method is to trace around a region on a paper grid.

BLMs 7, 8, & 11

Area and Perimeter

Middle school students should also begin to develop an understanding of the relationship between area and perimeter (the distance around a region) and the units used to measure them. Area and perimeter are continually a source of confusion for students. Perhaps it is because both involve regions to be measured or because students are asked to memorize formulas for both concepts and tend to get the formulas confused. Both formulas use the same linear measurements, length (*L*) and width (*W*), and if the formulas are not understood conceptually, students can easily forget which formula to use when.

Whatever the reason for students confusing area and perimeter, expect that even students in the middle grades will confuse these two ideas. An interesting approach to alleviating this confusion is to contrast the two ideas, as is done in the next activities.

ACTIVITY 8.7

Fixed Perimeters

Give students a loop of string that is exactly 24 units long. (Use a non-stretchy string. Double the string into a loop that is 1 foot in length and mark the strings at this length. Tie a knot just beyond the marks so that the resulting loop is 24 inches.) The task is to decide what different-sized rectangles can be made with a perimeter of 24 inches. Students may want to use a 1-inch grid to place their strings on. Each different rectangle can be recorded on grid paper with the area noted.

An alternative to the string loop is to simply use centimeter grid paper and ask students to find rectangles with a perimeter of 24.

The loop of string provides students with a concrete representation of the fixed perimeter. If the loop is untied and stretched in a straight line, it can be measured with a ruler to indicate that perimeter is a linear measure.

EXPANDED LESSON

(pages 263–264)
A complete lesson plan based on "Fixed Areas" can be found at the end of this chapter.

ACTIVITY 8.8

Fixed Areas

Provide students with 36 square tiles such as Color Tiles. The task is to see how many rectangles can be made with an area of 36—that is, using all 36 tiles to make filled-in rectangles, not just borders. Each new rectangle should be recorded by sketching the outline and the dimensions on grid paper. Centimeter or half-centimeter grids are good for recording. For each rectangle, students should determine and record the perimeter.

 Before reading further, think about the two previous activities. For "Fixed Areas," will all of the perimeters be the same? If not, what can you say about the shapes with longer or shorter perimeters? For "Fixed Perimeters," will the areas remain the same? Why or why not?

You may have been surprised to find out that two rectangles having the same area do not necessarily have the same perimeter. Similarly, two shapes with the same perimeter do not always have the same area. And, of course, this fact is not restricted to rectangles.

As students do Activities 8.7 and 8.8, have them keep track of the new areas and perimeters they find in a table. Using the table they can make graphs that illustrate the relationships between the side of the rectangle and both the area and perimeter. For the data found in the "Fixed Perimeters" activity, suggest that students plot the length against the width of the various rectangles. They should also plot the length against the area of the rectangles. These relationships are discussed in Chapter 10 as early examples of functions. Figure 10.2 (p. 288) shows what the two graphs should look like. For the

"Fixed Areas" activity, students will be able to find nine different rectangles, assuming that the 2 × 18 rectangle and the 18 × 2 rectangle are counted as two. The graph of the length against the perimeter (Figure 8.8) shows that as the rectangle approaches a square shape, the perimeter gets smaller.

Even though the equation of the graph in Figure 8.8 may be too difficult for students to determine, they can plot the points and draw the curve. To get the formula, note that $A = 36 = LW$. Therefore, $W = 36/L$. Substitute this in the formula $P = 2L + 2W$ and get $P = 2L + 2(36/L)$.

As an extension to "Fixed Perimeters," have students try the next activity. It can assess whether students can apply their findings from the "Fixed Perimeters" activity to irregular regions.

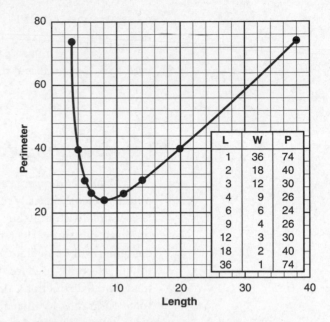

L	W	P
1	36	74
2	18	40
3	12	30
4	9	26
6	6	24
9	4	26
12	3	30
18	2	40
36	1	74

FIGURE 8.8 •

Rectangles are made using 36 square tiles. The graph shows how the length of each rectangle affects the perimeter. The smallest perimeter will always occur when the rectangle is the "fattest" or, in this case, a square. The graph can be drawn with no skills other than the ability to plot points.

ACTIVITY 8.9

"Out of Shape" Areas

Pose the following situation to students: Nathan wants to find the area of a lake on his uncle's property. Share Figure 8.9 with students as a representation of an aerial photograph of the lake that has been placed over a 1-cm square grid. Explain to students that Nathan has learned how to find the area of rectangles in school by counting the squares inside the rectangle. So he cuts a piece of string that goes all the way around the outside of the shape. He then forms the string into a square, places it on top of centimeter grid paper, and counts the number of square centimeters inside his string. He uses this estimate as the estimate for the area of the irregular shape. The students' task is to decide if Nathan's method gives a good estimate of the area of the lake and to explain why or why not.

Some students will need to repeat Nathan's strategy and compare their results to simply estimating the square centimeters inside the irregular shape. Provide them with a copy of an irregular shape drawn onto centimeter grid paper, as shown in Figure 8.9, and with nonstretchy string. Some students make the connection between the "Fixed Perimeters" activity and argue that, with a fixed perimeter, the area will vary and depends on the shape. Encourage students to continue to explore with the string and grid paper to see if they can find other shapes (i.e., nonpolygons) that have greater area than the square. (For

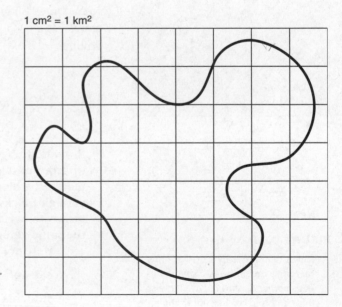

1 cm² = 1 km²

FIGURE 8.9 •

Finding the area of an irregular shape that represents a lake.

a fixed perimeter, a circle will have a larger area than any other shape with the same perimeter.)

The idea of a fixed perimeter can be extended to three dimensions. There a figure with a fixed volume and the smallest surface area will be a sphere.

Measuring Volume

Volume and *capacity* are both terms for measures of the "size" of three-dimensional objects. *Volume* typically refers to the amount of space that an object takes up. Volume is measured with units such as cubic inches or cubic centimeters—units that are based on linear measures. The term *capacity* is generally used to refer to the amount that a container will hold. Standard units of capacity include quarts and gallons, liters and milliliters—units used for liquids as well as the containers that hold them. Having made these distinctions, they are not ones to worry about. Many people use the terms *volume* and *capacity* interchangeably.

By middle school most students understand the concept of capacity and the corresponding units. They have also been introduced to the concept of volume in lower grades. However, many middle school students still experience some confusion about the concept. For example, some students are bothered by the fact that volume is measured with cubic units when the object that is being measured may or may not be a cube. Also, many students believe that if you know the volume of a three-dimensional object then you can figure out its surface area. (This works for a cube and a sphere but not for most three-dimensional objects.) Therefore, students' understanding of volume should be extended and deepened at the middle school level to address these and other misconceptions.

As with area, providing some opportunities for middle school students to measure volume by filling objects will be time well spent. The following activity is a good starting point to see what ideas your students have about volume.

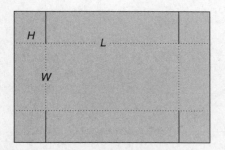

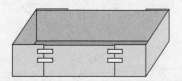

FIGURE 8.10 • • • • • • • • • • • •

Make small boxes by starting with a rectangle and drawing a square on each corner as shown. Cut on the solid lines and fold the box up, wrapping the corner squares to the outside and tape or glue them to the sides as shown.

ACTIVITY 8.10

Fill and Compare

Provide students with a pair of small boxes that you have folded up from posterboard. (See Figure 8.10.) Use unit dimensions that match the blocks that you have. Students are given two boxes and enough blocks to cover the bottom of both boxes. The students' task is to decide which box has the greater volume or if they have the same volume.

Here are some suggested box dimensions ($L \times W \times H$):

6 × 3 × 4   5 × 4 × 4   3 × 9 × 3   6 × 6 × 2   5 × 5 × 5

Students should use words, drawings, and numbers to explain their conclusions. The boxes can be filled with cubes to confirm conclusions. No formulas should be used unless students can explain them.

Assessment Note

As students decide which box has the greater volume, notice how they compare the boxes. Think about what their approach to comparing the boxes tells you about their understanding of volume. What part of the box do they focus on? Are they looking at the linear dimensions of the boxes and attempting to compare those? If so, are they aware of how these linear dimensions help them measure the *inside* of the box, or are they just attempting to apply the formula $L \times W \times H$? You may have to ask students questions to clarify for yourself exactly how they are reasoning.

The next activity offers students another opportunity to fill objects in order to compare volumes. This activity is actually easier to conduct but a bit more difficult to try to predict the outcome.

ACTIVITY 8.11

Comparing Tubes

Give each pair of students two sheets of construction paper and tape. They are to make a tube shape (cylinder) with one sheet by taping the two long edges together. Using the second sheet, they are to make a shorter, fatter tube by taping the short edges together. The task is for students to decide which cylinder (when placed upright) holds the most or whether they have the same capacity.

STOP Even adults have difficulty judging which of the two containers will hold more. Try it yourself before reading further.

The results may be surprising. Before doing this with your class, survey them to see how many select which option. Most groups split roughly in thirds between the short and fat, tall and skinny, or same options. Without using formulas, try using a lightweight filler such as Styrofoam packing peanuts. (Heavier fillers, like beans, tend to flow out the bottom of the cylinder unless you use card stock.) Place the skinny cylinder inside the fat one. Fill the inside tube and then lift it up, allowing the filler to empty into the fat cylinder.

Use this as an opportunity to point out that surface area is like the outer skin of three-dimensional objects. The manner in which the cylinders were constructed for this activity demonstrates that surface area of objects can be found by dissecting the objects into two-dimensional nets. This is further illustrated with spheres in the section on developing formulas.

The next activity continues to help students understand more about the relationship between an object's surface area and volume. This activity is exactly analogous to Activity 8.8, "Fixed Areas." Here the volume is fixed and students look for changes in surface area.

Fixed Volume: Comparing Prisms

Give each pair of students a supply of multilink cubes or wooden cubes. Their task is, for a fixed number of cubes, to build different rectangular prisms and record the surface area for each prism formed. A good number of cubes to suggest is 64, since a minimal surface area will occur with a 4 × 4 × 4 cube. With 64 cubes a lot of prisms can be made. However, if you are short of cubes, other good choices are 24 or 36 cubes. Using the tables students construct, they should observe any patterns that occur. In particular, what happens to the surface area as the prism becomes less like a tall, skinny box and more like a cube? Repeat the activity several times with different fixed volumes (i.e., numbers of cubes).

The goal here is for students to realize that volume does not dictate surface area and to recognize the pattern between surface area and volume that is similar to the one found between area and perimeter. Namely, prisms that are more cubelike have less surface area than those prisms with the same volume that are less cubelike.

Once students have developed formulas for computing area and volume, they can continue to explore the relationships between surface area and volume, and area and perimeter.

Having efficient ways to compute these measurements helps students to focus more easily on these relationships. Once they have these tools available to them, an interesting exploration for students is to determine what happens to the volume and surface area (area and perimeter) if the dimensions of the solid (two-dimensional shape) are increased by a factor of k. This idea is also explored in Activity 6.9 (p. 168). The way that area and volume change when the linear dimensions of the shapes change is a wonderful exploration in proportional reasoning.

Standard Units of Measure

As pointed out earlier, there are a number of reasons for teaching measurement using nonstandard units. However, measurement sense demands that students be familiar with the common measurement units and that they be able to make estimates in terms of these units and meaningfully interpret measures depicted with standard units.

Perhaps the biggest error in measurement instruction is the failure to recognize and separate two types of objectives: first, understanding the meaning and technique of measuring a particular attribute and, second, learning about the standard units commonly used to measure that attribute. These two objectives can be developed separately; when both objectives are attempted together, confusion is likely. Once students feel comfortable with measurement of an attribute, they can focus on standard units.

Instructional Goals

Three broad goals relative to standard units of measure can be identified:

1. *Familiarity with the unit.* Familiarity means that students should have a basic idea of the size of commonly used units and what they measure. Without this famil-

iarity, measurement sense is impossible. It is more important to know about how much 1 liter of water is or to be able to estimate a shelf as 5 feet long than to have the ability to measure either of these accurately.

2. *Ability to select an appropriate unit.* Related to unit familiarity is knowing what is a reasonable unit of measure in a given situation. The choice of an appropriate unit is also a matter of required precision. (Would you measure your lawn to purchase grass seed with the same precision as you would use in measuring a window to buy a pane of glass?) Students need practice in using common sense in the selection of appropriate standard units.

3. *Knowledge of a few important relationships between units.* The emphasis should be kept to those relationships that are commonly used, such as inches, feet, and yards or milliliters and liters. Tedious conversion exercises do little to enhance measurement sense. The goal of unit relationships is the least important of all measurement objectives.

Developing Unit Familiarity

The importance of familiarity with standard units of measure can be seen in the reluctance (even fear) on the part of a majority of U.S. citizens to adopt the metric system. The average adult develops a "feel" for units used throughout life: inch, foot, mile, pound, cup, gallon. These *customary* units are not easier to use than metric units, but they are familiar, whereas *metric* units are not. Helping students develop familiarity with the most frequently used units of measure in both systems is, thus, an important goal of instruction.

Two types of activities can help develop familiarity with standard units: (1) comparisons that focus on a single unit and (2) activities that develop personal referents or benchmarks for single units or easy multiples of units.

ACTIVITY 8.13

About One Unit

Give students a model of a standard unit and have them search for things that measure about the same as that one unit. For example, to develop familiarity with the meter, give students a piece of rope 1 meter long. Have them make lists of things that are about 1 meter. Keep separate lists for things that are a little less (or more) or twice as long (or half as long). Encourage students to find familiar items in their daily lives. In the case of lengths, be sure to include circular lengths. Later, students can try to predict if a given object is more than, less than, or close to 1 meter.

The same activity can be done with other unit lengths. Parents can be enlisted to help students find familiar distances that are about 1 mile or about 1 kilometer. Suggest in a letter that they check the distances around the neighborhood, to the school or shopping center, or along other frequently traveled paths.

For the standard weights of gram, kilogram, ounce, and pound, students can compare objects on a two-pan balance with single copies of these units. It may be more effective to work with 10 grams or 5 ounces. Students can be encouraged to bring in familiar objects from home to compare on the classroom scale.

Standard area units are thought of in terms of lengths. Rather than imagining the squared units, such as square inches or square feet, we imagine the length of one of

STANDARD UNITS OF MEASURE

these units. So familiarity with lengths is important. Familiarity with a single degree is not as important as some idea of 30, 45, 60, and 90 degrees.

The second approach to unit familiarity is to begin with very familiar items and use their measures as references or benchmarks. A doorway is a bit more than 2 meters. A bag of flour is a good reference for 5 pounds. Your bedroom may be about 10 feet long. A paper clip weighs about a gram and is about 1 centimeter wide. A gallon of milk weighs a little less than 4 kilograms.

Of special interest for length are benchmarks found on our bodies. These become quite familiar over time and can be used as approximate rulers in many situations.

ACTIVITY 8.14

Personal Benchmarks

Measure your body. About how long is your foot, your stride, your hand span (stretched and with fingers together), the width of your finger, your arm span (finger to finger and finger to nose), the distance around your wrist and around your waist, and your height to waist, to shoulder, and to head? Perhaps you cannot remember all of these, but some may prove to be useful benchmarks, and some may be excellent models for single units. Most people can find a 10-cm length somewhere on their hands or a fingernail width that is about 1 cm. Give students a card similar to Figure 8.11 to assist them in making their own body rulers.

To help remember these references, they must be used in activities in which lengths, volumes, and so on are compared to the benchmarks to estimate measurements.

Choosing Appropriate Units

Should the room be measured in meters or kilometers? Should the concrete blocks be weighed in grams or kilograms? The answers to questions such as these involve more than simply knowing how big the units are, although that is certainly required. Another consideration involves the need for precision. If you were measuring your wall in order to cut a piece of molding or woodwork to fit, you would need to measure it very precisely. The smallest unit would be an inch or a centimeter, and you would also use small fractional parts. But if you were determining how many 8-foot molding strips to buy, the nearest foot would probably be sufficient.

FIGURE 8.11 • • • • • •

Possible measures that students can find to create their personal body rulers.

_____'s Body Ruler
(Name of student)

My hand span is _____ cm.
(measure outstretched hand between tip of thumb and tip of little finger)

The width of my _____ fingernail is 1 cm or ____ mm.

The width of the back of my hand is _____ cm.

My height is _____ m or _____ cm.

My mass in kilograms is _____ kg.

ACTIVITY 8.15

Guess the Unit

Find examples of measurements of all types in newspapers, on signs, or in other everyday situations. Present the context and measures but without units. The task is to predict what units of measure were used. Have students discuss their choices.

Developing Relationships Between Units

The number of inches in a foot or a yard or the number of cups in a quart is the type of information that must eventually be committed to memory. Practice with conversions is something that lends itself well to pencil-and-paper work. This procedural aspect of unit familiarity has been overworked in the curriculum largely due to the ease of testing rather than the need to know.

Many students may know that there are 16 ounces in 1 pound, but when they try to determine how many pounds are in 90 ounces, they get confused over which operation to use. This is partly a matter of understanding the meanings of operations. However, simple common sense can help. In this example, since pounds are heavier than ounces, it is reasonable to end up with fewer pounds than ounces.

The customary system involves an unfortunate variety of conversion factors, and as long as the United States continues to use it, teachers will have to deal with helping students commit the most commonly used factors to memory.

Exact conversions between the metric and the customary systems should never be done. From the standpoint of familiarity with these systems, "soft" or "friendly" conversions are useful as long as we live in a country that seems bent on having two systems of measurement. For example, a liter is "a gulp more" than a quart (the "gulp" is about $\frac{1}{4}$ cup), and a meter is "a bit longer" than a yard. The same is true for benchmarks. One hundred meters is about one football field plus one end zone, or about 110 yards. One kilometer is a little more than half a mile.

Assessment Note

Consider what you as a teacher can learn from these two tasks:

1. 427 centimeters = _____ meters
2. Estimate the length of this rope in centimeters and in meters. What ideas did you use to help make your estimate?

Both tasks relate centimeters to meters. The second task requires a student to have unit familiarity as well. Does the student use a meter–centimeter relationship or make two independent estimates? How are the estimates made? Are familiar benchmarks for the unit being used? Feedback related to these questions is available as students do the second task but not the first. Much more information about a student's understanding of unit relationships and familiarity with units can be gained from the second task. As with all assessment, the information gained can be used to guide your instruction or for evaluation purposes.

TABLE 8.2 •
Commonly Encountered Units of Measure

	Metric System	Customary System
Length	millimeter	inch
	centimeter	foot
	meter	yard
	kilometer	mile
Area	square centimeter	square inch
	square meter	square foot
		square yard
Volume	cubic centimeter	cubic inch
	cubic meter	cubic foot
		cubic yard
Capacity	millimeter	ounce*
	liter	teaspoon
		tablespoon
		cup
		quart
		gallon
Weight	gram	ounce*
	kilogram	pound
	metric ton	ton

*In the U.S. customary system, the term *ounce* refers to a weight or *avoirdupois* unit, 16 of which make a pound, and also a volume or capacity unit, 8 of which make a cup. Though the two units have the same name, they are not related.

Important Standard Units

Both the customary and metric systems include many units that are not used in everyday living. Table 8.2 lists the units that are most common.

The Metric System

The metric system was developed in France about the time of the French Revolution (1790). At this time in history (called the Age of Enlightenment), the focus was on rational thought, and scientists were interested in organizing their disciplines in a rational way. The metric system, a rational system of measure, arose from this endeavor.

The metric system is designed to be consistent with the decimal system we already use. Also, the names of units follow a pattern. There is a base unit for each type of quantity to be measured (e.g., meter, liter, gram). Each related unit has a prefix that indicates its relationship to the base unit. For example, since the prefix *kilo-* means "thousand," *kilometer* means a "thousand meters." The prefix *centi-* means "one-hundredth," so *centimeter* means "one-hundredth of a meter." Furthermore, the structure of the metric system allows you to use a single unit for each measure. In contrast, the customary system frequently mixes units (3 pounds 6 ounces, or 6 feet 2 inches), which can make it difficult to combine measurements. It is much easier to combine measurements in the metric system.

Try your hand at combining these two lists of measurements:

2 yards, 1 foot, $5\frac{1}{2}$ inches	2.273 meters
1 yard, 2 feet, $7\frac{1}{4}$ inches	1.708 meters

Which system do you find is easier when it comes to combining measurements?

In both preceding columns, the total lengths are the same.

Unit familiarity with the popularly used units should be the principal focus of almost all instruction with standard units. Again, when possible, connect metric units to familiar reference points to help students make sense of these units (e.g., a nickel weighs about 5 grams). First and foremost, teach measuring in metric units by *doing* measuring in metric units.

Of course, those of you who teach in Canada are not faced with the issues surrounding a dual measurement system. We envy you that simplicity.

Perhaps one of the worst errors in the metric measurement curriculum is having students "move decimal points" to convert from one metric unit to another prior to a complete development of decimal notation. Confused, students memorize rules about moving decimals so many places this way or that, and the focus becomes rules and right answers.

As students begin to appreciate the structure of decimal notation, the metric system can and should be developed with all seven places: three prefixes for smaller units (*deci-, centi-, milli-*) and three for larger units (*deka-, hecto-, kilo-*). With decimal knowledge and familiarity with the basic and popularly used units, the complete metric system is easy to learn.

Making conversions within the metric system can be approached in two related ways. As we saw in Figure 4.6 in Chapter 4 (p. 112), a place-value chart gives a metric name to each of seven consecutive places. If it is understood that the decimal point always identifies the units position, then given any metric measurement, each digit is in a position with a metric name. The decimal point can be repositioned if the name of the unit is changed. In the measure 17.238 kg, the decimal indicates that the 7 is in the units position. The label "kg" indicates that the name of the position is kilograms. Therefore, the 2 is in the hectogram position, the 3 in the dekagram position, and the 8 in the gram position. Repositioning the decimal to indicate grams as the units makes the same measure read 17,238 g or 17,238.0 g.

An alternate rationale is to think of decimal point shifting as multiplying or dividing by powers of 10. In our example, since there are 1000 grams in a kilogram, change to grams by multiplying by 1000, or shift the decimal three places to the right.

It should be emphasized once again that unit conversion is perhaps the least important part of learning the metric system or any standard system. It is a skill that is not used frequently in daily life.

The Customary System

The "familiar" system of units is technically known as the U.S. customary system. After an attempt in the 1970s to go completely metric, most schools and textbooks have resigned themselves to teaching both metric and customary systems.

Conversion of units within the customary system is difficult for students for two reasons: There are more conversion ratios to memorize, and they are not conveniently related to the decimal system. For example, many children will add 3 feet 8 inches to 5 feet 6 inches and get 9 feet 4 inches instead of 9 feet 2 inches. (Why?) Similar difficulties occur with all conversions in the customary system. Once again, while it is important to know how many inches in a foot and a few other common relationships, overemphasis on conversions in the customary system is unwarranted.

Developing Formulas

The relationship between measurement and geometry is most evident in the development of formulas for measures of geometric figures. Formulas help us use easily made measures to determine indirectly some other measure that is not so easily found. For example, it is easy to measure the three dimensions of a box with a ruler, but it is not easy to actually measure the volume of the same box. By using a formula, the volume can be determined from the length measures.

Although formulas are efficient ways to determine measures, unfortunately they can mask what is being measured. For example, when the volume formula refers to linear measurements of the sides of the three-dimensional object, students are often befuddled by how linear units become cubic units. Participating in the development of the formulas can help students understand what is behind this perceived "mystical" transformation. It also contributes to students' understanding of the connectedness between formulas. Developing the formulas and seeing how they are interrelated is significantly more important than blindly plugging numbers into formulas—primarily a matter of computational tedium.

Common Difficulties

Many students become so encumbered with the use of formulas and rules that an understanding of what these formulas are all about is completely lost.

Overemphasizing Formulas

In the sixth National Assessment of Educational Progress, students were asked to draw on a square grid a rectangle with an area of 12 square units. Correct responses were given by 42 percent of fourth-grade and 66 percent of eighth-grade students. When asked for the area of a carpet 9 feet long and 6 feet wide, correct responses for these grades were given 19 percent and 65 percent of the time, respectively. Most fourth-grade students selected the sum of the dimensions (15) as their answer. The eighth-grade performance is consistent with that of drawing the 12-square-unit rectangle but is not a strong performance (Kenney & Kouba, 1997).

Many such items from this assessment and earlier NAEP studies indicate that students often have difficulty applying area measurement formulas and that formulas for area and perimeter are often confused.

Part of the problem may be the premature jump to formulas to determine these measurements and the fact that the formulas for both area and perimeter refer to linear measurements. This hides what is being measured in the area situation.

Another cause of this difficulty may be students' belief that the formula is the definition of the measurement. Tasks such as those shown in Figure 8.12 cannot be solved with simple formulas; they require an understanding of concepts and how formulas work. Many students believe that such shapes do not have areas or that the areas are impossible to determine because there are no formulas that "work" for such complex shapes. This difficulty for students comes when they believe that "length times width" is a definition of area.

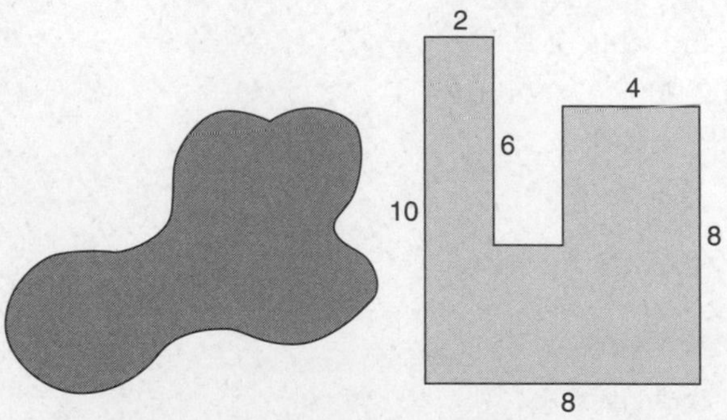

Height or Side

Another common error when students use formulas comes from failure to conceptualize the meaning of height in geometric figures, both two and three dimensional. The shapes in Figure 8.13 each have a slanted side and a height given. Students tend to confuse these two. Any side or flat surface of a figure can be called a *base* of the figure. For each base that a figure has, there is a corresponding height. If the figure were to slide into a room on its base, the *height* would be the height of the shortest door it could pass through without bending over—that is, the perpendicular distance to the base. Students have a lot of early experiences with the length-times-width formula for rectangles, in which the

"How would you determine the areas of these shapes?"

Note: Many children believe that such shapes do not have areas or that the areas are impossible to determine because there are no formulas.

FIGURE 8.12 ●

Understanding the attribute of area.

height is exactly the same as the length of a side. Perhaps this is the source of the confusion.

Before formulas involving heights are discussed, students should be able to identify where a height could be measured for any base that a figure has.

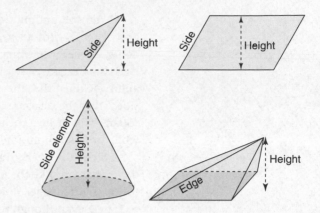

FIGURE 8.13 •

Heights of figures are not always measured along an edge or a surface.

The Area of Rectangles, Parallelograms, Triangles, and Trapezoids

The development of area formulas is a fantastic opportunity to follow the spirit of the NCTM *Principles and Standards*. First, a problem-solving approach can meaningfully involve students and help them see that mathematics is a sense-making endeavor. Second, the connectedness of mathematics is evident. Here you will see that all of the standard area formulas are intimately related and can be developed and learned as an integrated whole rather than as a collection of isolated facts.

Rectangles

The formula for the area of a rectangle is one of the first that is developed and is usually given as $A = L \times W$, "area equals length times width." Looking forward to other area formulas, an equivalent but more unifying idea might be $A = b \times h$, "area equals *base* times *height*." The base-times-height formulation can be generalized to all parallelograms and is useful in developing the area formulas for triangles and trapezoids. Furthermore, the same approach can be extended to three dimensions, where volumes of cylinders are given in terms of the *area of the base* times the height. Base times height, then, helps connect a large family of formulas that otherwise must be mastered independently.

The following activity is a good way to help students construct the formula for a rectangle using a strictly problem-based approach.

ACTIVITY 8.16

Rectangle Comparison—Square Units

Students are given a pair of rectangles that are either the same in area or are very close. They are also given a model or drawing of a single square unit and an appropriate ruler. The students are not permitted to cut out the rectangles or even draw on them. The task is to use their rulers to determine, in any way that they can, which rectangle is larger or whether they are the same. They should use words, drawings, and numbers to explain their conclusions. Some suggested pairs are as follows:

4×10 and 5×8 $\qquad$ 5×10 and 7×7 $\qquad$ 4×6 and 5×5

The first two pairs can be found in the Blackline Masters.

BLM 27

STOP **Before reading further, look at the Blackline Master for Activity 8.16 and see how you would solve this problem. Assume that you have not previously learned the $L \times W$ formula.**

You will undoubtedly find students who know the $L \times W$ formula and use it in Activity 8.16 without necessarily understanding why it works. For these and all students, demand that they develop a convincing argument for their comparisons. In your discussion of this activity, look for students who measured one side of the rectangle and concluded that the measure will tell how many of the squares will fit along that side. Then the measure of the other dimension will tell how many rows of these squares will fit into the rectangle. Some students may use a repeated addition approach while others will multiply.

Since the words that you use to talk about ideas are conventions, explain to students that you like the idea of measuring one side to tell how many squares will fit in a row along that side. You would like them to call or think of this side as the *base* of the rectangle even though some people call it the length or the width. Then the other side you can call the *height*. But which side is the base? Be sure that students conclude that either side could be the base. If you use the formula $A = b \times h$, then the same area will result using either side as the base.

Notice that having students fill in rectangles with squares is useful for understanding what it means to measure area, but research indicates that activities such as that have almost no effect in developing or understanding formulas. With Activity 8.16, students will clearly see that they are using linear measures to determine square units. Furthermore, they will develop the formula themselves rather than reading it in a book. Even if students have previously been exposed to the area formula, Activity 8.16 and the discussion that develops the $A = b \times h$ formula is well worth the time invested.

In moving to a formula for area, we sometimes rush to focus on the linear dimensions of the object being measured because the linear dimensions give us the numbers we need to compute the area. Unfortunately, the efficiency of this approach can mask what is actually being measured, making it appear to many students that something magical is happening to transform linear units to square units. When they ask how inches can become square inches, some teachers respond with the rule: "When you multiply the same thing by itself, it is squared. So when you multiply inches by inches, it becomes square inches." They may model this by writing: 2 inches × 3 inches = 6 inches × inches = 6 inches^2. This is not very helpful in convincing students that something short of a miracle has not occurred.

Consider the 3-cm by 6-cm rectangle in Figure 8.14. Revisit with students the need to use units of area to measure area. In this case, squares that are 1 centimeter on each side could be used to cover the region. Return to the meaning of multiplication: 3 × 6 means 3 groups of 6. You want students to think about what is being grouped in this situation. In terms of the previous activity, it is the row of squares that lie along the base. We have 3 groups of 6 square centimeters, or 18 square centimeters. We were not counting linear units but square units all along. Linear units were not somehow miraculously transformed. Being explicit about what we are measuring can convince students that formulas also make sense in mathematics.

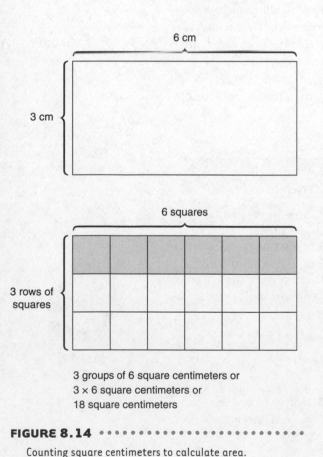

FIGURE 8.14 •••••••••••••••••••••••••••

Counting square centimeters to calculate area.

Chapter 8   DEVELOPING MEASUREMENT CONCEPTS AND FORMULAS

From Rectangles to Other Parallelograms

Once students understand the base-times-height formula for rectangles, the next challenge is to determine the areas of parallelograms. Do not provide a formula or other explanation. Rather, try the following activity, which again asks students to devise their own formula.

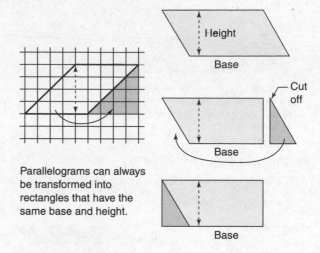

Parallelograms can always be transformed into rectangles that have the same base and height.

ACTIVITY 8.17

Area of a Parallelogram

Give students two or three parallelograms either drawn on grid paper or, for a slightly harder challenge, drawn on plane paper. If drawn on plane paper, provide all dimensions—the lengths of all four sides and the height. Their task is to use what they have learned about the area of rectangles to determine the area of these parallelograms. Students should find a method that will work for any parallelogram, even if not drawn on a grid.

FIGURE 8.15 •••••••••••••••••••••••

Area of a parallelogram.

If students are stuck finding the area of a parallelogram, ask them to examine ways that the parallelogram is like a rectangle or how it can be changed into a rectangle. As shown in Figure 8.15, a parallelogram can always be transformed into a rectangle with the same base, the same height, and the same area. Thus, the formula for the area of a parallelogram is exactly the same as for a rectangle: base times height.

From Parallelograms to Triangles

It is very important for students to understand the parallelogram formula before exploring triangle area. With that background, the area of a triangle is relatively simple. As with the other formulas, use a problem-based approach as in the next activity.

ACTIVITY 8.18

Area of a Triangle

Provide students with at least two triangles drawn on grid paper. Avoid right triangles because they are an easier special case. The challenge for students is to use what they have learned about the area of parallelograms to find the area of each of the triangles and to develop a method that will work for any triangle. They should be sure that their method works for all the triangles given to them as well as at least one more that they draw.

There are several hints that you might offer if students are stuck. *Can you find a parallelogram that is somehow related to your triangle?* If this is not sufficient, suggest that they fold a piece of paper in half, draw a triangle on the folded paper, and cut it out, making two identical copies. They should use the copies to find out how a triangle is related to a parallelogram.

As shown in Figure 8.16, two congruent triangles can always be arranged to form a parallelogram with the same base and the same height as the triangle. The area of the

A = base × height

Two copies of any triangle will always form a parallelogram with the same base and height; therefore, the triangle has an area of half of the parallelogram, $A = \frac{1}{2}$ (base × height).

FIGURE 8.16 •••••••••••••••••••••••••••••

Two triangles always make a parallelogram.

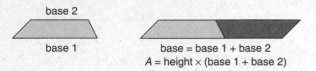

base 2

base 1

base = base 1 + base 2
A = height × (base 1 + base 2)

Two trapezoids always make a parallelogram with the same height and a base equal to the sum of the bases in the trapezoid. Therefore,

$$A = \frac{1}{2} \times height \times (base\ 1 + base\ 2)$$

FIGURE 8.17 ••••••••••••••••••••••••••••••

Two trapezoids always form a parallelogram.

triangle will, therefore, be one-half as much as the parallelogram. Have students further explore all three possible parallelograms, one for each triangle side serving as base. Will the computed areas always be the same?

From Parallelograms to Trapezoids

After developing formulas for parallelograms and triangles, your students may be interested in tackling trapezoids without any further assistance. There are at least ten different methods of arriving at a formula for trapezoids, each related to the area of parallelograms or triangles. One of the nicest methods uses the same general approach that was used for triangles. Suggest that students try working with two trapezoids that are identical, just as they did with triangles. Figure 8.17 shows how this method results in the formula. Now, not only are all of these formulas connected, but also similar methods were used to develop them.

Here are a few hints, each leading to a different approach to finding the area of a trapezoid.

- Make a parallelogram inside the given trapezoid using three of the sides.
- Make a parallelogram using three sides that surround the trapezoid.
- Draw a diagonal forming two triangles.
- Draw a line through the midpoints of the nonparallel sides. The length of that line is the average of the lengths of the two parallel sides.
- Draw a rectangle inside the trapezoid leaving two triangles and then put those two triangles together.

 Do you think that students should learn special formulas for the area of a square? Why or why not? Do you think students need formulas for the perimeters of squares and rectangles?

Circle Formulas

The relationship between the *circumference* of a circle (the distance around or the perimeter) and the length of the *diameter* (a line through the center joining two points on the circle) is one of the most interesting that children can discover. The circumference of every circle is about 3.14 times as long as the diameter. The exact ratio is an irrational number close to 3.14 and is represented by the Greek letter π. So $\pi = C/D$, the circumference divided by the diameter. In a slightly different form, $C = \pi D$. Half the diameter is the radius (r), so the same equation can be written $C = 2\pi r$. (Chapter 7 discussed in detail the concept of π and how students can discover this important ratio.)

Figure 8.18 presents an argument for the area formula $A = \pi r^2$. This development is one commonly found in textbooks.

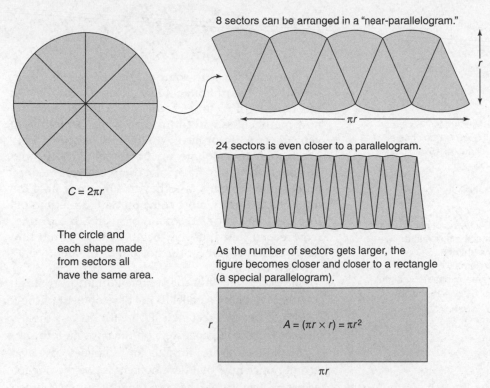

8 sectors can be arranged in a "near-parallelogram."

FIGURE 8.18 • • • • • • •

Development of the circle
area formula.

$C = 2\pi r$

24 sectors is even closer to a parallelogram.

The circle and
each shape made
from sectors all
have the same area.

As the number of sectors gets larger, the
figure becomes closer and closer to a rectangle
(a special parallelogram).

r $A = (\pi r \times r) = \pi r^2$

πr

Students can cut a circle into eight sectors or perhaps even more
and rearrange them to form a near-rectangle with dimensions
of half the circumference by the radius.

Regardless of the approach you use to develop the area formula, students should
be challenged to figure it out on their own. For example, show students how to arrange
8 or 12 sectors of a circle into an approximate parallelogram. Their task should be to
use this as a hint toward development of an area formula for the circle. You may need
to help them notice that the arrangement of sectors is an approximate parallelogram
and that the smaller the sectors, the closer the arrangement gets to a rectangle. But the
complete argument for the formula should come from your students.

Volumes of Common Solid Shapes

The relationships between the formulas for volume are completely analogous to
those for area. As you read, notice the similarities between rectangles and prisms,
between parallelograms and "sheered" (oblique) prisms, and between triangles and
pyramids. Not only are the formulas related, but also the process for development of
the formulas is similar.

Volumes of Cylinders

A *cylinder* is a solid with two congruent parallel bases and sides with parallel elements that join corresponding points on the bases. There are several special classes of
cylinders, including *prisms* (with polygons for bases), *right prisms, rectangular prisms,* and
cubes (see Chapter 7, p. 196). Interestingly, all of these solids have the same volume formula, and that one formula is analogous to the area formula for parallelograms.

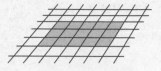

Base is 3 × 5.
Area of base is
15 squares.

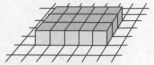

Base "holds" 15 cubes.
A 3 × 5 × 1 box has a
volume of 15 cubic units.

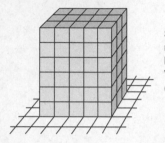

Six layers of cubic units
make a box with a
height of 6.
Volume =
(area of base) × (height)
= 15 × 6

FIGURE 8.19 •

Volume of a prism.

ACTIVITY 8.19

Volume of Boxes

Provide students with some cardboard shoe boxes or similar cardboard boxes, a few cubes, and a ruler. As was done with rectangles, the task is to determine how many cubes will fit inside the box. Most likely your boxes will not have whole-number dimensions, so tell students to ignore any fractional parts of cubes. Although they may have seen or used a volume formula before, for this task they may not rely on a formula. Rather, they must come up with a method or formula that they can explain or justify. If a hint is required, suggest that they begin by finding out how many cubes will fit on the bottom of the box.

The development of the volume formula from this box exploration is exactly parallel to the development of the formula for the area of a rectangle. Figure 8.19 shows the development as if the grid paper were on the bottom of the box.

Recall how the area formula for rectangles was developed and notice how that development is like the one for volume. Instead of *length* of the base × height (for *area* of rectangles), in three dimensions, the *volume* formula for the corresponding figure is *area* of the base × height.

Show students a stack of three or four decks of playing cards (or a stack of books or paper). When stacked straight, they form a rectangular solid. The volume, as just discussed, is $V = A \times h$, with A equal to the area of one card. Now if the stack is sheered or slanted to one side as shown in Figure 8.20, what will the volume of this new figure be? Students should be able to argue that this figure has the same volume (and same volume formula) as the original stack.

What if the cards in this activity were some other shape? If they were circular, the volume would still be the area of the base times the height; if they were triangular, still the same. The conclusion is that the volume of *any* cylinder is equal to the *area of the base* times the *height*.

Volumes of Cones and Pyramids

Recall that when parallelograms and triangles have the same base and height, the areas are in a 2-to-1 relationship. Interestingly, the relationship between the volumes of cylinders and cones with the same base and height is 3-to-1.

To investigate this relationship use plastic models of these related shapes such as Power Solids. Have students estimate the number of times the pyramid will fit into the prism. Then have them test their prediction by filling the pyramid with water or rice and emptying it into the prism. They will discover that exactly three pyramids will fill a prism with the same base and height. (See Figure 8.21.)

The 3-to-1 ratio of volumes is true of all cylinders and cones with the same base and height regardless of the shape of the base or the position of the vertex. That is, for any cone or pyramid, $V = \frac{1}{3}(A \times h)$.

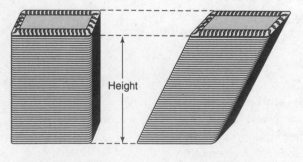

Height

FIGURE 8.20 •

Two cylinders with the same base and height have the same volume.

Surface Area and Volume of a Sphere

Polyhedra are three-dimensional objects with flat or plane faces consisting of polygons. Finding the surface area of polyhedra requires students to think about the two-dimensional polygons that cover the outside of the polyhedron. The surface area of a sphere is not so simple. There are no nets consisting of polygons that will cover the outside of a sphere. However, we can do some other measurements to help us approximate the surface area of a sphere. Two such approaches follow.

Select an orange that appears to be nearly spherical. Carefully cut it in half so that you have two congruent hemispheres. The face of each hemisphere should look like a circle. Lay the half orange on a sheet of paper and trace around the circumference of the hemisphere. Repeat this 3 more times so that you have 4 nonoverlapping circles on the paper. Now remove the orange peel in small sections so that the pieces of peel will lay flat onto the paper. Cover the inside of the 4 circles with the orange peel. The orange peel should cover or come close to covering the interior of all 4 circles. The orange peel represents the surface area of a sphere (the orange). Since the orange peel covers about 4 circles, it is equivalent to the area of 4 circles where r is the radius of the orange sphere as well as of the circle, or $4\pi r^2$. Thus, we can conclude, albeit somewhat imprecisely, that $4\pi r^2$ is the surface area of a sphere.

If you want to avoid the messiness of oranges, you can use Styrofoam hemispheres and felt cloth. Have students cover the outside of the ball in small sections of cloth so that the cloth lays as flat as possible on the surface of the sphere but does not overlap. Use U-shaped pins or pins with large heads to secure the felt to the ball. Straight pins with small heads often work their way through the cloth and disappear into the ball. After completely covering the ball, students remove the cloth and fit the pieces into the 4 circles drawn on the paper. They may need to cut the pieces to distribute them across the 4 circles. The result will be similar to using an orange.

Another approach to approximating the surface area of a sphere uses a Styrofoam hemisphere and some soft, cotton clothesline. (Plastic clothesline will not work well.) In the center of the flat circular surface of the hemisphere, pin the end of the rope to the Styrofoam. Then carefully coil the rope around this center starting point until the coiled rope exactly covers the circular surface. Mark the point on the rope where the coil ends. See Figure 8.22(a). This much rope is the amount needed to cover the circular region (the area of the circle). Now remove the rope and turn the hemisphere over, with the circular surface flat on the table. This time pin the end of the rope to the edge of the hemisphere next to the table. Coil the rope around the curved surface area of the hemisphere until it is completely covered as shown in Figure 8.22(b). Mark the

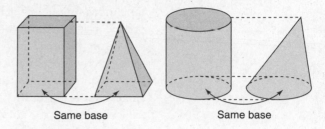

The volume of a pyramid or cone is one-third the volume of a prism or cylinder with the same base and same height.

FIGURE 8.21 •

Comparing volumes of prisms to pyramids and cones to cylinders.

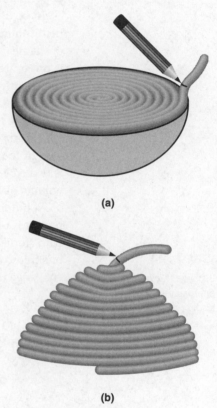

(a)

(b)

FIGURE 8.22 • • • • • • • • • • • • • • • • • •

Finding the curved surface area of a hemisphere in relationship to the flat surface of the circle. (a) Cotton clothesline is coiled first on the flat circular surface of the Styrofoam hemisphere. Begin by pinning the rope to the center of the disk. The rope is marked to indicate how much rope was used. (b) Using the same clothesline, pin the end of the rope at the bottom of the hemisphere and coil the rope around to the top. Mark the end. By comparing the two lengths found in parts a and b, you can compare the surface area of the hemisphere to the surface area of the circular disk.

rope indicating how much was used to cover the hemisphere. Now compare the length of rope used for each portion. If you used the same rope, you will be able to fold it into two nearly identical halves using the first mark as the fold point. That means that it took exactly twice as much rope to cover the curved hemisphere as to cover the circular surface. In other words, the curved surface of the hemisphere is twice that of the flat circular surface with the same radius. The surface area of the hemisphere is, therefore, $2\pi r^2$, or the area of 2 circles. Just as with the oranges, the surface of the full sphere is $4\pi r^2$, or the area of 4 circles.

Although a bit more tedious, the rope method for comparing the circular surface to the surface of the sphere is considerably more accurate and dramatic. It is best if two students work together to help hold the rope in place as it is wound around the Styrofoam surfaces.

With the knowledge that the surface area of a sphere is equal to $4\pi r^2$, we can also develop a formula for the volume of a sphere. What is more, the volume formula will again be directly connected to ideas already developed. Take a Styrofoam ball (or a hemisphere) and cut out a pyramid-like shape as shown in Figure 8.23(a). The height of the near-pyramid should be approximately the radius of the sphere. Of course, this is not quite a pyramid because the base is curved. Now cut out another pyramid-like shape with a smaller base. Comparing the bases of the two near-pyramids, you will notice that the base of the second is less curved. Imagine cutting the entire sphere into very, very tiny near-pyramids—each much smaller than those you cut out. In theory, the height of each near-pyramid should be equal to the radius of the sphere. As the base of the near-pyramid gets smaller and smaller, the less curve it has and the closer it is to a true pyramid. The sum of the volume of all these tiny pyramids will equal the volume of the sphere itself, as shown in Figure 8.23(b).

If doing this with your class, the process to this point is most likely a demonstration. It is unreasonable for students to cut into a Styrofoam ball. However, after discussing with students how the entire sphere could, at least in theory, be constructed of near-pyramids with very tiny bases and each with a height equal to the radius of the sphere, challenge them to use this information to find a formula for the volume of a sphere.

FIGURE 8.23 • • • • • • •

Using near-pyramids to approximate the volume of a sphere.

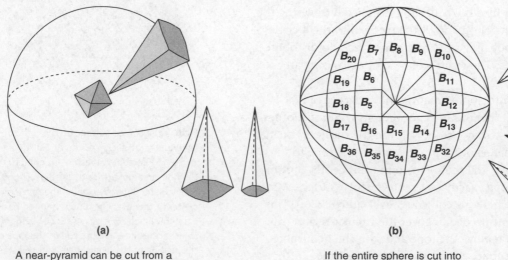

(a)

A near-pyramid can be cut from a sphere. The height of the pyramid is the radius of the sphere. The smaller the base, the flatter the base.

(b)

If the entire sphere is cut into near-pyramids, the combined volumes will be the same as the volume of the sphere

STOP Use the information you have read so far and see if you can develop a formula for the volume of a sphere.

Since we know how to determine the volume of a pyramid ($V = \frac{1}{3} \times B \times h$, where B is the area of the base and h is the height of the pyramid), we can express the volume of the sphere as:

$$V_{\text{sphere}} = \tfrac{1}{3}B_1 h + \tfrac{1}{3}B_2 h + \tfrac{1}{3}B_3 h + \tfrac{1}{3}B_4 h + \ldots + \tfrac{1}{3}B_n h$$

where n is the number of near-pyramids that make up the sphere. (See Figure 8.23b.) Substituting r for h and factoring out the common factors of $\frac{1}{3}$ and r, we get

$$V_{\text{sphere}} = \tfrac{1}{3}r \, (B_1 + B_2 + B_3 + B_4 + B_5 + \ldots + B_n)$$

Think about what the expression $(B_1 + B_2 + B_3 + B_4 + B_5 + \ldots + B_n)$ represents. It is the sum of the bases of all the near-pyramids, which is none other than the surface area of the sphere. Using the formula for surface area of a sphere that we developed before, we get

$$V_{\text{sphere}} = \tfrac{1}{3}r \, (4\pi r^2) \text{ or } \tfrac{4}{3}\pi r^3$$

Reviewing the Formulas

Notice how all of the formulas that we have discussed tie together:

- Parallelograms are really just rectangles that have been shifted to make the sides slanted. The area for both is $B \times h$ or *length of the base × height.*

- Triangles turn out to simply be half of a parallelogram with the same base and height. The area of a triangle is $\frac{1}{2}(B \times h)$.

- Trapezoids are also related to parallelograms and triangles. For example, all trapezoids can be made into two triangles. The heights of each are the same. Use B for the longer parallel side and b for the shorter, and the area of the trapezoid is $\frac{1}{2}(B \times h) + \frac{1}{2}(b \times h)$. (This can be simplified, but if derived this way, it is an easy way to remember it.)

- The area of a circle is found by using smaller and smaller sectors so that it can be rearranged into a parallelogram. The base of the near-parallelogram is half of the circumference (πr) and the height is the radius. So, $B \times h$ becomes (πr) $\times r$ or πr^2.

And then we moved to three dimensions and found very similar results.

- All cylinders (i.e., right prisms or boxes, slanted prisms, circular cylinders, and in fact cylinders with any shaped base) have the same volume formula. It is nearly identical to the formula for parallelograms: $B \times h$ where B represents the *area* of the base instead of the *length* of the base.

- Whereas triangles are *one-half* the area of related parallelograms, cones (including the special case of pyramids) are *one-third* the volume of related cylinders

DEVELOPING FORMULAS

(and prisms). That means that the volume of all pyramids and cones is one third that of the corresponding cylinders and prisms: $\frac{1}{3}(B \times h)$.

- There is an interesting 4-to-1 relationship between the surface area of a circle and that of a sphere with the same radius. Using this 4× factor for the surface area, and the $\frac{1}{3}$ factor for pyramids, we can move directly to the volume of a sphere: $\frac{1}{3}(4(\pi r^2)) \times r$. Here you should see the volume of a pyramid or $\frac{1}{3}(B \times h)$ where B is $4(\pi r^2)$ and r is the height. Simplified, this formula becomes $\frac{4}{3}(\pi r^3)$.

The connectedness of mathematical ideas can hardly be better illustrated than with the connections of all of these formulas to the single concept of base times height.

As illustrated throughout this last section, a conceptual approach to the development of formulas helps students understand these tools as meaningful yet efficient ways to measure different attributes of objects around us. After having developed formulas in meaningful ways, students are no longer required to memorize them as isolated pieces of mathematical facts, but they can derive formulas from what they already know. Mathematics does make sense!

EXPANDED LESSON

Fixed Areas
Based on Activity 8.8, p. 242

GRADE LEVEL: Fifth to eighth grades.

MATHEMATICS GOALS
- To help contrast the concepts of area and perimeter.
- To develop the relationship between area and perimeter of different shapes when the area is fixed.
- To compare and contrast the units used to measure perimeter and those used to measure area.

THINKING ABOUT THE STUDENTS
Students have worked with the ideas of area and perimeter. Most students can find the area and perimeter of given figures and can state the formulas for finding the perimeter and area of a rectangle. However, they still often become confused as to which formula to use.

MATERIALS AND PREPARATION
- Each student will need 36 square tiles such as Color Tiles, at least two sheets of centimeter or half-centimeter grid paper (see Blackline Masters 8 and 9), and a recording sheet (see Blackline Master L-2). Have extra sheets of grid paper on hand.
- This activity can be done in pairs. If students are paired, still provide each student 36 square tiles, as each student needs to explore how the rectangles can be constructed.
- Overhead tiles and a transparency of the grid paper and recording chart will be helpful to introduce the activity as well as to share students' ideas afterward. If overhead tiles are not available, the Color Tiles will suffice, although they will be opaque and more difficult for students to see the individual tiles.

lesson

BLM L-2

BEFORE

Begin with a simpler version of the task:

- Have students build a rectangle using 12 tiles at their desks. Explain that the rectangle should be filled in, not just borders. After eliciting some ideas, ask a student to come to the overhead and make a rectangle that has been described.
- Model sketching the rectangle on the grid transparency. Record the dimensions of the rectangle in the recording chart, for example, "2 by 6."
- Ask: *What do we mean by perimeter? How do we measure perimeter?* After helping students define perimeter and describe how it is measured, ask them for the perimeter of this rectangle. Ask a student to come to the overhead to measure the perimeter of the rectangle. (Use either the rectangle made from tiles or the one sketched on grid paper.) Emphasize that the units used to measure perimeter are one dimensional, or linear, and that perimeter is just the distance around an object. Record the perimeter in the chart.
- Ask: *What do we mean by area? How do we measure area?* After helping students define and describe how it is measured, ask for the area of this rectangle. Here you want to make explicit that the units used to measure area are two dimensional and, therefore, cover a region. After counting the tiles, record the area in the chart.
- Have students make a different rectangle using 12 tiles at their desks and record the perimeter and area as before. Students will need to decide what "different" means. Is a 2 by 6 rectangle different than a 6 by 2 rectangle? Although these are congruent, students may wish to consider these different. That is okay for this activity.

The Task
- See how many different rectangles can be made with 36 tiles. Determine and record the perimeter and area for each rectangle.

Establish Expectations

Write the directions on the board:

1. Find a rectangle using *all* 36 tiles.
2. Sketch the rectangle on the grid paper.
3. Measure and record the perimeter and area of the rectangle on the recording chart.
4. Find other rectangles using *all* 36 tiles. Record as before.

DURING

- Observe how students are generating new rectangles. Are they using some systematic way (e.g., changing the length of the rectangle by one each time) to ensure they have found all rectangles? Are they haphazardly finding rectangles with no apparent strategy?
- How do they measure the perimeters? Do they count or measure all four sides or do they double the sum of length and width? Are they aware that the perimeters change?
- Do students realize that the areas must remain the same since all of them use 36 tiles?

AFTER

- Ask students what they have found out about perimeter and area. Ask: *Did the perimeter stay the same? Is that what you expected? When is the perimeter big and when is it small?*
- Ask students how they can be sure they have all of the possible rectangles. As a class, decide on a systematic method of recording rectangles on the recording chart. For example, start with a side of 1, then 2, and so on. After everyone has had time to consider the information in the chart, have students describe what happens to the perimeter as the length and width change. (The perimeter gets shorter as the rectangle gets fatter. The square has the shortest perimeter.)

ASSESSMENT NOTES

- Are students confusing perimeter and area?
- How do students react to the idea that the perimeter changes? Do they think they made a mistake in determining the perimeter?
- Are students looking for patterns in how the perimeter changes before you guide them toward that idea?
- As they form new rectangles, are they aware that the area is not changing because they are using the same number of tiles each time? If not, these students may not know what area is, or they may be confusing it with perimeter.
- Are students looking for patterns in how the perimeter changes before you guide them toward that idea?

- Students who continue to confuse perimeter and area should engage in tasks that ask them to use various informal units of area to fill and compare regions. They can also use string to provide a concrete representation of perimeter of various shapes. The string can be stretched into a straight line and can be measured with a ruler to reinforce that perimeter is a linear measure.

next steps

- Activity 8.7, "Fixed Perimeters," is a good activity to pair with this one if you have not already done so.
- Even if both Activities 8.7 and 8.8 are successful, formulas may still need to be redeveloped in a conceptual manner.

ALGEBRAIC REASONING

*P*rinciples and Standards for School Mathematics (2000) lists algebra as one of the five content standards for pre-K–12 mathematics. Today, most states also have an algebra component in their curricula. Rather than the algebra you may remember from your high school days, the algebra intended for pre-K–12 focuses on patterns, relationships and functions, and the use of various representations—symbolic, numeric, and graphic—to help make sense of and communicate about all sorts of mathematical situations. As students become comfortable with these ideas and methods of representation, they will begin to utilize them in nearly all of mathematics, not just in a study of algebraic ideas.

Algebraic reasoning or *algebraic thinking* is a popular term used to indicate how students utilize the content of algebra—patterns, relationships, functions, and representations—to understand and communicate about mathematical situations. *Algebraic reasoning* involves analyzing, representing, and generalizing patterns and regularities in all aspects of mathematics.

In this chapter, we look specifically at activities that focus on algebraic reasoning in grades 5–8. As this type of reasoning develops, so must the language and symbolism that have been developed to support and communicate that thinking, specifically thinking about equations, variables, and functions. Functions and functional notation, significant components of algebraic reasoning, are such important ideas in mathematics that a separate chapter has been devoted to them.

big ideas

1 Logical patterns exist and are a regular occurrence in mathematics. They can be recognized, extended, and generalized with both words and symbols. The same pattern can be found in many different forms. Patterns are found in physical and geometric situations as well as in numbers.

2 A variety of representations such as diagrams, number lines, charts, and graphs can be used to illustrate mathematical situations and relationships. These representations help in conceptualizing ideas and in solving problems.

3 Symbolism, especially that involving equations and variables, is used to express generalizations of patterns and relationships.

4 Variables are symbols that take the place of numbers or ranges of numbers. They have different meanings depending on whether they are being used as representations of quantities that vary or change, representations of specific unknown values, or placeholders in a generalized expression or formula.

5 Equations and inequalities are used to express relationships between two quantities. Symbolism on either side of an equation or inequality represents a quantity. Thus, $3 + 8$ and $5n + 2$ are both expressions for numbers, not something "to do."

Growing Patterns

Identifying and extending patterns are important processes in algebraic thinking. Beginning at about the fourth grade and extending through the middle school years, students can explore patterns that involve a progression from step to step. In technical terms, these are called *sequences;* we will simply call them *growing patterns*. With these patterns, students not only extend patterns but also look for a generalization or an algebraic relationship that will tell them what the pattern will be at any point along the way. Growing patterns also demonstrate the concept of function and can be used as an entry point to this very important mathematical idea.

Figure 9.1 illustrates some growing patterns that are built with various materials or drawings. The patterns consist of a series of separate steps, each new step related to the previous one according to the pattern.

The first thing to do with patterns in the upper and middle grades is to get students comfortable with building patterns and talking about how they can be extended in a logical manner. Building the patterns with physical materials such as tiles, counters, or flat toothpicks allows students to make changes if necessary and to build on to one step to make a new step. It is also more fun! The following activity will introduce growing patterns.

ACTIVITY 9.1

Extend and Explain

Show students the first three or four steps of a pattern. Provide them with appropriate materials or grid paper, have them extend the patterns, and explain why their extension indeed follows the pattern.

FIGURE 9.1 • • • • • • •

Growing patterns with materials or drawings.

When discussing a pattern, students should try to determine how each step in the pattern differs from the preceding step. If each new step can be built by adding

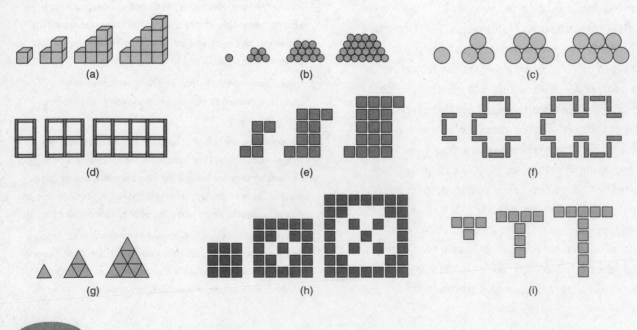

(a)   (b)   (c)

(d)   (e)   (f)

(g)   (h)   (i)

on to or changing the previous step, the discussion should include how this can be done. For example, each stairstep in Figure 9.1(a) can be made by adding a column of blocks to the preceding stairsteps. In contrast, the pattern of tiles in Figure 9.1(h) involves a form of expansion rather than adding on.

Growing patterns also have a numeric component, the number of objects in each step. As shown in Figure 9.2, a table can be made for any growing pattern. One row of the table or chart is always the number of steps, and the other is for recording how many objects are in that step. Frequently, a pattern grows so quickly and requires so many blocks or spaces to draw it that it is only reasonable to build or draw the first five or six steps. This leads to the following activity.

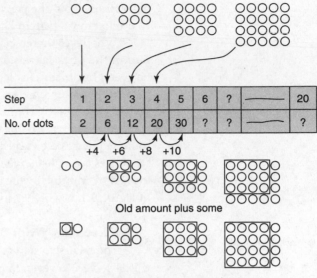

FIGURE 9.2 •
Two different relationships in a visual pattern.

ACTIVITY 9.2

Predict How Many

Have students begin to extend a growing pattern you provide. They should also make a table showing how many items are needed to make each step of the pattern. The task is to predict the number of items in the twentieth step of the pattern. The challenge is to see if there is a way to do this without filling in the first 19 entries of the table. Predictions should also be accompanied by an explanation.

Finding a way to determine the twentieth or even the hundredth entry in the table gets at the heart of finding a relationship that students will later understand is an example of a function. We next look at how to help students find these relationships.

Searching for Relationships

Once a table or chart is developed, students have two representations of the pattern: the one created with the drawing or materials and the numeric version that is in the table. When looking for relationships, some students will focus on the table and others will focus on the physical pattern. It is important for students to see that whatever relationships they discover, they exist in both forms. So if a relationship is found in a table, challenge students to see how that plays out in the physical version.

Patterns from Step to Step: Recursive Relationships

For most students, it is easier to see the patterns from one step to the next. When you have a chart constructed, the differences from one step to the next can be written next to or below it, as in Figure 9.2. In that example, the number in each step can be determined from the previous step by adding successive even numbers. The description that tells how a pattern changes from step to step is known as a *recursive relationship*.

Whenever there is a pattern in the table, see if students can find that same pattern in the physical version. In Figure 9.2, notice that in each step, the previous step has been outlined. That lets you examine the amount added and see how it creates the pattern of adding on even numbers. The picture or physical pattern and the table should be as closely connected as possible.

As students note the differences from one step to the next, they may realize that some sequences are created by adding or subtracting the same number each time. These sequences are called *arithmetic sequences*. Other sequences, called *geometric sequences,* are formed by multiplying by the same number each time. Find an example of each of these in Figure 9.1. (Figure 9.1 includes one geometric and four arithmetic sequences.)

Patterns from Step Number to Step: Functional Relationships

The recursive step-to-step pattern is almost certainly the first that your students will observe. However, to find the table entry for the hundredth step, the only way a recursive pattern can help is to find all of the prior 99 entries in the table. If a rule or relationship can be discovered that connects the number of objects in a step to the number of the step, any table entry can be determined without building or calculating all of the intermediate entries. A rule that determines the number of elements in a step from the step number is an example of a *functional relationship*.

There is no single best method for finding this relationship between step number and step. Some students may get insight by simply "playing around" with the numbers and asking, "How can I operate on the number of the step to get the corresponding number in the table?" Most will benefit from examining the physical pattern for regularities. For example, at the bottom of Figure 9.2, a square array is outlined for each step. Each successive square is one larger on a side. What relationship might exist between this subset of the pattern and the step numbers? In this example, the side of each square is the same as the step number. The row to the right of each square is also the step number.

 With that information, how would you describe the twentieth step? Can you determine how many elements will be in it without drawing the picture?

At this point, a significant activity is to write a numeric expression for each step number using the same pattern. For example, the first four steps in Figure 9.2 are $1^2 + 1$, $2^2 + 2$, $3^2 + 3$, and $4^2 + 4$.

It may take much searching and experimenting for students in groups or as a class to come up with an expression that is similar for each step. Do not get frustrated if students have difficulty. Encourage the search for relationships to continue, even if it takes more than one day. The search for relationships is the most significant portion of these activities.

Assessment Note

As students search for relationships, do they have difficulty identifying what is changing? What do their responses tell you about what they are focusing on in the table or the physical patterns? If they are having difficulty, encourage them to look for a geometric pattern in the physical or visual pattern (see the squares found in Figure 9.2). This representation can help them identify what is not changing. Then they can focus on what is changing.

Moving from Patterns to Function and Variable

When students have discovered numeric expressions for each step using step numbers, write them with brackets around the step numbers as shown in Figure 9.3. If this results in a pattern, the bracketed numbers will change from step to step, while the other numbers in the expressions remain the same. Now the bracketed numbers can be replaced by a letter or variable, resulting in a general formula. The formula defines the functional relationship between step numbers and step values.

 Before reading on, explore some of the patterns in Figure 9.1 to see if you can find formulas (functional relationships) for each. You should be able to "plug in" the step numbers in your formulas and get the value for that step. Some are a bit harder than others.

The discussion to this point is summarized in the following activity, an elaboration of "Predict How Many." It is best to do this in groups so that ideas can be generated more freely.

ACTIVITY 9.3

Find the Function in the Pattern

Give students the first three or four steps of a pattern. Their tasks are as follows:

1. **Extend the pattern several more steps until they are sure they understand the pattern. They should always look backward to the beginning of the pattern to see that their idea works for all steps. Record this in a drawing.**

(continued)

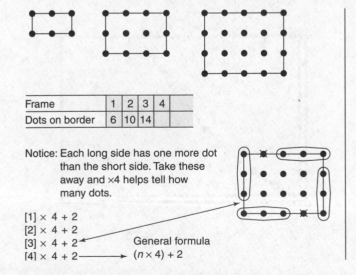

Frame	1	2	3	4	
Dots on border	6	10	14		

Notice: Each long side has one more dot than the short side. Take these away and ×4 helps tell how many dots.

[1] × 4 + 2
[2] × 4 + 2
[3] × 4 + 2
[4] × 4 + 2 → General formula $(n \times 4) + 2$

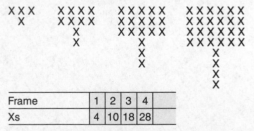

Frame	1	2	3	4	
Xs	4	10	18	28	

Notice: If the tail part is added to the side of the top part, there is always a square and three more columns.

[1] × [1] + (3 × [1])
[2] × [2] + (3 × [2])
[3] × [3] + (3 × [3])

FIGURE 9.3 • • • • • • • •

Finding functional relationships in patterns.

2. Make a table that shows the number of elements in each step they have constructed.
3. Find and describe in writing as many patterns as possible, both from the table and from the physical pattern. For each pattern found in the table, they should see how that idea can be found in the physical pattern. The most important pattern to look for is the one from steps to number of elements, the functional relationship.
4. Write the functional relationship as a formula in terms of the step number. Show how the formula works for each part of the table already constructed. Use the formula to predict the next entry in the table, and check this with an actual construction of the pattern, if possible. Use the formula to predict the twentieth entry in the table.

Graphing the Patterns

So far, growing patterns have been represented by the physical materials or drawings, by a chart, and by a symbolic rule. A graph adds a fourth representation. The individual points in a pattern can be plotted even if the physical pattern has not been discovered. Figure 9.4 shows the graph for each of the two patterns in Figure 9.3. Notice that the first is a straight-line (linear) relationship and the other is a curved line that would make half of a parabola if the points were joined.

Do not forget how easy it is both to plot points and to draw curves on the graphing calculator. The second graph in Figure 9.4 is also shown on a graphing calculator with the function $y = x^2 + 3x$ (same as $n^2 + 3n$) drawn through it.

Assessment Note

As students continue to work with growing patterns, have them predict what the graph will look like before they plot the points from the chart. Do they notice that when the recursive pattern is constant (i.e., the pattern is formed by an arithmetic sequence), as it is for the "Dots on the Border" pattern (Figure 9.3), the graph is a straight line or is linear? Or do they notice that

FIGURE 9.4

Graphs of growing patterns.

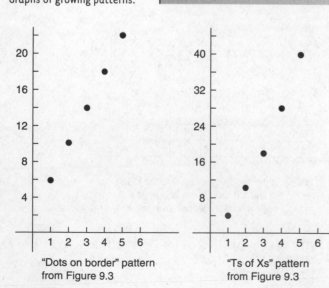

"Dots on border" pattern from Figure 9.3

"Ts of Xs" pattern from Figure 9.3

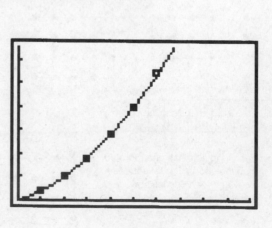

TI-83 graph of $y = x^2 + 3x$

when the recursive pattern is not constant, the graph is a curve? Can they analyze the change from step to step in the chart to determine why the graph results in a line or a curve? For the "Ts of Xs" pattern (Figure 9.3) the recursive pattern is +6, +8, +10, ... The amount of change from step to step is increasing, and the graph in Figure 9.4 reflects this as it curves upward in a steeper and steeper manner. Do students talk about the changes *in the changes* (the recursive relationship *in the recursive relationship*)? For straight lines, there is no change in the changes (i.e., the rate of change is 0), so the slope remains the same. For the "Ts of Xs," however, the change in the changes, or the rate of change, is increasing with each step. If students notice these connections and are able to articulate what is happening, they are well on their way to understanding slope of a graph as a rate of change.

Other Patterns to Explore

In elementary school, students begin their study of patterns through investigating repeating patterns (e.g., blue-green-green-blue-green-green . . .). As students enter the middle grades, their investigations should widen to include growing patterns as discussed so far. However, it would be misleading to leave the impression that this is all that students need to know about patterns. Mathematicians continue to search for and discover new patterns and relationships. Applications of mathematical patterns have led to solutions of real-world problems that were once thought to be unsolvable. Patterns are powerful ideas.

Number Patterns

Many worthwhile patterns can be observed with numbers alone. These can be simple repeating patterns such as 1, 2, 1, 2, . . . to more complicated patterns that involve some form of progression such as 1, 8, 27, 64, 125, . . . (cubes: $1^3, 2^3, 3^3$, etc.). Here are some more numeric patterns:

2, 4, 6, 8, 10, . . .	(even numbers; add 2 each time)
1, 4, 7, 10, 13, . . .	(start with 1; add 3 each time)
1, 4, 9, 16, . . .	(squares: $1^2, 2^2, 3^2$, etc.)
0, 1, 5, 14, 30, . . .	(add the next square number)
2, 5, 11, 23, . . .	(double the number and add 1)
2, 6, 12, 20, 30, . . .	(multiply successive pairs of counting numbers)
3, 3, 6, 9, 15, 24, . . .	(add the two preceding numbers—an example of a Fibonacci sequence)

The challenge in these patterns or sequences of numbers is not only to find and extend the pattern but also to try to determine a general rule to produce the *n*th number in the sequence. Informal or exploratory approaches are similar to those described for growing patterns.

Another form of number pattern is found in function machines as in the next activity.

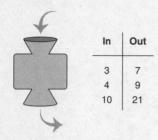

In	Out
3	7
4	9
10	21

FIGURE 9.5 • • • • • • • •

A simple function machine is used to play "Guess My Rule." Students suggest input numbers and the operator records the output value.

ACTIVITY 9.4

Guess My Rule

A simple in-out box is drawn on the board as in Figure 9.5. The machine "operator" knows the secret that is "stored" in the machine. For example, a rule might be $2n + 1$ (double the input number and add 1). Students try to guess the rule by putting numbers into the machine and observing what comes out. Students tell the operator what number to put in. The operator tells what number comes out. A list of "in-out" pairs are kept on the board. Students who think they have guessed the rule raise their hands. As more numbers are "put into the machine," those who think they know the rule tell what comes out. Continue until most have guessed the rule.

Students can play "Guess My Rule" in small groups. Provide a collection of rules on cards or let students make up their own rules. The rule should be in writing before the guessing begins.

A graphing calculator can easily be made into a true function machine to play "Guess My Rule."

On the TI-73 or TI-83, the following simple program will take an entry, display the output, and continue to accept inputs until you press Quit.

```
Prgm 1: GUESS
:Lbl 1
:Disp  ENTER X
:Input X
:2x + 5 => A    (This line stores the secret function.)
:Disp A
:Goto 1
```

Students using the program will see only

```
Prgm 1: GUESS
"ENTER X"
?3
                      11
ENTER X
?5
                      15
```

The function line of the program is easily changed.

The following activities also explore patterns with a calculator.

Amazing Digits

Enter $n \times 99$ where n is any number from 1 to 9. Press ☐. Now press other numbers followed by ☐. Each new press of ☐ multiplies the display by 99. Try other values of n followed by ☐. What is the pattern? Try $n \times 999$ and even $n \times 9999$. Students should play with and explore this idea as long as they wish. Next try using repeating digits for n (3333 or 66). Instead of using nines for the multiplier, try using 0.009 or 99.9. Also experiment with other repeat-digit multipliers. If students are interested, the patterns with nines might be analyzed by looking at 999 as $1000 - 1$ or as 9×111.

More Amazing Digits

Especially if students have shown interest in "Amazing Digits," try division by 9. Begin by just dividing single-digit numbers by 9. (The calculator remembers the last divisor, so after the first division, just enter the new number and press ☐.) After this, there are all sorts of variations to try:

a. Divide by 99, 999, . . .
b. Divide by 0.9, 0.09, 0.009, . . .
c. Divide by 9, but use two-digit dividends. Can you predict the results?
d. Try three-digit dividends and a divisor of 9.
e. Combine (a) or (b) with (c) or (d).

The patterns in "More Amazing Digits" are spectacular and interesting by themselves, but you may want to also try using a digit other than 9 in that exercise.

The Fibonacci Sequence

For a growing pattern that is just a little bit different, see Figure 9.6. It begins with a little square. Each successive step is formed by building a new and larger square onto the previous design. (Can you see how to continue drawing this pattern?) If the sides of the first two little squares are 1 each, then the sides of each new square are the numbers of most interest in this pattern. For those squares shown in the figure, the sides are 1, 1, 2, 3, 5, 8, and 13. What would the side of the next square be? This series of numbers, known as the *Fibonacci sequence,* is named for the Italian mathematician Leonardo Fibonacci (c. 1180–1250). The sequence occurs in a variety of living things. For example, if you count the sets of spirals that go in opposite directions on a pineapple or the seeds of a sunflower, the two numbers will be adjacent numbers in the Fibonacci sequence, usually 8 and 13 for a pineapple and 55 and 89 for sunflowers.

Another interesting fact about the Fibonacci sequence is that the ratio of adjacent numbers in the sequence gets closer and closer to a single fixed number known as the *golden ratio,* a

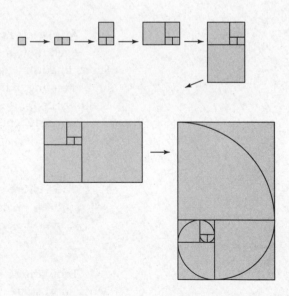

FIGURE 9.6 •

A growing pattern of squares: Each new rectangle is a little closer to a "golden rectangle."

number very close to 1.618. Each larger rectangle in Figure 9.6 has sides in ratio a little closer to the golden ratio. A rectangle in that ratio is called a *golden rectangle,* examples of which can be found in most of the prominent examples of ancient Greek architecture as well as in much art and architecture through the ages. The spiral that is drawn in the last rectangle shown (made from quarter circles drawn in each square) is the same spiral found in the shell of the chambered nautilus.

The Fibonacci sequence and the golden ratio are fascinating phenomena of mathematics. For those who would like to learn more about the connections of this sequence with nature, art, and mathematics, books by Runion (1990) and by Garland (1987) are highly recommended.

Variables and Equations

Variables constitute an extremely powerful method of expressing the regularities found in mathematics. Variables enable us to use mathematical symbolism as a tool to think and help better understand mathematical ideas in the same way physical objects and drawings are used. But if variables are to be included with these other "thinker toys," it is important to help students develop an understanding of the various ways they are used.

Variables

A *variable* is a symbol that can stand for any one of a set of numbers or other objects. Although correct, this simple-sounding definition has a variety of interpretations, depending on how the variables are used. A less than clear understanding can lead to a host of misinterpretations.

Misunderstandings About Variables

Even though students are exposed throughout the elementary years to boxes and letters in arithmetic expressions, studies indicate that most children have a very narrow understanding of the concept of "variable" (Booth, 1988; Chalouh & Herscovics, 1988; Lodholz, 1990).

Some students believe that $7w + 22 = 109$ and $7n + 22 = 109$ will have different solutions. Letters are sometimes taken to represent objects rather than numeric values.

 We all know there are 3 feet in a yard. Using *F* for feet and *Y* for yards, which of these equations correctly expresses this relationship: $3F = Y$ or $F = 3Y$? Make your choice before reading on.

Translating real relationships into symbolic equations is often difficult for students. Most students will pick the first equation, $3F = Y$. Perhaps you did also. Try putting some numbers in $3F = Y$. For example, if *F* is 3, then *Y* should be 1. But that does not work in $3F = Y$. It seems correct because it looks like the familiar relationship "three feet in one yard"—that is, if you are using the letters *F* and *Y* as labels or objects. Therein lies the problem. Many times we say, "Use *F* for feet and *Y* for yards," but we *mean* use *F* for the *number* of feet and *Y* for the *number* of yards. Thus, it can appear that we are using the variable as a label or object, but variables are *not* labels or objects—they represent numbers. Compare the statement that "there are three feet in one yard" with "the *number* of feet is three times the *number* of yards." When *F* stands for the *number* of feet and *Y* stands for the *number* of yards, the correct equation is $F = 3Y$.

Conventions of notation also compound the difficulty. For example, we use *ab* to mean $a \times b$, but $3 \times 5 \neq 35$. Similarly, $ab = ba$, but $35 \neq 53$; and $4 + 0.75 = 4.75$, but $2x + y \neq 2xy$.

Different Uses of Variables

Meanings of variables change with the way they are used. Usiskin (1988) identified three uses of variables that are commonly encountered in school mathematics:

1. *As a specific unknown.* In the early grades, this is the use found in equations such as $8 + \square = 12$. Later, we see exercises such as this: If $3x + 2 = 4x - 1$, solve for *x*.
2. *As a pattern generalizer.* Variables are used in statements that are true for all numbers. For example, $a \times b = b \times a$ for all real numbers.
3. *As quantities that vary in joint variation.* *Joint variation* occurs when change in one variable determines a change in another. In $y = 3x + 5$, as *x* changes or varies, so does *y*. Formulas are also an example of joint variation. In $C = 2\pi r$, as *r*, the radius, changes, so does *C*, the circumference.

Variables as Unknowns

The following activity is a reasonable way for students to experience the meaning of a variable as a placeholder for a specific unknown.

ACTIVITY 9.7

Story Translations

Read a simple story problem to students but omit the question. Their task is to write an equation that means the same thing. For example: *There are 3 full boxes of pencils and 5 extra pencils. There are 41 pencils in all.* ($3 \times \square + 5 = 41$). Be sure to include situations for all four operations. The activity can be reversed by providing an equation with an unknown and letting students make up a story to go with it. Once equations are agreed on, students should use whatever means they wish to find values that make the sentences true. Trial and error is a reasonable first strategy.

Sometimes students will write what may look like different equations. For example, for the situation *A hamburger costs $5.50 more than a shake*, some students may write $h = s + 5.50$ while other students may write $h - s = 5.50$. Students should decide how these equations are alike and how they are different.

Number Tricks

Have students do the following sequence of operations:

> **Write down any number.**
> **Add to it the number that comes after it.**
> **Add 9.**
> **Divide by 2.**
> **Subtract the number you began with.**

Now you can "magically" read their minds. Everyone ended up with 5!

The challenge is to see if students can discover how the trick works. If students need a hint, suggest that instead of using an actual number, they use a box or a letter to begin with. Start with N. Add the next number: $N + (N + 1) = 2N + 1$. Adding 9 gives $2N + 10$. Dividing by 2 leaves $N + 5$. Now subtract the number you began with, leaving 5.

There are endless trick sequences like the one in this activity. Here are two more:

- Pick a number between 1 and 9, multiply by 5, add 3, multiply by 2, add another number between 1 and 9, subtract 6. What do you see?

- Pick a number, multiply by 6, add 12, take half of the result, subtract 6, divide by 3. What happens?

These tricks can also be explored with models by using a small box or a cube for the unknown. Figure 9.7 shows how the first of the two tricks above might be modeled. Notice the place-value component required to understand the result.

FIGURE 9.7 ·········

Number tricks can be modeled using a block or a box for the unknown. Additional numbers are shown with counters or base-ten pieces.

 Pick a number between 1 and 9.

Multiply by 5 and add 3.

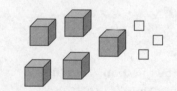

Multiply by 2 and add another 1-digit number.

Subtract 6, and then . . .

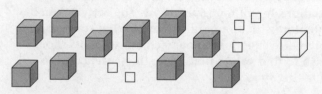

(a 2-digit number)

Variables as Pattern Generators

Variables are often used to illustrate rules or regularities that exist in our number system. We often write down these rules using variables without giving much thought to the fact that students may not understand the variables involved.

ACTIVITY 9.9

What's True for All Numbers?

Ask students how they know that 465 + 137 = 137 + 465 without doing the computation. Students' explanations should show evidence of understanding the commutative property for addition, although the name of the property is not important. How can this be written to show that it's a rule that is true for every number, even fractions and decimals? If students do not suggest it, offer the idea that letters or shapes could be used like this:

$$\Delta + \square = \square + \Delta \qquad \text{or} \qquad n + m = m + n$$

Be sure students understand that the choice of letter or shape is totally arbitrary as long as it is understood that each stands for any number and that when the same letter or shape appears in the same equation, it must represent the same value.

With this introduction, challenge students to find other statements that are true for all numbers.

Students may need some prodding to think about things that are always true, but it is best that they come up with the ideas themselves. One way to provide hints is to explore some specific examples. For example, draw a divided rectangle as shown in Figure 9.8. What are two ways to calculate the area? This can lead to the generalized version of the distributive property: $a(b + c) = (a \times b) + (a \times c)$. In addition to properties of the number system, also think about definitions of exponents or rules for negative numbers, all of which can be expressed in a general form using variables.

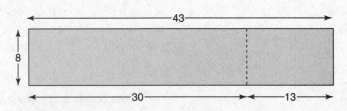

FIGURE 9.8 •

The distributive property is just one of many ideas that can be generalized using variables.

ACTIVITY 9.10

Special Quantities

What numeric expression would tell the number of chair legs on 376 chairs? (376 × 4) What about 195 chairs? (195 × 4) How would you write the number of legs on any number of chairs? ($N \times 4$) Using this as an example, challenge students to write expressions for other types of quantities: fingers on students, eggs in cartons, crayons in boxes, wheels on tractor trailers, hours in days, inches in feet, quarts in gallons, and so on. Similarly, use variables to express these special numbers: any odd number, any even number, any multiple of 7, a multiple of 3 plus a different multiple of 5, any two-digit number, any power of 2. Once students get the idea, have them make up their own special quantities and see if others can describe them verbally.

FIGURE 9.9 • • • • • • • •

A spreadsheet formula uses variables to represent values in other cells. The expression in a cell is a pattern generalizer for that cell. The same spreadsheet is shown twice here, once with the formula in each cell and once with the cell values calculated. Note that any change in column A will produce changes in the entire row.

	A	B	C	D	E	F	G	H	I
1	**Exploring Odd and Even Numbers**								
2									
3	N	Even	Odd	E + E	E + O	O + O	E × E	E × O	O × O
4	1	2	3	4	5	6	4	6	9
5	2	4	5	8	9	10	16	20	25
6	7	14	15	28	29	30	196	210	225
7	10	20	21	40	41	42	400	420	441
8	15	30	31	60	61	62	900	930	961

	A	B	C	D	E	F	G	H	I
1	**Exploring Odd and Even Numbers**								
2									
3	N	Even	Odd	E + E	E + O	O + O	E × E	E × O	O × O
4	1	=2*A4	=2*A4+1	=B4+B4	=B4+C4	=C4+C4	=B4*B4	=B4*C4	=C4*C4
5	2	=2*A5	=2*A5+1	=B5+B5	=B5+C5	=C5+C5	=B5*B5	=B5*C5	=C5*C5
6	7	=2*A6	=2*A6+1	=B6+B6	=B6+C6	=C6+C6	=B6*B6	=B6*C6	=C6*C6
7	10	=2*A7	=2*A7+1	=B7+B7	=B7+C7	=C7+C7	=B7*B7	=B7*C7	=C7*C7
8	15	=2*A8	=2*A8+1	=B8+B8	=B8+C8	=C8+C8	=B8*B8	=B8*C8	=C8*C8

The way that variables are used in the "Special Quantities" activity is essentially the way variables are used in spreadsheets. In Figure 9.9, odd and even numbers are generated from the numbers in column A. These values are then used in the sums and products columns.

Variables as Quantities That Vary

"Joint variation is at the heart of understanding patterns and functions. As students grow in their ability to derive meaning for variables in contexts, they encounter variables that are changing in relation to each other" (Lappan, 1998, p. 57). Whenever students develop charts that list the corresponding values of two related quantities, they are exploring the idea of *joint variation;* the value in one row varies according to the value in the other row. In the study of ratio and proportion, students make charts relating cost to the number of units purchased or relating miles driven to gallons of gasoline used. In measurement, charts are made that relate circumference to diameter or volume to the area of the base of a cylinder. In data analysis, best-fit lines produce generalizations of the way two variables are approximately related, for example, height and arm span. In this chapter, we have seen that the study of growing patterns results in formulas that connect the step number to the number of elements in that step of the pattern.

All of these are examples of joint variation—one value changing in relation to another. They are also examples of functions. Consequently, a rule can be written that describes the way that the two variables are related. Chapter 10 is devoted to helping students understand and analyze functions. There we will examine ways to help students explore joint variation of variables expressed in contextual situations, in equations, in charts, in graphs, and in words.

Equations and Inequalities

In the expression $3B + 7 = B - C$, the equal sign means that the quantity on the left *is the same as* the quantity on the right. To understand expressions in this way, students must interpret simple arithmetic expressions such as $3 + 5$ or 4×87 as *single quantities*.

Unfortunately, students tend to look on expressions such as $3 + 5$ and 4×87 as commands or things to do. The + tells you to add, and students think of *add* as a verb or an operator button, like pressing ⊟ on a calculator. As students read left to right in an equation, the = tells them, "Now give the answer." Because of this "get an answer" view of operations and equal signs, students fail to think of $5 + 2$ as another way to write 7.

A Balance-Pan Approach to Equality

The following activities are ways to help students with the basic concepts needed to understand equations.

ACTIVITY 9.11

Names for Numbers

Challenge students to find different ways to express a particular number, say, 10. Give a few simple examples, such as 2×5, $12 - 2$, or $30 \div 3$. Encourage the use of two or more different operations. "How many names for 8 can you find using only numbers less than 10 and at least three operations?" One example is: $\frac{6 \times 2 + 3 \times 4}{3}$. In your discussion, emphasize that each expression is a way of representing or writing a number.

The activity "Names for Numbers" is similar to the commercial game 24. However, in the basic game of 24 the student is given four particular numbers and is challenged to use all four numbers with any combination of the four operations to produce 24. You can use this game as another opportunity to discuss how these expressions are just another way to represent a number, namely, 24.

Notice that there are no equal signs used in Activity 9.11. The next activity develops the concept of the equal sign. It begins with numbers only but is quickly extended to include variables.

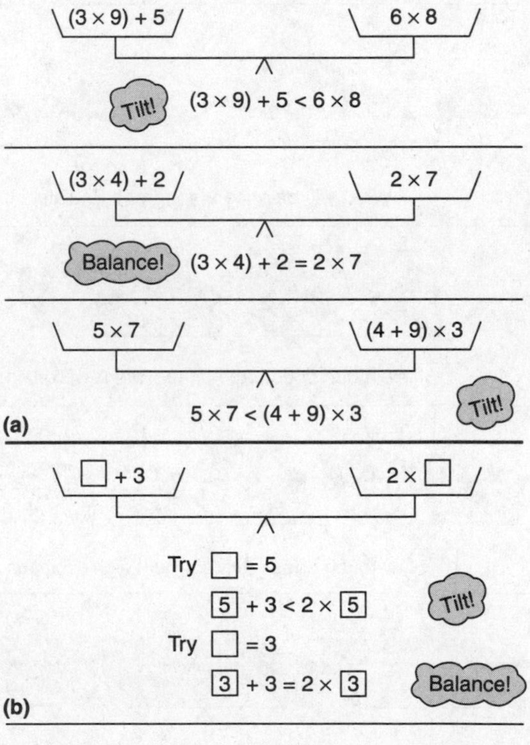

ACTIVITY 9.12

Tilt or Balance

On the board, draw a simple two-pan balance. In each pan, write a numeric expression, and ask which pan will go down or whether the two will balance (see Figure 9.10). Challenge students to write expressions for

(continued)

(a)

Tilt! $(3 \times 9) + 5 < 6 \times 8$

Balance! $(3 \times 4) + 2 = 2 \times 7$

$5 \times 7 < (4 + 9) \times 3$ Tilt!

(b)

Try $\square = 5$
$\boxed{5} + 3 < 2 \times \boxed{5}$ Tilt!
Try $\square = 3$
$\boxed{3} + 3 = 2 \times \boxed{3}$ Balance!

FIGURE 9.10 •

Using expressions and variables in equations and inequalities. The two-pan balance helps develop the meaning of =, <, and >.

EXPANDED LESSON

(pages 282–283)
A complete lesson plan
based on "Tilt or Balance"
can be found at the end
of this chapter.

each side of the scale to make it balance. For each, write a corresponding equation to illustrate the meaning of =. Note that when the scale "tilts," either a "greater than" or "less than" symbol (> or <) is used.

After a short time, add variables to the two-pan balance activity.

In Figure 9.11, a series of examples shows scale problems in which different shapes on the scales represent different values. Two or more scales for a single problem provide different information about the shapes or variables.

When no numbers are involved, as in the top two examples of Figure 9.11, students can find combinations of numbers for the shapes that make all of the balances balance. If an arbitrary value is given to one of the shapes, then values for the other shapes can be found accordingly. In the second example, if the sphere = 2, then the cylinder must be 4 and the cube = 8. If a different value is given to the sphere, the other shapes will change accordingly.

The scale problems (with a number for each scale) are to be solved for a unique value for each shape. There are usually several paths to finding a solution.

> **STOP** How would you solve the last problem in Figure 9.11? Can you solve it in two ways?

You (and your students) can tell if you are correct by checking your solutions with the original scale positions. Believe it or not, you have just solved a series of simultaneous equations, a skill generally left to a formal algebra class.

Solving Equations

To *solve an equation* means to find values of the variable that make the equation true. To help students develop skills of solving equations in one variable, it is advisable to maintain the image of the balance pans. The balance makes it reasonably clear to students that if you add or subtract value from one side, you must add or subtract a like value from the other side to keep the scales balanced.

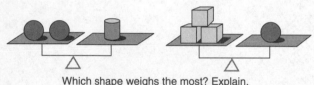

Which shape weighs the most? Explain.
Which shape weighs the least? Explain.

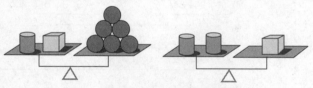

What will balance 2 spheres? Explain.

How much does each shape weigh? Explain.

How much does each shape weigh? Explain.

How much does each shape weigh? Explain.

FIGURE 9.11

Examples of problems with multiple scales (equations).

ACTIVITY 9.13

Adjust the Balance

Show a balance with variable expressions in each side. Use only one variable. Make the tasks such that a solution by trial and error is not reasonable. For example, the solution to $3x + 2 = 11 - x$ is not a whole number. Suggest that adjustments can be made to the quantities in each pan as long as the balance is maintained. If you begin with simple equations such as $x - 17 = 31 - x$, students should be able to develop skills and explain their rationale. Students should also be challenged to devise a method of proving that their solutions are correct. (Solutions can be tested by substitution in the original equation.)

Figure 9.12 shows solutions for two equations, one in a balance and the other without. Even after you have stopped using the balance, it is a good idea to refer to the scale or balance pan concept of equality and the idea of keeping the scales balanced.

As students begin to work with equations in two variables (i.e., equations they could graph on a coordinate plane), the equations will often be in a form in which neither variable is isolated. For example, in the equation $3A - B = 2A$, they may want A in terms of B or B in terms of A. The same technique of solving for one variable can be used to solve for one variable in terms of the other by adjusting the expressions on both sides while keeping the equation in balance.

Assessment Note

The main content of this chapter is found in the ideas pertaining to growing patterns and the related ideas of variables and equations. Your curriculum will likely specify particular skills in these areas. To assess this knowledge is straightforward. Can your students recognize and extend patterns of the appropriate type for their grade level? Do they use variables in ways that suggest an understanding of the various uses and meanings of *variable*? And do they solve equations appropriate for their grade level? Answers to these questions should be found in the way students respond to the activities you conduct in class or in end-of-unit tests that assess these ideas directly.

More pervasive than these specific ideas, however, is the general notion of algebraic reasoning. It is appropriate to gather data that indicate the degree to which students make generalizations based on their mathematical experiences and use appropriate language and symbolism to represent these generalizations. Since pattern and regularity can be found in nearly all areas of mathematics, algebraic reasoning should be developed and assessed throughout the curriculum. Students who ask questions like "Will that work for any numbers?" or who observe similarities from one area of mathematics to another are using algebraic reasoning. Students who have difficulty seeing and expressing relationships such as the way two patterns are alike or who have difficulty expressing rules and formulas are not as strong in their algebraic reasoning.

Make a conscious effort to observe and keep anecdotal records of behaviors that are indicative of algebraic reasoning. It is quite likely that such records over time will give you useful insights into the mathematical talents of your students.

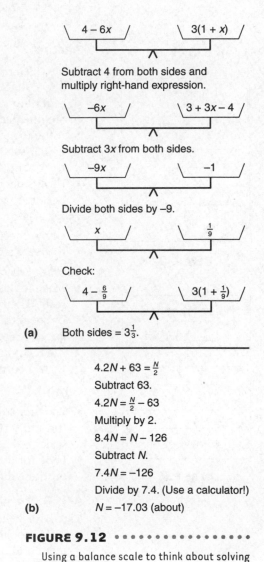

(a)

4 − 6x   3(1 + x)

Subtract 4 from both sides and multiply right-hand expression.

−6x   3 + 3x − 4

Subtract 3x from both sides.

−9x   −1

Divide both sides by −9.

x $\frac{1}{9}$

Check:

$4 - \frac{6}{9}$ $3(1 + \frac{1}{9})$

Both sides = $3\frac{1}{3}$.

(b)

$4.2N + 63 = \frac{N}{2}$

Subtract 63.

$4.2N = \frac{N}{2} - 63$

Multiply by 2.

$8.4N = N - 126$

Subtract N.

$7.4N = -126$

Divide by 7.4. (Use a calculator!)

$N = -17.03$ (about)

FIGURE 9.12

Using a balance scale to think about solving equations.

EXPANDED LESSON

Tilt or Balance

Based on Activity 9.12, pp. 279–280

GRADE LEVEL: Sixth or seventh grade.

MATHEMATICS GOALS
- To connect the symbols =, <, and > to the concept of equality, less than, and more than.
- To develop the notion of variables as unknowns.

THINKING ABOUT THE STUDENTS
Students have been challenged to find different ways to express numbers, as in Activity 9.11, "Names for Num-

bers." Students know how to apply the order of operations to an expression and are familiar with the symbols =, <, and >.

MATERIALS AND PREPARATION
- Prepare a transparency of Tilt or Balance? (Blackline Master L-3).
- Make a copy of the Tilt or Balance Challenge worksheet for each student (Blackline Master L-4).

lesson

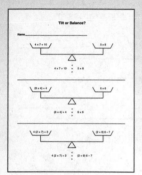

BLM L-3

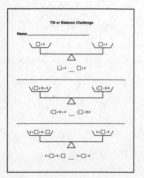

BLM L-4

BEFORE

Begin with a simpler version of the task:
- Show students the transparency, Tilt or Balance? Explain that the drawing is a representation of a pan balance, and since the drawing cannot tilt when the quantities are unequal, we can indicate the inequality by using < or >. Ask them to determine if the first scale tilts or balances. Have a volunteer explain his or her thinking and which symbol (<, >, or =) he or she would use to indicate the relationship between the quantities.
- Have students consider and discuss the next two balance scales in a similar manner. Be sure that students understand the correct use of < and >.

The Task
- Given the Tilt or Balance Challenge worksheet, substitute numbers for the □ symbol to create a numeric expression on each side of the scales to make them balance.

Establish Expectations
- Make it clear to students that the □ represents the same value on both sides of the scale. Their goal is to write expressions for each side of the scale to make it balance by substituting a number for the □. If they try a number that results in an unbalanced scale, they should write a corresponding inequality using < or > to indicate the relationship. For each successful attempt at balancing the scales, they should write a corresponding equation to illustrate the meaning of =.

DURING
- Look for students who are using different numbers for the variable on each side of the scale. The variable or unknown should be the same number on both sides of the scale.
- Look for different strategies used by students to determine the unknowns. Capitalize on these differences in the "after" portion of the lesson.

AFTER
- Ask for volunteers to share their thinking in determining the solution for the first scale problem. Do not evaluate students' ideas but encourage other students to comment and question their classmates' thinking. Ask for other ways to think about the task. Repeat for the next two scale problems.

- Ask students to write down what they think the symbol = means. Have students share with a partner and then discuss ideas as a class. It is important for the students to come to the consensus that = means *is the same as*.

ASSESSMENT NOTES

- Are students using a systematic approach to determine the solutions? In other words, are they using the results of their attempts to inform their next attempt? Or are they haphazardly trying numbers?
- Are students appropriately evaluating expressions using order of operations?
- Do students have a clear sense that = means that the expressions on either side of it are equivalent amounts? Do they understand this in equations without a reference to a scale?

- Pose scale problems, like those in Figure 9.11, p. 280, where each shape on the scales represents a different value.
- For students who are ready for a challenge, pose scale problems in which the solutions are not whole numbers.

This will quickly lead to methods of solving equations. See Activity 9.13, "Adjust the Balance."

next steps

EXPANDED LESSON

EXPLORING FUNCTIONS

Algebraic reasoning, as discussed in the previous chapter, involves a search for regularity in all of mathematics. Functions, the topic of this chapter, are one of the most powerful tools in this endeavor. They allow us to represent relationships symbolically, visually, and orally, and to generalize relationships between variables in every area of mathematics involving quantities that are related. This makes the concept of function one of the big ideas of mathematics.

Functions are the tool used for mathematically modeling all types of real-world change. Representing functions in different ways can lead to analysis and understanding of that change. Students in the middle grades should develop an understanding of the multiple methods of expressing real-world functional relationships (words, graphs, equations, and tables). Working with these different representations of functions will allow students to develop a fuller understanding of this important concept.

big ideas

1 Functions are relationships or rules that uniquely associate members of one set with members of another set.

2 In a functional relationship, one variable (the dependent variable) is defined in terms of the other variable (the independent variable).

3 Functional relationships can be expressed in real contexts, graphs, algebraic equations, tables, and words. Each representation for a given function is simply a different way of expressing the same idea. Each representation provides a different view of the function. The value of a particular representation depends on its purpose.

Function Concepts and Representations

A study of functions is a study of the way change in one variable affects change in another; it is a study of *joint variation* of variables. A *function* is a rule that uniquely defines how the first or independent variable affects the second or dependent variable.

There are five different ways to interpret or represent a function: through a context, table of values, language, graph, and, finally, the familiar equation. Each is a different way of communicating the same rule of correspondence or relationship. It is important to see that each representation expresses the same idea yet provides a different way of looking at or thinking about the relationship. We will use the context of a hot-dog vendor to illustrate all five representations.

Brian is trying to make money to help pay for college by selling hot dogs from a hot-dog cart at the coliseum during major performances and ball games. He pays the cart owner $35 per night for the use of the cart. He sells hot dogs for $1.25 each. His costs for the hot dogs, condiments, napkins, and other paper products are about 60 cents per hot dog on average. The income from a single hot dog is, therefore, 65 cents.

Contextual Representations of Functions

This function begins with a context: selling hot dogs and the resulting profit. The more hot dogs Brian sells, the more profit he will make. So, we are interested in Brian's profit in terms of the number of hot dogs sold. Brian does not begin to make a profit immediately because he must pay the $35 rent on the vending cart. Nonetheless, Brian's profit is dependent on—*is a function of*—the number of hot dogs he sells.

Not every function has a real-world context, but at the middle school level, it is useful to place functions in contexts that make sense to students. Here are some other contexts in which functional relationships are to be found:

- Suppose that the value of a new car depreciates at the rate of 20 percent each year. There is a definite relationship between the age of the car and its current value.

- If you measure the height and arm span of a lot of different people, from very short to very tall, you will likely find that there is a predictable relationship between these two measures. Arm span is related to height.

- A ride on a roller coaster has several possible relationships. As time passes from the beginning of the ride to the end of the ride, the height of the cars above the ground changes. It increases slowly at first, then most likely has a fast decrease followed by a series of lesser increases and decreases. The speed of the cars on the roller coaster is also a function of time. The speed of the cars has an effect on how loud the passengers scream, and so it is reasonable to say that speed and screams are related, although perhaps not as precisely as the height is related to the time.

- If you build rectangles so that all have the same fixed perimeter, the lengths of the rectangles will decrease as the widths increase. If you begin with a very small width and a longer length, the area of the rectangles first increases as the width increases from zero and then decreases.

These are all contexts in which there is a functional relationship. For the height versus arm span and the loudness of roller coaster passengers, a relationship is not easy

FUNCTION CONCEPTS AND REPRESENTATIONS

to determine precisely. Riders will not always scream at exactly the same decibel level, nor will everyone's height-to-arm span ratio be the same. However, all of these situations illustrate functions in meaningful contexts. Each has at least two values that vary jointly, with one being dependent on or related to the other.

Table Representations of Functions

Brian the hot-dog vendor might well sit down and calculate some possible income figures based on hypothetical sales. This will give him some idea of how many franks he must sell to break even and what his profit might be for an evening. For example, if he sells no hot dogs, he will be $35 in the hole, or his profit will be negative $35. (For the time being, let's not consider the cost of any hot dogs, condiments, napkins, and other paper products that Brian may have purchased that are not sold.) Selling 70 hot dogs would yield a profit of 70 × 0.65 – 35 = 45.50 – 35, or $10.50. A table of similar values might look like this:

Hot Dogs	Profit
0	–35.00
70	10.50
100	30.00
150	62.50

The number of hot dogs shown in the table is purely a matter of choice. One could calculate the profit for 10,000 hot dogs (10,000 × 0.65 – 35), even though it is not reasonable to expect Brian to sell that many in one evening. One of the values of contexts in thinking about functions is to see how mathematical representations can ignore reality. The person who interprets the table must take the context into consideration.

 When a set of data such as the height and arm span is organized in a table, it does not yet create a function. Why not?

A function must *uniquely* define the value of one variable in terms of the other. Heights can predict arm span but not precisely. There may be many different persons in the data set with the same height who have different arm spans. As you will see in Chapter 11, a line can be drawn to approximate data that are not perfectly organized. A best-fit line for the height—arm span data would define a functional relationship that approximates reality to the degree that the line fits or represents the data.

Language Expressions for Functions

Functional relationships are dependent relationships or rules of correspondence. In other words, the value of one variable is defined in terms of the other. In the hot-dog vendor situation, Brian's profit depends on the number of hot dogs sold. So, in functional language, we can say, "Profit *is a function of* the number of hot dogs sold." The phrase "is a function of" expresses the dependent relationship. The profit *depends on*—is a function of—the hot-dog sales.

Looking at the other examples, we would say that the current value of a car is a function of its age or its value depends on its age. If someone were to ask what speed the roller coaster is going, you might respond, "It depends on the time since the ride began," or, in functional terms, "That depends. The speed is a function of the time since the ride began."

 STOP See if you can express the relationships in the other examples in functional terms.

Assessment Note

Listening to how students describe a functional relationship in their own words provides you with valuable information about their understanding of independent and dependent variables and variables in general. Expressing a functional relationship in words requires the student to first identify the variables at play and then to think about which variable is defined in terms of the other. They have to think about what is changing and how that change is taking place. Check to see if students have first identified the pertinent variables that are changing. If students have difficulty with this first step, discussing what is not changing can help some students focus on what is changing. What do their responses tell you about how they understand the idea that one variable can depend on another? Do they describe the dependency relationship; that is, have they correctly identified which variable is the independent variable? Just as in so many other situations, putting ideas into their own words helps students to make sense of what is happening. It also provides you with a window into their understanding.

Graphical Representations of Functions

They say that a picture is worth a thousand words. This is certainly true of functions. In the case of a function the picture is a graph. In Figure 10.1, six different values of hot-dog sales are plotted on a graph. The horizontal axis represents the number of hot dogs sold, and the vertical axis, the profit. As we have already established, the profit goes up as the sales go up. There is, in this situation, a very clear pattern to the six values.

The graph shows that the relationship between sales and profits is *linear*—a straight line—and is increasing. It also allows us easily to answer questions about Brian's profits. How many hot dogs must be sold to break even? The graph shows zero profit (the break-even point) where the line crosses the horizontal axis. (Why?) It looks to be near 53 or 54. What is Brian's profit for 130 hot dogs? How many hot dogs must be sold to make a profit of $100? The context gives meaning to the graph, and the graph adds understanding to the context.

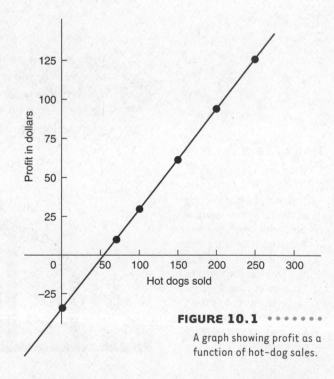

FIGURE 10.1 ·······

A graph showing profit as a function of hot-dog sales.

FUNCTION CONCEPTS AND REPRESENTATIONS

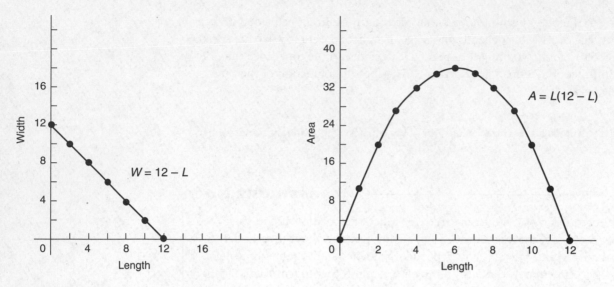

FIGURE 10.2 • • • • • • •

The width and area graphs as functions of the length of a rectangle with a fixed perimeter of 24 units.

The graph is another mathematical model that, in terms of the context, does not make sense for all portions of the picture. If the line is extended indefinitely, there would be values where Brian's sales were negative (to the left of the vertical axis). This clearly does not make sense. Nor is it reasonable to talk about sales of millions of hot dogs even though the graph can extend as far as is wished.

Not all functions have straight-line graphs. For example, if you start with a rectangle that has a fixed perimeter of 24 inches and increase the length beginning at 1 inch, both the width and the area will vary accordingly (see Figure 10.2). The width graph is linear. It decreases at a constant rate. By contrast, the area graph rises in a curve, reaches a maximum value, and then goes back down.

Figure 10.3 shows a simple roller coaster. Suppose that it takes just 120 seconds to ride.

Try to sketch a graph that shows the *height* of the roller coaster throughout the ride. Why will your graph not be exactly the same as the path of the roller coaster? Now make another graph that shows the *speed* of the car over the 120 seconds of the ride. Share your sketches with a friend. How are these two graphs related to each other?

FIGURE 10.3 • • • • • • • • • •

If it takes 120 seconds to ride this roller coaster, sketch a graph of the height of the car as a function of time. How should the points A through H be spaced along the time line? Sketch a second graph of the speed as a function of time. The time axis with points A to H should be the same. What would a graph of "scream decibels" look like?

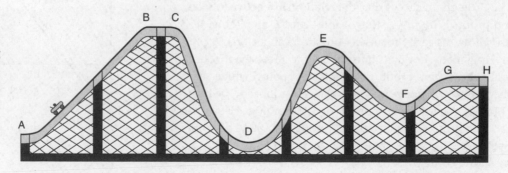

Equations to Represent Functions

Suppose that we pick a letter, say, *H,* to represent the number of hot dogs Brian sells. For each hot dog sold, his income is $1.25 \times H$ dollars. But to determine his profit, we have to subtract from his income the rental cost of the cart and 60 cents cost per hot dog. Therefore, Brian's profit is represented by $(1.25 \times H) - (0.60 \times H) - 35$, or $(0.65 \times H) - 35$. To make an equation, we can assign another letter to stand for profit: $P = (0.65 \times H) - 35$. This equation defines a mathematical relationship between two values or two variables, profit and hot dogs. Taken out of context, it is simply a relationship between P and H. It is the same as the relationship between x and y in the equation $y = 0.65x - 35$.

By expressing a function as an equation, it can be examined in its most abstract form. Different types of equations have different properties. When the properties are understood, they can be applied to the context as well. In our hot-dog example, the equation has the general form of a linear equation, $Y = mX + b$. In this form, the value of m tells us how quickly or steeply the line goes up or down moving from left to right. The value of b tells where the graph will cross the vertical axis.

In the rectangle context, the following two equations represent the width and area, respectively, as functions of the length (assuming that the perimeter is fixed at 24 units):

$$W(L) = \frac{24 - 2L}{2} = 12 - L$$

$$A(L) = L(12 - L) = 12L - L^2$$

Expressing functions in an equation can make it easier to see what is happening. In this example, the function notations $W(L)$ and $A(L)$ were used instead of a single letter for each. $W(L)$ stands for the width. Within this efficient notation is an indication that the width is a function of the length L. "The width when the length is 3" can now be represented symbolically as $W(3)$. The symbolic name for the function itself—the relationship between the length and width—is represented by the letter W. Similarly for the area function A: $A(L)$ is the area for any given value of L; $A(4)$ is the area when the length is 4. The area is a function of the length.

Equations also make it easier to calculate values of the function. The equation can be entered into a graphing calculator, and the calculator can do the calculations to produce a table or draw a graph. Without the equation representation of the function, the graphing calculator is much less useful. Figure 10.4 shows the screen of a TI-83 calculator with both the width and the area graphs drawn. The table to the right computes the area for every length in steps of one-half. It requires very little expertise to do this on the calculator and allows the middle school student the chance to see and explore graphs without the tedium of having to plot points.

Sometimes equations come from selecting a curve (and its corresponding equation) that seems to "fit" the data available. That is how an equation for the height–arm span relationship would be determined. A "best-fit curve" would be determined to fit the data. A complete discussion of finding a best-fit line—including an example—is found in Chapter 12.

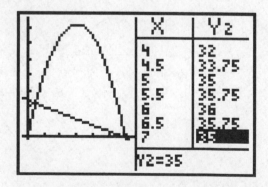

FIGURE 10.4 • • • • • • • • • • • • • • • • • • •

This graphing calculator shows graphs of both the width and the area of a rectangle of fixed perimeter as functions of the length. The table can show all possible length and area values.

Developing Function Concepts in the Classroom

If the discussion so far had focused only on Brian the hot-dog vendor, the development would be similar to the approach in a middle school classroom. Begin with a context, explore the relationships, and develop different representations to show what has been found.

Begin with Meaningful Contexts

Today, algebra is dominated by the study of functions and should begin with meaningful situations in which functions can be found. Numerous contexts contain functional relationships that are completely accessible to students, even as early as fifth grade. By exploring a context and making sense of it, the function relationship is already developed.

In the context of Brian's sales, a discussion can involve finding the number of hot dogs that need to be sold to make a given amount of money and how much profit is made by selling a particular number of hot dogs. By examining and explaining these questions, students are working with the joint variation between hot dogs sold and profit made. They are actually using a function before they have been asked to worry about symbols and definitions.

Our lives abound with situations that involve functional relationships. Making money and the ideas related to profit and loss are both realistic and interesting. Social studies provides many relationships. For example, populations of various regions may be related to health, income, production levels, education levels, death rates, and so on. Science offers another area of investigations. Pendulums can be swung to investigate period as a function of length. The distance a toy car will roll down a ramp can be compared to the angle of the ramp. Plant growth can be related to quantities of fertilizer or to the number of days since germination. These are just a few real contexts that can make the study of functions meaningful.

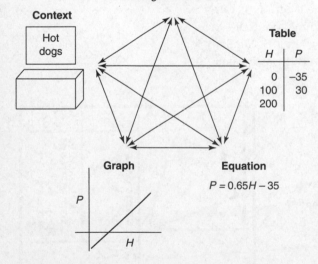

FIGURE 10.5 •

Five different representations of a function. For any given function, students should see that all these representations are connected and illustrate the same relationship. Each representation provides a different perspective on the function.

Connect Different Representations

Figure 10.5 illustrates the five representations of functions that we explored earlier. The most important idea is to see that for a given function, each of these representations illustrates the same relationship. The *context* provides an embodiment of the relationship outside the world of mathematics. *Language* helps express the relationship in a meaningful and useful manner. *Tables* explicitly match up selected elements that are paired by the function. The joint variation is implicit in the pairings of numbers. The *graph* translates the number pairs into a picture. Any point on the graph of a function has two coordinates. The function

Chapter 10 EXPLORING FUNCTIONS

is the rule that relates the first coordinate to the second. The *equation* expresses the same functional relationship with the economy and power of mathematical symbolism.

Use Technology

In the past, when students had to plot points and do by hand all the computations that were involved, functions were limited to very simple examples. Eighth-grade students would probably never see a function with an equation much more complicated than $y = 3x + 2$. The tedium of computing and plotting function values meant that examples had to use numbers that were small and relatively easy to work with, making the link to real contexts almost impossible. Thanks to technology, we can now explore realistic contexts involving not-so-nice numbers. Students can investigate all sorts of functions as long as a relationship can be identified.

Consider the examples in the first part of this chapter. The profit example is the easiest to work with and could probably be examined without technology. The car depreciation is an exponential function. The area for a fixed perimeter is a quadratic function. If students can come up with an equation to go with a function rule, technology can be used to make a graph and do the necessary number crunching to make a table. The technology is not "thinking" for the students; on the contrary, student effort is focused on the thinking and not on the mechanics of computation and plotting points.

Students who have talked about exponents and about percents—both middle grades topics—are equipped to develop an equation for the car depreciation situation. That exploration might go like this: If the car loses 20 percent of its value in 1 year, then it must be worth 80 percent of its value after a year. So after 1 year, the $15,000 car is worth $15,000 × 0.8. In the second year, it loses 20 percent of that value, so it will be worth only 80 percent of its value at the end of year one: ($15,000 × 0.8) × 0.8 = $15,000 × 0.8^2. At the end of the third year, the value will be $15,000 × 0.8^3, and so on. In general, at the end of n years, the value of the car can be expressed in this equation: $V = \$15,000 \times 0.8^n$. Figure 10.6 shows the graph and the table of values on a graphing calculator. This equation is no more difficult to enter into a graphing calculator or a computer graphing utility than $y = 3x + 2$. The idea is to see that there are functional relationships and that these can be expressed in different ways.

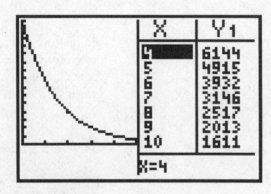

FIGURE 10.6 ••••••••••••••••••••••••

The graph and table for $V = 15,000 \times 0.8^n$. The graph shows n for values 0 to 15. The vertical axis runs from 0 to 15,000.

Functions from Patterns

Growing patterns can be used to introduce the idea of function rules connected to a context. Growing patterns or sequences developed from physical or pictorial drawings were discussed at length in Chapter 9. Now that we have a more complete view of the function concept and the various representations of functions, let's explore one more example of a growing pattern and see how all of these ideas fit together in that context.

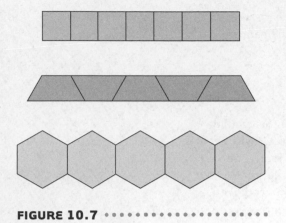

FIGURE 10.7 ·

What is the perimeter of a string of *N* pattern blocks?

Perimeter Patterns

In this activity, students explore the perimeters of strings of regular polygons. Each string is made up of tiles of the same shape. Adjoining tiles share one side, as shown in Figure 10.7. For a given shape, the task is to develop a rule or formula for the perimeter of strings of any number of tiles. For example, if the tiles are square, the perimeter for one square is 4, for two squares is 6, for three squares is 8, and so on. What is a formula for the perimeter of a string of *N* squares? Figure 10.7 shows strings for three different shapes. Pattern blocks are an excellent manipulative for this task because all edges are 1 inch long except for the trapezoid, which has a long side of 2 inches.

Students working at "Perimeter Patterns" should first develop a table by adding tiles to their string one at a time and recording the perimeters in a table as they go. A recursive relationship is easy to determine. For hexagons, it is "add 4 to the preceding perimeter." A table for hexagons looks like this:

1	2	3	4	5	6	7	8	. . .	N
6	10	14	18	22	26	30	34	. . .	?

So now we have a table and a contextual situation. The next challenge is the most interesting: Find a rule or equation that tells the perimeter for *N* hexagons. What students come up with depends on whether they focus on the table of numbers or the string of tiles. In either case, they are likely to have a variety of ideas.

Assessment Note

As you listen to and observe students during this activity, pay attention to the strategies they use to search for patterns and generalizations. Do they use the differences from one step to the next? Do they only look for regularities in the physical patterns or in the table? Do they or can they coordinate step numbers with different aspects of the physical pattern? Do they distinguish between a recursive relationship in a pattern and a functional rule that will produce the step value for any step?

 Before reading further, see if you can come up with at least two different formulas for the perimeter of *N* hexagons.

Here are five different-looking formulas:

$$4N + 2 \qquad 2(2N + 1) \qquad 6 + (N - 1)4 \qquad (N - 2)4 + (2 \times 5) \qquad 2N + 2N + 2$$

Are your formulas in this list? Perhaps you found a different one. When students share different formulas for the same pattern, others might be challenged to see how they arrived at the patterns. The following three ideas generate three of the five formulas given:

- *The first tile has a perimeter of 6. Each new tile adds 4 more.* (This idea can be found in the table as well as the block pattern.)
- *Each tile has two edges on the top. Include the one extra edge on the left along with the top edges. The bottom edges plus the right edge are the same as this.*
- *Each tile has two edges on the top and two on the bottom plus the two end edges.*

 Match these three ways of thinking of the perimeter with three of the formulas. Then try to figure how one may have been thinking to generate the other two. Of course, all of these "different" formulas are equivalent, with the simplest form being 4N + 2.

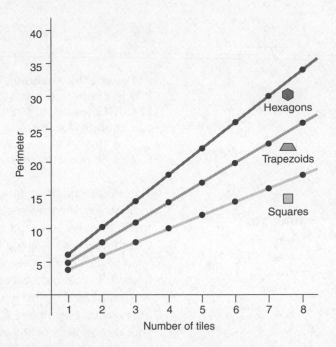

FIGURE 10.8 •

Graphs of the perimeters of three different pattern-block strings.

To add language to our representations, we can say, "The perimeter of a string of hexagons is a function of the number of hexagons in the string."

Next, a graph of the perimeter relationship provides the fifth representation. The points on the graph will lie along a straight line and go up 4 units for every added tile. The graphs for each of the other tile shapes will go up at different rates or with different *slopes* (see Figure 10.8).

The perimeter problem has an interesting extension. If different groups of students have been working on strings of shapes using different polygons, the resulting formulas will be similar. See if students can find an even more general formula with two variables: *N* representing the number of tiles and *S* representing the number of sides per tile. (This challenge is left to you.)

Functions from the Real World

. . . . investigation of functions. Here are some other ideas that develop the same concepts.

Relationships Found in the Real World

Real-world situations, such as the example of Brian selling hot dogs, can be explored with students by having them make tables of data using the information given. By computing several entries in the table, students will begin to see a pattern develop. Consider the following activity.

How Many Gallons Left?

Present this situation to students: A car gets 23 miles per gallon of gas. It has a gas tank that holds 20 gallons. Suppose that you were on a trip and had filled the tank at the outset. Make a table showing the number of gallons remaining in the tank for at least three different points in a trip of 350 miles. Plot the data on a graph. Show how you calculated each entry in your table and be prepared to discuss with the class what you did.

Notice that very little direction is given in this activity. However, the situation presented to the students is fairly clear. Some teachers may prefer to use numbers that would be easier to compute, but that takes much of the realism out of the situation. If a student decides to make a table entry for 50 miles, he or she will first have to figure out what to do. On a calculator, $50 \div 23 = 2.173913$. This amount should be subtracted from 20 to find out how many gallons remain in the tank. Should you subtract 2 or 2.17 or 2.173913? This is a good example to use to discuss numbers in real contexts. Avoid being prescriptive so that students will do their own thinking and not rely on your directions. Students are bound to make errors in reasoning as well as in computation. Class discussion will sort things out.

As part of the discussion, help students develop functional language to represent the situation. Here the number of gallons in the tank is dependent on how far the car has been driven. Thus, the number of gallons remaining is *a function of* the miles driven. In addition to the language, work toward student development of an equation that represents the relationship in the situation. In this case, one possible equation is $g = 20 - \frac{m}{23}$. Or, using functional notation, you might say $G(m) = 20 - \frac{m}{23}$.

Students can draw a line through their plotted points, or with a computer or graphing calculator they can enter the equation and have technology do the graphing. In either case, use the graph to answer questions about the situation: "How can you tell from the graph how much gas will be left after driving 300 miles?" "How many miles can you drive before the gas tank has only 3 gallons left?" "What will happen to the graph if the driver stops to fill the tank after driving 350 miles?" The *trace* feature on a graphing calculator is a great help for getting values from a graph.

Here are a few suggestions for similar explorations.

Mr. Calloway wants to build a fenced pen against one side of his shed. The shed is 15 feet long, and he wants to use the full side of the shed. The pen is to be in the shape of a rectangle with two sides 15 feet long. How much fence will he have to buy if he knows how long the other two sides of the pen will be (side versus fence length)? Add in a gate that is 3 feet long and costs $32. If fencing is $4.25 per foot, rethink the problem in terms of side versus cost. You can also discuss area and side length.

Mark is an avid cyclist. He can average 17 miles per hour for about 4 hours. He leaves home and travels for $2\frac{1}{2}$ hours at this rate, stops for lunch for $\frac{1}{2}$ hour, and then starts home. What is his distance from home at any given time? Suppose he goes faster for 1 hour and slower for 2 more hours

and then returns home. Suppose he has a flat tire and has to stop for 15 minutes to repair it. How fast will he have to go in order to return home at the same time as scheduled, including the same lunch break? Does it make any difference where the breakdown occurs?

Pleasant's Hardware buys widgets for $4.17 each, marks them up 35 percent over wholesale, and sells them at that price. Relate widgets sold to total income. Consider profit instead of income. Incorporate a sale using a reduced price.

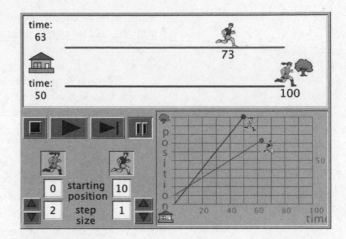

FIGURE 10.9 •

Applet 5.2, "Understanding Distance, Speed, and Time Relationships Using Simulation Software."

Used with permission from NCTM *e-Standards*. Copyright © 2003 by the National Council of Teachers of Mathematics, Inc. All rights reserved. The presence of the screenshot from NCTM *e-Standards*, http://standards.nctm.org/document/ examples/chap5/5.2/index.htm, does not constitute or imply an endorsement by NCTM.

The NCTM *e-Standards* has two applets that demonstrate the connection between a real-world context and graphs, tables, and equations. In Applet 5.2 students can adjust the speed, direction, and starting position of two runners. As the runners are set in motion, a time–distance graph is generated dynamically for each runner (see Figure 10.9). In Applet 6.2, when the cost per minute of a phone call is adjusted, a graph and equation of the total cost are adjusted accordingly. Two rates on the same graph help illustrate rate (slope) visually.

Proportional Situations

Many relationships involving rates or proportions offer a valuable opportunity for examining functions. The following is a typical proportion problem.

Two out of every three students who eat in the cafeteria drink a pint of white milk. If 450 students eat in the cafeteria, how many gallons of milk are consumed?

As the problem is stated, there is a fixed number of students (450) and a single answer to the problem. Students would be expected to set up a proportion and solve for the unknown. But if only the first sentence of the problem is provided, students can be asked to create a table showing the number of pints (or gallons) of milk consumed for four or five different numbers of students, plot the data on a graph, and create an equation that shows the relationship between students in the cafeteria and milk consumed. Functional language can be discussed: The number of pints of milk consumed in the cafeteria is a *function* of the number of students who eat there. The graph can be used to answer the question about milk for 450 students. Students can be challenged to find an equation that gives the amount of milk in terms of the number of students.

The following problem has been converted to a function investigation by asking for an answer in terms of an unknown instead of a specific number.

....

If each lemonade recipe will serve 20 people, how many recipes are needed to serve _n_ people? If it takes three cans of concentrate to make one recipe, how many cans should be purchased to serve _n_ people?

....

This example has two questions. One equation can be written to relate the number of recipes as a function of the number of people [$r(n) = \frac{n}{20}$], and a second equation to give the number of cans of concentrate as a function of the number of recipes [$c(r) = 3r$]. Using these equations you can find an equation that gives cans of concentrate as a function of the number of people.

Notice that the graphs of all proportional situations are straight lines that pass through the origin. Students will find that the slope of these lines is also the rate between the two variables.

Functions from Formulas

Geometric formulas relate various dimensions, areas, and volumes of shapes. Each of these formulas involves at least one functional relationship.

Consider any familiar formula for measuring a geometric shape. For example, $V = \frac{1}{3}\pi r^2 h$ is the formula for the volume of a circular cone. Here the volume is related to both the height of the cone and the radius. If the radius is held constant, the volume is a function of the height. Similarly, for a fixed height, the volume is a function of the radius. Figure 10.10 shows how both of these ideas might be illustrated and the graph that would be associated with each.

The following activity is an example of using functions in a practical way.

ACTIVITY 10.3

Designing the Largest Box

Begin with a rectangular sheet of cardboard, and from each corner, cut a square. Fold up the four resulting flaps, and tape them together to form an open box. The volume of the box will vary, depending on the size of the squares. (The sheet in Figure 10.11 measures 9 by 12 inches.) Write a formula that gives the volume of the box as a function of the size of the cutout squares. Use the function to determine what size the squares should be to create the box with the largest volume.

In "Designing the Largest Box," the resulting equation is a cubic or third-power polynomial. However, any seventh-grade student who knows that the volume of a box is the product of the three dimensions could develop this formula. A table of values and a graph are easily produced on a graphing calculator.

As with some other contexts we have looked at, this function is defined for values that do not make sense in the context. The largest square that could be cut out is 4.5 inches on a side, in which case the squares from adjacent corners would touch and there would be no flap to turn up. But the function will produce "negative volumes"

Volume of a cone
$$V = \frac{1}{3}\pi r^2 h$$

Fix the radius, and vary the heights.

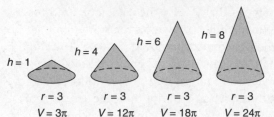

$h = 1$ $h = 4$ $h = 6$ $h = 8$

$r = 3$ $r = 3$ $r = 3$ $r = 3$
$V = 3\pi$ $V = 12\pi$ $V = 18\pi$ $V = 24\pi$

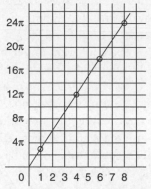

Volume as a function of height or radius. If the radius is fixed, changes in height produce a straight-line graph, but if the height is fixed, changes in the radius produce a curved line.

Fix the heights, and vary the radius.

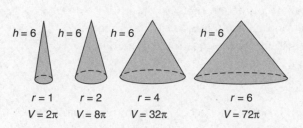

$h = 6$ $h = 6$ $h = 6$ $h = 6$

$r = 1$ $r = 2$ $r = 4$ $r = 6$
$V = 2\pi$ $V = 8\pi$ $V = 32\pi$ $V = 72\pi$

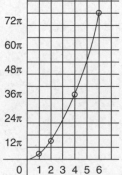

for values between 4.5 and 6 and positive volumes for values of the variable greater than 6. The equation representation of the function makes sense in this context *only* for values between 0 and 4.5. This is a useful discussion for students to help them realize that a mathematical model cannot be completely divorced from the context. Figure 10.12 shows the graph on a calculator. The tracer is near the point at which a maximum volume will occur.

Functions from Scatter Plot Data

Often in the real world, phenomena are observed that seem to suggest a functional relationship but not necessarily as clean or as well defined as the situations we have observed so far. In these cases, the data are generally plotted on a graph to produce a scatter plot of points. A visual inspection of the graphed data may suggest what kind of relationship, if any, exists. When a functional relationship seems to be suggested, an equation can be sought that defines a function approximating the data.

Situations like this are explored in Chapter 11. For example, data representing the heights and weights of people in a sample are plotted on a graph as a set of points, one for each person in the sample. The plot suggests a straight-line relationship between the heights and

FIGURE 10.11

If squares are cut from a 9-by-12-inch piece of cardboard so that the four flaps can be folded up, what size squares should be cut so that the volume of the box is the largest possible?

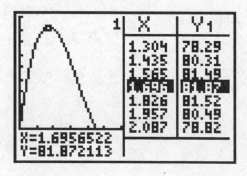

FIGURE 10.12

A graphing calculator plot of the volume function for the problem in Figure 10.11.

weights. A median-median line—a best-fit line—is found and, in this case, is the function (in graphical form) that approximates the data and is used to define the observed relationship between height and weight. In functional language, we could say that weight appears to be a function of height. (See pp. 326–330.)

Students in the middle grades might easily gather data found in an interesting context and perform this same type of analysis—that is, plot the data, look for a possible relationship, and find a best-fit line. When a line is drawn on the scatter plot, all representations of the function are present. The context produced the data. The graph of the best-fit line is a graphical representation of the function, and functional language can easily be used. A table can be made from points on the best-fit line. (Why would the table be made from the line or the equation and not from the actual data?) The equation can be found using the method described in Chapter 11, or the graphing calculator can be used to generate the equation.

Assessment Note

When gathered data only approximate a function rule, as in scatter plot activities, do students indicate an understanding of the difference between the real data and the best-fit line or the constructed function rule?

In cases where a simple equation is not readily accessible technology can be used to produce the equation. There seems little reason to stop students from using graphing calculators or curve-fitting software to see that methods do exist for finding best-fit curves. The calculator permits students to see what these best-fit curves and equations may look like, even though the techniques of finding the equations without technology may have to wait.

ACTIVITY 10.4

Pendulum Swings

Give pairs of students string and a small weight that can be tied to the string (a large washer or a tennis ball, for example). Assign each pair a different length for their pendulum, from about 30 cm to 3 m (if the room is tall enough). The pendulum should be measured from the suspension point to the bottom of the weight. Have students carefully time the swing of the pendulum through ten full (back-and-forth) swings. If time permits, they can perform the experiment several times and take an average of their times to report to the class.

In the pendulum experiment, the data will form a surprisingly accurate curve. Students can use their hand-drawn curve to predict the times for other pendulum lengths. The curve is the top half of a parabola that opens to the right. It can be found on the graphing calculator by experimenting with the equation $y = a\sqrt{x}$ for different values of a until a curve is found that fits nicely. What is most important at this level is seeing how a physical law can be expressed as a function and represented in table and graphical form.

Electronic Data Gathering

Technology now offers students a way to gather physical data that has exciting implications for connecting function concepts to the real world. The Calculator-Based Laboratory (CBL) is a device that interfaces between the graphing calculator and data sensors to gather and record real data directly into the calculator. Experiments that measure things such as temperature of a liquid, motion of a rolling car or a bouncing ball, light intensity, pH, and force can be conducted, with no pencil-and-paper record keeping. Theories of science that before could only be described can now be observed with real data gathered and analyzed.

Figure 10.13 shows a simple experiment using two different sensors connected through the CBL to a graphing calculator. The motion detector senses the motion back and forth as the hand stretches the rubber bands. The force sensor is connected to the rubber bands and measures the force applied and transmitted through them. A program available with Texas Instruments' manual (Brueningsen, Bower, Antinone, & Brueningsen, 1994) is loaded into the calculator. The program directs the CBL to collect data at regular intervals and store them in the calculator. Like any other data, these can then be plotted and a best-fit line determined. Figure 10.14 shows a scatter plot of data from running this experiment. It is fairly clear that there is a linear relationship and that a best-fit line would likely go through the origin. It is appropriate to say that the force applied to the rubber band is directly proportional to the distance the rubber band is stretched. In functional language, the force *is a function of* the amount the rubber band is stretched.

The following activity uses a motion detector and graphing calculator to help students develop an intuitive feel for slope in the context of walking rates. Prior to engaging in the next activity, ask students to think about and discuss the measures of time, distance, and speed and how these measurements are related.

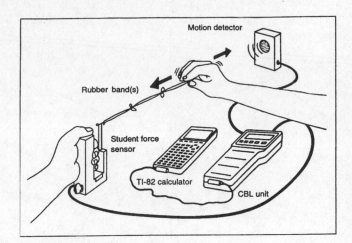

FIGURE 10.13 •

Two data probes are used to deliver force and motion data directly to a graphing calculator.

Source: "Real-World Math with the CBL System." Copyright Texas Instruments Inc., Dallas, TX. Reprinted by permission of Texas Instruments Inc.

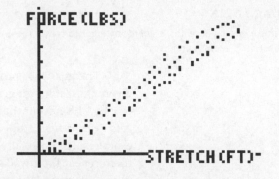

FIGURE 10.14 •

A graphing calculator scatter plot of data gathered in a rubber-band-stretching experiment as depicted in Figure 10.13.

ACTIVITY 10.5

Walk This Way

Set up a motion detector and display screen so that all students can see the resulting graph.

Enlist a few students to walk in front of the motion detector to get a "feel" for how it works. Draw students' attention to what the vertical and horizontal axes represent (distance and time) and how the rate at which students walk in front of the motion detector is reflected on the resulting graph. (This

(continued)

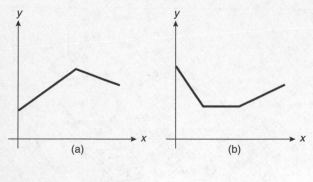

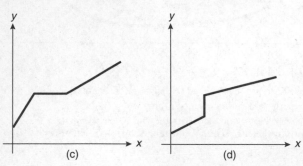

FIGURE 10.15

Using a motion detector, students attempt to create these constant piecewise graphs.

is best done by asking students to describe what they notice as their classmate moves in front of the motion detector.) Ask students to predict what the graph would look like if they traveled at a constant speed and went a long distance in a short time. Likewise, ask them to predict what the graph would look like if they traveled at a constant speed and went a short distance in a long time. Have students think of real-world situations in which they might travel in each of these ways. After the discussion, have a student try to produce the graphs the class has described by walking in front of the motion detector. Discuss what happens as a result and have students try it again with any adjustments if need be. In groups of three to four students, have students examine piecewise linear graphs (graphs that are made of two or three linear pieces) as in Figure 10.15. In groups, they are to plan their walks and be ready to describe and execute them for the rest of the class. After each group describes a plan for one of the graphs and then executes it, discuss what students notice. Continue to draw students' attention to how the rate of the walker relates to the steepness of the resulting graph.

The goal is to produce graphs that are reasonably close, but not exact, to the given graphs. If you get bogged down in trying to get students to recreate the graphs exactly, the notion that the rate of the walker determines the steepness of the graph gets lost. At first, students may want to try their walk several times in an effort to get exact results, especially as they are learning how the motion detector works. Having them repeat their walks with adjustments is fine as long as they are attempting to produce the general shape of the given graph and are not getting mired in the details.

Assessment Note

As students describe their plans and execute their walk, are they aware that their rate of walking is connected to the steepness of the resulting graph? Can they articulate how fast they should walk if the graph is not very steep or if it is quite steep? Some students will attempt to mimic the shape of the graph in their walk. For example, for the graph in Figure 10.15a, a student may attempt to walk an inverted V path in front of the motion detector. When he does this, he walks out of the range of the detector and the graphing calculator stops plotting points until he comes back into range. If this happens, ask the class to figure out what happened and why, and to provide suggestions to the student walker that can help him produce the given graph. The student's choice of the inverted V path should tell you that he (and the other students in his group) do not understand what the given graph is modeling. It is paramount that you, through well-placed questions, keep students' attention drawn to how their motion is connected to the slope of the graph.

Although difficult to reproduce using a motion detector, students can discuss time–distance graphs like those in Figure 10.16. In those graphs, the rate is not constant but rather is constantly changing.

> Graphs (a) and (b) in Figure 10.16 show motion that changes both direction and speed at the same point. In graph (c), the motion is always forward but the speed (slope) varies. What makes one portion of graph (c) different from the other, and where does it change?

Imagine beginning a walk very quickly. With every step, however, you walk just a bit slower than before. Eventually, you slow quite a bit with each step until you stop (very briefly) and turn toward home. As you head home, your speed increases just as it decreased before. (See graph (a), Figure 10.16.) *Speed* is seen in the steepness of the graph, whether up or down. In graph (c), the speed changes but the direction remains forward. *Velocity* is positive for forward directions and negative for reverse directions.

In addition to developing the idea of how one variable can be dependent on another, activities with time and distance help to develop another key idea in the study of functions—the idea of slope, or rate of change. We will return to the concept of slope later. (Slope is also defined in coordinate geometry. See Figure 7.35 on p. 222.)

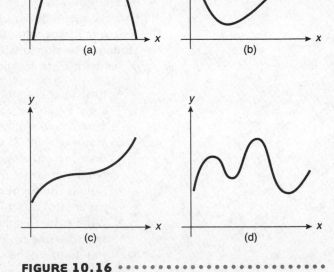

FIGURE 10.16 ●

Curved time–distance graphs involve motion that is not a constant rate. Discuss how the rate of speed changes in each of these graphs.

Other Scatter Plot Ideas

Consider gathering information that may be of personal interest to students. For example, do grades earned in social studies predict grades earned in mathematics? What about science and mathematics? What would the functional relationships be here? Even if a scatter plot of some information that was gathered showed no particular trend, functional language could still be employed—for example, "The grades on last week's mathematics test do *not* appear to be a function of the number of hours' sleep students got the night before the test."

Data can also be obtained from sports records, census reports, the business section of the newspaper, and many other sources. The Internet has lots of sites where data can be found. You can find these sites listed on p. 310 in Chapter 11.

Fun Experiments

There are all sorts of experiments that students can design to see what functional relationships, if any, exist between two variables.

Fun Function Experiments

The task is to try to develop a functional relationship between two variables by conducting an experiment. Data should be entered in a table and plotted on a graph. The goal is to determine an equation (function) that can be used to make predictions. A graphing calculator or computer will be a useful tool for curve fitting, although for some experiments that may not be necessary. Students should explain which is the independent variable and which is the dependent. Here are some ideas for experiments:*

- How long would it take for 100 students standing in a row to complete a wave like the ones done at football games? Experiment with different numbers of students from 5 to 25. Can the relationship predict how many students it would take for a given wave time?
- How far will a Matchbox car roll off of a ramp, based on the height the ramp is raised?
- How is the flight time of a paper airplane affected by the number of paper clips attached to the nose of the plane?
- What is the relationship between the number of dominoes in a row and the time required for them to fall over? (Use multiples of 100 dominoes.)
- Make wadded newspaper balls using different numbers of sheets of newspaper. Rubber bands help hold the paper in a ball. What is the relationship between the number of sheets and the distance the ball can be thrown?
- If colored water is dropped on a paper towel, what is the relationship between the number of drops and the diameter of the spot? Is the relationship different for different brands of towels?
- How much weight can a toothpick bridge hold? Lay toothpicks in a bunch to span a 2-inch gap between two boards. From the toothpicks, hang a bag or other container into which weights can be added until the toothpicks break. Begin with only one toothpick.

Experiments like these are fun. They also provide an opportunity for students to engage in experimental design. Students need practice in identifying independent and dependent variables, controlling experiments for other variables, measuring and recording results, and analyzing data. This is a perfect blend of mathematics and science.

Graphs Without Equations

The graph is one of the most powerful representations of a function. It is both fun and profitable to interpret and construct graphs related to real situations but without using any specific data, equations, or numbers. The advantage of activities such as these is the focus on how a graph can express the relationships involved.

---

*Most of these experiments were inspired by the article "Algebra: Real-Life Investigations in a Lab Setting" (McCoy, 1997), which contains additional ideas and useful suggestions.

ACTIVITY 10.7

Sketch a Graph

Sketch a graph for each of these situations. No numbers or formulas are to be used.

  a. The temperature of a frozen dinner from 30 minutes before it is removed from the freezer until it is removed from the microwave and placed on the table. (Consider time 0 to be the moment the dinner is removed from the freezer.)
  b. The value of a 1970 Volkswagen Beetle from the time it was purchased to the present. (It was kept by a loving owner and is in top condition.)
  c. The level of water in the bathtub from the time you begin to fill it to the time it is completely empty after your bath.
  d. Profit in terms of number of items sold.
  e. The height of a baseball in terms of time from when it is thrown straight up to the time it hits the ground.
  f. The speed of the baseball in the situation in (e).

 Stop for a moment and sketch graphs for each of the situations in the last activity.

It is fun to have students sketch their graphs on transparencies without identifying which situation is being graphed (no labels on the graphs). Let students examine the graphs to see if they can determine which situation goes with each graph that is presented. Examine the graphs for one situation drawn by several students to decide which graph represents a situation best and why. Figure 10.17 contains six graphs that match the six situations described in the "Sketch a Graph" activity. Can you match these graphs with the six situations? How do these graphs compare to the graphs that you sketched?

A similar example of rates is found in situations involving time and distance. Consider the following:

A car is traveling along a road at about 45 mph and comes to a stop sign. It stops for the sign and then accelerates to the same 45-mph speed.

Sketch a graph of the *distance* the car has traveled from the beginning of the story to the end. The horizontal axis should be *time.* In other words, the graph should show distance as a function of time. How would a graph of the *speed* of the car look over the same interval?

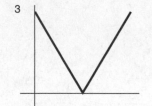
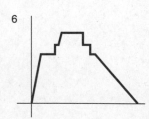

FIGURE 10.17

Match each graph with the situations described in Activity 10.7. Talk about what is happening in each case.

303

FUNCTIONS FROM THE REAL WORLD

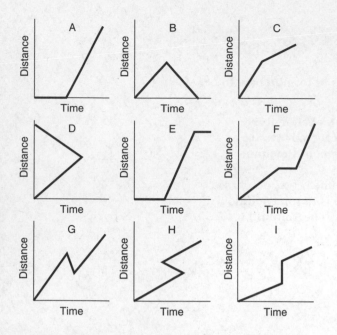

FIGURE 10.18 • • • • • • • • • • • • • • • •

Which graphs could not possibly describe a journey? Why?
Invent a journey story for each of the possible graphs.

The following activity could be done after students
have sketched graphs for a variety of time and distance
situations.

EXPANDED LESSON

(pages 306–307)

A complete lesson plan
based on "Create a Journey
Story" can be found at
the end of this chapter.

ACTIVITY 10.8

Create a Journey Story

Suppose that a student has created the time–
distance graphs shown in Figure 10.18. Each is
supposed to represent the journey of a single vehicle or person. Some of them are impossible and
could not represent any journey. First identify
the impossible graphs. Then make up a plausible
journey story for each of the remaining graphs.

Students could share their stories without telling
which graph each story was supposed to match. The class
could then discuss which graph best fits each tale.

The next activity is similar but begins to develop
the idea of rate of change—how rapidly or slowly something changes.

ACTIVITY 10.9

Bottles and Volume Graphs

Figure 10.19 shows six bottles and six graphs. Assume that the bottles are
filled at a constant rate. Because of their shapes, the height of the liquid in
the bottles will increase either more slowly or more quickly as the bottle gets
wider or narrower. Match the graphs with the bottles.

FIGURE 10.19 • • • • • •

If the bottles are filled at
a constant rate, match the
graphs with the bottles.

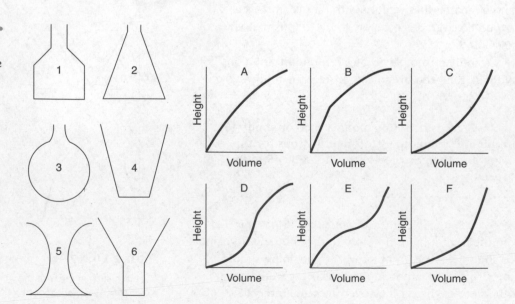

Find some bottles or glasses that have different shapes. One place to look is in the science lab. Using a small container such as a medicine cup, pour water into each bottle. Measure the height after each small containerful is poured. Make a graph of the heights as a function of the volume. If students do an actual experiment, the discussion of which graph fits which bottle and why will be much more meaningful. This is another opportunity for students to explore the concept of slope, or rate of change. See how this discussion is like the time–distance graphs in Figures 10.15 and 10.16.

Assessment Note

The main thrust of the ideas in this chapter is that students should begin to see functional relationships in a variety of situations—relationships where the change in one quantity has a predictable effect on the change in another.

An equally important idea is communication of these functional relationships. Functions can be expressed in terms of context, language, tables, graphs, and equations. What is most important is that students see these representations as different but related methods of telling about a function.

If you keep these big ideas in mind, your assessment plans should be focused accordingly.

EXPANDED LESSON

Create a Journey Story

Based on Activity 10.8, p. 304

GRADE LEVEL: Seventh or eighth grade.

MATHEMATICS GOALS
• To develop the way that graphs express relationships.

THINKING ABOUT THE STUDENTS
Students have explored their rate of walking with a Calculator-Based Ranger (motion detector) to learn how walking rates are modeled in a graph. For instance, they understand that the faster they walk, the steeper the line that is generated in the display. Students have experienced graphing ordered pairs in a coordinate plane. (The motion-detector experience is not a prerequisite for this lesson.)

MATERIALS AND PREPARATION
• Make copies of the Create a Journey Story worksheet for each student (Blackline Master L-5).
• Make a transparency of the Create a Journey Story worksheet.

- -

lesson

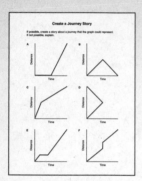

BLM L-5

BEFORE

Begin with a simpler version of the task:
• Ask students to sketch a graph of the distance a car travels in the following story:

  A car is traveling along a road at a steady speed and comes to a stop sign. It stops for the sign and then accelerates to the same speed as before.

• Point out that the horizontal axis should represent *time* and the vertical axis should represent *distance*.
• Have students share their sketches. Resist evaluating the sketches. Encourage students to comment on and question classmates' ideas. Draw attention to different periods of time on the horizontal axis and how the distance changes within that period. A reasonable sketch might look like one of these:
• The graph on the right has a curve following the stopped (horizontal) segment, indicating speeding up from stopped to the former speed. The left graph is quite adequate.

The Task
• The Create a Journey Story worksheet shows time–distance graphs created by a student. Each is supposed to represent the journey of a single vehicle or person. For each of the graphs, make up a plausible journey story or explain why it is not possible to do so.

Establish Expectations
• For those graphs that can represent a journey, students should make up a simple yet plausible journey story. The story may involve walking, running, or driving a car.
• Point out that some of the graphs cannot represent any credible journey. For those graphs, they are to explain why.

DURING
• As individual students write their stories, ask them to explain to you what is happening in their stories at various points in the graph.

- If a student is having trouble getting started, cover up all but the first part of the graph he or she is working on. Ask the student to think about what that part of the graph tells him or her about the distance traveled or the time elapsed. Help the student translate that information into a story context. Repeat with the next part of the graph.
- For students ready for a challenge, ask them to graph the *speed* of the car in the "before" portion of the lesson over the same interval of time.

AFTER

- Have students share one of their stories without telling which graph the story is supposed to match. Have the class discuss which graph best fits the story.
- Ask students to explain why the impossible graphs are impossible. (Graph D is impossible because it shows different positions at the same time. Graph F is impossible because in the vertical segment the position changes but no time elapses.)
- Discuss the steepness (slope) of lines in different segments of the graph. Ask what it means if the graph is steeper in one portion than in another.
- After identifying stories for each graph, compare stories for the same graph. Have students discuss the similarities and the differences.

ASSESSMENT NOTES

- Look for students who create journey stories that mimic the shape of the graph by the movement of the journey but that do not reflect the relationship of distance versus time. For example, for graph A, such a student might describe walking on a straight path and then veering off the path to the left. This story does not interpret the graph as a relationship between distance and time but rather as a map.
- Are students able to articulate through their stories the reason for different slopes in different parts of the graph? That is, steeper lines indicate faster speeds. Downward sloping lines indicate moving backward or toward the starting point. (A person/car could turn around and move forward or go backward without turning around. The graph would be the same.)

- For students who are experiencing difficulty, more work with a Calculator-Based Ranger to graph distance versus time data can help students test their conjectures.
- Activity 10.7, "Sketch a Graph," is a good partner to this activity. There students sketch graphs to match stories.

- To begin to develop the idea of rate of change (indicated by the slope of a graph), have students do Activity 10.9, "Bottles and Volume Graphs."

next steps

EXPLORING DATA ANALYSIS

Graphs and statistics bombard the public in advertising, opinion polls, reliability estimates, population trends, health risks, and progress of students in schools, just to name a few areas. We hear that the average amount of rainfall this summer is more than it was last summer; that the average American household consists of 2.53 people; that the national median value of a house is $134,100; that about 17 percent of the U.S. population has a college degree; and that 9 out of 10 dentists recommend a particular brand of toothpaste. Magazines and newspapers use various types of graphs to provide the reader with a snapshot of such information.

To deal with this information, students should have ample informal yet meaningful experiences with basic concepts of data analysis throughout their school years. By the time students are fifth graders, they should have had many experiences collecting and organizing sets of data as well as representing data in graphs—mainly bar, picture, line, and circle graphs. They have likely worked with range and the measures of central tendency, median and mode, and quite possibly mean. In the middle grades, students should continue to build on this basic knowledge, developing a better understanding of these representations and statistics as they learn about new representations such as box plots, stem-and-leaf plots, and scatter plots. The emphasis in middle grades should first be placed on activities leading to intuitive understanding and conceptual knowledge. Computations and formulas should be developed based on these concepts.

big ideas

1 A collection of objects with various attributes can be classified or sorted in different ways. A single object can belong to more than one class. Classification is the first step in the organization of data.

2 Data are gathered and organized in order to answer questions about the populations from which the data come. With data from only a sample of the population, inferences are made about the population. Increased sample size improves confidence in inferences made.

3 Data sets can be analyzed in various ways to provide a sense of the shape of the data, including how spread out they are (range, variance) and how they are centered (mean, median, mode). Measures that describe data with numbers are called statistics.

4 Data can be organized in various graphical forms to visually convey information. The use of a particular graph or statistic can mediate what the data tell about the population.

Gathering Data to Answer Questions

Data analysis is about more than calculating statistics. It includes both asking and answering questions about our world. To answer the questions, data must be gathered and organized and then an analysis made.

The first goal in the Data Analysis and Probability standard of *Principles and Standards* says that students should "formulate questions that can be addressed with data and collect, organize, and display relevant data to answer them" (NCTM, 2000, p. 48). Notice that data collection should be for a purpose, to answer a question, just as in the real world. The analysis of data should have the agenda of adding information about some aspect of our world. This is what political pollsters, advertising agencies, market researchers, census takers, wildlife managers, and hosts of others do: gather data to answer questions.

Many times the teacher or textbook provides middle school students with the questions to answer and the data with which to answer them. Students in this age range often need to see the connection between what they are learning in school and their own lives. Although information about the range of population in different regions, the average cost of housing, or the average commute time in various cities may be interesting to adults, these are not necessarily the same questions that will interest middle school students. Also, sports data, a very common context used in data analysis, do not have universal appeal. Students should be afforded opportunities to generate their own questions, design their own collection methods, and collect their own data.

When students formulate the questions they want to ask, the data they gather become more and more meaningful. How they organize the data and the techniques for analyzing them have a purpose. For example, one class of students gathered data concerning which cafeteria foods were most often thrown in the garbage. As a result of these efforts, certain items were removed from the regular menu. The activity illustrated to students the power of organized data, and it helped them get food that they liked better.

Ideas for Questions and Data

Often the need to gather data will come from the class naturally in the course of discussion or from questions arising in other content areas. Science, of course, is full of measurements and, thus, abounds in data requiring analysis. Social studies is also full of opportunities to pose questions requiring data analysis. The next few sections suggest some additional ideas.

Classroom Questions

Students may be interested to learn about themselves, their families and pets, measures such as arm span or time to get to school, their likes and dislikes, and so on. The easiest questions to deal with are those that can be answered by each class member contributing one piece of data. When there are lots of possibilities, suggest that students restrict the number of choices. Here are a few ideas:

Favorites: TV show, games, vehicles, type of music, musical band, music CD, movie, sport, sports team, ice cream shop, video game platform.

Numbers: Number of pets, sisters, or brothers; hours watching TV or hours of sleep; hours on Instant Messaging or on the computer; number of music CDs.

Measures: Sitting height, arm span, area of foot, long-jump distance, shadow length, time on the mile run, time on the bus.

Beyond the Classroom

Students in the middle grades often begin to think about various populations and differences between them. For example, how are fifth graders similar or different from middle school students? Students might examine questions concerning boys versus girls, adults or teachers versus students, or categories of workers or college graduates. These situations involve issues of sampling and making generalizations and comparisons.

The news media frequently report what the latest survey reveals about the "typical" family, business, teenager, drug addict, or member of some other population or group. How did they survey everyone, and what does "typical" mean? Do the students in your classroom believe they are typical? Are they like those in the next classroom or the next grade level? To describe a group usually involves asking a variety of questions, and deciding on which questions to ask is not nearly as easy as it may sound. How many questions should be asked? Should they be multiple choice? If not, how will the answers be handled? To describe a large group (say, the school), how many people should be surveyed? How should they be selected? Students should be involved in making these decisions as they formulate their questions and design surveys.

Wilson and Krapfl (1995) describe how students in a middle school classroom decided on the information that they would gather about each other in order to provide a future exchange student a good description of an average student in the classroom. Through this experience, not only did students have to grapple with what information to gather but also how to gather and then describe that information.

Other Sources of Information

Gathering data can mean using data that have been collected by others. For example, newspapers, almanacs, sports record books, maps, and various government publications are sources of data that may be used to answer student questions. Students may be interested in facts about another country as a result of a social studies unit. Olympic records in various events over the years or data related to space flight are other examples of topics around which student questions may be formulated. For these and hundreds of other questions, data can be found on the World Wide Web. Here are three websites with lots of interesting data:

- U.S. Census Bureau (www.census.gov): This website contains copious statistical information by state, county, or voting district.

- The World Fact Book (www.odci.gov/cia/publications/factbook/index.html): This website provides demographic information for every nation in the world, including population, age distributions, death and birth rates, and information on the economy, government, transportation, and geography. Maps are included as well.

- Internet Movie Database (www.imdb.com): This website offers information about movies of all genres. In Activity 11.11, data gathered from this site are used to explore scatter plots.

Classification of Data

Once data have been collected, the next decision involves how to classify or categorize the information to make sense of it. This is a fundamental activity in data analysis. In order to begin to answer questions and to formulate and answer further questions, data must be grouped into categories. For example, vehicles might be categorized based on manufacturer, gas mileage, year, or type (e.g., truck, car, minivan, sports-utility vehicle). For another example, favorite cold beverages might be grouped as caffeinated and noncaffeinated or as soda, water, juice, tea, and other. Each of these groupings is based on a different attribute of the data.

Students need experiences with categorizing data in numerous ways so that they begin to understand that different classifications can provide different and sometimes more meaningful information about the data. Suppose from a survey about students' favorite games, 25 different games are named. A bar graph with 25 categories is not particularly helpful. However, categorizing the games as board games, electronic games, or sports games provides more meaningful information about the data collected, such as which type of game is most popular.

The Shape of Data

A big conceptual idea in data analysis can be referred to as the *shape of data:* a sense of how data are spread or grouped, what characteristics they have, and what they tell us in a global way about the population from which they are taken.

Statistical techniques provide a numeric picture of the shape of the data. The numbers can be thought of as measures of the shape. For example, the median tells us where the center is. The range tells about the spread of the data.

Each of the graphical techniques we will discuss gives a visual picture of the shape of data. Students should learn that different graphs provide different snapshots of the data. For the particular question being answered, the choice of graphs is made around the notion of the shape of the data.

Descriptive Statistics

Although graphs provide visual images of data, measures of the data are a different and important way to describe data. Numbers that describe data are *statistics,* measures of the data that quantify some attribute of them. The things that are most often described numerically about a set of data are the distance between the highest and lowest data values (the *range*), some measure of where the center of the data is (an *average*), and how dispersed the data are within the range (the *variance* or *dispersion*). Students can get an idea of the importance of these statistics by exploring the ideas informally.

Averages

The term *average* is heard quite frequently in everyday usage. Sometimes it refers to an exact arithmetic average, as in "the average daily rainfall." Sometimes it is used quite loosely, as in "She is about average height." In either situation, an average is a single number or measure that is descriptive of a larger collection of numbers. If your test average is 92, it is assumed that somehow all of your test scores are reflected by this number.

The *mean, median,* and *mode* are specific types of averages or *measures of central tendency.* The *mode* is the value that occurs most frequently in the data set. Of these three statistics, the mode is the least useful as a descriptor of a data set as a whole. Consider the following set of numbers:

1, 1, 3, 5, 6, 7, 8, 9

The mode of this set is 1 and not a very good description of this set. If the 8 in this string of numbers were a 9, there would be two modes. If one of the ones were changed to a 2, there would be no mode at all. In short, the mode is a statistic that does not always exist, does not necessarily reflect the center of the data, and can be highly unstable, changeable with very small changes in the data.

The *mean* is computed by adding all of the numbers in the set and dividing the sum by the number of elements added. This is the statistic that is sometimes referred to as the *average,* although the terms are not synonymous. The mean of our sample set is 5 (40 ÷ 8). The mean is discussed in more detail in the next section.

The *median* is the middle value in an ordered set of data. Half of all values lie at or above the median and half below. For the eight numbers in our sample set, the median is between 5 and 6, or 5.5. The median is easier to understand and to compute and is not affected, as the mean is, by one or two extremely large or extremely small values outside the range of the rest of the data.

In the following activity students begin to develop definitions for *mean, median, mode,* and *range* by examining sets of data and their corresponding statistics.

ACTIVITY 11.1

What's the Meaning of This?

Provide groups of students with several data sets and the corresponding mean, median, mode, and range. Four data sets with corresponding statistics are provided for this purpose in Table 11.1. The task is for students to examine the data sets and their corresponding statistics to make conjectures about the meaning of mean, median, mode, and range. You may need to suggest to students to start with Data Set A and make a conjecture about the meanings of these terms. Then as they move to the next data set, they can revise their conjectures. Discuss as a class the meanings they have developed and how those meanings evolved as they examined each new data set.

Having students examine these statistics over several data sets and create their own definitions is a much more powerful and meaningful way to help students understand what these statistics are about than simply providing the definitions to them.

TABLE 11.1 •

Data Sets and Corresponding Statistics for Generating Definitions of Mean, Median, Mode, and Range

	Data Set A	Data Set B	Data Set C	Data Set D
	1, 1, 3, 4, 5, 5, 7, 9, 9, 10	10, 12, 17, 24, 25, 32, 34, 34, 42, 47, 54, 68, 71, 79, 80, 85, 86, 87, 98, 99	8, 9, 11, 14, 32	0, 2, 2, 3, 3, 3.5, 3.75, 4, 4.25, 4.5
Mean	5.4	54.2	14.8	3.0
Median	5	50.5	11	3.25
Mode	1, 5, 9	34	None	2, 3
Range	9	89	24	4.5

You may need to help them tweak their definitions to better reflect the conventional definitions; however, the conventional definitions will make much more sense to students after attempting to generate their own.

Understanding the Mean: Two Concepts

Due to ease of computation and stability, the median when compared to the mean has some advantages as a practical average. However, the mean will continue to be used in popular media and in books. For smaller sets of data such as your test scores, the mean is perhaps a more meaningful statistic. Finally, the mean is used in the computation of other statistics such as the standard deviation. Therefore, it remains important that students have a good concept of what the mean tells them about a set of numbers.

There are actually two different ways to think about the mean. First, it is a number that represents what all of the data items would be if they were leveled out. In this sense, the mean represents all of the data items. Statisticians prefer to think of the mean as a central balance point. This concept of the mean is more in keeping with the notion of a measure of the "center" of the data or a measure of central tendency. Both concepts are discussed in the following sections.

A Leveling Concept of the Mean

Suppose that the average number of family members for the students in your class is 5. One way to interpret this is to think about distributing the entire collection of moms, dads, sisters, and brothers to each of the students so that each would have a "family" of the same size. To say that you have an average of 93 for the four tests in your class is like spreading the total of all of your points evenly across the four tests. It is as if each student had the same family size and each test score were the same, but the totals matched the actual distributions. This concept of the mean is easy to understand and explain and has the added benefit that it leads directly to the algorithm for computing the mean.

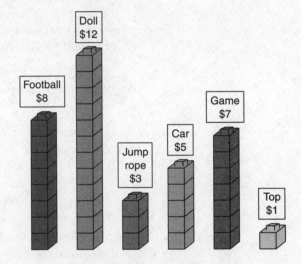

Bar graph made with plastic snap cubes

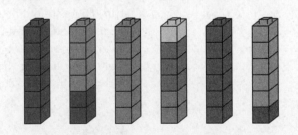

The same cubes rearranged into equal stacks.
Their height is the <u>mean</u> value of the bars above.

FIGURE 11.1 ●

Understanding the mean as a leveling of the data.

ACTIVITY 11.2

Leveling the Bars

Have students make a bar graph of some data using plastic connecting cubes such as Unifix. Choose a situation with 5 or 6 bars with no more than 10 or 12 cubes in each. For example, the graph in Figure 11.1 shows prices for six toys. The task for students is to use the graph itself to determine what the price would be if all of the toys were the same price, assuming that the total for all the toys remained the same. Students will use various techniques to rearrange the cubes in the graph but will eventually create six equal bars, possibly with some leftovers that could mentally be distributed in fractional amounts. (In the example, the total

(continued)

DESCRIPTIVE STATISTICS

number of cubes is a multiple of six.) Do not tell students they are finding the average or mean, only that they are to find equal-length bars.

Explain to students that the size of the leveled bars is the *mean* of the data—the amount that each item would cost if all items cost the same amount but the total of the prices remained fixed.

Follow "Leveling the Bars" with the next activity to help students develop an algorithm for finding the mean.

ACTIVITY 11.3

The Mean Foot

Pose the following question: What is the mean length of our feet in inches? Have each student cut a strip of adding machine tape that matches the length of his or her foot. Students record their names and the length of their feet in inches on the strips. Suggest that before finding a mean for the class, you will first get means for smaller groups. Put students into groups of four, six, or eight students. (Groups of five or seven will prove to be problematic.) In each group, have the students tape their foot strips end to end. The task for each group is to come up with a method of finding the mean without using any of the lengths written on the strips. They can only use the combined strip. Each group will share their method with the class. From this work, they will devise a method for determining the mean for the whole class.

 STOP **Before reading on, what is a method that the students could use in "The Mean Foot"?**

To evenly distribute the inches for each student's foot among the members of the group, they can fold the strip into equal parts so that there are as many sections as students in the group. Then they can measure the length of any one part.

How can you find the mean for the whole class? Suppose there are 23 students in the class. Using the strips already taped together, make one very long strip for the whole class. It is not reasonable to fold this long strip into 23 equal sections. But if you wanted to know how long the resulting strip would be, how could that be done? The total length of the strip is the sum of the lengths of the 23 individual foot strips. To find the length of one section if the strip were actually folded in 23 equal parts, simply divide the entire length by 23. In fact, students can mark off "mean feet" along the strip. There should be very close to 23 equal-length "feet." This dramatically illustrates the usual add-up-and-divide algorithm for finding the mean.

Some students believe that they can always find the mean of two data sets together by finding the mean of the means of the two sets. It will be beneficial to conduct the following activity with students to address this possible misconception.

ACTIVITY 11.4

The Mean of Means

Pose the following situation to students: At the first two track meets, Jacob had the following standing broad jump performances: 6.0 feet, 5.5 feet, 2.4 feet, 4.2 feet, 5.5 feet, 5.0 feet, 3.8 feet, and 5.5 feet. He found that the mean for his standing broad jump so far was 4.74 feet. At the third track meet, his jumps were 6.3, 6.5, 6.6, and 6.2. The mean for these jumps was 6.35 feet. Jacob claims that he can find the mean of all his broad jumps so far by finding the mean of these two means. In other words, he claims that the mean for all his broad jumps so far is

$$\frac{4.74 \text{ feet} + 6.35 \text{ feet}}{2} \text{ or } \frac{11.09 \text{ feet}}{2} \text{ or } 5.55 \text{ feet}$$

Do students think Jacob's method is correct? Ask them to compare the "average" of 5.55 feet to all the data. Does it seem too high? Too low? Now have them calculate the mean of all 12 jumps. First in pairs and then as a class, have students discuss why they think Jacob's method does not work.

STOP **Before reading further, try to figure out why Jacob's strategy does not work. Think about the notion of fair sharing. Is that really happening with Jacob's method?**

If need be, provide students with two more data sets that have the same number of items in each set and have students find the mean Jacob's way and also by adding up all data items and dividing by the total number of items. Each way should yield the same result. Encourage students to consider why having an equal number of data items in each set would make a difference.

A Balance Point Concept of the Mean

Statisticians think about the mean as a point on a number line where the data on either side of the point are balanced. To help think about the mean in this way, it is useful to think about the data placed on a line plot rather than as bar graphs. What is important is not how many pieces of data are on either side of the mean or balance point but the distances of data from the mean that must balance.

To illustrate, draw a number line on the board, and arrange eight sticky notes above the number 3 as shown in Figure 11.2a. Each sticky note represents one family. The notes are positioned on the line to indicate how many pets are owned by the family. Stacked up like this would indicate that all families have the same number of pets. The mean is three pets. But different families are likely to have different numbers of pets. So we could think of eight families with a range of numbers of pets. Some may have zero pets, and some may have as many as ten or even more. How could you

FIGURE 11.2 • • • • • • •

(a) If all data points are the same, the mean is that value. (b) By moving data points away from the mean in a balanced manner, different distributions can be found that have the same mean.

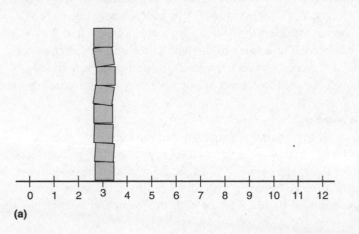

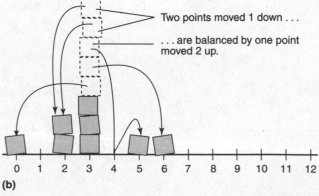

Two points moved 1 down . . .

. . . are balanced by one point moved 2 up.

(a)

(b)

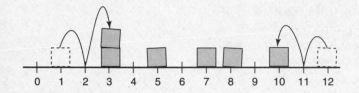

FIGURE 11.3 ●

Move data points in toward the center or balance point without changing the balance around that point. When you have all points at the same value, that is the balance or the mean.

change the number of pets for these eight families so that the mean remains at 3? Students will suggest moving the sticky notes in opposite directions, probably in pairs. This will result in a symmetrical arrangement. But what if one of the families has eight pets, a move of five spaces from the 3? This might be balanced by moving two families to the left, one three spaces to the 0, and one two spaces to the 1. Figure 11.2b shows one way the families could be rearranged to maintain a mean of 3. You should stop here and find at least two other distributions of the families, each having a mean of 3.

Use the next activity to find the mean or balance point given the data.

ACTIVITY 11.5

Finding the Balance Point

Have students draw a number line from 0 to 12 with about an inch between the numbers. Use six small sticky notes to represent the prices of six toys as shown in Figure 11.3. Have them place a light pencil mark on the line where they think the mean might be. For the moment, avoid the add-up-and-divide computation. The task is to determine the actual mean by moving the sticky notes in toward the "center." That is, the students are finding out what price or point on the number line balances out the six prices on the line. For each move of a sticky one space to the left (a toy with a lower price), a different sticky must be moved one space to the right (a toy with a higher price). Eventually, all stickies should be stacked above the same number, the balance point or mean.

Stop now and try this exercise yourself. Notice that after any pair of moves that keeps the distribution balanced, you actually have a new distribution of prices with the same mean. The same was true when you moved the stickies out from the mean when they were all stacked on the same point.

The balance concept does not lead to the add-up-and-divide algorithm for computing the mean. However, it is useful to do the following side-by-side approach. Make bars of cubes for the original data in Figure 11.3. Level the bars by moving only one cube at a time from a longer bar to a shorter bar. Each time you move a cube off of a bar, the sticky note for that bar must be moved one space to the left. At the same time, the sticky note for the bar to which the cube was added must be moved one space to the right. As you continue to move cubes one at a time, adjust the sticky notes accordingly.

Starting with the Mean

Notice that the mean (or for that matter the median and mode) is only a single number that is used to describe the central tendency of a set of data and so by itself is not a very useful description of the shape of the data. In fact, the balance approach to the mean clearly illustrates that many different distributions can have the same mean. The next activity reinforces this notion by first starting with the mean and asking students to generate possible data sets. One purpose of this activity is to see if and how students use the meanings of mean to help them generate different sets of data.

ACTIVITY 11.6

Equal Means

Pose this task to students: Tickets to the school talent show at Hillyard Middle School went on sale this week. The school newspaper reported that the mean for tickets sold during lunch each day this week was 10. How many tickets could have been sold each day? Have students create at least three different data sets for this situation.

Changes in Data, Changes in Averages

The following activities investigate how changes in the data affect the mean, median, and mode.

ACTIVITY 11.7

Toying with the Measures

Give students a list of toys with prices, such as the following, that someone has supposedly purchased: football ($8), doll ($12), jump rope ($3), car ($5), game ($7), and a top ($1). Have students calculate the mean, median, and mode for this data set. Now add another toy that cost $20 to the list of purchased toys and ask them to predict how the mean, median, and mode will change. After sharing their predictions and justifications, students should calculate the statistics and compare them to their predictions. Modify the set of toys by removing the $1 toy. (Perhaps the $1 toy was returned to the store.) Students should predict how the mean, median, and mode will be affected by this removal. Again have students share their predictions and reasoning and then compare their predictions with what actually happens. Continue to pose questions, such as the following, each time asking for predictions and justifications: Suppose that one new toy is added that increases the mean from $6 to $7. How much does the new toy cost? Suppose you had a coupon for a free toy. Will adding zero to the set of data change the mean of the set? Describe why or why not. Will it change the median? Mode? Explain.

The following activity is similar to "Toying with the Measures" but provides a different context.

EXPANDED LESSON

(pages 331–332)
A complete lesson plan based on "Toying with the Measures" can be found at the end of this chapter.

ACTIVITY 11.8

Bus Time

Show students data from a seventh-grade class that kept track of how long students were on the bus in the afternoon. (See Table 11.2.) After students find the mean, median, and mode of this data set, tell them that the bus breaks down before the last stop. Nathan, who is the last one off the bus in the afternoon, spends 90 minutes on the bus instead of 30. Students are to

(continued)

TABLE 11.2 •••••••
Data Showing Time
Spent on the Bus by
20 Students

Student	Time (min)
Alberto	6
Amy	6
Zach	8
Cam	9
Sergio	9
Taylor	9
Spencer	10
Matt	12
Ben	12
Jacob	12
Will	12
Natalie	15
Sophie	15
Andre	17
Su	20
Kristina	22
Kate	25
Jenny	26
Lyle	27
Nathan	30

predict and then check how this change in the data will affect the mean, median, and mode. After discussing predictions, change the data set again by explaining that right before the bus left in the afternoon, Nathan remembered he had play practice after school. He got off the bus and his time spent on the bus goes from 30 minutes to 1 minute. Have students predict the effect of this change and then check their predictions. In pairs and then as a class, discuss what effect outliers (data that are much greater or smaller than the rest of the data in the set) seem to have on the mean, median, and mode and which one(s) are affected more by an outlier. For further exploration, ask students what they think would happen if one outlier is greater and one outlier is smaller than the rest of the data. Based on their findings, which measure of central tendency do they think would be a better representation of a data set that contains one or more outliers?

Based on the findings from the previous activities, students should realize that the mean is significantly affected by extreme values, especially for small sets of data. Each data point affects the mean; however, even large variations at the extremes of a data set have no effect on the median.

Which Average Is the Best?

Each of the measures of central tendency has strengths that make it a better choice to represent a set of data in various situations. Students should learn to select the most appropriate average to describe a typical item of a data set. After investigating how each measure of central tendency is affected by the distribution of the data, students can make more informed decisions about which average to use for a given purpose. Activities, such as the following, focus on the differences among the mean, median, and mode and can help students use and interpret these measures correctly.

ACTIVITY 11.9

What's in an Average?

Give students the following descriptions of possible data sets. Their task is to decide which average (mean, median, or mode) is the most appropriate average to describe a typical item in each of the following data sets.

- Size of shoes sold in a shoe store
- Salaries in a large company
- Salaries in a small company
- Cost of houses in your local area
- Test scores for a student
- Size of cereal boxes in a grocery store
- Cost of hotel rooms at a particular hotel
- A person's monthly telephone bill for a year

It may be helpful to suggest to students to generate sample data sets for each situation. Students should be ready to justify their choice of an average.

In the next activity, different statistics can be used in order to make various arguments concerning the data.

You Be the Judge

In the high school gymnastics meet, Jena and Kya were the top two competitors. Five judges gave them the following scores. Who won the competition, or was it a tie?

Judge	Jena	Kya
1	8	9
2	6	9
3	10	7
4	9	8
5	7	7

How are the two sets of scores similar? How are they different? Which statistic (mean, median, mode, range) seems to be the fairest way to judge the competition?

A clever choice of statistics is often used as a convincing method to make an argument or sway opinion. It is important for students in the upper grades to begin to see how this is often done in politics, advertising, or even in supposedly objective news reporting. Another numerical measure that you may not think of as a statistic is often used in this manner—percentage gain or loss. For example, it may sound impressive to talk about a 25 percent-off sale when the original price of the item is small, say $8. This same $2 discount, however cannot be touted as 25 percent if the original price of the item is $50. In other words, sometimes it is useful to talk about a percentage increase or decrease, whereas other times an actual amount makes the better argument. Statistics can often be misleading or used to make an argument sound better than it really is. Look for newspaper ads or stories in which statistics are used to sway opinion.

Assessment Note

When assessing your students' understanding of descriptive statistics, there are at least two quite different aspects of their knowledge you should keep distinct. The first is their procedural knowledge. For example, can they compute the mean using the balance method as well as the add-it-up-and-divide method? Procedural skills are relatively simple to assess with a traditional test question.

Second, can the students describe in conceptual terms what the statistic tells us? For example, "The mean, median, and mode are called measures of central tendency. What is meant by central tendency and how does each statistic measure it?" Or you might ask students to explain why the median might be a better measure of central tendency for a small data set than the mean.

Graphical Representations

Students should be involved in deciding how they want to represent their data. Sometimes you can suggest a new way of displaying data and have children learn to construct that type of graph or chart. Once they have made the display, they can discuss its value. Did this graph (or chart or picture) tell about our data in a clear way? Compared to other ways of displaying data, how is this better?

The emphasis or goal of this instruction should be to help students see that graphs and charts tell about information, that different types of representations tell different things about the same data. The value of having students actually construct their own graphs is not so much that they learn the techniques but that they are personally invested in the data and that they learn how a graph conveys information. Once a graph is constructed, the most important activity is discussing what it tells the people who see it, especially those who were not involved in making the graph. Discussions about graphs of real data that the students have themselves been involved in gathering will help them interpret other graphs and charts that they see in newspapers and on TV.

In this section we focus on graphical representations that have not been emphasized in the earlier grades: stem-and-leaf plots, histograms, line graphs, box plots, and scatter plots. Line plots and circle graphs will also be briefly addressed. What we should *not* do is get overly anxious about the tedious details of graph construction. The issues of analysis and communication are your agendas and are much more important than the technique! In the real world, technology will take care of details of graph construction.

There are two equally good possibilities you may consider when planning to have your students construct graphs or charts. First, you can simply encourage students to do their best and make, by hand, charts and graphs that make sense to them and that they feel communicate the information they wish to convey. This is not to say that students do not need guidance. They should have seen and been involved in group constructions of various types of graphs and charts. This provides them with some ideas from which to choose for their own graphs.

The second option is to use technology. The computer and graphing calculators have provided us with many tools for constructing simple yet powerful representations. With the help of technology, it is possible to construct several different pictures of the same data with very little effort. The discussion can then focus on the message or information that each format provides. A word of caution is warranted here. Computers and calculators will make graphs even when they are inappropriate to your needs. Consequently, students should make their own selections of various graphs and justify their choice based on their intended purposes.

No matter which approach you take when having students construct graphs, it is important to pose situations that include a real context and have students decide what statistics and what graphs would best serve the purposes. Is a bar graph or a line graph more appropriate? Why? Which statistic is better in this situation, the mean or median?

Once a graph has been constructed, engage the class in a discussion of what information the graph tells or conveys. "What can you tell about our class by looking at this shoe graph?" Graphs convey factual information (more people wear sneakers than any other kind of shoe) and also provide opportunities to make inferences that are not directly observable in the graph (kids in this class do not like to wear leather shoes). The difference between actual facts and inferences is an important idea in graph construction and is also an important idea in science. Students can examine graphs found in newspapers or magazines and discuss the *facts* in the graphs and the *message* that may have been intended by the person who made the graph.

Interpretation

"Making the graph or computing the statistic does not help me understand what it tells me about the data." There are a number of ways to get at interpretation. For example, several graphs and statistics for the same situation and data can be presented. "Suppose you were a newspaper editor. Which of these statistics and graphs should you use in your story? Explain your selection. Are any of these statistics of no value to the message?" In this type of interpretation, several options are provided, and the choice is based on the intended audience and purpose. There is no need actually to compute the statistics or create the graphs.

Another idea is to provide graphs and statistics for two related situations: your class and the rest of the school, your state and the rest of the country, hamburgers at McDonald's and hamburgers at Burger King. What can be determined for sure from these data? What inferences can be made? What would help you make a decision about _____ that you cannot determine from the information gathered? How could you use this information to argue in favor of _____? How could you use the same information to argue on the reverse side of the issue?

(a) First make the stem.

Stem-and-Leaf Plots

Stem-and-leaf plots are a combination of a table and a graph. They are actually a form of bar graph in which numeric data are plotted by using the actual numerals in the data to form the graph. By way of example, suppose that the American League baseball teams had posted the following record of wins over the past season:

Baltimore	45	Milwaukee	91
Boston	94	Minnesota	98
California	85	New York	100
Chicago	72	Oakland	101
Cleveland	91	Seattle	48
Detroit	102	Toronto	64
Kansas City	96	Texas	65

(b) Write in the leaves directly from the data.

If the data are to be grouped by tens, list the tens digits in order and draw a line to the right, as in Figure 11.4a. These form the "stem" of the graph. Next, go through the list of scores, and write the ones digits next to the appropriate tens digit, as in Figure 11.4b. These are the "leaves." The process of making the graph groups the data for you. Furthermore, every piece of data can be retrieved from the graph. (Notice that stem-and-leaf plots are best made on graph paper so that each digit takes up the same amount of space.)

To provide more information, the graph can be quickly rewritten, ordering each leaf from least to most, as in Figure 11.4c. In this form, it may be useful to identify the number that belongs to a particular team, indicating its relative place within the grouped listing.

Stem-and-leaf graphs are not limited to two-digit data. For example, if the data ranged from 600 to 1300, the stem could be the numerals from 6 to 13 and the leaves made of two-digit numbers separated by commas.

(c) It is easy to rewrite each leaf in numeric order. This puts all of the data in order.

FIGURE 11.4 ● ● ● ● ● ● ●

Making a stem-and-leaf plot.

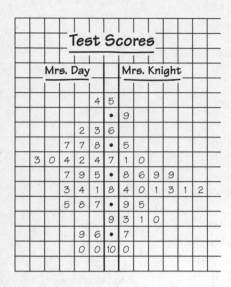

FIGURE 11.5 • • • • • • • • • • • • • •

Stem-and-leaf plots can be used to compare two sets of data.

Figure 11.5 illustrates two additional variations. When two sets of data are to be compared, the leaves can extend in opposite directions from the same stem. In the same example, notice that the data are grouped by fives instead of tens. When plotting 62, the 2 is written next to the 6; for 67, the 7 is written next to the dot below the 6.

Stem-and-leaf plots are significantly easier for students to make than bar graphs, all of the data are maintained, they provide an efficient method of ordering data, and individual elements of data can be identified.

Continuous Data Graphs

Bar graphs or picture graphs are useful for illustrating categories of data that have no numeric ordering—for example, types of vehicles or favorite TV shows. This type of data is composed for independent units and is called discrete data. When data are grouped along a continuous scale, they should be ordered along a number line. Examples of such information include temperatures that occur over time, height or weight over age, and percentages of test takers scoring in different intervals along the scale of possible scores. This type of data is called *continuous data*.

Line Plots

Line plots are useful *counts* of things along a numeric scale. To make a line plot, a number line is drawn and an X is made above the corresponding value on the line for every corresponding data element. One advantage of a line plot is that every piece of data is shown on the graph. It is also a very easy type of graph for students to make. It is essentially a bar graph with a potential bar for every possible value. A simple example is shown in Figure 11.6.

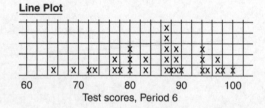

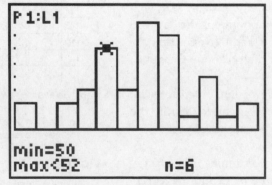

Age of U.S. presidents at inauguration

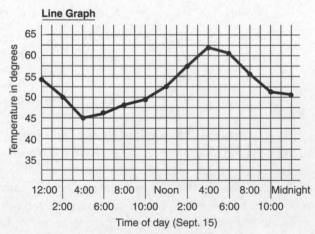

Temperature change over 24 hours

FIGURE 11.6 •

Three approaches to graphing data over continuous intervals. Notice that the horizontal scale must show some progression and is not just a grouping, as in a bar graph.

Chapter 11 EXPLORING DATA ANALYSIS

Histograms

A *histogram* is a form of bar graph in which the categories are consecutive equal intervals along a numeric scale. The height of each bar is determined by the number of data elements falling into that particular interval. Histograms are not difficult in concept but can cause problems for the students constructing them. What is the appropriate interval to use for the bar width? What is a good scale to use for the height of the bars? That all of the data must be grouped and counted within each interval causes further difficulty. Technology helps us with all of these decisions, allowing students to focus on the graph and its message. Graphing calculators, for example, produce histograms without much difficulty. They allow for the size of the interval to be specified and easily changed. By connecting the calculator to a computer, the graphs can be printed out or pasted into a word processor for inclusion in a student report. Figure 11.6 shows an example of a histogram produced on a TI-83.

The little figure that looks like a bug on top of one of the bars is the trace indicator. It can be moved from bar to bar. For each bar, the trace indicates the number of data points in that interval. On this bar, there are six data points indicated by "$n = 6$" in the lower part of the screen.

Line Graphs

A *line graph* is used when there is a numeric value associated with equally spaced points along a continuous number scale. Points are plotted to represent two related pieces of data, and a line is drawn to connect the points. For example, a line graph might be used to show how the length of a flagpole shadow changed from one hour to the next during the day. The horizontal scale would be time, and the vertical scale would be the length of the shadow. Discrete points can be plotted and straight lines drawn connecting them. In the example of the shadow, a shadow did exist at all times, but its length did not jump or drop from one plotted value to the other. The graph should show a continuous change. See a similar example involving temperature change in Figure 11.6.

Students have a tendency to graph discrete data using continuous data graphs like the line graph. For example, consider Figure 11.7 in which a student has graphed the number of siblings of each of his classmates using a line graph. The arrows have been added to the graph, highlighting the problem with displaying this type of data with a line graph. Every point on the line should have a value. What are the values where the arrows are pointing? A more appropriate choice would be a bar graph or a circle graph as shown in Figure 11.8.

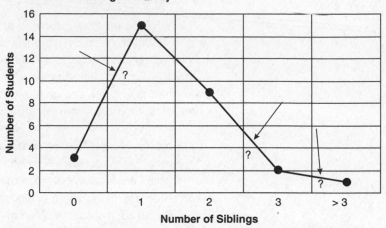

Number of Siblings in Family

FIGURE 11.7 ●

A line graph is used inappropriately to graph discrete data. What would the values be for the points indicated by the arrows?

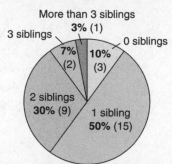

Number of Siblings in Family

More than 3 siblings
3% (1)
3 siblings
7% (2)
0 siblings
10% (3)
2 siblings **30%** (9)
1 sibling **50%** (15)

Fifth Grade: Mrs. Jones
30 students

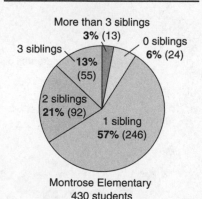

More than 3 siblings
3% (13)
3 siblings
13% (55)
0 siblings
6% (24)
2 siblings **21%** (92)
1 sibling **57%** (246)

Montrose Elementary
430 students

FIGURE 11.8 ● ● ● ● ● ● ● ● ● ● ● ● ●

Circle graphs show ratios of part to whole and can be used to compare ratios.

GRAPHICAL REPRESENTATIONS

Circle Graphs

A circle or pie graph is used when data have been partitioned into parts and interest is in the ratio of each part to the whole. In Figure 11.8, each of two graphs shows the percentages of students with different numbers of siblings. One graph is based on classroom data and the other on schoolwide data. Because pie graphs display ratios rather than quantities, the small set of class data can be compared to the large set of school data. That could not be done with bar graphs.

Easily Made Circle Graphs

Nearly every spreadsheet program has circle graph capabilities. Even without technology, there are a variety of ways that circle graphs can be made easily. Circle graphs of the students in your room can be made quickly and quite dramatically. Suppose, for example, that each student picked his or her favorite basketball team in the NCAA tournament's "Final Four." Line up all of the students in the room so that students favoring the same team are together. Now form the entire group into a circle of students. Tape the ends of four long strings to the floor in the center of the circle, and extend them to the circle at each point where the teams change. Voilà! A very nice pie graph with no measuring and no percentages. If you copy and cut out a hundredths disk (one is in the Blackline Masters) and place it on the center of the circle, the strings will show approximate percentages for each part of your graph (see Figure 11.9).

Another easy approach to circle graphs is similar to the human pie graph. Begin by having students make a bar graph of the data. Once complete, cut out the bars themselves, and tape them together end to end. Next, tape the two ends together to form a circle. Estimate where the center of the circle is, draw lines to the points where different bars meet, and trace around the full loop. You can estimate percentages using the hundredths disk as before.

From Percentages to Pie Graphs

If students have experienced either of the two methods just described, using their own calculations to make pie graphs will make more sense. The numbers in each category are added to form the total or whole. (That's the same as taping all of the strips together or lining up the students.) By dividing each of the parts by the whole with a calculator, numbers between 0 and 1 result—fractional parts of the whole. If rounded to hundredths, these numbers are now percentages of the whole. Rounding may cause some error. With a copy of the hundredths disk, students can easily make a pie chart and never have to mess with degrees and protractors. Trace around the disk to make the outline of the pie. Mark the center through a small hole in the disk, and draw a line to the circle. Start from that point, and use the disk to measure hundredths around the outside.

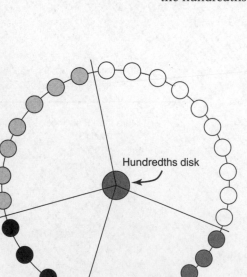

Hundredths disk

FIGURE 11.9 • • • • • • • • • • • • • • • • •

A human pie graph: Students are arranged in a circle, with string stretched between them to show the divisions.

Box-and-Whisker Plots

Box-and-whisker plots (or just *box plots*) are an easy method for visually displaying not only the median statistic but also information about the range and distribution or variance of data. In Fig-

The following numbers represent the ages in months of a class of sixth-grade students.

Boys		Girls	
132	122	140	131
140	130	129	128
133	134	141	131
142	125	134	132
134 *Joe B.*	147	124	130
(137)	131	129 *Whitney*	127
139	129	(125) *Whitney*	

All students

12	2, 4
•	5, 5, 7, 8, (9), 9, 9,
13	0, 0, 1, 1, (1), 2, 2, 3, 4, 4, 4
•	(7), 9
14	0, 0, 1, 2
•	7

Boys

12	2
•	5, 9
13	(0), 1, 2, 3, |4, 4
•	7, (9)
14	0, 2
•	7

Girls

12	4
•	5, 7,|8, 9,|9
13	(0), 1, 1, 2, |4
•	
14	0, 1
•	

FIGURE 11.10 ● ● ● ● ● ●

Ordered stem-and-leaf plots grouped by fives. Medians and upper and lower quartiles are found on the stem-and-leaf plots. Medians and quartiles are circled or are represented by a bar (I) if they fall between two elements.

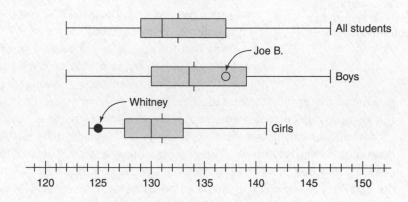

Age (months) of 27 sixth-grade students

FIGURE 11.11 ● ● ● ● ● ●

Box-and-whisker plots show a lot of informaiton.

ure 11.10, the ages in months for 27 sixth-grade students are given, along with stem-and-leaf plots for the full class and the boys and girls separately. Box-and-whisker plots are shown in Figure 11.11.

Each box-and-whisker plot has these three features:

1. A box that contains the "middle half" of the data, one-fourth to the left and right of the median. The ends of the box are at the *lower quartile,* the median of the lower half of the data, and the *upper quartile,* the median of the upper half of the data. Twenty-five percent of the data lie at or below the lower quartile, while 75 percent of the data lie at or below the upper quartile.
2. A line inside the box at the median of the data.
3. A line extending from the end of each box to the *lower extreme* and *upper extreme* of the data. Each line, therefore, covers the upper and lower fourths of the data.

Look at the information these box plots provide at a glance! The box and the lengths of the lines provide a quick indication of how the data are spread out or bunched together. Since the median is shown, this spreading or bunching can be determined for each quarter of the data. The entire class in this example is much more spread out in the upper half than the lower half. The girls are much more closely grouped in age than either the boys or the class as a whole. It is immediately obvious

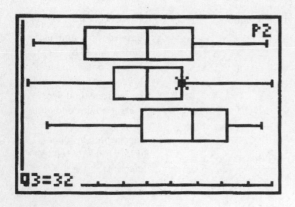

FIGURE 11.12 •

Three box plots of data falling between the values of 0 and 50. Twenty-three items are represented by the top plot, 122 by the middle plot, and 48 by the bottom plot. The cursor on the middle plot shows that the third quartile is 32. What other information can be determined from this plot?

that at least three-fourths of the girls are younger than the median age of the boys. The *range* of the data (difference between upper and lower extremes) is represented by the length of the plot, and the extreme values can be read directly. It is easy to mark and label entries of particular interest. For example, Joe B. and Whitney might be the class officers.

Making box-and-whisker plots is quite simple. First, put the data in order. An easy and valuable method is to make a stem-and-leaf plot and order the leaves, providing another visual image as well. Next, find the median. Simply count the number of values and determine the middle one. This can be done directly on the stem-and-leaf plots as was done in Figure 11.10. To find the two quartiles, ignore the median itself, and find the medians of the upper and lower halves of the data. Mark the two extremes, the two quartiles, and the median above an appropriate number line. Draw the box and the lines. Box plots can also be drawn vertically.

Note that the means for the data in our example are each just slightly higher than the medians (class = 132.4; boys = 133.9; girls = 130.8). For this example, the means themselves do not provide nearly as much information as the box plots. In Figure 11.11, the means are shown with small marks extending above and below each box.

Graphing calculators and several computer programs draw box-and-whisker plots, making this relatively simple process even more accessible. The TI-73 and TI-83 calculators can draw box plots for up to three sets of data on the same axis. In Figure 11.12, the data for the top box plot are based on 23 items. The second plot has 122 items. The third plot has 48 items of data. When you compare both large and small sets of data in this manner, the spread or lack of spread of the data becomes much more obvious.

> Notice that in Figure 11.11 the box for the boys is actually a bit longer than the box for the whole class. How can that be when there are clearly more students in the full class than there are boys? How would you explain this apparent discrepancy to a class of seventh graders?

Scatter Plots and Relationships

Data are often analyzed to search for or demonstrate relationships between two sets of data or phenomena. For example, what are the relationships, if any, between time spent watching television and overall grades? Does the size of a college have anything to do with the cost of attending?

All sorts of real situations exist where we are interested in relationships between two variables or two numeric phenomena. The world of science abounds with experimental data. How far does a toy car roll down an inclined plane as compared to the angle of the plane? How tall do beans grow over a 21-day period from the day they sprout? Such data are generally gathered from some sort of experiment that is set up and observed, with measurements taken. The experiment defines the various variables to look at.

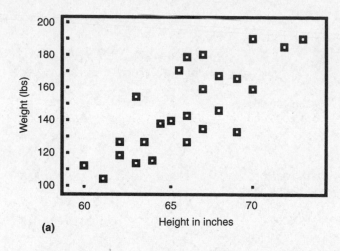

(a) Height in inches

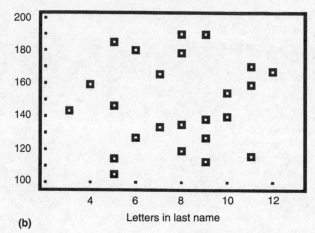

(b) Letters in last name

FIGURE 11.13 • • • • • •

Scatter plots show potential relationships or lack of relationships.

Data that may be related are gathered in pairs. For example, if you were going to examine the possible relationship between hours of TV watched and grades, each person in the survey or sample would produce a pair of numbers, one for TV time and one for grade point average.

Scatter Plots

Regardless of the source of the data, a good first attempt at examining them for possible relationships is to create a *scatter plot* of the two variables involved, a graph of points on a coordinate grid with each axis representing one of the two variables. Each pair of numbers from the two sets of data, when plotted, produces a visual image of the data as well as a hint concerning any possible relationships. Suppose that the following information was gathered from 25 eighth-grade boys: height in inches, weight in pounds, and number of letters in their last name. The two graphs in Figure 11.13 show two possibilities. Graph (a) is a scatter plot of height to weight, and graph (b) is a plot of name length to weight. Both were made with a graphing calculator.

As you would expect, the boys' weights seem to increase as their heights increase. However, the relationship is far from perfect. There is no reason to expect any relationship between name length and weight, and indeed the dots appear to be almost randomly distributed.

The following activity provides sets of data for students to examine for possible relationships.

ACTIVITY 11.11

Searching for Relationships

Provide students with a data set within which numerous potential relationships can be explored. For example, data about some popular movies are shown in Table 11.3. Have students consider the different relationships that they might explore with these data. For example, is there a relationship between the budget of a movie and its box office sales? Between the number of screens the movie is showing on and a movie's opening weekend sales? After choosing two variables to explore, students should construct scatter plots with the given data. They should be ready to discuss what the shape of

TABLE 11.3 •
Data on Recent Movies

Movie	Running Time (in minutes)	Box Office Sales	Budget	Number of Screens Opening Weekend	Opening Weekend Sales
Shrek	90	$267,652,016	$60,000,000	3,587	$42,347,760
Monsters, Inc.	88	$255,870,172	$115,000,000	3,237	$62,577,067
Lord of the Rings: Return of the King	201	$376,958,965	$94,000,000	3,703	$72,629,713
Harry Potter and the Chamber of Secrets	161	$261,970,615	$100,000,000	3,682	$88,357,488
Spider-Man	121	$403,706,375	$139,000,000	3,615	$114,844,116
Elf	95	$173,381,405	$33,000,000	3,337	$31,113,501
Bruce Almighty	101	$242,589,580	$81,000,000	3,483	$85,734,045
Pirates of the Caribbean: The Curse of the Black Pearl	143	$305,388,685	$125,000,000	3,269	$46,630,690
Finding Nemo	100	$339,714,367	$94,000,000	3,374	$70,251,710
Cheaper by the Dozen	98	$138,604,245	$40,000,000	3,298	$27,557,647
The Matrix: Revolutions	129	$139,259,759	$110,000,000	3,502	$48,475,154

Source: Data obtained from www.imdb.com.

the scatter plot tells them. Students can continue to choose other variables to explore, each time comparing the new scatter plots to previous ones, looking for similarities and differences about their shapes.

Best-Fit Lines

If your scatter plot indicates a relationship, it can be simply described in words. "As boys get taller, they tend to get heavier." This is correct but not particularly useful. What exactly is the relationship? If I knew the height of a boy, could I predict what his weight might be based on this information? Like much of statistical analysis, the value of a statistic is to predict what has not yet been observed. We poll a small sample of voters before an election to predict how the full population will vote. Here, can a sample of 30 students predict the weights of other students?

The relationship in these cases is not a number like a mean or a standard deviation but rather a line or curve. Is there a line that can be drawn through the scatter plot that represents the "best" approximation of all of the dots and reflects the observed trend? If the scatter plot seems to indicate a steadily decreasing or steadily increasing relationship (as in the height–weight graph), you would probably try to find a straight line that approximates the dots. Sometimes the plot will indicate a curved relationship, in which case you might try to draw a smooth curve like a parabola to approximate the dots.

What Determines Best Fit?

From a strictly visual standpoint, the line you select defines the observed relationship and could be used to predict other values not in the data set. The more closely the dots in the scatter plot hug the line you select, the greater the confidence you would have in the predictive value of the line. Certainly you could draw a straight line somewhere in the length–weight graph, but you would not have much faith in its predictive capability because the dots would be quite dispersed from any line you might draw.

ACTIVITY 11.12

Best-Fit Line

Once students have collected related data and prepared a scatter plot, duplicate an accurate version of the plot for each group of students. Provide the groups with a piece of spaghetti to use as a line. The task is to tape the line on the plot so that it is the "best" line to represent the relationship in the dots. Furthermore, the students are to develop a rationale for why they positioned the line as they did.

Using an overhead transparency of the plot, compare the lines chosen by various groups and their rationales.

Before reading further, return to the height–weight plot in Figure 11.13, graph (a), and draw a straight line that you think would make a good line of best fit. (You may want to make a photo enlargement of that figure to use with your class.) What reason would you offer for why you drew the line where you did?

Many of the reasons students will give for their best-fit line will be rather subjective: "It just looks right" or "There are just as many points above as below." Others will see how many points they can make the line touch. Most intuitive ideas fail to consider all of the points. Two different people using the same criteria might well come up with very different lines. There is a need for a better definition of a best-fit line.

Encourage students to use a more "mathematical" reason for why a line might be best. Since a good line is one around which most dots cluster, a good-fitting line is one where the distances from all of the dots to the line is minimal. This general notion of least distance to the line for all points can lead to an algorithm that will always produce a unique line for a given set of points. Two such algorithms are well known and used in statistics. The more complicated approach is called the *least squares regression* line. It is an algebraic procedure that is not accessible to middle grade students and is also rather tedious to compute. The second algorithm produces what is called the *median-median* line and is quite easy to determine.

Median–Median Line

The median-median line can be determined either directly from the graph or from the data. It is based on the simple median statistic. The method for determining the median-median line essentially consists of these steps:

1. Separate the data into three "equal" sets of points along the horizontal axis. (In the example of Figure 11.14, since there are 25 points, put the extra point into the middle third.)
2. Find the *median point* in each third of the points. (This is described in the text that follows.)
3. Connect the median points in the first and third sets of data. This line takes into consideration all points in these two sections but ignores the points in the middle third.
4. Draw a parallel line one-third of the distance from this first line to the center median point. This gives the center collection of points a proportional influence on the position of the line.

329

SCATTER PLOTS AND RELATIONSHIPS

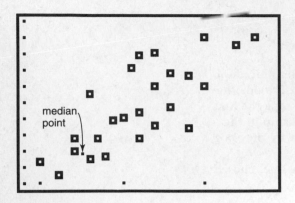

FIGURE 11.14 •

A height-versus-weight scatter plot. Use the graph to find the median-median line. The single pixel in the lower left is the median point for the left third of the points.

A *median point* in a scattered collection of points is the point with its first coordinate equal to the median of all the first coordinates and its second coordinate equal to the median of all the second coordinates. Another way of saying this is that the median point is one that is midway vertically and midway horizontally. Using this second formulation, the median point can be found by counting points from the bottom up until you have half the points below and half above. With an odd number of points, draw a horizontal line through the middle point. With an even number of points, draw the line halfway between the two middle points. The median point will fall on this horizontal line. Repeat the process, moving from left to right. The vertical line you find this way will intersect the horizontal line at the median point. Note that it is not necessary for the median point to be a data point.

In Figure 11.14, the median point in the left-hand third of the data (the first eight points counting left to right) is shown as a single pixel.

STOP **Find the other two median points on your own, and complete steps 3 and 4. Use Figure 11.14.**

Median–Median Lines with a Calculator

The TI-73 and TI-83 calculators will compute the median-median line for you. Figure 11.15 shows the calculator plot of the median-median line for the same height-versus-weight data.

Thinking About Functional Relationships

It is worth noting that the median-median line is a graphical representation of a function relating the variable on the horizontal axis to the variable on the vertical axis.

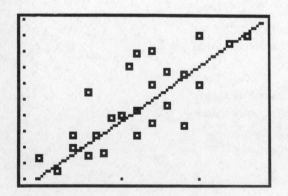

FIGURE 11.15 •

The median-median line for the points plotted in Figure 11.14.

Using the height–weight example, it is appropriate to say that *the weight of a boy is a function of his height.* The best-fit line is a mathematical method of determining what the function might be. Different methods of finding the best-fit line will likely develop slightly different lines.

Note that if the function (line) that we found accurately predicted the weight of a boy based on his height, all of the data points would fall along a perfectly straight line. That they do not is a vivid picture of the difference between data found in the world (the points on the graph) and a mathematical model of the real world (the line).

Scatter plots and best-fit lines are discussed again in Chapter 10 on functions. The connection among the real world, statistics, and algebraic ideas is a valuable one to make.

Chapter 11 **EXPLORING DATA ANALYSIS**

EXPANDED LESSON

Toying with the Measures

Based on Activity 11.7, p. 317

GRADE LEVEL: Sixth to eighth grades.

MATHEMATICS GOALS

To develop an understanding of how characteristics of a data set (e.g., distribution of data, outliers) affect the mean, median, and mode.

THINKING ABOUT THE STUDENTS

Students know how to find the mean, median, and mode of a data set.

MATERIALS AND PREPARATION

- Prepare a transparency of "Toy Purchases" (Blackline Master L-6) to use in the "before" portion of the lesson.
- Provide a copy of the "Toying with Measures" worksheet (Blackline Master L-7) for each student.

lesson

BLM L-6

BLM L-7

BEFORE

Begin with a simpler version of the task:

- Give the students the following data set: 3, 3, 3, 3, 3. Ask them to determine the mean, median, and mode. After verifying that the mean, median, and mode for this set is 3, ask the students to predict what, if any, changes in these statistics would occur if the number 15 was added to the set. Elicit students' ideas and rationales, asking others to comment on or question the ideas.
- Students should be able to compute the new statistics mentally. Clearly, the median and mode for this new data set remain unchanged. The mean changes from 3 to 5. For each of these statistics, discuss why changes occurred or did not occur.

The Task

- On the transparency of "Toying with Measures," show students the six toys that they have purchased and their prices. Have students calculate the mean, median, and mode for this data set and share those values to ensure that all students have found the correct values.
- The task is to make a series of changes to this original data set of six prices. For each change, first predict—*without computation*—the mean, median, and mode for the new data set and give a reason for the predictions. Do this for each change. Second, compute the actual statistics for the changed set and compare these to the predictions.

  Each of the following changes to the data set are made to the original set of six toy prices:

  1. You decide to buy a seventh toy that costs $20.
  2. You return the $1 toy to the store (leaving only five toys).
  3. By buying six toys the store gives you a free toy.
  4. You decide to buy a second doll for $12.
  5. Make a change you think will be interesting.

Establish Expectations

- Students first record their predictions on the "Toying with Measures" worksheet of the new mean, median, and mode along with their reason for the prediction for each of the five changes. Be sure students understand that each change is to the original set of six toys. The fifth change is one that they think might make an interesting change in the statistics.

- After sharing predictions and reasons with a partner, students should calculate the statistics and compare those with their predictions. If a prediction is very different from the calculation, they should try to find an error in their reasoning.

DURING

- Listen to individual students' predictions and justifications for those predictions. Is there evidence in students' explanations of their understanding the meaning of the different statistics?
- How are students incorporating the free toy into the set? Do they believe it will affect the mean, median, and mode? (The free toy adds a data point of $0. The mean and median will change.)
- Be sure students do not change their predictions after doing the calculations.
- For a challenge, ask the following question: Suppose that one new toy is added that increases the mean from $6 to $7. How much does the new toy cost?

AFTER

- Have students share their predictions and reasoning and discuss how their predictions compared with the actual statistics.
- Discuss what effect outliers (data that are much greater or smaller than the rest of the data in the set) seem to have on the mean, median, and mode and which statistic(s) are affected more by an outlier.
- Based on their findings, which measure of central tendency do they think would be a better representation of a data set that contains one or more outliers? Students should realize that the mean is significantly affected by extreme values, especially for small sets of data.
- Discuss the fact that these have been very small data sets. How would similar changes affect the mean and median if there were about 100 items in the data set?

ASSESSMENT NOTES

- How are students using current values for mean, median, and mode to make predictions? Are their predictions reasonable?
- Do students seem dependent on procedures to determine mean, median, and mode?

- For further exploration, ask students what they think would happen if one outlier is greater and one outlier is smaller than the rest of the data.

- Students can continue to investigate how changes in the data affect the mean, median, and mode in Activity 11.8, "Bus Time."

next steps

EXPLORING CONCEPTS OF PROBABILITY

References to probability are all around us: The weather forecaster predicts a 60 percent chance of snow; medical researchers predict people with certain diets have a high chance of heart disease; the fine print on a lottery ticket states that you have a 1 in 5 million chance of winning the lottery this week; or airlines, in an effort to ensure the public's confidence in air travel, calculate the chance of a person dying in an airplane crash is 1 in 10 million while being hurt in a car accident is 1 in 75. Simulations of complex situations are frequently based on probabilities and are then used in the design process of such things as spacecraft, highways, and storm sewers or plans for reactions to disasters.

Because the ideas and methods of probability are so prevalent in today's world, this strand of mathematics has risen in visibility in the school curriculum. To make sense of the ideas and methods of probability, middle school students need to collect and analyze data from experiments that they conduct. It is important for students to explore probability situations using a variety of random generator

big ideas

1 The occurrence of an event can be characterized along a continuum from impossible to certain. The *probability of an event* is a number between 0 (impossible) and 1 (certain) that is a measure of the chance that a given event will occur. A probability of $\frac{1}{2}$ indicates an even chance of the event occurring.

2 Probability is about predictions over the long term rather than predictions of individual events. For example, when rolling a die we expect a 2 to occur about one-sixth of the time when we conduct a large number of rolls. However, we cannot predict with much certainty what the next roll of the die will be.

3 The relative frequency of outcomes of an event (*experimental probability*) can be used as an estimate of the exact probability of an event. The larger the number of trials, the better the estimate will be. The results for a small number of trials may be quite different from a result experienced in the long run. For some events, the exact probability can be determined by an analysis of the event itself. A probability determined in this manner is called a *theoretical probability*.

4 Two events are either independent or dependent. If the occurrence of one event does not influence the occurrence of the other event, they are called *independent*. For example, the first flip of a coin does not influence the second flip of the coin. If eight heads in a row come up, the chance that the next toss of the coin will be a head remains exactly $\frac{1}{2}$. Chance has no memory! Two events are dependent if the occurrence of one has an impact on the occurrence of the other. For example, if you are dealt one ace in a game of cards, the chance of being dealt a second ace is diminished since there are now only three aces remaining.

5 Simulation is a technique used for answering real-world questions or making decisions in complex situations in which an element of chance is involved. To see what is likely to happen in the real event, a model must be designed that has the same probabilities as the real situation.

devices (e.g., coins, dice, colored chips, spinners) and methods of analysis (e.g., organized lists, tree diagrams, area models) across a variety of contexts. Without these varied explorations, students will find it difficult to move from the relatively simple (and at times faulty) reasoning prevalent in elementary school to the more formal reasoning that will be developed after middle school.

Theoretical Versus Experimental Probability

Simply stated, a *probability* is a measure of the likelihood of an event occurring. But how do you measure a chance? In many situations, there are actually two ways to determine this measure. One way is through logical analysis of the situation (*theoretical probability*) and the other is generated through data collection (*experimental probability*). Let's consider a simple experiment as an illustration: What is the probability or likelihood of obtaining a head when tossing one coin?

Logically, we could argue that if it is a fair coin, obtaining a head is just as likely as obtaining a tail. Since there are two possible outcomes that are equally likely, each has a probability of $\frac{1}{2}$. Hence, the theoretical probability of obtaining a head is $\frac{1}{2}$.

When all possible outcomes of a simple experiment are equally likely, the *theoretical probability* of an event is

$$\frac{\text{Number of outcomes in the event}}{\text{Number of possible outcomes}}$$

Now let's determine the probability of obtaining a head through data collection. Take a fair coin and toss it 10 times, recording the result of the toss in a frequency table (number of heads and number of tails). In 10 tosses, you might have had 3 tails and 7 heads ($\frac{7}{10}$ for heads), or 8 tails and 2 heads ($\frac{2}{10}$ for heads). These ratios are called *relative frequencies*. The *relative frequency* of an event is

$$\frac{\text{Number of observed occurrences of the event}}{\text{Total number of trials}}$$

These numbers ($\frac{7}{10}$ and $\frac{2}{10}$) are not close to the theoretical probability of $\frac{1}{2}$. Continue to collect data until you have completed 100 tosses. (A quick way to do this experiment is to work in groups. If 10 people each do 10 trials and pool their data, the time needed for 100 trials is not long.) The more tosses made, the closer the relative frequency gets to the theoretical probability, and you can become more confident in the results. Since it is impossible to conduct an infinite number of trials, we can only consider the relative frequency or *experimental probability* for a very large number of trials as an approximation of the theoretical probability. This emphasizes the notion that probability is more about predictions over the long term than predictions of individual events.

Theoretical Probability

In the following activity, students play a game and keep track of the outcomes for each turn—gathering data. The results of the game—the experimental probability—will very likely be contrary to students' intuitive ideas. This in turn will cause them to analyze the game in a logical manner and find out why things happened as they did—theoretical probability.

ACTIVITY 12.1

Fair or Unfair?

Three students toss 2 like coins (e.g., 2 pennies, 2 nickels, 2 quarters) and are assigned points according to the following rules: Player A gets 1 point if the coin toss results in "two heads"; player B gets 1 point if the toss results in "two tails"; and player C gets 1 point if the toss results are "mixed" (one head, one tail). The game is over after 20 tosses. The player who has the most points wins. Have students play the game at least two or three times. After each game, the players are to stop and discuss if they think the game is fair and make predictions about who will win the next game.

When the full class has played the game several times, conduct a discussion on the fairness of the game. Challenge students to make an argument *not* based on the data as to whether the game is fair or not and why.

EXPANDED LESSON

(pages 350–351)
A complete lesson plan based on "Fair or Unfair?" can be found at the end of this chapter.

Having students explain the outcomes to an experiment or make predictions about future events can provide teachers with insight into how students are thinking about probability. A simple analysis of the game in Activity 12.1 might go like this: You can get 2 tails, 1 head and 1 tail, or 2 heads. There are three outcomes and, therefore, each has an equal chance. The game should be fair. However, after playing "Fair or Unfair?" students will find that player C (gets points for a mixed result) appears to have an unfair advantage (especially if they have played several games or the class has pooled its data). This observation seems to contradict the notion that the outcomes are equally likely. If students cannot reconcile this discrepancy between their initial idea that the game is fair and the actual results, have them play the game once again. However, this time they should play the game using two different coins, say, a penny and a nickel. Have them record results separately for each coin. For example, a toss may result in "head on penny, head on nickel," "head on penny, tail on nickel," or "tail on penny, head on nickel." The distinction between these last two outcomes can help students understand why player C has an unfair advantage.

Some students may be able to analyze the situation and generate all the possible outcomes. An explanation may be as follows:

> *There is only one way for two heads to occur and one way for two tails to occur, but there are two ways for a head and a tail to occur: Either the first coin is heads and the second tails, or vice versa. That makes a total of four possible outcomes, not three. (See Figure 12.1.) Getting a head and a tail happens in two out of the four possible outcomes. Since each outcome is equally likely, getting a head and a tail has a probability of $\frac{2}{4}$ or $\frac{1}{2}$.*

This theoretical probability is based on a logical analysis of the experiment, not on experimental results.

First Coin	Second Coin
Head	Head
Head	Tail
Tail	Head
Tail	Tail

FIGURE 12.1 • • • • • • •

Four possible outcomes of flipping two coins.

THEORETICAL VERSUS EXPERIMENTAL PROBABILITY

Experimental Probability

In the preceding discussion, it should be clear that our intuition about the chance of an event is often misleading. It might seem, therefore, that we should always make an attempt to find the theoretical probability. But some situations cannot be analyzed mathematically to determine a theoretical probability. In other words, the probability of some events can be determined only through data collection (experimental probability), conducting a sufficiently large number of trials to become confident that the resulting relative frequency is an approximation of the theoretical probability. The following activity provides students with such a situation.

ACTIVITY 12.2

Cup Toss

Provide a small plastic "portion" cup or other small cup to pairs of students. Ask them to list the possible ways that the cup could land if they tossed it in the air and let it land on the floor. Which of the possibilities (upside down, right side up, or on its side) do they think is most and least likely? Why? Inform them that they will toss the cup 20 times, each time recording how it lands on the floor. Students should agree on a uniform method of tossing the cups to ensure unbiased data (e.g., standing up, flipping the cups at the same height, and letting them land on the floor). Have students share their results for 20 trials. Discuss the differences and generate reasons for them. Have students predict what will happen if they pool their data. Pool the data and compute the three ratios (upside down, right side up, and on the side) to the total number of tosses at various points, say after 100, 200, 300, 400, 500, and so on up to 1000 tosses. List the ratios in a chart with column headings: number of tosses, side, up, and down. As the pooled sample grows, continue to ask students to make and revise their predictions. The relative frequency should begin to converge toward and approximate the actual probability.

In the cup-tossing experiment (Activity 12.2), there is no practical way to determine the results before you start. However, once you had results for 200 flips, you would undoubtedly feel more confident in predicting the results of the next 100 flips. After gathering data on that same cup for 1000 trials, you would feel even more confident. Say that your cup lands on its side 78 times out of the first 100 tosses. You might choose a round figure of 75 or 80 sideways landings for any 100 tosses as a possible probability. If, after 200 flips, there were 163 sideways landings, you would feel even more confident about a 4-out-of-5 ratio and predict about 800 sideways landings for 1000 tosses. The more flips that are made, the more confident you become. You have determined an *experimental probability* of $\frac{4}{5}$ or 80 percent for the cup to land on its side. It is experimental because it is based on the results of an experiment rather than a theoretical analysis of the cup.

The Law of Large Numbers

The phenomenon that the relative frequency becomes a closer approximation of the actual probability or the theoretical probability as the size of the data set (sample) increases is referred to as *the law of large numbers*. The larger the size of the data set, the more representative the sample is of the population. Thinking about statistics, a survey of 1000 people provides more reliable and convincing data about the larger population than a survey of 5 people. The larger the number of trials (or surveys), the more confident you can be that the data reflect the larger population. The same is true when you are attempting to determine the probability of an event through data collection.

The next activity provides an informal assessment of students' understanding that small sample sizes may or may not be reflective of the larger population.

ACTIVITY 12.3

Guess What's in the Box

Tell the students about an experiment conducted in another class. A box contained colored tiles. Students could not see into the box. They reached in and pulled out one tile at a time. After recording the color of the tile, it was placed back into the box, the box was shaken to mix the tiles, and another tile was pulled from the box. After drawing tiles from the box in this manner 10 times, they found they had drawn 5 blue, 3 green, 1 red, and 1 yellow.

Have students respond to these questions: What colors of the tiles might be in the box? How many of each color might there be?

In "Guess What's in the Box," the sample size is very small. In fact there is almost no way to know with any certainty the distribution of colors. There may very well be other colors that were not drawn. Whatever the distribution of tiles, any multiple of that distribution would have the same probabilities. As you listen to students' reasoning, do not provide this information; rather, let the ideas come out in discussion.

The following activity is meant to reinforce this notion that better inferences can be drawn from larger samples than from smaller ones.

ACTIVITY 12.4

Short Run/Long Run

Students roll two dice and record the sum in the corresponding column of a chart (see Figure 12.2). They continue to roll the dice until one of the columns is completely filled. Before beginning play, have students predict which column they think will "win" and explain their prediction. Similarly, have them predict which number will have the fewest entries and explain this prediction as well. After playing, compare what happened to their predictions. As they do the recording, they put a circle around the X or tally that is the first one in the rows indicated on the left by a circle. (In Figure 12.2, a sum of 5 was the first to occur twice and 6 was the first to occur five times.)

After all students have played at least once, list all the sums that were circled, that is, leading in row 2. In separate lists, put the circled sums for row 5, row 8, and row 10—the winners.

Discuss with students which number won most often and which number had the fewest marks at the end of the game and why that might be. Compare the lists of leading numbers. Students should notice that there are fewer different leading numbers as the game goes on. Discuss why this is so. Ask students to examine the shape of the data displays for their individual results. What do they notice and what does this tell them? Ask them if they

(continued)

THEORETICAL VERSUS EXPERIMENTAL PROBABILITY

Figure 12.2

Number of times sum appears	2	3	4	5	6	7	8	9	10	11	12
(10)											
9											
(8)											
7											
6											
(5)					(X)						
4					X		X				
3			X	X	X	X	X				
(2)			X	(X)	X	X	X	X			
1	X	X	X	X	X	X	X	X	X	X	

FIGURE 12.2 •••••••••••••••

Chart for recording the number of times a sum appears on two dice in the activity "Short Run/Long Run." Students circle the first tally that is marked in rows 2, 5, 8, and 10. This chart has been partially filled in.

Figure 12.3

	2	3	4	5	6	7	8	9	10	11	12
						X					
						X					
						X					
						X					
						X	X				
						X	X				
					X	X	X				
					X	X	X				
				X	X	X	X				
					X	X	X	X			
					X	X	X	X			
					X	X	X	X			
			X	X	X	X	X	X	X		
					X	X	X	X	X	X	
					X	X	X	X	X	X	
					X	X	X	X	X	X	
			X	X	X	X	X	X	X		
		X	X	X	X	X	X	X	X		
			X	X	X	X	X	X	X	X	
			X	X	X	X	X	X	X	X	
	X	X	X	X	X	X	X	X	X	X	X
	X	X	X	X	X	X	X	X	X	X	X
	X	X	X	X	X	X	X	X	X	X	X
	X	X	X	X	X	X	X	X	X	X	X
	2	**3**	**4**	**5**	**6**	**7**	**8**	**9**	**10**	**11**	**12**

FIGURE 12.3 •••••••••••••••

Sample chart of pooled data for Activity 12.4, "Short Run/Long Run."

Chapter 12 EXPLORING CONCEPTS OF PROBABILITY

played the game again, which number do they think would win and why? Ask students to predict what would happen if they continued to roll the dice and collected more data. What would the data display look like and what would it mean?

To examine what happens if there are more data, combine the results of three to four students into one chart as shown in Figure 12.3.

In "Short Run/Long Run" one of the most interesting observations will likely be a discussion of the lists of numbers circled in rows 2, 5, 8, and 10. If the data do not clearly show that the variability is not decreasing from 2 to 5 to 8, have students play again, at least up until row 5.

 Why should there be a range of numbers in the row 2 list and fewer numbers in the row 8 list?

It is possible for almost any number from 2 to 12 to be circled in row 2 since it does not take many rolls to get to row 2. These results might be called the effects of the "law of small numbers"—not enough data to get a handle on the situation. However, as more and more rolls are made, the law of large numbers begins to take over. The sum of 7 has the greatest probability of winning. The sums of 6 and 8 are the next most likely, 5 and 9 somewhat less likely than that, and so on down to 2 and 12. This reality of the probabilities is what will cause a pooled graph to have a nearly symmetrical appearance with 6, 7, or 8 almost certainly at the top. As more and more rolls are accumulated, the results will be more and more symmetrical. The law of large numbers causes the experimental results to get closer to the theoretical probability.

Implications for Instruction

There are many reasons why an experimental approach to probability, actually conducting experiments and examining outcomes, is important in the middle grades classroom.

- It is significantly more intuitive. Results begin to make sense and do not result from some abstract rule.

- It eliminates guessing at probabilities and wondering, "Did I get it right?" Counting or trying to determine the number of elements in a sample space can be very difficult without some intuitive background information.

- It provides an experiential background for examining the theoretical model. When you begin to sense that the probability of two heads is $\frac{1}{4}$ instead of $\frac{1}{3}$, the analysis in Figure 12.1 seems more reasonable.

- It helps students see how the ratio of a particular outcome to the total number of trials begins to converge to a fixed number. For an infinite number of trials, the relative frequency and theoretical probability would be the same.

- It develops an appreciation for a simulation approach to solving problems. Many real-world problems are actually solved by conducting experiments or simulations.

- It is a lot more fun and interesting! Even searching for a correct explanation in the theoretical model is more interesting.

Whenever possible, try to use an experimental approach in the classroom. If a theoretical analysis (such as with the two-coin experiment in "Fair or Unfair?") is possible, it should also be examined, and the results should be compared. Rather than correcting a student error in an initial analysis, we can let experimental results guide and correct student thinking.

Technology Note

Truly random events often occur in unexpected groups; a fair coin may turn up heads five times in a row. A 100-year flood may hit a town twice in ten years. Hands-on random devices such as spinners, dice, or cubes drawn from a bag give students an intuitive feel for the imperfect distribution of randomness. Students believe in the unbiased outcomes of these devices. The downside is that hands-on devices require a lot of time to produce a large number of trials. This is where technology can help enormously.

Electronic devices, including some relatively simple calculators and graphing calculators, are designed to produce random outcomes at the press of a button. Computer software is available that flips coins, spins spinners, or draws numbers from a hat. Calculators produce random numbers that can then be interpreted in terms of the desired device. As long as students accept the results generated by the technology as truly random or equivalent to the hands-on device, they offer significant advantages for performing experiments. A possible downfall of using technology is that it may mask what is happening, such as how sample spaces are generated, which can hinder students' understanding of probability. Having students actually spin spinners, roll dice, draw chips out of bags, and so on is a useful first approach.

Software for exploring probability concepts can generally be described as computer-animated random devices. Graphics show students the coins being flipped or the spinner being spun. Most allow different speeds. In a slow version, students may watch each spin of a spinner or coin flip. Faster speeds show the recording of each trial but omit the graphics. An even quicker mode simply shows the cumulative results. The number of trials can be set by the user.

Tangible Math: The Probability Constructor (Riverdeep, 2002), designed for students at the middle grades, is sophisticated and offers many options. Within each of six devices, the probability of the outcomes is adjustable and outcomes can be displayed in a variety of ways.

Even with only one computer in the room, a good probability program is a worthwhile investment.

Assessment Note

You can add to the list of reasons for beginning probability explorations with experiments rather than theoretical analysis the opportunity that these explorations provide for authentic assessment of student ideas. By engaging students first in conduct of an experiment, you can ask the following:

- What does it mean that an event has a probability of 89 percent or of $\frac{2}{3}$?
- How many times do you think you should conduct the experiment before you feel confident?
- What should you do if your results don't make sense to you?
- If you know the probability of an event, can you predict the result of the next trial?
- What does "confidence in your results" mean?

Sample Space and Determining Probabilities

Understanding the concepts of outcome and sample space is central to understanding probability. A *sample space* for an experiment or chance situation is the set of all possible outcomes for that experiment. An *outcome* or *event* is a subset of the sample space. For example, the possible outcomes or the sample space for rolling a single die can be represented as {1, 2, 3, 4, 5, 6}. One event from this sample space is rolling an even number: {2, 4, 6}. Rolling a single die, drawing one colored chip from a bag, or the occurrence of rain tomorrow are all examples of what are called *single-stage* experiments. A *single-stage* or *one-stage* experiment is an experiment that requires only one activity to determine an outcome: one roll, one draw from the bag, one new day. A *two-stage* or *multistage* experiment is an experiment that requires two (or more) activities to determine an outcome. Examples include rolling two dice, drawing two cubes from a bag, and the occurrence of rain and forgetting your umbrella.

Middle grades students should be able to list the sample space for a one-stage experiment. However, determining sample spaces for experiments with two or more stages can often present a challenge.

When exploring two-stage experiments, there is another factor to consider: Does the occurrence of the event in one stage have an effect on the occurrence of the event in the other? In the following sections we will consider two-stage experiments of both types—those with independent events and those with dependent events.

Independent Events

Recall that in Activity 12.1, "Fair or Unfair?," students explored the results of tossing two coins. The toss of one coin had no effect on the other. These were examples of *independent events;* the occurrence or nonoccurrence of one event has no effect on the other. In that instance and in "Short Run/Long Run" (Activity 12.4), the challenge is to determine the sample space and the number of outcomes in the various events. The common error for both tossing two coins or rolling two dice is a failure to distinguish between the two events, especially when the outcomes are combined, as in "a head and a tail" or adding the numbers on the dice.

We've already solved the problem of tossing two coins. Let's explore rolling two dice and adding the results as was done in "Short Run/Long Run," Activity 12.4. The results of the sums of two dice might look like Figure 12.4a. (Figure 12.3 is another example.) These results show clearly that these events are not equally likely and that in fact the sum of 7 has the best chance of occurring. To explain this, they might

FIGURE 12.4 ••••••••

Tallies can account only for the total (a) or keep track of the individual die (b).

Sum of Two Dice

2	卌 l
3	卌 卌
4	卌 卌 卌 llll
5	卌 卌 卌 llll
6	卌 卌 卌 卌 卌 llll
7	卌 卌 卌 卌 卌 卌 卌 llll
8	卌 卌 卌 卌 卌 卌 llll
9	卌 卌 卌 卌 卌
10	卌 卌 卌 l
11	卌 ll
12	卌 卌

(a)

Red Die

	1	2	3	4	5	6
1	卌	卌 l	卌	卌 ll	卌 llll	卌 ll
2	卌 llll	卌 lll	卌 l	卌	卌 lll	卌 ll
3	卌 卌	卌	卌 lll	卌	卌 卌 ll	卌
4	卌 ll	卌 卌	卌 llll	卌	卌 卌 ll	卌 ll
5	卌 lll	卌 卌 ll	卌 卌	卌	卌	卌 llll
6	卌 lll	卌 llll	卌 lll	卌 ll	卌 llll	卌 lll

Green Die

There are six ways to get 7.

(b)

look for the combinations that make 7: 1 and 6, 2 and 5, and 3 and 4. But there are also three combinations for 8. It seems as though 8 should be just as likely as 7, and yet it is not.

Now suppose that the experiment is repeated. This time, for the sake of clarity, suggest that students roll two different-colored dice and that they keep the tallies in a chart like the one in part (b) of Figure 12.4.

The results of a large number of dice rolls indicate what one would expect, namely, that all 36 cells of this chart are equally likely. But there are more cells with a sum of 7 than any other number. Therefore, students were really looking for the event that consists of any of the six ways, not three ways, that two dice can add to 7. There are six outcomes in the desired event out of a total of 36, for a probability of $\frac{6}{36}$, or $\frac{1}{6}$.

To create the sample space for two independent events, it is helpful to use a chart or diagram that keeps the two events separate and illustrates the combinations. The matrix in Figure 12.4(b) is one good suggestion when there are only two events. A tree diagram (Figure 12.5) is another method of creating sample spaces that can be used with any number of events.

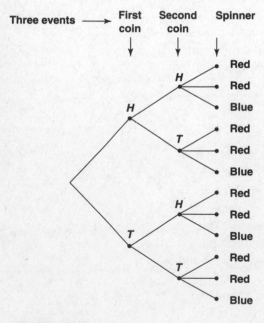

Three events ⟶ First coin   Second coin   Spinner

FIGURE 12.5 ••••••••••••••••••••••

A tree diagram showing all possible outcomes for two coins and a spinner that is $\frac{2}{3}$ red.

ACTIVITY 12.5

Multistage Events

The following are examples of multistage events composed of independent events.

Rolling an even sum with two dice
Spinning blue and flipping a cup on end
Getting two blues out of three spins (depends on the spinner)
Having a tack or a cup land up if each is tossed once
Getting *at least* two heads from a toss of four coins

342

••••••••••••••••••••••••••••••

Chapter **12** EXPLORING CONCEPTS OF PROBABILITY

Have students first make and defend a prediction of the probability of the event. Then they should conduct an experiment with a large number of trials, comparing their results to their predicted probabilities. Finally, they should reconcile differences. Where appropriate, students can try to determine the theoretical probability as part of their final analysis of the experiment.

Words and phrases such as *and, or, at least,* and *no more than* can also cause children some trouble. Of special note is the word *or,* since its everyday usage is generally not the same as its strict logical use in mathematics. In mathematics, *or* includes the case of *both.* So in the tack-and-cup example, the event includes tack up, cup up, and *both* tack *and* cup up.

One way to determine the theoretical probability of a multistage event is to list all possible outcomes and count those that are favorable, that is, those that make up the event. This is useful and intuitive as a first approach. However, it has some limitations. First, what if the events are not all equally likely? For example, the spinner may be only $\frac{1}{4}$ blue. Second, it is difficult to move from that approach to even slightly more sophisticated methods. An area model approach has been used successfully with fifth-grade students and is quite helpful for some reasonably difficult problems.

Suppose that after many experiences, you have decided that your cup lands on its side 82 percent of the time. The experiment is to toss the cup and then draw a card from a deck. What is the probability that the cup will land on its side *and* you will draw a spade? Draw a square to represent one whole. First partition the square to represent the cup toss, 82 percent and 18 percent, as in Figure 12.6(a). Now partition the square in the other direction to represent the four equal card suits. As shown in Figure 12.6(b), one region is the proportion of time that both events, sideways and spades, happen. The area of this region is $\frac{1}{4}$ of 82 percent, or 20.5 percent.

You can use the same drawing to determine the probability of other events in the same experiment. For example, what is the probability of the cup landing on either end *or* drawing a red card? As shown in Figure 12.6(c), half of the area of the square corresponds to drawing a red card. This section includes the case of drawing a red card *and* an end landing. The other half of the 18 percent end landings happen when a red card is not drawn. Half of 18 percent is 9 percent of the area. The total area for a red card *or* an end landing is 59 percent.

The area approach is easy for students to use and understand for experiments involving two independent events when the probability of each is known. For more than two independent events, further subdivision of each region is required but is still quite reasonable (see Figure 12.7). The use of *and* and *or* connectives is easily dealt with. It is quite clear to students, without memorization of formulas, how probabilities should be combined.

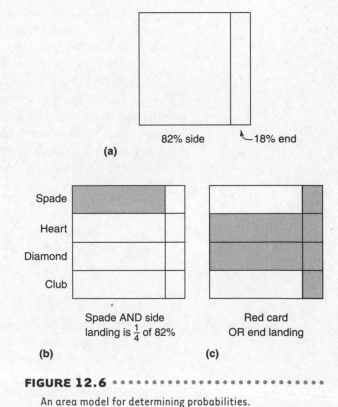

(a)

82% side   18% end

(b) Spade AND side landing is $\frac{1}{4}$ of 82%

(c) Red card OR end landing

FIGURE 12.6

An area model for determining probabilities.

SAMPLE SPACE AND DETERMINING PROBABILITIES

FIGURE 12.7 ·······

Area model for experiments of tossing 2 and 3 coins.

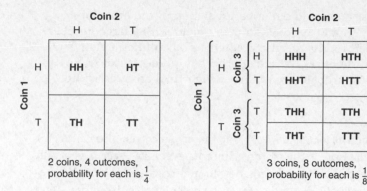

2 coins, 4 outcomes, probability for each is $\frac{1}{4}$

3 coins, 8 outcomes, probability for each is $\frac{1}{8}$

Dependent Events

The next level of difficulty occurs when the probability of one event depends on the result of the first. For example, suppose that there are two identical boxes. In one box is a dollar bill and two counterfeit bills. In the other box is one of each. You may choose one box and from that box select one bill without looking. What are your chances of getting a genuine dollar? Here there are two events: selecting a box and selecting a bill. The probability of getting a dollar in the second event depends on which box is chosen in the first event. These events are *dependent,* not independent.

As another example, suppose you are riding a new water ride at the local theme park. The raft you are riding in can take three paths. The raft will go down path A $\frac{1}{2}$ of the time. It will go down path B $\frac{1}{4}$ of the time and the rest of the time it will go down path C. On path A you have a 75 percent chance of getting wet from the waterfall. On path B you are certain to get wet, a 100 percent chance. On path C you have a 50 percent chance of getting wet. What's the probability that you will be wet by the time you get off the ride? Notice that the probability of getting wet is dependent on which path the raft goes down.

Any of these problems could be explored with an experimental approach, a simulation. Remember that an experimental approach should always be used first. A second approach to these problems is to use the area model to determine the theoretical probabilities. An area model solution to the water ride problem is shown in Figure 12.8. How would the area model for the water ride problem be different if the probability of getting wet on path C was two-thirds rather than one-fourth?

 It would be good to stop at this point and try the area approach for the problem of the counterfeit bills. The chance of getting a dollar is $\frac{5}{12}$. Can you get this result?

The area model will not solve all probability problems. However, it fits very well into a developmental approach to the subject because it is conceptual, it is based on existing knowledge of fractions, and more symbolic approaches can be derived from it. Figure 12.9 shows a tree diagram for the same problem, with the probability of each path of the tree written in. After some experience with probability situations, the tree diagram model is probably easier to use and adapts to a wider range of situations. You should be able to match up each branch of the tree diagram in Figure 12.9 with a sec-

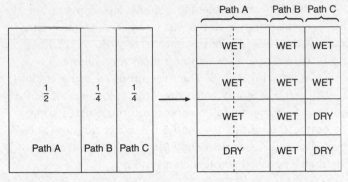

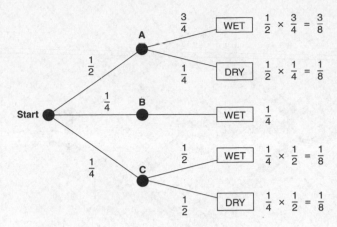

On Path A, $\frac{3}{4}$ of the time you will get wet. (Note: Not $\frac{3}{4}$ of the square but $\frac{3}{4}$ of the times you go down Path A.

On Path B, you will get wet 100 percent of the time (or $\frac{4}{16}$ of the total time). On Path C, $\frac{1}{2}$ of these times (or $\frac{2}{16}$ of the total time) you will get wet.

Therefore, you will get wet $\frac{12}{16}$ of the time and you will not get wet $\frac{4}{16}$ of the time.

FIGURE 12.8 •

Using an area model to solve the water ride problem.

FIGURE 12.9 •

A tree diagram is another way to model the outcomes of a multistage experiments with dependent events.

tion of the square in Figure 12.8. Use the area model to explain why the probability for each complete branch of the tree is determined by multiplying the probabilities along the branch.

Simulations

Simulation is a technique used for answering real-world questions or making decisions in complex situations where an element of chance is involved. Many times simulations are conducted because it is too dangerous, complex, or expensive to manipulate the real situation. To see what is likely to happen in the real event, a model must be designed that has the same probabilities as the real situation. For example, in designing a rocket, a large number of related systems all have some chance of failure. Various combinations of failures might cause serious problems with the rocket. Knowing the probability of serious failures will help determine if redesign or backup systems are required. It is not reasonable to make repeated tests of the actual rocket. Instead, a model that simulates all of the chance situations is designed and run repeatedly with the help of a computer. The computer model can simulate thousands of flights, and an estimate of the chance of failure can be made.

Many real-world situations lend themselves to simulation analysis. In a business venture, the probability of selling a product might depend on a variety of chance factors, some of which can be controlled or changed and others not. Will advertising help? Should high-cost materials be used? What location provides the best chance of sales? If a reasonable model can be set up that simulates these factors, an experiment can be run before actually entering into the venture to determine the best choices.

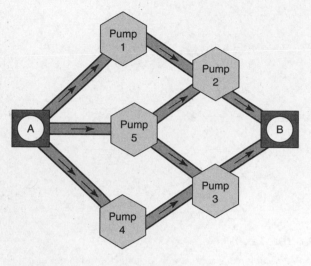

FIGURE 12.10 •

Each of these five pumps has a 50 percent chance of failure. What is the probability that some path from A to B is working?

The following problem and model are adapted from the excellent materials developed by the Quantitative Literacy Project (Gnanadesikan, Schaeffer, & Swift, 1987). In Figure 12.10, a diagram shows water pipes for a pumping system connecting A to B. The five pumps are aging, and it is estimated that at any given time, the probability of pump failure is $\frac{1}{2}$. If a pump fails, water cannot pass that station. For example, if pumps 1, 2, and 5 fail, water can flow only through 4 and 3. Consider the following questions that might well be asked about such a system:

- What is the probability that water will flow at any time?
- On the average, about how many stations need repair at any time?
- What is the probability that the 1–2 path is working at any time?

For any simulation, a series of steps or a model can serve as a useful guide.

1. *Identify key components and assumptions of the problem.* The key component in the water problem is the condition of a pump. Each pump is either working or not. The assumption is that the probability that a pump is working is $\frac{1}{2}$.
2. *Select a random device for the key components.* Any random device can be selected that has outcomes with the same probability as the key component—in this case, the pumps. Here a simple choice might be tossing a coin, with heads representing a working pump.
3. *Define a trial.* A *trial* consists of simulating a series of key components until the situation has been completely modeled one time. In this problem, a trial could consist of tossing a coin five times, each toss representing a different pump.
4. *Conduct a large number of trials, and record the information.* For this problem, it would be good to keep the record of heads and tails in groups of five because each set of five is one trial and represents all of the pumps.
5. *Use the data to draw conclusions.* There are four possible paths for the water, each flowing through two of the five pumps. As they are numbered in the drawing, if any one of the pairs 1–2, 5–2, 5–3, and 4–3 is open, it makes no difference whether the other pumps are working. By counting the trials in which at least one of these four pairs of coins both came up heads, we can estimate the probability of water flowing. To answer the second question, the number of tails per trial can be averaged.

 STOP **How would you answer the third question concerning the 1–2 path's being open?**

Steps 4 and 5 are the same as solving a probability problem by experimental means. The interesting problem-solving aspects of simulation activities are in the first three steps, where the real-world situation is translated into a model. Translation of real-world information into models is the essence of applied mathematics.

The following is a common problem that lends itself to simulation. It has a sur-prising result that can help students appreciate the need for large samples.

......

Two hospitals keep records about the gender of the babies born at their facilities each day. Hospital Big is a large urban hospital where 25 babies are born each day on average. Hospital Small is a small regional facility where only 5 babies are born on most days. On any given day, which of the follow-ing statements is more likely to be true? Or are the two events equally likely?

1. At least 20 out of 25 babies born in Hospital Big are female.
2. At least 4 out of 5 babies born in Hospital Small are female.

......

The following is a description of how a simulation might be devised to solve the hospital–babies problem.

Key components and assumptions: More babies are born in Hospital Big than Hospi-tal Small. The assumption is that the event of having a female baby and the event of having a male baby is equally likely ($\frac{1}{2}$ for each).

Random device: In this situation, we need to use a random device that has two possible outcomes, so we could use a coin or a two-colored chip.

Define a trial: A trial consists of a set of 25 tosses (Hospital Big) and a second set of 5 tosses (Hospital Small).

Conduct a large number of trials: Pool the data generated by the class to increase the size of the data set.

Use the data to draw conclusions: Unexpected or unusual outcomes occur more often with smaller sets of data because they do not necessarily reflect the char-acteristics of the larger population. Larger samples are more reflective of the larger population, so the results of the simulation with the larger data set should be closer to $\frac{1}{2}$ for boy babies and $\frac{1}{2}$ for girl babies.

Here are a few more examples of problems that can be solved by simulation and are easy enough to be tackled by middle school students.

......

In a true-or-false test, what is the probability of getting 7 out of 10 ques-tions correct by guessing alone? (*Key component:* answering a question. *Assumption:* Chance of getting it correct is $\frac{1}{2}$.) What if the test were multiple choice with 4 choices?

......

......

In a group of five people, what is the chance that two were born in the same month? (*Key component:* month of birth. *Assumption:* All 12 months are equally likely.)

......

Casey's batting average is .350. What is the chance he will go hitless in a complete nine-inning game? (*Key component:* getting a hit. *Assumptions:* Probability of a hit for each at-bat is .35. Casey will get to bat four times in the average game.)

Krunch-a-Munch cereal packs one of five games in each box. About how many boxes should you expect to buy before you get a complete set? (*Key component:* getting one game. *Assumption:* Each game has a $\frac{1}{5}$ chance. *Trial:* Use a $\frac{1}{5}$ random device repeatedly until all five outcomes appear; the average length of a trial answers the question.) What is the chance of getting a set in eight or fewer boxes?

The conditions of the problem suggest the random devices that may be used in the simulation. Thinking of random devices that generate probabilities of $\frac{1}{2}$ (coin, two-colored chip) and $\frac{1}{6}$ (die) are relatively easier than identifying random devices that generate other probabilities. Spinners can be flexibly divided into the needed areas to generate appropriate probabilities. Dice can also be used flexibly. For instance, suppose you need a random device that generates probabilities of $\frac{2}{3}$ and $\frac{1}{3}$. You can use the values 1, 2, 3, 4 on the dice to represent the probabilities of $\frac{2}{3}$ and the values 5, 6 to represent the probabilities of $\frac{1}{3}$.

There are dice available from educational distributors with 4, 8, 12, and 20 sides that can be used for various probability activities. However, asking students to create new devices or use existing ones in different ways helps them reflect about how probabilities result from the different random generators.

Assessment Note

It is useful to have a list of the conceptual ideas that are involved in learning about probability so that as you assess your students, you will not simply focus on the procedural skills. Nearly every idea we have discussed in this chapter is explored via a problem-based task that involves an analysis of an experiment. These tasks, or ones very similar to them, can be used as assessment activities. Instead of discussions with the class, have students write explanations to questions you include with the activity. Here is a list of the main ideas we have discussed in this chapter:

- *The distinction between theoretical and experimental probability.* Students can write about the results that occur in an experiment with, say, 50 or 100 trials and discuss the relationship of the relative frequency of an event to the true probability. What do you do if the theoretical probability cannot be determined? Ask for examples.
- *The law of large numbers.* Have students write about the results of an experiment in the short run and in the long run. Why are the relative frequencies usually different? Which results are most reliable?

- *Sample spaces for independent and dependent events*. Rather than have students simply give definitions of these two types of two-stage experiments, have students describe the sample space for experiments. Do they utilize the dependency of events if applicable? Do they use effectively a matrix, tree diagram, or area model? Which do they select to determine the sample spaces and probabilities? Do they use the models with understanding?

- *Simulations*. The most effective assessment is simply to have a student construct an assessment plan for a given simulation. It is not necessary for the student to actually conduct the simulation if there is not time; rather, ask for written explanations for each decision made in designing the simulation. Within this task there are numerous ideas about probability that very likely will illustrate understanding of many of the concepts listed here.

EXPANDED LESSON

Fair or Unfair?

Based on Activity 12.1, p. 335

GRADE LEVEL: Sixth to eighth grades.

MATHEMATICS GOALS

- To develop the notion that probability is more about predictions over the long term than predictions of individual events.
- To develop the need to analyze a situation and consider its theoretical probability.
- To compare experimental probability and theoretical probability.

THINKING ABOUT THE STUDENTS

Students have experience in identifying events that lie on the continuum between impossible and certain, and they understand that a number between 0 and 1 can indicate the chance that a given event will occur.

MATERIALS AND PREPARATION

- Provide each group of three students a pair of like coins, such as 2 pennies or 2 nickels. Two-color plastic counters are another possible choice.

lesson

BEFORE

Begin with a simpler version of the task:

- Ask students what they think "fair" means. As you listen to students, write their ideas on the board. Some students may think it means that everyone should win an equal number of times. Other students are a bit more egocentric and believe that fair means that they will win. The definition that you want to steer them toward is that *fair* means that no one player has an advantage over anyone else to win.
- Have students consider a game in which player A gets 1 point if a tossed coin results in a head and player B gets 1 point if the coin toss results in a tail. In other words, does player A or player B have an unfair advantage over the other one? Why or why not? Use this simple game to further discuss the idea of a fair game.

The Task

- In groups of three, play the coin toss game described here at least two or three times and decide if the game is fair or not and why.

> ### The Coin Toss Game
> *Three players take turns tossing two like coins. On each toss, points are assigned as follows:*
> > *Player A gets a point if the result is two heads.*
> > *Player B gets a point if the result is two tails.*
> > *Player C gets a point if the result is one head and one tail.*
>
> *The game is over after 20 tosses. The player with the most points wins.*

Establish Expectations

- Students should play the game at least two times. After the first game, students are to stop and discuss if they think the game is fair and make predictions about who will win the next game.
- After playing twice, the group should decide if they think the game is fair and try to decide why they think as they do. If they are clear on an argument and there is time, they can play a third time.

DURING

- Be sure students are playing and scoring the game correctly.
- After students have played two games, be sure that they are engaging in a discussion concerning their ideas about the fairness of the game.

- Some students may be able to analyze the situation without playing the game. Others will need to play the game several times and reflect on why they are getting results that contradict their predictions.

AFTER

- When groups have played the game several times and had group discussions, conduct a whole-class discussion about the fairness of the game. You may want to pool the class data to see how many points players A, B, and C received. This pooled data should significantly favor player C (one head and one tail).
- Challenge students to make their argument about the fairness of the game based on reasons other than their data. Do not evaluate students' ideas but allow them to comment and question each other's ideas.
- There are essentially two likely arguments, one that is correct and one that is flawed. The correct explanation is: There is only one way for two heads to occur and one way for two tails to occur, but there are two ways for a head and a tail to occur—either the first coin is heads and the second coin is tails, or vice versa. That makes a total of four possible outcomes, not three. Getting a head and a tail happens in two out of the four possible outcomes. The flawed explanation is: There are three possible outcomes with one way for each to happen.
- Many students are likely to struggle with the notion that there are two different ways to generate a tail and a head. If students have this difficulty, have groups trade one coin with another group so that each group has two different coins. Alternatively, they can mark one of their coins. Now have the groups play the game again, recording results separately for each coin. For example, a toss may result in "head on penny, head on nickel," "head on penny, tail on nickel," "tail on penny, head on nickel," or "tail on penny, tail on nickel." Have students share their findings. The distinction between the two middle results can help students understand why player C has an unfair advantage.

ASSESSMENT NOTES

- Are students able to analyze the situation without playing the game? Or do they need to play the game several times, and possibly use different coins, to help them understand why the game is not fair?
- Are there any students who still think that the result of the next toss is somehow dependent on previous tosses?

- If students have difficulty grasping the idea that a tail on the first coin and a head on the second coin is different from a head on the first coin and a tail on the other, have them engage in more activities that have this same feature. For example, rolling two six-sided dice, have students find the sums. They are to determine if it is more likely to get an odd sum or an even sum. It will be helpful to have students use one white die and one colored die to help them distinguish between different outcomes.
- This activity involves another concept that is explored later in the chapter: The Coin Toss Game is an example

of a two-stage event in which the combined outcomes are independent. Other multi-stage events are suggested in Activity 12.5, "Multistage Events."

next steps

- A possible next step is to examine events in which it is not possible to determine the probability. "Cup Toss" (Activity 12.2) is one such event. These and similar activities also lead to the discussion of long-term results versus short-term results—the law of large numbers.

EXPANDED LESSON

APPENDIX A

PRINCIPLES AND STANDARDS FOR SCHOOL MATHEMATICS

Content Standards and Grade Level Expectations

NUMBER AND OPERATIONS

STANDARD

Instructional programs from prekindergarten through grade 12 should enable all students to—

Understand numbers, ways of representing numbers, relationships among numbers, and number systems

Understand meanings of operations and how they relate to one another

Compute fluently and make reasonable estimates

PRE-K–2

Expectations

In prekindergarten through grade 2 all students should—

- count with understanding and recognize "how many" in sets of objects;
- use multiple models to develop initial understandings of place value and the base-ten number system;
- develop understanding of the relative position and magnitude of whole numbers and of ordinal and cardinal numbers and their connections;
- develop a sense of whole numbers and represent and use them in flexible ways, including relating, composing, and decomposing numbers;
- connect number words and numerals to the quantities they represent, using various physical models and representations;
- understand and represent commonly used fractions, such as $\frac{1}{4}$, $\frac{1}{3}$, and $\frac{1}{2}$.

- understand various meanings of addition and subtraction of whole numbers and the relationship between the two operations;
- understand the effects of adding and subtracting whole numbers;
- understand situations that entail multiplication and division, such as equal groupings of objects and sharing equally.

- develop and use strategies for whole-number computations, with a focus on addition and subtraction;
- develop fluency with basic number combinations for addition and subtraction;
- use a variety of methods and tools to compute, including objects, mental computation, estimation, paper and pencil, and calculators.

GRADES 3–5

Expectations

In grades 3–5 all students should—

- understand the place-value structure of the base-ten number system and be able to represent and compare whole numbers and decimals;
- recognize equivalent representations for the same number and generate them by decomposing and composing numbers;
- develop understanding of fractions as parts of unit wholes, as parts of a collection, as locations on number lines, and as divisions of whole numbers;
- use models, benchmarks, and equivalent forms to judge the size of fractions;
- recognize and generate equivalent forms of commonly used fractions, decimals, and percents;
- explore numbers less than 0 by extending the number line and through familiar applications;
- describe classes of numbers according to characteristics such as the nature of their factors.

- understand various meanings of multiplication and division;
- understand the effects of multiplying and dividing whole numbers;
- identify and use relationships between operations, such as division as the inverse of multiplication, to solve problems;
- understand and use properties of operations, such as the distributivity of multiplication over addition.

- develop fluency with basic number combinations for multiplication and division and use these combinations to mentally compute related problems, such as 30×50;
- develop fluency in adding, subtracting, multiplying, and dividing whole numbers;
- develop and use strategies to estimate the results of whole-number computations and to judge the reasonableness of such results;
- develop and use strategies to estimate computations involving fractions and decimals in situations relevant to students' experience;
- use visual models, benchmarks, and equivalent forms to add and subtract commonly used fractions and decimals;
- select appropriate methods and tools for computing with whole numbers from among mental computation, estimation, calculators, and paper and pencil according to the context and nature of the computation and use the selected method or tool.

NUMBER AND OPERATIONS

STANDARD

Instructional programs from prekindergarten through grade 12 should enable all students to—

Understand numbers, ways of representing numbers, relationships among numbers, and number systems

GRADES 6–8

Expectations

In grades 6–8 all students should—

- work flexibly with fractions, decimals, and percents to solve problems;
- compare and order fractions, decimals, and percents efficiently and find their approximate locations on a number line;
- develop meaning for percents greater than 100 and less than 1;
- understand and use ratios and proportions to represent quantitative relationships;
- develop an understanding of large numbers and recognize and appropriately use exponential, scientific, and calculator notation;
- use factors, multiples, prime factorization, and relatively prime numbers to solve problems;
- develop meaning for integers and represent and compare quantities with them.

GRADES 9–12

Expectations

In grades 9–12 all students should—

- develop a deeper understanding of very large and very small numbers and of various representations of them;
- compare and contrast the properties of numbers and number systems, including the rational and real numbers, and understand complex numbers as solutions to quadratic equations that do not have real solutions;
- understand vectors and matrices as systems that have some of the properties of the real-number system;
- use number-theory arguments to justify relationships involving whole numbers.

Understand meanings of operations and how they relate to one another

- understand the meaning and effects of arithmetic operations with fractions, decimals, and integers;
- use the associative and commutative properties of addition and multiplication and the distributive property of multiplication over addition to simplify computations with integers, fractions, and decimals;
- understand and use the inverse relationships of addition and subtraction, multiplication and division, and squaring and finding square roots to simplify computations and solve problems.

- judge the effects of such operations as multiplication, division, and computing powers and roots on the magnitudes of quantities;
- develop an understanding of properties of, and representations for, the addition and multiplication of vectors and matrices;
- develop an understanding of permutations and combinations as counting techniques.

Compute fluently and make reasonable estimates

- select appropriate methods and tools for computing with fractions and decimals from among mental computation, estimation, calculators or computers, and paper and pencil, depending on the situation, and apply the selected methods;
- develop and analyze algorithms for computing with fractions, decimals, and integers and develop fluency in their use;
- develop and use strategies to estimate the results of rational-number computations and judge the reasonableness of the results;
- develop, analyze, and explain methods for solving problems involving proportions, such as scaling and finding equivalent ratios.

- develop fluency in operations with real numbers, vectors, and matrices, using mental computation or paper-and-pencil calculations for simple cases and technology for more-complicated cases;
- judge the reasonableness of numerical computations and their results.

ALGEBRA

STANDARD

Instructional programs from prekindergarten through grade 12 should enable all students to—

Understand patterns, relations, and functions

Represent and analyze mathematical situations and structures using algebraic symbols

Use mathematical models to represent and understand quantitative relationships

Analyze change in various contexts

PRE-K–2

Expectations

In prekindergarten through grade 2 all students should—

- sort, classify, and order objects by size, number, and other properties;
- recognize, describe, and extend patterns such as sequences of sounds and shapes or simple numeric patterns and translate from one representation to another;
- analyze how both repeating and growing patterns are generated.

- illustrate general principles and properties of operations, such as commutativity, using specific numbers;
- use concrete, pictorial, and verbal representations to develop an understanding of invented and conventional symbolic notations.

- model situations that involve the addition and subtraction of whole numbers, using objects, pictures, and symbols.

- describe qualitative change, such as a student's growing taller;
- describe quantitative change, such as a student's growing two inches in one year.

GRADES 3–5

Expectations

In grades 3–5 all students should—

- describe, extend, and make generalizations about geometric and numeric patterns;
- represent and analyze patterns and functions, using words, tables, and graphs.

- identify such properties as commutativity, associativity, and distributivity and use them to compute with whole numbers;
- represent the idea of a variable as an unknown quantity using a letter or a symbol;
- express mathematical relationships using equations.

- model problem situations with objects and use representations such as graphs, tables, and equations to draw conclusions.

- investigate how a change in one variable relates to a change in a second variable;
- identify and describe situations with constant or varying rates of change and compare them.

ALGEBRA

STANDARD

Instructional programs from prekindergarten through grade 12 should enable all students to—

Understand patterns, relations, and functions

Represent and analyze mathematical situations and structures using algebraic symbols

Use mathematical models to represent and understand quantitative relationships

Analyze change in various contexts

GRADES 6–8

Expectations

In grades 6–8 all students should—

- represent, analyze, and generalize a variety of patterns with tables, graphs, words, and, when possible, symbolic rules;
- relate and compare different forms of representation for a relationship;
- identify functions as linear or nonlinear and contrast their properties from tables, graphs, or equations.

- develop an initial conceptual understanding of different uses of variables;
- explore relationships between symbolic expressions and graphs of lines, paying particular attention to the meaning of intercept and slope;
- use symbolic algebra to represent situations and to solve problems, especially those that involve linear relationships;
- recognize and generate equivalent forms for simple algebraic expressions and solve linear equations.

- model and solve contextualized problems using various representations, such as graphs, tables, and equations.

- use graphs to analyze the nature of changes in quantities in linear relationships.

GRADES 9–12

Expectations

In grades 9–12 all students should—

- generalize patterns using explicitly defined and recursively defined functions;
- understand relations and functions and select, convert flexibly among, and use various representations for them;
- analyze functions of one variable by investigating rates of change, intercepts, zeros, asymptotes, and local and global behavior;
- understand and perform transformations such as arithmetically combining, composing, and inverting commonly used functions, using technology to perform such operations on more-complicated symbolic expressions;
- understand and compare the properties of classes of functions, including exponential, polynomial, rational, logarithmic, and periodic functions;
- interpret representations of functions of two variables.

- understand the meaning of equivalent forms of expressions, equations, inequalities, and relations;
- write equivalent forms of equations, inequalities, and systems of equations and solve them with fluency—mentally or with paper and pencil in simple cases and using technology in all cases;
- use symbolic algebra to represent and explain mathematical relationships;
- use a variety of symbolic representations, including recursive and parametric equations, for functions and relations;
- judge the meaning, utility, and reasonableness of the results of symbol manipulations, including those carried out by technology.

- identify essential quantitative relationships in a situation and determine the class or classes of functions that might model the relationships;
- use symbolic expressions, including iterative and recursive forms, to represent relationships arising from various contexts;
- draw reasonable conclusions about a situation being modeled.

- approximate and interpret rates of change from graphical and numerical data.

GEOMETRY

STANDARD

Instructional programs from prekindergarten through grade 12 should enable all students to—

Analyze characteristics and properties of two- and three-dimensional geometric shapes and develop mathematical arguments about geometric relationships

Specify locations and describe spatial relationships using coordinate geometry and other representational systems

Apply transformations and use symmetry to analyze mathematical situations

Use visualization, spatial reasoning, and geometric modeling to solve problems

PRE-K–2

Expectations

In prekindergarten through grade 2 all students should—

- recognize, name, build, draw, compare, and sort two- and three-dimensional shapes;
- describe attributes and parts of two- and three-dimensional shapes;
- investigate and predict the results of putting together and taking apart two- and three-dimensional shapes.

- describe, name, and interpret relative positions in space and apply ideas about relative position;
- describe, name, and interpret direction and distance in navigating space and apply ideas about direction and distance;
- find and name locations with simple relationships such as "near to" and in coordinate systems such as maps.

- recognize and apply slides, flips, and turns;
- recognize and create shapes that have symmetry.

- create mental images of geometric shapes using spatial memory and spatial visualization;
- recognize and represent shapes from different perspectives;
- relate ideas in geometry to ideas in number and measurement;
- recognize geometric shapes and structures in the environment and specify their location.

GRADES 3–5

Expectations

In grades 3–5 all students should—

- identify, compare, and analyze attributes of two- and three-dimensional shapes and develop vocabulary to describe the attributes;
- classify two- and three-dimensional shapes according to their properties and develop definitions of classes of shapes such as triangles and pyramids;
- investigate, describe, and reason about the results of subdividing, combining, and transforming shapes;
- explore congruence and similarity;
- make and test conjectures about geometric properties and relationships and develop logical arguments to justify conclusions.

- describe location and movement using common language and geometric vocabulary;
- make and use coordinate systems to specify locations and to describe paths;
- find the distance between points along horizontal and vertical lines of a coordinate system.

- predict and describe the results of sliding, flipping, and turning two-dimensional shapes;
- describe a motion or a series of motions that will show that two shapes are congruent;
- identify and describe line and rotational symmetry in two- and three-dimensional shapes and designs.

- build and draw geometric objects;
- create and describe mental images of objects, patterns, and paths;
- identify and build a three-dimensional object from two-dimensional representations of that object;
- identify and build a two-dimensional representation of a three-dimensional object;
- use geometric models to solve problems in other areas of mathematics, such as number and measurement;
- recognize geometric ideas and relationships and apply them to other disciplines and to problems that arise in the classroom or in everyday life.

GEOMETRY

STANDARD

Instructional programs from prekindergarten through grade 12 should enable all students to—

Analyze characteristics and properties of two- and three-dimensional geometric shapes and develop mathematical arguments about geometric relationships

Specify locations and describe spatial relationships using coordinate geometry and other representational systems

Apply transformations and use symmetry to analyze mathematical situations

Use visualization, spatial reasoning, and geometric modeling to solve problems

GRADES 6–8

Expectations

In grades 6–8 all students should—

- precisely describe, classify, and understand relationships among types of two- and three-dimensional objects using their defining properties;
- understand relationships among the angles, side lengths, perimeters, areas, and volumes of similar objects;
- create and critique inductive and deductive arguments concerning geometric ideas and relationships, such as congruence, similarity, and the Pythagorean relationship.

- use coordinate geometry to represent and examine the properties of geometric shapes;
- use coordinate geometry to examine special geometric shapes, such as regular polygons or those with pairs of parallel or perpendicular sides.

- describe sizes, positions, and orientations of shapes under informal transformations such as flips, turns, slides, and scaling;
- examine the congruence, similarity, and line or rotational symmetry of objects using transformations.

- draw geometric objects with specified properties, such as side lengths or angle measures;
- use two-dimensional representations of three-dimensional objects to visualize and solve problems such as those involving surface area and volume;
- use visual tools such as networks to represent and solve problems;
- use geometric models to represent and explain numerical and algebraic relationships;
- recognize and apply geometric ideas and relationships in areas outside the mathematics classroom, such as art, science, and everyday life.

GRADES 9–12

Expectations

In grades 9–12 all students should—

- analyze properties and determine attributes of two- and three-dimensional objects;
- explore relationships (including congruence and similarity) among classes of two- and three-dimensional geometric objects, make and test conjectures about them, and solve problems involving them;
- establish the validity of geometric conjectures using deduction, prove theorems, and critique arguments made by others;
- use trigonometric relationships to determine lengths and angle measures.

- use Cartesian coordinates and other coordinate systems, such as navigational, polar, or spherical systems, to analyze geometric situations;
- investigate conjectures and solve problems involving two- and three-dimensional objects represented with Cartesian coordinates.

- understand and represent translations, reflections, rotations, and dilations of objects in the plane by using sketches, coordinates, vectors, function notation, and matrices;
- use various representations to help understand the effects of simple transformations and their compositions.

- draw and construct representations of two- and three-dimensional geometric objects using a variety of tools;
- visualize three-dimensional objects from different perspectives and analyze their cross sections;
- use vertex-edge graphs to model and solve problems;
- use geometric models to gain insights into, and answer questions in, other areas of mathematics;
- use geometric ideas to solve problems in, and gain insights into, other disciplines and other areas of interest such as art and architecture.

MEASUREMENT

STANDARD

Instructional programs from prekindergarten through grade 12 should enable all students to—

Understand measurable attributes of objects and the units, systems, and processes of measurement

Apply appropriate techniques, tools, and formulas to determine measurements

PRE-K–2

Expectations

In prekindergarten through grade 2 all students should—

- recognize the attributes of length, volume, weight, area, and time;
- compare and order objects according to these attributes;
- understand how to measure using nonstandard and standard units;
- select an appropriate unit and tool for the attribute being measured.

- measure with multiple copies of units of the same size, such as paper clips laid end to end;
- use repetition of a single unit to measure something larger than the unit, for instance, measuring the length of a room with a single meterstick;
- use tools to measure;
- develop common referents for measures to make comparisons and estimates.

GRADES 3–5

Expectations

In grades 3–5 all students should—

- understand such attributes as length, area, weight, volume, and size of angle and select the appropriate type of unit for measuring each attribute;
- understand the need for measuring with standard units and become familiar with standard units in the customary and metric systems;
- carry out simple unit conversions, such as from centimeters to meters, within a system of measurement;
- understand that measurements are approximations and understand how differences in units affect precision;
- explore what happens to measurements of a two-dimensional shape such as its perimeter and area when the shape is changed in some way.

- develop strategies for estimating the perimeters, areas, and volumes of irregular shapes;
- select and apply appropriate standard units and tools to measure length, area, volume, weight, time, temperature, and the size of angles;
- select and use benchmarks to estimate measurements;
- develop, understand, and use formulas to find the area of rectangles and related triangles and parallelograms;
- develop strategies to determine the surface areas and volumes of rectangular solids.

MEASUREMENT

STANDARD

Instructional programs from prekindergarten through grade 12 should enable all students to—

Understand measurable attributes of objects and the units, systems, and processes of measurement

Apply appropriate techniques, tools, and formulas to determine measurements

GRADES 6–8

Expectations

In grades 6–8 all students should—

- understand both metric and customary systems of measurement;
- understand relationships among units and convert from one unit to another within the same system;
- understand, select, and use units of appropriate size and type to measure angles, perimeter, area, surface area, and volume.

- use common benchmarks to select appropriate methods for estimating measurements;
- select and apply techniques and tools to accurately find length, area, volume, and angle measures to appropriate levels of precision;
- develop and use formulas to determine the circumference of circles and the area of triangles, parallelograms, trapezoids, and circles and develop strategies to find the area of more-complex shapes;
- develop strategies to determine the surface area and volume of selected prisms, pyramids, and cylinders;
- solve problems involving scale factors, using ratio and proportion;
- solve simple problems involving rates and derived measurements for such attributes as velocity and density.

GRADES 9–12

Expectations

In grades 9–12 all students should—

- make decisions about units and scales that are appropriate for problem situations involving measurement.

- analyze precision, accuracy, and approximate error in measurement situations;
- understand and use formulas for the area, surface area, and volume of geometric figures, including cones, spheres, and cylinders;
- apply informal concepts of successive approximation, upper and lower bounds, and limit in measurement situations;
- use unit analysis to check measurement computations.

DATA ANALYSIS AND PROBABILITY

STANDARD

Instructional programs from prekindergarten through grade 12 should enable all students to—

Formulate questions that can be addressed with data and collect, organize, and display relevant data to answer them

Select and use appropriate statistical methods to analyze data

Develop and evaluate inferences and predictions that are based on data

Understand and apply basic concepts of probability

PRE-K–2

Expectations

In prekindergarten through grade 2 all students should—

- pose questions and gather data about themselves and their surroundings;
- sort and classify objects according to their attributes and organize data about the objects;
- represent data using concrete objects, pictures, and graphs.

- describe parts of the data and the set of data as a whole to determine what the data show.

- discuss events related to students' experiences as likely or unlikely.

GRADES 3–5

Expectations

In grades 3–5 all students should—

- design investigations to address a question and consider how data-collection methods affect the nature of the data set;
- collect data using observations, surveys, and experiments;
- represent data using tables and graphs such as line plots, bar graphs, and line graphs;
- recognize the differences in representing categorical and numerical data.

- describe the shape and important features of a set of data and compare related data sets, with an emphasis on how the data are distributed;
- use measures of center, focusing on the median, and understand what each does and does not indicate about the data set;
- compare different representations of the same data and evaluate how well each representation shows important aspects of the data.

- propose and justify conclusions and predictions that are based on data and design studies to further investigate the conclusions or predictions.

- describe events as likely or unlikely and discuss the degree of likelihood using such words as certain, equally likely, and impossible;
- predict the probability of outcomes of simple experiments and test the predictions;
- understand that the measure of the likelihood of an event can be represented by a number from 0 to 1.

DATA ANALYSIS AND PROBABILITY

STANDARD

Instructional programs from prekindergarten through grade 12 should enable all students to—

Formulate questions that can be addressed with data and collect, organize, and display relevant data to answer them

Select and use appropriate statistical methods to analyze data

Develop and evaluate inferences and predictions that are based on data

Understand and apply basic concepts of probability

GRADES 6–8

Expectations

In grades 6–8 all students should—

- formulate questions, design studies, and collect data about a characteristic shared by two populations or different characteristics within one population;
- select, create, and use appropriate graphical representations of data, including histograms, box plots, and scatterplots.

- find, use, and interpret measures of center and spread, including mean and interquartile range;
- discuss and understand the correspondence between data sets and their graphical representations, especially histograms, stem-and-leaf plots, box plots, and scatterplots.

- use observations about differences between two or more samples to make conjectures about the populations from which the samples were taken;
- make conjectures about possible relationships between two characteristics of a sample on the basis of scatterplots of the data and approximate lines of fit;
- use conjectures to formulate new questions and plan new studies to answer them.

- understand and use appropriate terminology to describe complementary and mutually exclusive events;
- use proportionality and a basic understanding of probability to make and test conjectures about the results of experiments and simulations;
- compute probabilities for simple compound events, using such methods as organized lists, tree diagrams, and area models.

GRADES 9–12

Expectations

In grades 9–12 all students should—

- understand the differences among various kinds of studies and which types of inferences can legitimately be drawn from each;
- know the characteristics of well-designed studies, including the role of randomization in surveys and experiments;
- understand the meaning of measurement data and categorical data, of univariate and bivariate data, and of the term variable;
- understand histograms, parallel box plots, and scatterplots and use them to display data;
- compute basic statistics and understand the distinction between a statistic and a parameter.

- for univariate measurement data, be able to display the distribution, describe its shape, and select and calculate summary statistics;
- for bivariate measurement data, be able to display a scatterplot, describe its shape, and determine regression coefficients, regression equations, and correlation coefficients using technological tools;
- display and discuss bivariate data where at least one variable is categorical;
- recognize how linear transformations of univariate data affect shape, center, and spread;
- identify trends in bivariate data and find functions that model the data or transform the data so that they can be modeled.

- use simulations to explore the variability of sample statistics from a known population and to construct sampling distributions;
- understand how sample statistics reflect the values of population parameters and use sampling distributions as the basis for informal inference;
- evaluate published reports that are based on data by examining the design of the study, the appropriateness of the data analysis, and the validity of conclusions;
- understand how basic statistical techniques are used to monitor process characteristics in the workplace.

- understand the concepts of sample space and probability distribution and construct sample spaces and distributions in simple cases;
- use simulations to construct empirical probability distributions;
- compute and interpret the expected value of random variables in simple cases;
- understand the concepts of conditional probability and independent events;
- understand how to compute the probability of a compound event.

APPENDIX B

A GUIDE TO THE BLACKLINE MASTERS

This appendix contains thumbnails of all of the Blackline Masters that are referenced throughout the book. Those introduced in the Expanded Lessons appear at the end and are numbered separately. Go to the companion website at www.ablongman. com/vandewalleseries to download the full-sized Blackline Masters.

Tips for the Use of the Blackline Masters

When a Blackline Master is to be used either as a workmat for students or to be cut apart into smaller pieces, the best advice is to duplicate the master on card stock. Card stock (also known as index stock) is heavy paper that comes in a variety of colors and can be found at copy or office supply stores.

With materials that require cutting into smaller pieces, we suggest that you laminate the card stock before you cut out the pieces. This will preserve the materials for several years and save valuable time in the future. For the Assorted Shapes (BLMs 12–18), make each set of seven pages a different color. Otherwise, it is very difficult to tell to which set a stray shape belongs.

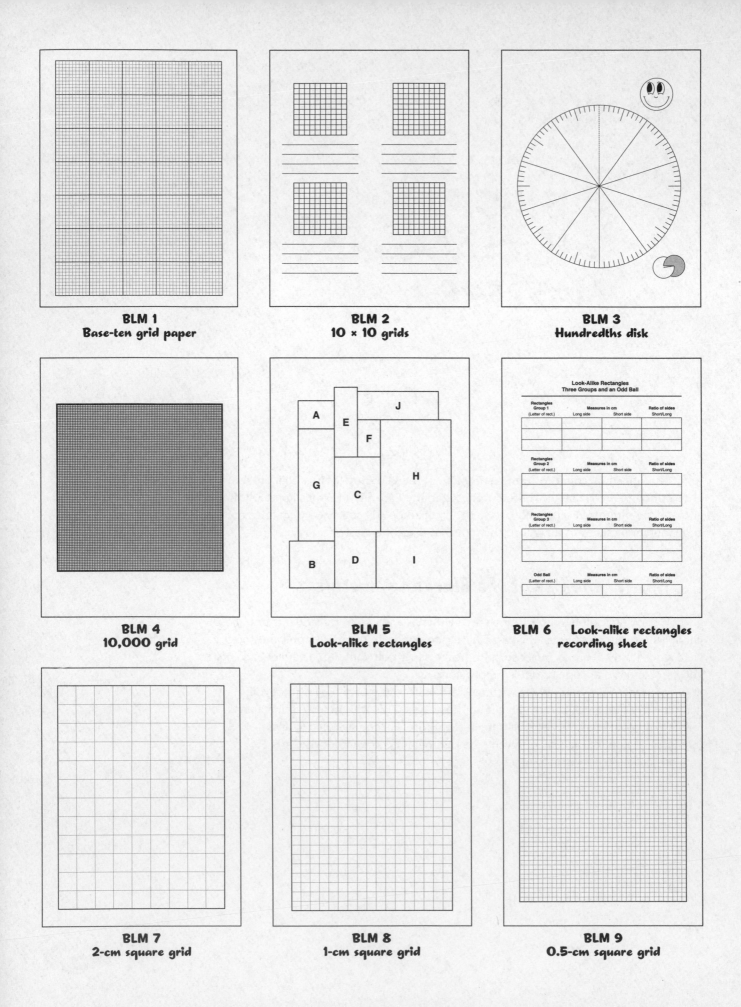

BLM 1
Base-ten grid paper

BLM 2
10 × 10 grids

BLM 3
Hundredths disk

BLM 4
10,000 grid

BLM 5
Look-alike rectangles

BLM 6   Look-alike rectangles recording sheet

BLM 7
2-cm square grid

BLM 8
1-cm square grid

BLM 9
0.5-cm square grid

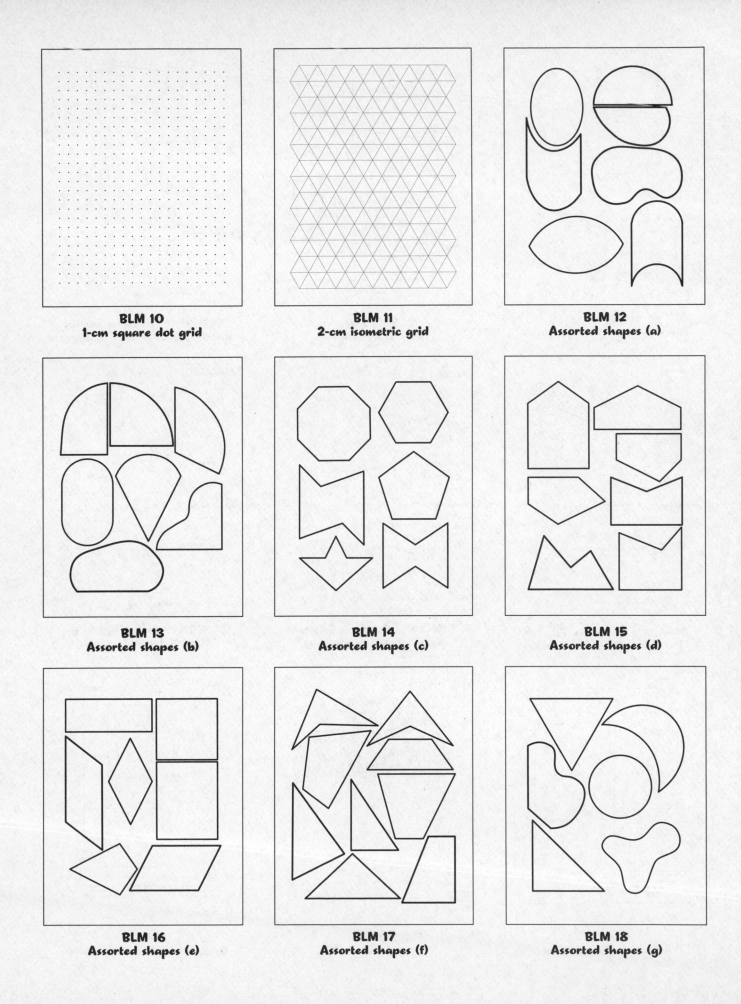

BLM 10
1-cm square dot grid

BLM 11
2-cm isometric grid

BLM 12
Assorted shapes (a)

BLM 13
Assorted shapes (b)

BLM 14
Assorted shapes (c)

BLM 15
Assorted shapes (d)

BLM 16
Assorted shapes (e)

BLM 17
Assorted shapes (f)

BLM 18
Assorted shapes (g)

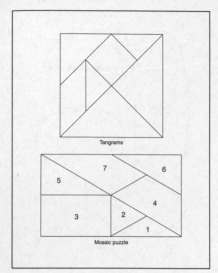

Tangrams

Mosaic puzzle

BLM 19
Tangrams and Mosaic Puzzle

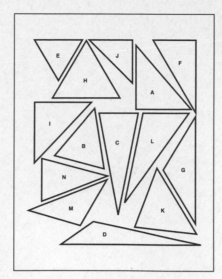

BLM 20
Assorted triangles

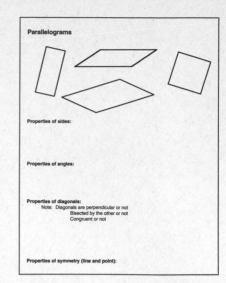

Parallelograms

Properties of sides:

Properties of angles:

Properties of diagonals:
Note: Diagonals are perpendicular or not
Bisected by the other or not
Congruent or not

Properties of symmetry (line and point):

BLM 21   Property lists for
quadrilaterals (parallelograms)

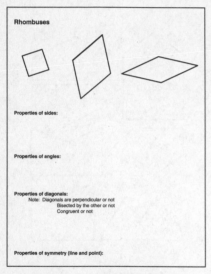

Rhombuses

Properties of sides:

Properties of angles:

Properties of diagonals:
Note: Diagonals are perpendicular or not
Bisected by the other or not
Congruent or not

Properties of symmetry (line and point):

BLM 22   Property lists for
quadrilaterals (rhombuses)

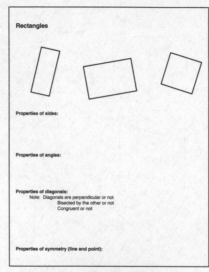

Rectangles

Properties of sides:

Properties of angles:

Properties of diagonals:
Note: Diagonals are perpendicular or not
Bisected by the other or not
Congruent or not

Properties of symmetry (line and point):

BLM 23   Property lists for
quadrilaterals (rectangles)

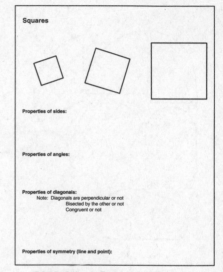

Squares

Properties of sides:

Properties of angles:

Properties of diagonals:
Note: Diagonals are perpendicular or not
Bisected by the other or not
Congruent or not

Properties of symmetry (line and point):

BLM 24   Property lists for
quadrilaterals (squares)

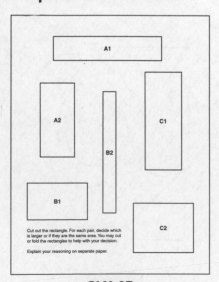

Cut out the rectangle. For each pair, decide which
is larger or if they are the same area. You may cut
or fold the rectangles to help with your decision.

Explain your reasoning on separate paper.

BLM 25
Rectangle Comparison

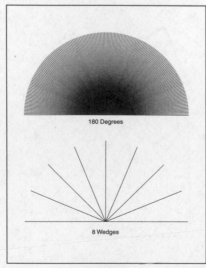

180 Degrees

8 Wedges

BLM 26
Degrees and wedges

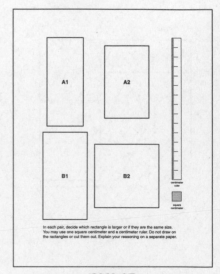

In each pair, decide which rectangle is larger or if they are the same size.
You may use one square centimeter and a centimeter ruler. Do not draw on
the rectangles or cut them out. Explain your reasoning on a separate paper.

BLM 27
Rectangle Comparison—Units

It's a Matter of Rates

1. Terry can run 4 laps in 12 minutes. Susan can run 3 laps in 9 minutes. Who is the faster runner?

2. Jack and Jill were picking strawberries at the Pick Your Own Berry Patch. Jack "sampled" 5 berries every 25 minutes. Jill ate 3 berries every 10 minutes. If they both pick at about the same speed, who will bring home more berries?

3. Some of the hens in Farmer Brown's chicken farm lay brown eggs and the others lay white eggs. Farmer Brown noticed that in the large hen house he collected about 4 brown eggs for every 10 white ones. In the smaller hen house the ratio of brown to white was 1 to 3. In which hen house do the hens lay more brown eggs?

4. The Talks-a-Lot Phone Company charges 70¢ for every 15 minutes. Reaching Out Phone Company charges $1.00 for 20 minutes. Which company is offering the cheaper rate?

BLM L-1

Name _____

Rectangles made with 36 tiles

Rectangle Dimensions	Area	Perimeter

BLM L-2

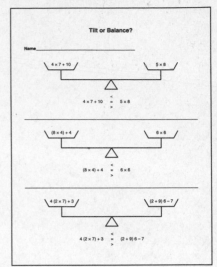

Tilt or Balance?

Name _____

$4 \times 7 + 10$ 5×8

$$4 \times 7 + 10 \quad \begin{array}{c} < \\ = \\ > \end{array} \quad 5 \times 8$$

$(8 \times 4) + 4$ 6×6

$$(8 \times 4) + 4 \quad \begin{array}{c} < \\ = \\ > \end{array} \quad 6 \times 6$$

$4 (2 \times 7) + 3$ $(2 + 9) 6 - 7$

$$4 (2 \times 7) + 3 \quad \begin{array}{c} < \\ = \\ > \end{array} \quad (2 + 9) 6 - 7$$

BLM L-3

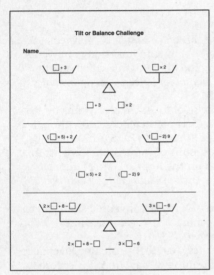

Tilt or Balance Challenge

Name _____

$\square + 3$ $\square \times 2$

$$\square + 3 \quad \rule{1cm}{0.4pt} \quad \square \times 2$$

$(\square \times 5) + 2$ $(\square - 2) 9$

$$(\square \times 5) + 2 \quad \rule{1cm}{0.4pt} \quad (\square - 2) 9$$

$2 \times \square + 8 - \square$ $3 \times \square - 6$

$$2 \times \square + 8 - \square \quad \rule{1cm}{0.4pt} \quad 3 \times \square - 6$$

BLM L-4

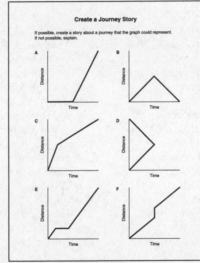

Create a Journey Story

If possible, create a story about a journey that the graph could represent. If not possible, explain.

A — Distance / Time
B — Distance / Time
C — Distance / Time
D — Distance / Time
E — Distance / Time
F — Distance / Time

BLM L-5

Toy Purchases

$8 $12 $3 $5 $7 $1

BLM L-6

Toying with Measures

Name _____

	Mean	Median	Mode
Original Set of 6			

Make predictions based on these changes. Give reasons for your predictions.

Add a $20 toy			
Reasons			
Return the $1 toy			
Reasons			
Get a free toy			
Reasons			
Buy a second $12 toy			
Reasons			
Your change:			
Reasons			

Calculate the actual statistics for each of the changes.

Add a $20 toy			
Return the $1 toy			
Get a free toy			
Buy a second $12 toy			
Your change:			

BLM L-7

REFERENCES

Backhouse, J., Haggarty, L., Pirie, S., & Stratton, J. (1992). *Improving the learning of mathematics.* Portsmouth, NH: Heinemann.

Ball, D. L. (1992). Magical hopes: Manipulatives and the reform of math education. *American Educator, 16*(2), 14–18, 46–47.

Battista, M. C. (1999). The mathematical miseducation of America's youth: Ignoring research and scientific study in education. *Phi Delta Kappan, 80,* 424–433.

Booth, L. R. (1988). Children's difficulties in beginning algebra. In A. F. Coxford (Ed.), *The ideas of algebra, K–12* (pp. 20–32). Reston, VA: National Council of Teachers of Mathematics.

Bresser, R. (1995). *Math and literature (grades 4–6).* White Plains, NY: Cuisenaire (distributor).

Brueningsen, C., Bower, B., Antinone, L., & Brueningsen, E. (1994). *Real-world math with the CBL system: 25 activities using the CBL and TI-82.* Dallas: Texas Instruments.

Burger, W. F. (1985). Geometry. *Arithmetic Teacher, 32*(6), 52–56.

Burns, M. (1999). *Making sense of mathematics: A look toward the twenty-first century.* Presentation at the annual meeting of the National Council of Teachers of Mathematics, San Francisco.

Campbell, P. B. (1995). Redefining the "girl problem in mathematics." In W. G. Secada, E. Fennema, & L. B. Adajian (Eds.), *New directions for equity in mathematics education* (pp. 225–241). New York: Cambridge University Press.

Campbell, P. F. (1996). Empowering children and teachers in the elementary mathematics classrooms of urban schools. *Urban Education, 30,* 449–475.

Campbell, P. F., Rowan, T. E., & Suarez, A. R. (1998). What criteria for student-invented algorithms? In L. J. Morrow (Ed.), *The teaching and learning of algorithms in school mathematics* (pp. 49–55). Reston, VA: National Council of Teachers of Mathematics.

Carpenter, T. P., Franke, M. L., Jacobs, V. R., Fennema, E., & Empson, S. B. (1998). A longitudinal study of invention and understanding in children's multidigit addition and subtraction. *Journal for Research in Mathematics Education, 29,* 3–20.

Carroll, W. M. (1996). Use of invented algorithms by second graders in a reform mathematics curriculum. *Journal of Mathematical Behaviour, 15,* 137–150.

Carroll, W. M. (1997). Results of third-grade students in a reform curriculum on the Illinois State Mathematics Test. *Journal for Research in Mathematics Education, 28,* 237–242.

Carroll, W. M., & Porter, D. (1997). Invented strategies can develop meaningful mathematical procedures. *Teaching Children Mathematics, 3,* 370–374.

Chalouh, L., & Herscovics, N. (1988). Teaching algebraic expressions in a meaningful way. In A. F. Coxford (Ed.), *The ideas of algebra, K–12* (pp. 33–42). Reston, VA: National Council of Teachers of Mathematics.

Chambers, D. (1996). Direct modeling and invented procedures: Building on students' informal strategies. *Teaching Children Mathematics, 3,* 92–95.

Clements, D. H., & Battista, M. T. (1990). Constructivist learning and teaching. *Arithmetic Teacher, 38*(1), 34–35.

Clements, D. H., & Battista, M. T. (1992). Geometry and spatial reasoning. In D. A. Grouws (Ed.), *Handbook of research on mathematics teaching and learning* (pp. 420–464). Old Tappan, NJ: Macmillan.

Cobb, P. (1996). Where is the mind? A coordination of sociocultural and cognitive constructivist perspectives. In C. T. Fosnot (Ed.), *Constructivism: Theory, perspectives, and practice* (pp. 34–52). New York: Teachers College Press.

Davis, R. B. (1986). *Learning mathematics: The cognitive science approach to mathematics education.* Norwood, NJ: Ablex.

De Villiers, M. D. (1999). *Rethinking proof with the Geometer's Sketchpad.* Emeryville, CA: Key Curriculum Press.

Fuys, D., Geddes, D., & Tischler, R. (1988). The van Hiele model of thinking in geometry among adolescents. *Journal for Research in Mathematics Education Monograph, 3.*

Garland, T. H. (1987). *Fascinating Fibonaccis: Mystery and magic in numbers.* Palo Alto, CA: Dale Seymour.

Gavin, M. K., Belkin, L. P., Spinelli, A. M., & St. Marie, J. (2001). *Navigating through geometry in grades 3–5.* Reston, VA: National Council of Teachers of Mathematics.

Geddes, D., & Fortunato, I. (1993). Geometry: Research and classroom activities. In D. T. Owens (Ed.), *Research ideas for the classroom: Middle grades mathematics* (pp. 199–222). New York: Macmillan.

Gnanadesikan, M., Schaeffer, R. L., & Swift, J. (1987). *The art and techniques of simulation: Quantitative literacy series.* Palo Alto, CA: Dale Seymour.

Hiebert, J. (1990). The role of routine procedures in the development of mathematical competence. In T. J. Cooney (Ed.), *Teaching and learning mathematics in the 1990s* (pp. 31–40). Reston, VA: National Council of Teachers of Mathematics.

Hiebert, J., & Carpenter, T. P. (1992). Learning and teaching with understanding. In D. A. Grouws (Ed.), *Handbook of research on mathematics teaching and learning* (pp. 65–97). Old Tappan, NJ: Macmillan.

Hiebert, J., Carpenter, T. P., Fennema, E., Fuson, K., Human, P., Murray, H., Olivier, A., & Wearne, D. (1996). Problem solving as a basis for reform in curriculum and instruction: The case of mathematics. *Educational Researcher, 25* (May), 12–21.

Hiebert, J., Carpenter, T. P., Fennema, E., Fuson, K., Wearne, D., Murray, H., Olivier, A., & Human, P. (1997). *Making sense: Teaching and learning mathematics with understanding.* Portsmouth, NH: Heinemann.

Hiebert, J., & Wearne, D. (1996). Instruction, understanding, and skill in multidigit addition and subtraction. *Cognition and Instruction, 14,* 251–283.

Hoffer, A. R. (1983). Van Hiele–based research. In R. A. Lesh & M. Landau (Eds.), *Acquisition of mathematics concepts and processes* (pp. 205–227). Orlando, FL: Academic Press.

Hoffer, A. R., & Hoffer, S. A. K. (1992). Ratios and proportional thinking. In T. R. Post (Ed.), *Teaching mathematics in grades K–8: Research-based methods* (2nd ed.) (pp. 303–330). Needham Heights, MA: Allyn & Bacon.

Huinker, D. (1998). Letting fraction algorithms emerge through problem solving. In L. J. Morrow (Ed.), *The teaching and learning of algorithms in school mathematics* (pp. 170–182). Reston, VA: National Council of Teachers of Mathematics.

Janvier, C. (Ed.). (1987). *Problems of representation in the teaching and learning of mathematics.* Hillsdale, NJ: Erlbaum.

Kamii, C. K. (1985). *Young children reinvent arithmetic.* New York: Teachers College Press.

Kamii, C. K. (1989). *Young children continue to reinvent arithmetic: 2nd grade.* New York: Teachers College Press.

Kamii, C. K., & Clark, F. B. (1995). Equivalent fractions: Their difficulty and educational implications. *The Journal of Mathematical Behavior, 14,* 365–378.

Kamii, C. K., & Dominick, A. (1997). To teach or not to teach the algorithms. *Journal of Mathematical Behavior, 16,* 51–62.

Kamii, C. K., & Dominick, A. (1998). The harmful effects of algorithms in grades 1–4. In L. J. Morrow (Ed.), *The teaching and learning of algorithms in school mathematics* (pp. 130–140). Reston, VA: National Council of Teachers of Mathematics.

Karplus, R., Pulos, S., & Stage, E. K. (1983). Proportional reasoning of early adolescents. In R. A. Lesh & M. Landau (Eds.), *Acquisition of mathematics concepts and processes* (pp. 45–90). Orlando, FL: Academic Press.

Kenney, P. A., & Kouba, V. L. (1997). What do students know about measurement? In P. A. Kenney & E. Silver (Eds.), *Results from the sixth mathematics assessment of the National Assessment of Educational Progress* (pp. 141–163). Reston, VA: National Council of Teachers of Mathematics.

Key Curriculum Press. (2001). *The geometer's sketchpad* (Version 4.0). Berkeley, CA: Key Curriculum Press.

Knuth, E., Choppin, J., Slaughter, M., & Sutherland, J. (2002). Mapping the conceptual terrain of middle school students' competencies in justifying and proving. *Proceedings of the Twenty-Fourth Annual Meeting of the Psychology of Mathematics Education, North American Chapter,* Vol. 4 (pp. 1693–1700). Athens, GA.

Kouba, V. L., Brown, C. A., Carpenter, T. P., Lindquist, M. M., Silver, E. A., & Swafford, J. O. (1988a). Results of the fourth NAEP assessment of mathematics: Number, operations, and word problems. *Arithmetic Teacher, 35*(8), 14–19.

Kouba, V. L., Zawojewski, J. S., & Strutchens, M. E. (1997). What do students know about numbers and operations. In P. A. Kenney & E. Silver (Eds.), *Results from the sixth mathematics assessment of the National Assessment of Educational Progress* (pp. 87–140). Reston, VA: National Council of Teachers of Mathematics.

Krause, E. (1987). *Taxi-cab geometry: An adventure in non-Euclidean geometry.* New York: Dover.

Kulm, G. (1994). *Mathematics and assessment: What works in the classroom.* San Francisco: Jossey-Bass.

Labinowicz, E. (1985). *Learning from children: New beginnings for teaching numerical thinking.* Menlo Park, CA: AWL Supplemental.

Labinowicz, E. (1987). Assessing for learning: The interview method. *Arithmetic Teacher, 35*(3), 22–24.

Lamon, S. J. (1993). Ratio and proportion: Connecting content and children's thinking. *Journal for Research in Mathematics Education, 24,* 41–61.

Lamon, S. J. (1999a). *More: In-depth discussion of the reasoning activities in "Teaching fractions and ratios for understanding."* Mahwah, NJ: Lawrence Erlbaum.

Lamon, S. J. (1999b). *Teaching fractions and ratios for understanding: Essential content knowledge and instructional strategies for teachers.* Mahwah, NJ: Lawrence Erlbaum.

Lamon, S. J. (2002). Part-whole comparisons with unitizing. In B. Litwiller (Ed.), *Making sense of fractions, ratios, and proportions* (pp. 79–86). Reston, VA: National Council of Teachers of Mathematics.

Lappan, G. (1998). Capturing patterns and functions: Variables and joint variation. In *The nature and role of algebra in the K–14 curriculum: Proceedings of national symposium* (pp. 57–59). Washington, DC: National Academy Press.

Learning Co. (1994). *TesselMania!* Mahwah, NJ: Author.

Lesh, R. A., Post, T. R., & Behr, M. J. (1987). Representations and translations among representations in mathematics learning and problem solving. In C. Janvier (Ed.), *Problems of representation in the teaching and learning of mathematics* (pp. 33–40). Hillsdale, NJ: Erlbaum.

Liedtke, W. (1988). Diagnosis in mathematics: The advantages of an interview. *Arithmetic Teacher, 36*(3), 26–29.

Lindquist, M. M. (1987). Problem solving with five easy pieces. In J. M. Hill (Ed.), *Geometry for grades K–6: Readings from the Arithmetic Teacher* (pp. 152–156). Reston, VA: National Council of Teachers of Mathematics.

Lo, J., & Watanabe, T. (1997). Developing ratio and proportion schemes: A story of a fifth grader. *Journal for Research in Mathematics Education, 28,* 216–236.

Lodholz, R. D. (1990). The transition from arithmetic to algebra. In E. L. Edwards, Jr. (Ed.), *Algebra for everyone* (pp. 24–33). Reston, VA: National Council of Teachers of Mathematics.

Ma, L. (1999). *Knowing and teaching elementary mathematics: Teachers' understanding of fundamental mathematics in China and the United States.* Mahwah, NJ: Lawrence Erlbaum.

Mack, N. K. (1995). Confounding whole-number and fraction concepts when building on informal knowledge. *Journal for Research in Mathematics Education, 26,* 422–441.

Martin, G., & Strutchens, M. E. (2000). Geometry and measurement. In E. A. Silver & P. A. Kenney (Eds.), *Results from the seventh mathematics assessment of the National Assessment of Educational Progress* (pp. 193–234). Reston, VA: National Council of Teachers of Mathematics.

Mathews, L. (1979). *Gator pie.* New York: Dodd, Mead.

McCoy, L. (1997). Algebra: Real-life investigations in a lab setting. *Mathematics Teaching in the Middle School, 2,* 220–224.

Mokros, J., Russell, S. J., & Economopoulos, K. (1995). *Beyond arithmetic: Changing mathematics in the elementary classroom.* Palo Alto, CA: Dale Seymour Publications.

National Council of Teachers of Mathematics. (1989). *Curriculum and evaluation standards for school mathematics.* Reston, VA: Author.

National Council of Teachers of Mathematics. (1995). *Assessment standards for school mathematics.* Reston, VA: Author.

National Council of Teachers of Mathematics. (2000). *Principles and standards for school mathematics.* Reston, VA: Author.

National Research Council. (2001). *Adding it up: Helping children learn mathematics.* J. Kilpatrick, J. Swafford, & B. Findell (Eds.). Mathematics Learning Study Committee, Center for Education Division of Behavioral and Social Sciences and Education. Washington, DC: National Academy Press.

Nelson, R. B. (1993). *Proofs without words: Exercises in visual thinking.* Washington, DC: MAA.

Noddings, N. (1993). Constuctivism and caring. In R. B. Davis & C. A. Maher (Eds.), *Schools, mathematics, and the world of reality* (pp. 35–50). Needham Heights, MA: Allyn & Bacon.

Noelting, G. (1980). The development of proportional reasoning and the ratio concept: 1. Differentiation of stages. *Educational Studies in Mathematics, 11,* 217–253.

O'Brien, T. C. (1999). Parrot math. *Phi Delta Kappan, 80,* 434–438.

Post, T. R. (1981). Fractions: Results and implications from the national assessment. *Arithmetic Teacher, 28*(9), 26–31.

Post, T. R., Behr, M. J., & Lesh, R. A. (1988). Proportionality and the development of prealgebra understandings. In A. F. Coxford (Ed.), *The ideas of algebra, K–12* (pp. 78–90). Reston, VA: National Council of Teachers of Mathematics.

Pugalee, D. K., Frykholm, J., Johnson, A., Slovin, H., Malloy, C., & Preston, R. (2002). *Navigating through geometry in grades 6–8.* Reston, VA: National Council of Teachers of Mathematics.

Reys, R. E. (1998). Computation versus number sense. *Mathematics Teaching in the Middle School, 4,* 110–113.

Riverdeep. (1994a). *Tangible math: The geometry inventor.* Cambridge, MA: Author.

Riverdeep. (1994b). *Tangible math: The probability constructor.* Cambridge, MA: Author.

Rowan, T. E., & Bourne, B. (1994). *Thinking like mathematicians: Putting the K–4 standards into practice.* Portsmouth, NH: Heinemann.

Runion, G. E. (1990). *The golden section.* Palo Alto, CA: Dale Seymour.

Scheer, J. K. (1980). The etiquette of diagnosis. *Arithmetic Teacher, 27*(9), 18–19.

Schifter, D., Bastable, V., & Russell, S. J. (1999a). *Developing mathematical understanding: Numbers and operations, Part 1, Building a system of tens (Casebook).* Parsippany, NJ: Dale Seymour Publications.

Schifter, D., Bastable, V., & Russell, S. J. (1999b). *Developing mathematical understanding: Numbers and operations, Part 2, Making meaning for operations (Casebook).* Parsippany, NJ: Dale Seymour Publications.

Schroeder, T. L., & Lester, F. K., Jr. (1989). Developing understanding in mathematics via problem solving. In P. R. Trafton (Ed.), *New directions for elementary school mathematics* (pp. 31–42). Reston, VA: National Council of Teachers of Mathematics.

Schwartz, S. L. (1996). Hidden messages in teacher talk: Praise and empowerment. *Teaching Children Mathematics, 2,* 396–401.

Sconyers, J. M. (1995). Proof and the middle school mathematics student. *Mathematics Teaching in the Middle School, 1,* 516–518.

Silver, E. A., & Stein, M. K. (1996). The QUASAR project: The "revolution of the possible" in mathematics instructional reform in urban middle schools. *Urban Education, 30,* 476–521.

REFERENCES

Smith, J. P., III. (2002). The development of students' knowledge of fractions and ratios. In B. Litwiller (Ed.), *Making sense of fractions, ratios, and proportions* (pp. 3–17). Reston, VA: National Council of Teachers of Mathematics.

Taber, S. B. (2002). Go ask Alice about multiplication of fractions. In B. Litwiller (Ed.), *Making sense of fractions, ratios, and proportions* (pp. 61–71). Reston, VA: National Council of Teachers of Mathematics.

Tahan, M. (1993). *The man who counted: A collection of mathematical adventures* (Trans. L. Clark & A. Reid). New York: Norton.

Texas Instruments. (1994). *Cabri geometry II* [Computer Software]. Dallas: Author.

Thompson, P. W. (1994). Concrete materials and teaching for mathematical understanding. *Arithmetic Teacher, 41,* 556–558.

Usiskin, Z. (1988). Conceptions of school algebra and uses of variables. In A. F. Coxford (Ed.), *The ideas of algebra, K–12* (pp. 8–19). Reston, VA: National Council of Teachers of Mathematics.

van Hiele, P. M. (1999). Developing geometric thinking through activities that begin with play. *Teaching Children Mathematics, 5,* 310–316.

Walter, M. I. (1970). *Boxes, squares and other things: A teacher's guide for a unit in informal geometry.* Reston, VA: National Council of Teachers of Mathematics.

Wearne, D., & Kouba, V. L. (2000). Rational numbers. In E. A. Silver & P. A. Kenney (Eds.), *Results from the seventh mathematics assessment of the National Assessment of Educational Progress* (pp. 163–191). Reston, VA: National Council of Teachers of Mathematics.

Wilson, M. & and Krapfl, C. (1995). Exploring mean, median, and mode with a spreadsheet. *Mathematics Teaching in the Middle School, 1,* 490–495.

Winter, M. J., Lappan, G., Phillips, E., & Fitzgerald, W. (1986). *Middle grades mathematics project: Spatial visualization.* Menlo Park, CA: AWL Supplemental.

Wood, T., & Turner-Vorbeck, T. (2001). Extending the conception of mathematics teaching. In T. Wood, B. S. Nelson, & J. Warfield (Eds.), *Beyond classical pedagogy: Teaching elementary school mathematics* (pp. 185–208). Mahwah, NJ: Lawrence Erlbaum.

INDEX

INDEX